ANCIENT
ROME

*For Mum and Dad, who took me to castles, forts and museums
and waited patiently for me to come out.*

*And for Tiddles, Bunty, Whisky, Lady Cat, Socks, Bobby,
Wendy, Tibby, Trajan, Tiger, Cleo, Tiddy, Felix, Stripy Kitten,
and Slasher.*

ANCIENT ROME

THE RISE AND FALL OF
AN EMPIRE 753 BC – AD 476

PATRICIA SOUTHERN

About the Author

Patricia Southern is an authority on the history of ancient Rome and the author of twelve books on the subject, including *The Roman Cavalry*; *Augustus* ('A reliable up-to-date guide through the snakepits of Roman politics' *THE SUNDAY TIMES*); *Caesar* ('Her style is delightfully approachable: lean and lucid, witty and pacy' *ANTIQUITY*); and *Cleopatra* ('In the absence of Cleopatra's memoirs, Southern's commendably balanced biography will do very well' *THE SUNDAY TELEGRAPH*, 'Scholarly and readable' DR PETER JONES). She lives in Northumberland.

This edition first published 2014

Amberley Publishing
The Hill, Merrywalks
Stroud, GL5 4EP

www.amberley-books.com

British Library Cataloguing in Publication Data.
A catalogue record for this book is available from the British Library.

ISBN 978 1 4456 1978 1

Typesetting and origination by Amberley Publishing
Printed in Great Britain

Contents

Preface & Acknowledgements

Judging by the number of new books that have appeared and the frequent programmes on television, there has been an upsurge in the popularity of ancient Rome in the past decade or so, which provides an excuse, if an excuse is required, for writing another one. Most of the books and television programmes have concentrated on one period or one aspect of Roman life and history, such as the rule of one particular emperor, or on the city of Pompeii, or on Rome's enemies such as Hannibal or Attila. There was a television history slot dealing solely with Cicero and the trial of Roscius, which was very well done and thoroughly enjoyable – many more like that would be very welcome, at least to this author. This book attempts to tell the story of Rome from the beginning to the fifth century, to provide the background for all the particular aspects that have achieved popular coverage, and many that haven't. As far as possible it is arranged chronologically, but when Rome became a world power, and things were happening simultaneously in different countries, the linear treatment is not always feasible. One advantage of a chronological approach is that it can be seen how Rome evolved, adapting to circumstances by amending political and military procedures. The Romans continually developed the system of government that had been intended for one relatively small Italian city so that it could fulfil the demands of a growing empire. They adjusted their fighting methods as new enemies were encountered. As time went on, after an initial intransigence, they shared their citizenship with selected individuals and peoples, and admitted them into their government. The longevity of the Roman Republic and Empire makes it impossible to cover all events and all aspects in a book of this length, so inevitably some details have to be selected and others left out, otherwise twenty volumes would still not be enough. Another point to note is that history is about people, whose mind-set we cannot totally penetrate, but the Romans were not too different from ourselves, and we know a great deal about some of the many personalities who shaped Rome. This book describes who they were and what they did, and sometimes why they did it. It is intended for the non-specialist audience, who might want to find out more from the selection of books listed in the bibliography.

My thanks are due as always to a number of people who have helped in the production of the book. Jonathan Reeve of Amberley Publishing was always willing to discuss details and answer questions, Jacqui Taylor, Jim Eden and Graeme Stobbs let me raid their photos and use their maps, and Cleo and Tiddy provided feline assistance with the typing, though the mistakes belong wholly to me, and cannot be laid at their paws.

Patricia Southern
Northumberland
2009

A Note About Dates

The starting point and end point for the Romans is problematic. The traditional dates of 753 BC for the foundation of the city, and AD 476 for the fall of the western Empire, are convenient but artificial, since people were settled near the River Tiber before 753 BC, and life went on after AD 476. History does not start and stop, nor does it change as abruptly as the choice of dates for turning points would suggest.

In the study of ancient Rome, modern scholars have typically utilized historical divisions largely based on significant events – significant, that is, according to our modern views, retrospectively applied. Such divisions are necessarily artificial, and may not have been so obvious to contemporaries who lived through these significant events, nor even to the ancient historians who examined the events at a later date. Turning points are not always recognized as such until comparison can be made, with the benefit of hindsight, between what went before and what came afterwards.

The great advantage of the use of artificial historical divisions, utilized throughout this book, is that such a scheme facilitates the study of the subject by creating manageable chunks, with a starting point and an end point before the next epoch begins. The dates of these starting points and end points always demand the addition of the qualifying symbol 'circa' because they are not absolute. The inhabitants of early Rome did not keep records of their activities, or if they did, such records have not survived, so it was left to their descendants to work out the age of their city and the probable time slots when military and political developments took place, or the most likely dates of the achievements of important men. Ancient historians were sincere in their attempts to reconcile their mythology with ascertainable facts, but there is considerable discrepancy in their opinions, just as there is still debate among modern scholars about the controversial issues in Roman history, of which there is no lack, especially for the early years.

Proud Tyrants:
The Kings of Rome *c.*753–*c.*509 BC

The site where Rome was to develop enjoyed several advantages. It lay in the area called Latium, on the banks of the River Tiber, on the fertile western side of the Italian peninsula. The land to the east of the central ridge of the Apennines is not so fertile or conducive to prosperous settlement, nor does it boast as many benign coastal landing places. For the first settlers at Rome, a good defensible site and a water supply would be of prime importance and the seven hills near the Tiber offered both. The route along the south bank of the Tiber gave access to the salt beds near the mouth of the river, and there was also an easy crossing point, in a bend of the river downstream of what was later to be called the Capitol Hill. This facilitated north–south communications through the regions of Latium and Etruria. Other considerations were the distance of the site from the western coast, not too far for trade and transport, but far enough for early warning of attacks.

The full impact of these geographical and social advantages were not perhaps appreciated or utilized all at once by the first inhabitants. To expound them all in one place might give the impression that the founder of the city arrived at the site, took a swift look round, dug in his spear at the intended spot, and harangued his followers about the fact that they could grow plentiful crops, use the trade routes, bring in supplies by river from the sea and use the same route in reverse to export goods, tax travellers and merchants, make a profit from controlling the route to the salt pans, defend themselves on the hills if they were attacked, and use the settlement as a base for expanding into everyone else's territory all around them. That is what eventually happened, but not because this was the original intent of the first Romans, pursued with unrelenting vigour after they had identified the best location on which to settle. It was the nature of their site, with its considerable advantages, that explains in part why Rome survived and expanded. The geographical setting facilitated such development, but geography in isolation would not have helped the early Romans to flourish. If it had not been for the social and political character of their succeeding generations, their capacity to overcome calamities, to adapt their procedures to circumstances and absorb the ideas of others, the prehistoric settlement may have petered out and failed. The combination of all the above circumstances helped the inhabitants to prosper and to dominate much of the ancient world.

The foundation of the city of Rome is the stuff of legend, only dimly illuminated by modern tools of archaeological, historical and literary investigation. Each of these lines of exploration can answer some, but not all, of the questions about how the settlement on the banks of the Tiber became the leading city of the Mediterranean world and the ruler of most of modern Europe and the Middle East. Archaeology can provide information about which artefacts or buildings were in use before or after other types, and about the origins of artefacts, thereby giving some clues about the chronology of various cultures. This provides an invaluable framework on which to build a more complete picture of the people who used the artefacts and buildings, and their relationships with other groups. Archaeological evidence can reveal how people lived and died, though it has to be admitted that the evidence accruing from excavations more commonly illustrates the way of death rather than the way of life of any given people, since cemeteries often survive longer and yield more evidence than ruined or abandoned settlements. In isolation, archaeology cannot tell us everything we would like to know about the people who used the artefacts or lived in the settlements, what they were like or how they thought. For that, documentary evidence is necessary, but even the information contained in archives and literature does not necessarily flesh out the details of daily life, nor is it always reliable. Writers often worked to their own or someone else's agendas, with a consequent bias, and archival documents can be forged or tampered with.

Each method of investigation of the past naturally has its limitations, especially if used without regard to other methods, but the difficulty lies in amalgamating the disparate information from the myths and legends, from the works of the ancient historians, and from archaeology. The production of a rounded picture of the remote past, using all the available but often limited evidence, ultimately and inevitably requires the addition of large amounts of speculation.

One of the major problems concerning the origins of Rome is the lack of any historical record for at least five centuries after the supposed date of foundation in the eighth century BC. The earliest recorded view of the Romans is provided by the Greeks, who began to establish colonies in southern Italy from about 750 BC. Their most northerly settlement was founded at Cumae in the bay of Naples at some time before 725 BC. While the Greeks were building their new colonies in Italy, Rome was quite unremarkable and unimportant, merely one city, or perhaps not yet worthy of that description, among several others in the region of Latium. From about the fifth century BC, the Greek historians took only cursory notice of the emergent settlement on the Tiber, but they were eventually alerted to the growing power of Rome when her armies gave a good account of themselves in fighting the Greek general Pyrrhus at Heraclea in 280 BC, where the phrase 'Pyrrhic victory' was born. The Romans were defeated and had to withdraw but they had inflicted such tremendous losses on the Greeks that Pyrrhus could not risk another battle. The Romans stood up to Pyrrhus once again in 275 BC near Beneventum. In less than a century after that, the Romans began to develop more than a passing interest in the Greeks and embarked on the gradual process of absorbing them.

The first acknowledged Roman historian who wrote about his native city is Quintus Fabius Pictor, who lived and worked towards the end of the third century BC. Little is known of him except that he was a senator, who went as an ambassador to Delphi in 216 BC. Although he was a Roman, he wrote his history in Greek, not Latin, possibly with the aim of presenting Roman politics and way of life to a Greek audience. The Romans of the late third century BC were anxious to make overtures of friendship to the various Greek states because at that time they were at war with the Carthaginians. From 218 onwards the Carthaginian general Hannibal was in Italy with his victorious army, inflicting defeat after defeat on the Romans. An alliance of the Carthaginians with any of the Greek states was to be feared, and in 215 Philip of Macedon did ally with Hannibal.

The next most important historian to document the rise of Rome was the Greek Polybius, brought to Rome after the Romans defeated the Greeks at the battle of Pydna in 168 BC. Polybius started out as a political prisoner, but soon became a protégé of the influential family of the Scipios, so when he wrote his history there was a strong bias towards the achievements of the various members of this family, but the total contribution of the Scipios to Roman glory was undoubtedly important. Polybius was, and still is, a singularly reliable writer who acknowledged his sources, and weighed the evidence, dismissing some tales out of hand and then trying to make sense of them according to the state of current knowledge. Since he wrote in Greek for a predominantly Greek audience, he took the trouble to explain things that would not have been familiar to his fellow countrymen, an extremely fortuitous and useful device for modern historians.

Dionysius of Halicarnassus was another Greek historian, who migrated to Rome in the late first century BC. He taught the art of rhetoric for a living, and wrote a history of Rome in Greek, but of his original twenty books, nine have been lost. The extant work covers the development of Rome up to the middle of the fifth century BC, consisting mostly of stories and legends, but Dionysius tried to assess their historical accuracy rather than simply relaying the tales.

A contemporary of Dionysius was the Roman Titus Livius, who was born in the mid-first century BC and died at some time between AD 12 and AD 17. He embarked on the mammoth task of producing a history of Rome from the foundation to the end of the civil wars which brought Augustus to power. Augustus is commonly regarded as the first emperor, though he would not have used such a title in his own day. He portrayed himself as first among equals, but in reality was in total command. The historian Livy was therefore not entirely free to write what he wanted to say, and he relied on the legends and stories and the works of other writers such as Fabius Pictor and Polybius. His other sources are unidentified. He reproduced what he found in these sources, without checking all the facts or evaluating the legends, sometimes including anachronisms, perhaps without realizing that he was doing so. This would not detract from his main purpose, which was to glorify Rome and the Romans, but nonetheless the 35 books that survive from his original 142 are objective enough, and modern historians can corroborate some of his facts from other documents, inscriptions and archaeological evidence.

For the Romans themselves, of course, the foundation of their city was quite straightforward. When they had begun to think of themselves as a distinct people they naturally wanted to explain where they had come from and to outline their history. The modern historian Eric Hobsbawm categorized embryonic nations as a people sharing a common misconception about their origins and a common antipathy towards their neighbours. This description can be applied to many emergent peoples, including the formation of various tribes as well as settled communities, but with regard to the Romans it fits the situation perfectly. Weaving together the various strands of myth, legend, and tradition, the Romans adopted and exploited Greek models and managed to combine a variety of legendary events into the narrative of their origins. After the conquest of Troy, they said, the Trojan hero Aeneas came to Italy and founded the city of Lavinium, then his son Ascanius founded Alba Longa. Romulus, who was allegedly related to the rulers of Alba Longa, founded Rome. The foundation of Alba Longa is traditionally dated to 1152 BC, and the Romans reckoned that Romulus founded their city in 753 BC, so that four centuries separate Ascanius and Alba Longa from Romulus and the foundation of Rome. The legend blithely ignores the impossible chronology, and embarrassed ancient historians, trying to take it seriously, had to jump through hoops in their attempts to account for the discrepancy.

The Romulus legend serves to explain, in part, the historically attested and long standing connection of Rome with Alba Longa. The story goes that Numitor, the King of Alba, had an evil brother called Amulius, who deposed the king and took his place, though he did not kill him. When he became king, Amulius secured his position by forcing Rhea Silvia, the daughter of Numitor, to become a Vestal Virgin. This meant that the right to marry and have children was denied her, so she could not produce an heir to challenge Amulius. These evil plans went awry when the god Mars himself came down to earth and impregnated her. When Romulus and Remus, the twin sons of Mars and Rhea Silvia, were born, Amulius had them thrown into the Tiber in some sort of small vessel, which washed up on the river bank where they were rescued by the famous she-wolf, and then found and reared by the shepherd Faustulus and his wife Acca Larentia. When they grew up, the twins kicked out Amulius from Alba Longa and replaced Numitor on the throne there. Then they founded Rome.

The association of Romulus and Remus with Alba Longa neatly explained an archaic ritual whose origins were lost in the mists of time. During the annual festival of the Feriae Latinae, a religious rite common to the tribes of Latium as the title suggests, most of the magistrates, officials and the populace of Rome trekked out from the city to journey to the Alban Mount south-east of Rome, to observe religious ceremonies there. This festival was important to the Romans, and was celebrated until the late Empire, even though reliable information about its origins was lacking even in Republican times. Neither the ancient nor the modern authors agree upon the exact site of the supposed city of Ascanius. Nowadays, the most famous buildings on the site are the vast palace built by the Emperor Domitian, of which only scant remains are known, and Castel Gandolfo, where the Pope's summer residence was established. Nothing has so far come to light to suggest that there was ever a city full of people dwelling near the Alban Mount, but there are abundant traces of the dead from the extensive cemeteries, dating to remote times, as far back as the tenth century BC. The cemeteries yield evidence of a common heritage, identified as a Latin culture, and it is thought that Alba was the chief gathering place of an ancient league that had expired by the time that the Romans got around to writing their own history. Nevertheless, the ancient festival endured.

The Romulus story attained iconic status, though it was the she-wolf that became the symbol of Rome, not necessarily accompanied by the twins that she protected and reared. According to Livy, a statue of the wolf together with the twins was dedicated in Rome in 206 BC, but the somewhat wary and worried wolf in the Capitoline Museum conveys the message more than adequately without the addition of the twins. The rotund infants that accompany the wolf now are the creation of the sculptor Pallaiolo, who produced them at some time in the fifteenth century AD.

It was said that Romulus built a fortified enclosure on the Palatine Hill, but his brother Remus persistently leapt over the walls, or perhaps kept on destroying part of them, and Romulus, or one of his entourage, killed Remus for this transgression. In the words of a dry-stone waller, wearily resigned to repairing field walls broken down by inconsiderate tourists, this was a perfectly justifiable homicide. But it was a sinister precedent that the city of Rome was said to have begun with a fratricide.

The Romulus legend may not even be very ancient. It cannot be shown to have begun at the same time as the traditional foundation date in the eighth century BC. It has been argued that it was current at least by the sixth century BC, but on the other hand it has also been suggested that the story may have circulated only from about the fourth century. The heroic tale has a Greek parallel in the story of the sons of Poseidon, the twins Neleus and Pelias, who were left for dead as babies but rescued and suckled by a bitch. The Romulus story may have been a deliberate fabrication utilizing elements of the Greek version.

After founding the city, Romulus offered the Capitol Hill as a refuge for men fleeing from various oppressors or perhaps from justice, and he followed this by kidnapping some of the women of the neighbouring tribe of Sabines, so that the original settlers would be able to marry and produce descendants, ensuring that the new city would flourish. A leader of the Sabines called Titus Tatius was said to have joined Romulus and brought some of his people to live in Rome. According to this version, Tatius and Romulus settled their differences, agreed to share the kingship, and ruled amicably together. Far from being a courageous leader, especially in the modern age of the anti-hero, Romulus has been designated the chief of a band of mongrel thugs and criminals. On the other hand, regarded in a more positive light, the open invitation for outsiders to join the settlers does foreshadow the Roman practice of integration and extension of citizenship to non-Romans, a practice that endured throughout the Republic and Empire.

The date of the foundation of the city of Rome was calculated retrospectively by its later inhabitants, when the settlement had evolved into a city state and the Republic had been constituted. Even among the ancient authors there was no real agreement on the exact moment of the foundation. Various dates were suggested, ranging from about 814 to 725 BC, but largely due to the work of the late Republican historian and polymath Terentius Varro, a date was finally established, probably by extrapolating backwards from the equally traditional date of the formation of the Republic in 509 BC, to arrive at c.753 BC, according to our modern calendar. When they began to keep records, this date became year one of the Roman calendar, and all subsequent dates were reckoned from this time onwards, *ab urbe condita*, abbreviated to *a.u.c.*, meaning 'from the foundation of the city'.

The first habitations on the Palatine Hill were primitive huts, nothing like the sophisticated dwellings of the Greek cities or those of the later version of Rome itself. The Romans of the Republic proudly acknowledged their humble beginnings by displaying a diligently preserved shepherd's hut that they said Romulus had lived in on the Palatine, their museum piece shown to visitors so that they could marvel at the contrast between what Rome once was and what she had become. There is plenty of room for jeering scepticism about the authenticity of Romulus's hut, allegedly preserved with due reverence throughout the centuries, but excavations on the Palatine in the 1930s revealed the remains of just such primitive huts, which have been dated to the middle years of the eighth century BC. The traces of fortifications which were discovered on the north-eastern side of the Palatine Hill have been dated to the same period. It is not certain that the huts and the defences are contemporary, but it is virtually impossible to resist the notion that the legend of the foundation of a settlement at Rome and the establishment of its early fortifications probably contains some elements of truth.

It does not matter whether the Romans firmly believed in the foundation myths, or the truth or otherwise of the actual date. The stories were embedded in the life of the Republic and the Empire and were never seriously challenged. In AD 248 the Emperor Philip celebrated 1,000 years of Rome, declaring a public holiday of several days, with splendid gladiatorial combats, sports and games, chariot races, theatrical productions, musical shows, literary and artistic exhibitions.

The huts on the Palatine that have been dated to the eighth century BC are not the only examples from the city. More huts have been found near the later Forum Boarium, and there were people living on some of the other hills, especially on the Quirinal and the Caelian. It is probable that settlers also colonized the other four of the famous seven hills of Rome, but archaeologists have always tended to concentrate much more on the Palatine than anywhere else, and therefore more and better detail derives from this location than from any of the others.

The primitive hut groups of the eighth century BC do not constitute the first settlement in the area that eventually became the city of Rome. Archaeological evidence attests that people were living there, or at least cremating their dead there, as early as 1,000 BC, but the nature of this early settlement is not fully understood. Only the cremations have been found without accompanying traces of habitation at the same time, so it cannot be demonstrated beyond doubt that there were any huts or houses contemporary with the cemeteries of 1,000 BC. There may have been no permanent dwellings, but transient peoples may have built flimsy huts and then moved on after a short stay, leaving behind their dead. On present evidence it cannot be said that there was a city in embryo, dating back to 1,000 BC.

On the other hand it is clear that even if Romulus really did exist and if he was the founder of a settlement on the Palatine c.753 BC, he did not choose a virgin site that was completely devoid of population. The famous phrase, 'Rome wasn't built in a day' is very true, but Rome was not founded in a day, either.

ITALY BEFORE THE ROMANS

Although the foundation myth may contain no elements of truth whatsoever, it cannot be summarily dismissed in its entirety. If the Romulus legend was fabricated during the Republic, and made to fit the way in which the Romans wished to portray themselves, then at least the traditional date for the foundation does have some plausibility. Cultural, political and social stirrings are detectable in the eighth century BC. It was definitely a time of change, affecting much of Italy.

Society all over Italy at the time of the traditional foundation of Rome was organized on a tribal basis. The tribesmen did not think of themselves as Italians, or even as a group of peoples living in a country called Italia, which is a later concept. The tribes would not necessarily have entertained notions of unity, or of loyalty to other tribes. Despite the division into tribal groups, during the centuries preceding the foundation of Rome, in the late Bronze Age, there seems to have been a remarkably uniform culture, with a similar way of life and type of settlement all over Italy, but this culture started to diversify from about 1,000 BC, when different regional cultures started to appear. At the beginning of the Iron Age, around 900 BC, the phenomenon was already entrenched and continued to develop. Generalization always contains an element of hyperbole or even untruth, but there was a detectable north–south divide in the way in which people disposed of their dead. The southern tribes buried their dead, while the peoples further north, including those of Latium, Campania and Etruria, preferred to cremate theirs. There were slight variations in the treatment of the ashes. There was a recognizable sub-group, called by modern archaeologists the Villanovan culture. These peoples placed the cremated remains in a vessel with a lid, and placed the vessel in the earth, marking the spot with a stone laid on top.

In Latium, people fashioned cremation urns in the shape of houses or huts, sometimes including with the ashes miniature utensils, presumably symbolic tools for use in the afterlife. Then the urn and the artefacts were placed into a large jar and buried in a pit. This practice was sufficiently widespread for archaeologists to give it a separate label, the Latial culture. It is indicative of a shared sense of identity among the Latins. They spoke the same language, adopted the same customs, shared the same religious beliefs and observed the same religious ceremonies. The Romans were part of this shared culture, sharing the Latin language and customs, and cremating their dead in the same way.

The multicultural nature of the peoples of the Italian peninsula was not entirely eradicated, even when Rome had taken over the whole country and started to expand into the rest of what was to become Europe. People still spoke different languages and followed different cultures in Italy, with the Roman veneer spread over them, even in the time of Augustus. A major problem in studying the different tribes who inhabited the territories around early Rome is the fact that they were only recorded by the Romans themselves at a comparatively late date. Several nuances about tribal life, readily apparent to the early Romans, may have been missed altogether or misinterpreted by the later writers.

In the eighth century BC, the Romans were surrounded by peoples of diverse origins. In the far north, up to and beyond the Alps, were the Celtic tribes. On the coasts around a large part of the south of the peninsula, there were Greek colonies, bringing Greek culture, art and architecture, and language to the attention of the early Romans. In the centre of Italy on either side of the Apennines were a group of tribes, including the Sabines, the Marsi, the Picenes and probably the Aequi and Volsci, who spoke a language called Oscan. And from the Tiber up to the north of Italy were the Etruscans, the most mysterious of all the ancient Italian peoples.

'Etruscan' is the name by which we know this tribe, the name coined for them by the Romans, with an alternative name Tusci, which was applied to the area we now know as Tuscany. The Greeks called them Tyrrhenians, and the Etruscans called themselves the Rasenna. Their origins are entirely unknown, and therefore very much disputed. To a previous generation of modern historians, this strange people seemed to have come from the east, perhaps Asia Minor, because their art, their artefacts and their luxury goods have discernible connections with oriental cultures. The Etruscans are not just set apart by their culture, but mostly by their language, still not fully understood. It is not part of the Indo-European group, though the Etruscans borrowed and adapted Greek symbols to write it down. Archaeologists and philologists do not have sufficient material to be able to decipher this language, and unfortunately the Romans absorbed into Latin only a few Etruscan terms. More extensive Roman borrowings may have enlightened modern historians about the Etruscans, their language and their origins.

An ancient Roman tradition maintains that their early society comprised three tribes, called the Ramnes, the Tities and the Luceres. Each tribe was subdivided into ten smaller groups called *curiae*, thirty in all, which formed the basis of the political assemblies, and of the early Roman army. Possibly these three tribes represent three different groups of settlers, the Ramnes representing the Romans, originally under Romulus, living on the Palatine. The Tities represented the Sabines under Titus Tatius on the Quirinal, and the Luceres were perhaps Etruscans living on the Caelian Hill, under a certain Lucumo, who was said to have rendered some assistance to the Romans. This is mostly conjecture, but in the absence of any other theory it seems perfectly feasible.

Unfortunately, different ethnic backgrounds cannot be so clearly revealed by archaeological means, though it used to be thought that the cremations and inhumations that were discovered in the early cemeteries in the vicinity of the Forum may represent the two different races of Romans and Sabines, who favoured different kinds of funerary arrangements. The facts would bear that interpretation but without further corroborative evidence it remains unproven. In modern society, cremations and burials take place contemporaneously, representing for the most part personal choice, not purely ethnic or even cultural preferences.

The early inhabitants of Rome were probably farmers, as their traditional stories seem to indicate. Not much is known about how they subsisted, but they would need to grow crops and engage in animal husbandry, and perhaps import foodstuffs as well. The Romans of the Republic looked back nostalgically to the time when simple farmers served as soldiers, when even great generals laid down their powers when the battles and times of danger were ended, and returned to their ploughs. Towards the end of the eighth century BC it is possible that a wealthy land-owning class had begun to emerge, who became the elite rulers of the settlement. How this wealth was reckoned in the early days is uncertain. It was probably assessed on property and land, perhaps also on livestock and crops. Coinage was not in general use in Rome at the end of the eighth century BC, although the Greeks had already started to issue coins round about then. By 500 BC it is generally agreed that the Romans had adopted a rudimentary system using bronze of a standardized weight.

The first steps towards urbanization were made during the seventh century, though Rome was not the only nascent city to develop in this way. Archaeological investigations at other cities of Latium, such as Lavinium, Satricum and Fidenae reveal that urbanization was taking place at the same time, so what was happening at Rome was not a unique phenomenon. Urban development in the city was neither sudden nor rapid, but progressed steadily. The first signs of corporate activity are detectable from about the middle of the seventh century BC, and round about 600 BC the first communal area was laid out and paved, at the expense of some hut dwellings which were destroyed, in what was to become the Forum. The first Senate House probably belongs to this epoch, and also the first building, one of several, on the site of the Regia, whose name indicates the dwelling place of kings. This first edifice was perhaps not labelled as such from the very beginning, but it may have been intended as an official and probably public building, associated with the early kings of Rome.

ROME UNDER THE KINGS

The sensational discovery at the end of the nineteenth century of the Black Stone, or *Lapis Niger*, in the assembly area in the centre of the city was one of those rare occasions when archaeological evidence could be married up with ancient literature. The ancient historians wrote about the *lapis niger in comitia* which was said to mark the burial place of Romulus, slightly puzzling if he had indeed simply disappeared and become a god, but as a commemorative site the area was generally associated with him by the historians. It was probably the shrine to the god Vulcan. Various finds buried underneath the stone yielded a date in the middle of the sixth century BC. It bore an inscription written in *boustrophedon* fashion, just as early Greek inscriptions were carved, with every second line in reverse direction, just as a ploughman ploughs a field, which is the original meaning of the Greek word *boustrophedon*. The language of the inscription was an older version of Latin, containing the word *recei*, from *rex*, or king, thus providing proof, if any were needed, that early Rome was definitely ruled by kings.

According to Roman tradition, from 753 BC until the foundation of the Republic in 509 BC, there were seven kings of Rome, starting with Romulus and ending with Tarquinius Superbus. The number seven may have significance, an ancient magical number, perhaps not just coincidentally equal to the number of hills of Rome. An immediate problem concerns this vast time span occupied by so few kings, seven rulers in nearly two and a half centuries. If the tradition is to be taken seriously, each king enjoyed or endured an extremely long reign. At first sight, this defies normal human stamina on such a consistent basis, but it is worth pointing out that during a comparable time span, the English monarchy can show a similar track record. Discounting Edward VIII, who was never crowned and abdicated after only a few months in 1936, there have been only eight kings or queens from the accession of George III in 1760 to the current monarch, Queen Elizabeth II, so the alleged long reigns of the seven ancient kings of Rome is not perhaps such a physical impossibility.

One suggestion is that there may have been more kings of Rome whose names have not been recorded or passed down to the later Romans, but there is not a shred of evidence to support such a theory. Another solution is to bring forward the dates of the seven kings, discounting the probably mythical Romulus in the mid-eighth century, and equate the reigns of the succeeding six kings with the tangible developments in Rome from the middle of the seventh century, when it seems that corporate policies, centrally directed, were being put into operation.

The nature of Roman kingship differed from the monarchical rule of later centuries, as modern Europeans would understand it. The kings of Rome qualified as tyrants, in the ancient Greek sense of rule by one man, rather than in the modern sense with all the connotations of cruel and unjust despots. Although family connections played a part in the selection of the kings, the kingship was not a hereditary institution, so there was no ruling dynasty passing its powers down through the generations and retaining its position with regard to other families and other cities by means of diplomatic marriages. Roman kings were not exactly elected but were appointed with the approval of the aristocracy and the people.

The king in Rome was head of state, the director of political life and of all administration, supreme military commander, chief priest and religious leader, lawgiver and chief justice. His power was embodied in his *imperium*, specifically in the command of the armies, and the symbols of his power, borrowed from the Etruscans, were the bundles of rods signifying his right to punish malefactors by flogging, grouped round an axe, signifying his right to execute them. This was the *fasces*, taken over by the consuls when the monarchy was abolished.

When a king died, there was an *interregnum*, literally a period of between rule, and an *interrex* was chosen to take the place of the king. The heads of the leading aristocratic families took up this office for five days at a time, laying down their powers in favour of the next man, and the process went on probably for a year, until the new king was chosen.

Each king was credited in Roman tradition with various attributes, achievements or innovations. The historical truth of the alleged actions and successes of the kings is beyond retrieval. In archaeological terms, certain developments or changes are detectable in Rome and can be roughly dated, but not necessarily assigned to a particular king. For social, legal and administrative events which do not involve buildings or leave any tangible trace, there can be no proof whatsoever of the legendary innovations set in motion by the Roman kings. What follows is based on ancient Roman tradition, only tenuously related to attested archaeological or historical facts.

Romulus was said to have ruled from *c*.753 to *c*.716 BC. He brought in the Sabines under their king, Titus Tatius, and reconciled the two peoples by marrying Hersilia, a woman of the Sabines. He was a formidable warrior, continually fighting against Rome's neighbours and then taking them over to absorb them into the new Roman state. It was said that he chose one hundred men to be his advisers, perhaps the embryonic Senate, though to hazard such a guess is fraught with difficulties. The heads of Roman households habitually surrounded themselves with a group of friends and acquaintances to advise and help them, so Romulus's circle may not have been an official organ of state. It was a common enough model. Other cities were governed by kings or a ruler by some other name, with a group of men acting as counsellors and/or councillors, and the rest of the populace divided into more manageable sub groups.

Romulus's followers, loyal or otherwise, were present at his death, which occurred during a religious ceremony taking place near the River Tiber. A furious storm broke, and most people dispersed. Romulus simply disappeared. He was nowhere to be found when the wind and rain ceased. No one knew what had happened, but it was said that he had died and become a god. More prosaically, it was also murmured that his loyal followers, tired of his increasingly autocratic rule, had assassinated him and carved him into portable sections to spirit him away, as it were. It is permissible to ask if the assassins managed to convince everyone that all the blood and gore really did come from the sacrificial animals. Whatever his fate, henceforth Romulus was worshipped as the god Quirinus.

The choice of the next king was supposedly made by the Sabines. They opted for Numa Pompilius, whose wife was the daughter of Titus Tatius. Numa's reign was dated from c.716 to c.673 BC. He was a good organizer, whose strengths lay in administration and law. He reformed the calendar, establishing a year of 360 days, and ensured that the appropriate religious ceremonies were celebrated at the proper times. He was responsible for the installation of the Vestal Virgins at Rome, importing the cult from Alba Longa, and he built the Temple of Janus, where the doors were open at all times except when the whole Roman world was at peace, when they were closed with great rejoicing and ceremonial.

When Numa Pompilius died, the Romans chose a Latin to rule them, called Tullus Hostilius, whose reign lasted from c.673 to c.641 BC. He was a successful leader who declared war on Alba Longa, ruled by their king, Mettius. Instead of campaigning with their whole armies, the two kings agreed to appoint their own champions to fight each other, and swore an oath that the losing side would submit to the victors. This is the context of the story of the three Horatii brothers, who fought successfully against three brothers from Alba Longa. Whether or not this event really took place, it is clear that Alba Longa never developed as did Rome and the other Latin cities, and it retained its importance only as the site of the annual religious festival of the Feriae Latinae. Tullus Hostilius was said to have built a new Senate House, called the Curia Hostilia, to accommodate the larger numbers of senators that resulted from Rome's expanding population and increased settlement in the city. The later, successive, Senate Houses were on a different alignment.

Ancus Marcius, the fourth King of Rome, was the grandson of Numa Pompilius. He ruled from c.641 to c.616 BC, his main achievement being the extension of Roman control along the Tiber as far as the coast, where he founded the port of Ostia at the mouth of the river. None of this can be proved, since nothing has come to light from the extensive archaeological excavations of Ostia Antica to verify the date or the name of the founder. Another achievement was the successful repulse of an attempt by the Latin cities to check growing Roman supremacy. He destroyed one of the Latin cities and settled the population in Rome itself, and he was said to have destroyed the settlements of Tellenae, Politorium and Ficana.

The fifth king, Tarquinius Priscus, or Tarquin the Elder, was an Etruscan citizen from the city with the same name, Tarquinii, but traditionally he was probably of Greek origin, since it was said that his father Demaratus left his native Corinth to avoid persecution and settled in Etruria. Priscus was closely associated with Ancus Marcius, and more or less seized power, though he did at least have the grace to wait until the king died. Then he manoeuvred himself into the kingship, bloodlessly it seems, and set about strengthening his own and the city's position, during a reign that lasted from *c.*616 to *c.*579 BC. He is said to have increased the size of the Senate, though it is not certain that the Senate at this stage was a permanent body whose members could be labelled senators, as in the Republic. The size of the Senate, if it existed as such, is not known for certain at this period, nor what were the conditions for entry to its ranks. There may have been a Senate House, attributed to Tullus Hostilius, but the group that met in it may have consisted of men from the leading families, not necessarily all aristocrats, who were chosen by the king on an *ad hoc* basis for deliberation about specific problems, perhaps with a changing membership according to the nature of the problem.

Another innovation was the increase in the size of the Roman cavalry. Romulus allegedly created three cavalry units, based on each of the three tribes of Ramnes, Tities, and Luceres, and Tarquinius wanted to create three more, but there was opposition on religious grounds, so in the end he kept the original three units and doubled their size.

Leaving aside the uncertain fate of Romulus, Tarquinius Priscus was the first king to be assassinated. The aggrieved sons of Ancus Marcius, who probably hoped to be made kings themselves, hired two assassins who killed Tarquinius by a blow from an axe as he presided over a court sitting. If the sons of the previous king were hoping to take over the government and install themselves as rulers after the assassination, their plot was foiled because Tarquinius's wife, Tanaquil, acted quickly and concealed the body, pretending that he was badly wounded, but still alive and would recover. She persuaded the Romans that all would be well if, in the meantime, her favourite Servius Tullius took over the reins of state as deputy of the king. By the time the truth emerged, Servius was firmly entrenched in power, and unassailable. He had not been appointed in the proper fashion, and worse still he was said to have started life as a slave, taken prisoner with his mother when Tarquinius captured the town of Corniculum. Later Roman historians tried hard to compensate for his origins, by inventing noble ancestry for him, which, in a perverse way, indicates that they accepted the story that he was low-born. His origins did not seem to bother Tarquinius

Priscus, who recognized the talents and abilities of Servius and offered him one of his daughters in marriage.

During his reign from about 579 to 535 BC, Servius restructured the administration of Rome. The so-called Servian reforms were far-reaching and pragmatic, but it is impossible now to extricate precisely what Servius set in motion, since his achievements were not described until centuries later by ancient historians whose viewpoint was influenced by the customs and procedures of their own day, in other words by the fully evolved system.

The extent of Roman territorial control had certainly increased since the days of the early settlers. The population of the city itself had no doubt increased, and even more people had been transferred to the city itself to be added to the citizen body, so the original division of the populace into three tribes was probably unwieldy and obsolete. Servius replaced this system, possibly creating a fourth tribe in the city of Rome. Each of the postulated four tribes may have had a section of the surrounding territory attached to it, or alternatively Servius may have created extra tribes for the periphery, though this is much disputed. In the Republic there were four tribes in the city and thirty-one in the regions surrounding Rome, but it is unlikely that this represents the reforms that Servius instigated. He can be credited with laying the foundations for such a scheme, whereby more tribes could be added in modular fashion as the expanding population outdistanced the previous tribal divisions.

The tribes were subdivided into smaller groups called centuries, which applied to the electoral systems and to the organization of the army. There was, presumably, a close connection with the centuriate assembly, the *comitia centuriata*, but the details of precisely what the connection was and how it worked are obscure. During the Republic, the *comitia centuriata* was responsible for the election of the more important magistrates such as the consuls and praetors, for enacting laws, and declaring war and peace.

The first census of the population of Rome was conducted perhaps as a preliminary to this reorganization. The tribal organisation was based on place of residence, and so cut across the different strata, mixing rich and poor alike in one tribe. The census was conducted to collect information about the status and circumstances of each man, so that he could be slotted into the relevant category or class based on wealth. The Latin word used for these divisions is *classis*, the original meaning of which is far removed from the construction put upon it by modern English speakers: it concerns calling up men to serve in the army. These class divisions were used to determine the contribution that each man should make when the army was assembled. Once again, the ancient historians were influenced by the fully evolved Republican system of five classes, with the wealthiest citizens providing full armour and weapons, down to the poorest, the last two classes, who went into battle virtually unprotected and bearing only light weapons. This brief description is an oversimplification that demands further elaboration. In the context of the Servian reforms, the five class system would probably have been too elaborate. Servius may have divided the Romans into only two classes, or even one class and a sub-group who did not qualify for inclusion in the class.

The new system arose as part of Servius's reorganization of the army. The king was concerned not only with the political divisions and assemblies, but with military command, a matter of importance to him since he had not been made king in the usual manner, and could be categorized as a usurper. More than any of his predecessors, Servius needed the army as the infrastructure of his power, and at this time it seems that he adopted the formation of the hoplite phalanx, heavy-armed troops who fought *en masse*, shield to shield. The Romans said that they had learned this formation from the Etruscans, but it was originally of Greek derivation. It is perhaps not important to debate where the Romans found their model, only that they did so around the time when Servius Tullius was allegedly the king. For the hoplite army, he would need only two classes, one class of those men who could afford the armour, the long lance and the shield of the hoplite soldiers, and one of the poorer men who served as light-armed troops. It is likely that this more simple system was the origin of the five classes of later times, further divisions being made as circumstances altered during the history of the Republic. Debate on these issues will probably continue until the end of time, unless by some fortuitous means, incontrovertible evidence comes to light dating from the early sixth century.

The reorganization of the tribes and the division of the population into classes had a political purpose as well as a military one, but it is not entirely clear how government was carried on under these schemes in the time of the kings. What emerges from later Roman history is on the one hand their conservatism, and on the other their capacity for adaptation, when circumstances demanded it. The Romans successfully modified and amended the systems they had inherited from the reforms of Servius Tullius for the next five centuries.

Servius attended to the defence of the city, as all the other kings were said to have done, but the wall named after him proves to be more elusive than previously thought. The ancient wall still standing near to the central railway station in Rome probably has nothing to do with King Servius, though tradition associates it with him. It is not easy to date the ancient walls of Rome and attribute them to any of the kings. Work on the defences was probably an ongoing perennial concern, either to establish walls or to repair them. There may never have been a complete enclosure, though it could be assumed that points of easy access would be protected somehow, and a king such as Servius, efficient and thorough, would probably make sure that everything was in order. According to Strabo and Dionysius of Halicarnassus he fortified the section between the Esquiline and the Viminal Hills, but it is impossible to verify this.

Another of Servius's achievements may have concerned the extension of the city boundary, which was not necessarily directly connected with the defensive walls. The actual boundary probably took in territory beyond the walls. It was called the *pomerium*, and had religious significance as well as marking the outer edge of the city. A general at the head of troops was supposed to lay down his command and disband his army before he crossed the *pomerium*. Centuries later, Lucius Cornelius Sulla infamously led his soldiers across it into the city to obtain what he wanted from the Senate and People of Rome. It was not his only encounter with the *pomerium*. When he had taken full control of Rome, Sulla extended the Servian boundary.

The seventh and last King of Rome, Tarquinius Superbus, 'the Proud' was an Etruscan, perhaps the grandson of Tarquinius Priscus. He is portrayed as an unscrupulous criminal with autocratic tendencies, which served, of course, to provide the excuse for his eventual expulsion and the overthrow of the monarchy. In 535 or 534 BC he allegedly arranged a *coup d'état*, seizing power by forcing the Senate to recognize him as king, even though the aged Servius was still alive. There was a fracas in which Servius was physically ejected from the Senate House and then murdered on his way home.

Despite his unlawful seizure of power and his subsequent anti-aristocratic behaviour, snubbing the senators and ruling without their advice, Rome flourished under his rule, which lasted from *c.*535 to *c.*509, when the Republic was established. Tarquinius was probably the founder of the Temple of Jupiter Optimus Maximus, Jupiter Best and Greatest, the chief deity of Rome, on the Capitoline Hill. Tradition also credits him with road building, further attention to the defences of the city, and a concern for health, safety and plumbing, demonstrated by the construction of the great sewer, the Cloaca Maxima. In order to hurry along his public building schemes, it was said that he forcibly assembled a large workforce of the poorer elements among the populace, thus keeping them occupied and giving them no time to foment trouble.

External relations were pursued with the same energetic determination. The Latin cities were brought under Roman domination, and their citizens contributed contingents to the Roman army. Rome was recognized as the chief city of Latium, a situation that is corroborated by a treaty arranged between Rome and Carthage, during the very first years of the Republic, probably in 507 BC. Carthage was a city state founded in North Africa by the Phoenicians. The Romans would fight several bitter wars with the

Carthaginians in the future. The treaty of the sixth century BC is described by the reliable and respected Greek historian Polybius, who may even have seen the original. He is not suspected of elaboration or distortion of the facts. True, he was writing some centuries later, so it is possible that someone could have forged the document at any time between Polybius's day and the alleged date of the treaty, but it is generally accepted as authentic by modern scholars. Part of the text of the treaty mentions Latin cities which were subject to Rome, and also Latins who were not subjects, indicating that there were still some parts of the area not yet under Roman hegemony. The Latin League is a convenient modern term applied to this amalgamation of the Latin cities, conveying something of how it worked, but it is not backed up by any evidence that the Romans ever used such a description. They usually dealt with the Latin cities on an individual basis rather than as a uniform group.

By the end of Tarquinius's reign, Romans from all walks of life had been given serious cause for resentment, but rebellion did not arise from a united people standing for their rights, until an event that started out as a family vendetta turned into a political revolution. The story was told that Tarquinius's younger son Sextus raped the virtuous Lucretia, who then killed herself, prompting Tarquinius's nephew, Lucius Junius Brutus, and Lucretia's husband, Lucius Tarquinius Collatinus, to lead the rebellion against their kinsman, who was reportedly absent from Rome at the time, besieging the city of Ardea. Tarquinius hurried back, but was denied entry to the city and went off to rally the Etruscan cities of Caere, Veii and Tarquinii to fight for him.

In the meantime, Junius Brutus and Tarquinius Collatinus took control of the state. It was said that they became the first consuls, though this may be an anachronistic interpolation, since it is not certain that this magistracy was established quite so early. Whatever their actual titles were, Brutus and Tarquinius held supreme power, but Brutus passed a decree banishing all the Tarquinii from Rome, and Collatinus had to go into exile. Tarquinius Superbus remained a thorn in the side of the Romans, even suborning the two sons of Brutus to agitate for his reinstatement. Brutus chose the noble path, and obeyed the law that he himself had passed, advocating the death penalty for anyone who tried to restore the monarchy. He executed his own sons, setting the precedent for the stern Roman virtues that sustained the Republic. Family loyalties and personal feelings were subordinated to the law and the security of Rome.

The Etruscan allies of Tarquinius met the Romans in battle *c.*509 BC. Junius Brutus was killed but the Romans won the battle, discouraging the Etruscans from further action, until Lars Porsenna, the King of Clusium in Campania, managed to unite them again and marched on Rome, probably in 506 BC. Here the tale becomes even more confused, one version insisting that the Romans repulsed Porsenna when the heroic Horatius Cocles held the bridge across the Tiber until it could be destroyed, and another version, repeated in the first century AD by Tacitus and Pliny, declaring that King Porsenna occupied the city for a while, perhaps even imposing a treaty on the Romans. If he did so, then he signally failed to reinstate Tarquinius Superbus as he had supposedly promised to do, or make himself king in place of Tarquinius. His role in the affair is not understood. A modern theory is that Porsenna actually put the final touches to the eradication of the Roman monarchy, though Tarquinius Superbus did not abandon hope of reinstatement as King of Rome, until his death in *c.*495 BC. He ended his days as an exile, living at Clusium.

The battles against Tarquinius's Etruscan allies, and the Etruscan origins of the family of Tarquinius Priscus and Tarquinius Superbus, lend support to the theory, now discounted, that the foundation of the Republic was in reality a rebellion against Etruscan political domination, but there is no real evidence that Rome was dominated by the Etruscans at any time during its development. The struggle was not between the supposedly inferior civilization of the Romans and the superior civilization of their masters, nor was it an ethnic war between the Latins and the Etruscans. In the spheres of art and architecture, systems of government and the insignia that went with them, and in general culture, the Etruscans definitely influenced the Romans, who were eclectic borrowers of all things practical and useful, but there is no evidence of oppression or racial strife. There was probably no immediate eradication from Rome of all settlers of Etruscan origin, nor any attempt to reduce their influence and subordinate them. Indeed some Etruscan names appear in the lists of consuls, though some historians have found ways of rejecting them as part of an attempt to prove that all things Etruscan were anathema to the Romans after the overthrow of Tarquinius Superbus.

The somewhat impossible and garbled tales of the end of the monarchy and the beginning of the Republic are probably mythical, at least in part, but even though the chronology is all wrong and even though some the main participants may be fictional, the accounts cannot be entirely rejected. Archaeological evidence of destruction dated to about 500 BC indicates that the expulsion of the kings and perhaps the struggle against Tarquinius's allies, may have been violent and bloody. The buildings and areas associated with the kings, or at least with government, were destroyed, such as the Regia and the Comitium, or place of assembly.

The revolution at Rome may not have occurred in isolation. At the turn of the sixth and fifth centuries BC other cities in Italy were in the process of changing their governments, sometimes ejecting their rulers with violence. The end of the monarchy at Rome can be seen as part of a more widespread movement. It was a time of political upheaval and warfare, which probably contributed directly to the archaeologically detectable economic decline of the middle years of the fifth century, when in several cities, including Rome itself, the import and manufacture of fine wares and luxury goods, and the public building programmes, all came to a halt.

Thus it was in the midst of rebellion and warfare that the Roman Republic was born, *c.*509 BC. The new government would have to reorganize itself to overcome the many problems that faced it. Rome was surrounded by various states and tribes who might seize their chance to overcome her in this period of weakness. Lars Porsenna was not finally defeated until *c.*504 at the battle of Aricia, and Tarquinius Superbus was still at large trying to persuade various cities to help him to reinstate himself as King of Rome. The Latin cities were beginning to agitate against Roman supremacy, and the Etruscans could not be counted on or trusted as allies. After the expulsion of the kings of Rome, there was no guarantee that the infant Republic would survive.

2

Fierce Neighbours: The Expansion of Rome in Italy 509–290 BC

The traditional date for the foundation of the Republic in 509 BC derives from the *Fasti*, or lists of the annually elected consuls. There is more than one version, but there are not too many alarming discrepancies in these different versions, all of which start at some date towards the end of the sixth century. The most complete version is that of Marcus Terentius Varro who compiled the *Fasti Capitolini* with a start date in 509 BC. Varro's list contains some inaccuracies, perhaps not due to fabricated entries on his part – he was too conscientious for that – but possibly in some cases his sources were erroneous, or there were gaps that he filled with informed speculation. The *Fasti Capitolini* provides better information than anything else that is available, so scholars use it despite the problems.

The ancient historians who tried to reconstruct the establishment and development of the early Republic could use a variety of materials, some of which are now lost. Information is quite sparse for the initial years, gathering momentum in volume and depth as the Republic grew, with the result that extrapolation backwards from what was known, to explain what was not known, may have distorted the opinions of the historians about the first years of Republican Rome. There would be some official archival sources, such as those that Varro used to document the names of the first consuls. The Pontifex Maximus, or high priest, kept annual records known as the *Annales Maximi*, citing the names of the annually elected state officials and noting selected events. The information for the early years of the Republic is sporadic and of dubious worth, but from the end of the fifth century BC the records are considered to be more reliable, so the ancient historians who used them are also more trustworthy. The Romans kept records of the laws that were enacted, and the treaties that were made with other states and powers. Senatorial decrees would need to be recorded if they were to be given validity. All types of records may have been inscribed on stone, while others may have been written on less durable materials. Some of the leading families recorded and archived the exploits and achievements of their ancestors, and even if they kept no physical records, they still had a body of oral traditions about their part in the progress of the Roman Republic. Around these documents, coupled with the traditional tales handed down by successive generations of the aristocratic families, historians could hang a fairly credible narrative.

It has been questioned whether the roots of the Republican system of government could have been organized and put into operation immediately after the expulsion of the kings. A few modern scholars prefer to interpret the growth of the system in evolutionary terms, as a gradual accretion of procedures and personnel built up empirically, based on experience and changing circumstances. It is unlikely that the truth will ever be revealed, but it is permissible to ask why the leading citizens of Rome are not considered capable of holding discussions to decide on how to govern from the first moment that they were free to do so, *c.*509 BC. At a distance of over twenty-five centuries it is perhaps too easy to overlook the fact that the largely anonymous men who guided the transition of Rome from monarchy to Republic were real people, endowed with the same brain capacity as modern humans. Whoever they were, collectively they most likely possessed all the attributes that were necessary in their new situation, and were probably courageous, efficient, capable of deliberation and making decisions, and sufficiently powerful, authoritative and ruthless to ensure that their decisions were not overruled. The heads of the most important families would have been able to hand down to their descendants a group consciousness of the government of Rome, derived from their association with the kings and from their tours of duty serving for five days, turn and turn about, as *interreges* when the kings died. They would not approach the art of ruling as complete novices, devoid of any experience at all. There is no reason why they could not have combined innovation with evolution, starting with an immediate improvisation which laid the foundations of the government, and constantly monitoring and adapting as time went on. The Romans usually dealt with new or changed situations by reshaping established systems that were already in place and of proven worth, which may be the method adopted by the first administrators of the Republic. The problem is that there is scarcely any information about the administrative system of the monarchy, and therefore it is impossible to discern how much of the Republican government grew out of that of the kings.

It was not as though the leaders of the newly established state could afford the luxury of indecisive vacillation, burying their heads in the sand and hoping that things would turn out all right in the end. There were several problems that beset the nascent Republic, some of them downright dangerous, and someone had to take over the government and make it function, attending to the administration, the economy, the food supply, the law, state security, and religion, without too much of a confused hiatus which could be exploited by neighbouring states or tribes. As well as being surrounded by potential external enemies, Rome faced internal upheavals as well, and it all had to be dealt with if Rome was not to be annihilated by combination of these dangers.

GOVERNMENT OF THE REPUBLIC

The governmental system of the Republic consisted of an advisory body of the leading men of the state, collectively called the Senate. The people were grouped together in assemblies, with certain limited powers, but sufficient to justify the proud title *Senatus Populusque Romanus*, the Senate and People of Rome. Administration was carried out by annually elected magistrates, who could serve for further terms, but never more than one year at a time, so that theoretically no single individual could legitimately retain power for a longer period, though it must be acknowledged that many of the internal problems of the Roman Republic arose from ambitious men trying to bend the rules to achieve and retain power, until finally someone accomplished it without upsetting too many people and created the Empire.

The Senate was probably already in existence before the Republic was formed, as the advisory body of the kings, though it may not have been a permanent establishment consisting of members appointed for life. It may not have been a body of a standard predetermined size, all of whose members were eligible to attend regular meetings. The kings may have summoned advisors on an *ad hoc* basis to debate specific problems, and then dismissed them, choosing a different set of senators when the next matter for discussion arose. The concept of the Senate as an advisory body, and no doubt many of the individual senators, survived the transition to the Republic, but the new Senate enjoyed considerably greater power than an advisory council.

Membership of the Senate was always based on wealth. In the Republic the property qualification was 400,000 sesterces (*sestertii*), and it remained at that figure until Augustus increased the minimum qualification to 1 million sesterces. The senators were mainly land-owners, but the Senate was not necessarily a totally aristocratic institution. Sons of senators did not automatically follow their fathers into the Senate since membership was not purely hereditary. Unsuitable men were not admitted, or if they had managed to become senators, they could be weeded out. From the middle of the fifth century BC, two magistrates called censors were elected by the people's assembly every four years, later changed to every five years. Their principal duties were to carry out a census of the Roman populace, as their name suggests, but during their tenure of office, which lasted for a year and a half, the censors could tidy up membership of the Senate and eject men whose behaviour or character did not conform to the desirable specifications.

The size of the Senate varied from time to time, according to requirements. There were 300 members in the second century BC, rising to 900 in the following century under Julius Caesar, who elevated certain individuals to senatorial status. At the end of the civil wars between Caesar and Pompey, and then between Mark Antony and Octavian, there were 1,000 senators, but Augustus reduced the number to a more manageable 600 in 18 BC. This remained the norm until the third century AD.

The senators shared a considerable collective experience of government, which qualified them for the supervision of domestic and foreign policy, the law, and religion. During the later Republic foreign embassies coming into Rome reported not to the magistrates but to the Senate, and likewise it was the Senate that collectively monitored the government of the Italian states, with the authority to interfere if it was considered necessary. The Senate delegated and despatched embassies to other countries outside Italy. Public trials for serious crimes, such as treason, conspiracy and assassination, were presided over by the Senate. Since the administration of finance was also under senatorial control, the commanders of the army were dependent on the goodwill of the senators, because it was only the Senate that had the power to authorize the provision of food, clothing, and pay to the troops. Campaigns could grind to a halt for lack of supplies and pay if the Senate was not feeling generous, as attested when the youthful general Gnaeus Pompeius Magnus wrote scathing letters from Spain, threatening to abandon the war because he had used up all his own money in buying food and paying his soldiers. He was exaggerating of course, since he was one of the wealthiest landowners in Rome, but he was not alone in having to go cap in hand to an intransigent Senate who wanted results without having to pay for them.

As time went on and the territory controlled by Rome increased, membership of the Senate was gradually modified and regulated, and a career path emerged, usually combining a succession of military and civilian posts. Senators were expected to take on many different tasks without very much training. They commanded armies and governed provinces, as well as taking part in the government at Rome. When the Empire was established, membership of the Senate was still the gateway to an administrative and political career, but the Emperor alone took control of military affairs and financial policy.

The people's assemblies of Republican Rome had some limited powers. They voted for candidates for the annual magistracies, and they accepted or rejected proposals that were put to them by the magistrates, but they had no right to discuss or to amend anything contained in the proposals. The two main assemblies were the *comitia curiata* and the *comitia centuriata*. The former assembly was the oldest, operative during the reigns of the kings of Rome, based on the thirty *curiae* or divisions of the tribes. The *comitia curiata* confirmed the appointment of the magistrates, and passed the necessary law (*lex curiata de imperio*) to bestow military power (*imperium*) on those magistrates who were to command armies.

The *comitia centuriata* was formed some time later than the *comitia curiata*, as part of the so-called Servian reforms, whereby the voting centuries and the military centuries were the same, so the functions of the *comitia centuriata* were related to those of the army. Perhaps its most important function with regard to the army was that this assembly was responsible for the declaration or rejection of war, and contrary to the popular image of the Romans as a totally warlike people, the assembly sometimes did not approve of going to war. In later years, as army organization changed, the divisions of the *comitia centuriata* lost their relationship to the composition of the army, but the assembly continued to carry out its political functions, declaring for or against wars, enacting laws, and electing the censors, consuls, and praetors.

Government by the Senate and People required personnel to carry out the various functions. The most powerful official, with supreme command of all things military and civilian, was the Dictator. This was not a regular appointment. A Dictator was usually chosen only in times of emergencies, for a period of six months. Everyone was subject to his rule, even the chief magistrates, the consuls, who were not removed from office. They resumed their own powers when the Dictator resigned.

In the later Republic, the supreme magistrates were the two annually elected consuls. It is generally assumed from the information contained in the *Fasti*, or lists of the consuls, that these magistrates were installed immediately after the ejection of Tarquinius Superbus, but this is not accepted by all scholars, and the nature of the consulship and the date of its institution have been questioned. One suggestion is that for an unspecified length of time, the chief magistrates of early Republican Rome may have originally been called praetors, a title that derives from the verb *prae-ire*, meaning 'to go before'. There may have been only one praetor, though there are references from the early Republic to a *praetor maximus*, implying that since there was a most important praetor, there may have been at least two lesser ones, but there is no definite information from which to draw firm conclusions about the rank or the number of praetors in the very early Republic, so informed speculation is the ultimate recourse for historians.

Alternatively it has been argued that the first magistrates after the fall of the monarchy were Dictators, elected annually and ruling without a colleague, and only later was this post limited to a six month term and adopted solely for times of emergency. The concept of a single all-powerful ruler was supposed to be anathema to the Romans, and the death penalty could be imposed on anyone who aspired to *regnum*, or kingship, so the story goes that the Romans adopted the collegiate principle of electing two chief magistrates so that one of them could check the over-weaning ambitions of the other, if such a situation should arise. In the fully fledged system, if one of the consuls died before the termination of his office, the other consul was obliged to hold elections to replace him, presumably to remove the temptation for the surviving consul to exercise supreme power even for a few months.

Despite the Roman aversion to sole rule, it is possible that the collegiate system was not observed when the very first consuls were installed. Some scholars suggest that the consuls were not originally elected in pairs, but this too remains speculative. A further complication is that the consuls were not elected in unbroken succession every year from the foundation of the Republic. Interspersed with the consuls, for blocks of several years in succession, a number of officials were appointed, called *tribuni militum consulari potestate*, military tribunes with consular power. The concept of consular power was retained but the magistrates exercising this power were not consuls, and they were not paired. There were never less than three at a time, sometimes four, and most commonly six. This situation lasted, on and off, from the middle of the fifth century until 367 BC.

During the later Republic, the consuls attended to all aspects of government, and were responsible for raising and commanding the armies. It was the summit of a politician's career to reach the consulship, and there was considerable cachet in belonging to a consular family, whose ancestors had all been consuls, sometimes more than once. It was permissible to stand for election after attaining the first consulship, and some men held the office several times, especially in times of danger. At the end of the second century BC when Italy was threatened by invasion from roving Celtic tribes, Gaius Marius was elected for six years in succession, mostly without even having to present himself in the city, because he was with the army, preparing for the next attack by the tribes. Other politicians tried to manoeuvre themselves into more than one year as consul, because they felt that holding office for only one year, and working with a colleague who could oppose any proposals, restricted the development of their policies, and it was especially irksome for the implementation of long-term plans. Hence men like Lucius Cornelius Sulla and Gaius Julius Caesar accepted the Dictatorship, eventually having it conferred on them for life, in order to push through their reforms with a tenuous semblance of legality. At the demise of the Republic, Augustus was much more covert and subtle, and managed to arrogate all power to himself without using inflammatory titles. The office of consul still held attractions for ambitious men under the Empire. Although it was the Emperor who was supreme commander of the armies and the master of the government, consulars were required to fill the posts as provincial governors and subordinate army commanders, and anyone who impressed the Emperor could rise to prominence and wealth.

Probably in 367 BC, after the Licinian-Sextian law was passed implementing reforms of the consulship, the praetors appeared, or possibly reappeared. These magistrates were elected annually and were subordinate to the consuls, and the post eventually became one of the stages on the path to the consulship. Originally only one praetor was elected. He could hold *imperium*, meaning that he was empowered to command armies, and he was left in full charge of the city when the consuls were absent. His principal duties involved legal functions as well as government of the city and military command. As Rome extended control over Italy, and then over countries outside Italy, the government required more personnel to carry out the increased administration, so the number of praetors was continually increased to cope with a growing workload. From the middle of the third century BC, there were two praetors, one to deal with internal affairs (*praetor urbanus*) and one to deal with foreigners (*praetor inter peregrinos*). The first provinces were governed by praetors. For a short time under Julius Caesar there were sixteen praetors, but the final total under Augustus was twelve. After holding office, the ex-praetor's subsequent post was usually as legate of a legion or as governor of a senatorial province.

Viewed retrospectively from the later Republic, this was the basis of the system that the Romans adopted once the monarchy was abolished. Whether they arrived at this level of sophistication soon after the ejection of the kings, or over a period of time, is still debated, but with a rudimentary form of the government that lasted for several centuries, the first Republican Romans faced their future. There was a long way to go and several problems to overcome. Internal upheavals and external wars occurred sometimes simultaneously and sometimes in succession, and occasionally one was linked directly to the other. Roman political life could never be long removed from war.

PATRICIANS & PLEBEIANS

Within the Roman populace, as with any other people, there were several divisions and dissensions. Perhaps the most important of these divisions, and the most problematic both for the Romans and for modern historians trying to analyse it, was the split between the aristocrats, the patricians, and the ordinary people, called plebeians, or the plebs. At a casual glance this seems quite straightforward, but on investigation it becomes more complicated. The ancient historians, accustomed to the patrician/plebeian divide, assumed that the division had begun in the days of the kings, probably dating back to Romulus and the foundation of the city. This is by no means proven, and no one can say definitely what was the distinction between patricians and plebs, nor when the differences became crystallized. It is not clear by what criteria patricians and plebs distinguished themselves, or how they recognized their own status and that of the other group.

Perennially, the differences between the patricians and plebs are categorized as the diametrically opposed rich and poor, landowners and landless, senators and people, none of which is accurate and none of which completely rationalizes the situation. Modern historians have suggested various origins for the two groups. Some of them subscribed to the theory that the patricians may have been the original settlers who came with Romulus, so the Greek and Roman scholars may have been correct in their assumption that the division went back to the foundation of Rome. More alarmingly for modern audiences, some historians preferred to explain the distinction as racial, the patricians being Romans and the plebs Sabine, or alternatively the patricians were the first settlers and the plebs were the hangers-on who came to Rome either voluntarily or were brought there as captives after their cities had been defeated and the inhabitants transferred. This neatly accounts for the inferior status of the plebs.

Another theory turns the problem on its head, preferring to label the plebs as the original residents of Rome, and the patricians as the non-Roman aristocracy who imposed their authority over the indigenous population, who were relegated to a lower status. This theory accounts for the fact that the patricians were confined to a few clans, or *gentes*, from *gens*, denoting members of a family all descended from a common ancestor.

The political friction between the patricians and plebs has been described as the 'struggle of the orders', a label invented by historians to describe a common thread that ran through many years of Roman history, but one of the side-effects of this label is that it also gives the impression that there was a prolonged campaign in which the plebs consistently strove towards their goal of political and social equality, and in response, the patricians fought to retain their supremacy. The reality is more like a series of squabbles over different grievances, sparked off by specific events or by legislation, and resolved, eventually, one at a time.

The plebeians were free-born Roman citizens who were not patricians, but it is not certain that every member of the population who did not belong to the patrician clans was necessarily a plebeian. There seem to have been other divisions or cross sections which are not clearly elucidated, and it is possible that people could belong to a selection of them. Plebeian and patrician status was hereditary. The plebeians were not all in dire poverty, and patricians did not derive their status solely from wealth, or to put it another way, wealth could not buy patrician status. In the later Republic, some plebeians were wealthier than some of the patricians, and a plebeian nobility arose, side by side with the patricians. Marriages between plebs and patricians were initially forbidden by law, but this legislation was quickly rescinded. Marriage liaisons took place between the two orders, but the plebeians remained plebeians and the patricians remained patricians, so it is clear that even over a prolonged period, intermarriage did not annul the differences between the two.

The so-called 'struggle of the orders' did not emerge until the fifth century BC. According to tradition, in 494 and again in 471 BC, the plebs uprooted themselves and left Rome, events known as the first and second secessions, the first one being somewhat doubtful. The legend says that in 494 the plebs occupied a hill, perhaps the Sacred Mount near the Tiber a few miles downstream from Rome, or possibly the Aventine, which was still outside the city boundary at the time. Some time later the Temple of Ceres on the Aventine became the cult centre for the plebs. It is not certain what gave rise to this first secession, nor is it clear whether the whole of the non-patrician population left the city, or even if all the plebeians were included in the dissident group.

It may have been mounting debts, or a decline in the standard of living, or oppression by the patricians, or all these burdens and more, that caused the plebs to rebel. Oppression by the patricians was a theme that ran through all agitation by the plebs. Debt and land distribution also featured constantly. In the context of the fifth century BC, the constant warfare with neighbouring tribes most likely contributed to the economic decline that is archaeologically attested for the same period in Rome and many of the cities in surrounding Roman territory. It would be the poorer people who felt the pinch more than the aristocrats, and most likely the plebs borrowed from the patricians just to keep going. Men could be legally imprisoned for debt, but creditors did not always have recourse to legal proceedings, and stories were told of men being beaten up, or arbitrarily imprisoned when they could not repay their loans. There is probably a basis of truth in the tales, even if hyperbole did the rest.

There may have been food shortages when the plebs seceded from Rome, perhaps the most inflammatory problem of all because the effects would be felt more rapidly than mounting debts. There were several occasions when food shortages were serious enough to be recorded in the annals of the fifth century BC. Once again the constant warfare probably contributed to and exacerbated the problem of the food supply by limiting production. Agriculture suffered when the farmer soldiers could not attend to their farms, or if the enemy destroyed the crops or stole them. Raiding of this sort and encroachment on agricultural land was probably the most common cause of the wars in the fifth century.

It was not only Rome's enemies who encroached on land, however. Another perennial problem that surfaced from time to time throughout the Republic was the distribution of public lands, the *ager publicus*. Theoretically this land was open to all citizens but in reality it was dominated by the aristocrats who were powerful enough and rich enough to drive people off the land and install their favourites, or their clients (*clientes*) with whom each patrician family surrounded themselves in a mutually supporting group.

The Romans were nearly always fighting some enemy or other from the tribes that surrounded them, and at the time of the so-called first secession in 494 BC they were involved in an ongoing war with the Latin cities, so the bargaining tool of the plebs was a refusal to serve in the army. But to serve as what? It is considered unlikely that the plebs formed the bulk of the main Roman army of the time, the hoplite phalanx, so if the plebs normally served as light-armed troops, this would leave the phalanx intact, and would probably not represent a crippling disadvantage to the Romans.

The first and second secessions in 494 and 471 BC are not unassailable truths and may have been fabricated, in whole or in part. The only certainties are the long term results of plebeian agitation in the early fifth century, beginning with the eventual establishment of the *concilium plebis* and the annual election of tribunes of the plebs. The *concilium plebis* was an assembly of the plebeians, distinct from the other assemblies called the *comitia curiata* and *comitia centuriata*. In its fully established form, the *concilium plebis* was responsible for the election of the tribunes of the plebs, and two magistrates called aediles, who were answerable to the tribunes, serving as their executive assistants. The principal duties of the aediles concerned the supervision and maintenance of the temples of Diana and Ceres on the Aventine Hill. From 367 BC onwards, two more aediles were elected, this time by the patricians, but all four of these magistrates protected the interests of the plebs, and were responsible for the maintenance and administration of the city, the streets and markets, and the organization of the public games. The post of aedile was a multi-tasking occupation, and a good grounding for participation in administration and government. Eventually the *concilium plebis* was called *comitia plebis*, like the other assemblies, probably after 471 when its voting mechanisms were reformed by the tribune Volero Publilius. It is not clear how votes were cast before this date, but when the system was reorganized, local tribes were taken as the voting units, decisions being made on the majority vote. The method by which Publilius reorganized the voting system was known as a plebiscite. He put forward his proposal, and the plebs voted on it (by whatever method was in use at the time), which is how the tribunes operated in the plebeian assembly. The plebiscites were designed to regulate the organization of the plebs alone, but from about the middle of the fifth century they were recognized as laws affecting the whole community, provided that they were approved by the patrician senators. In the third century BC this need for this approval was no longer necessary and plebiscites had the validity of laws.

The tribunes of the plebs understandably had to be of plebeian origin. They were not magistrates, and were not eligible to command armies, being quite distinct from the military tribunes who shared the title but not the functions. Using their political powers (all embraced under the heading of *tribunicia potestas*) the main duty of the *tribuni plebis* was to protect the plebs from harm. Their most important political tool was the right of *intercessio*, or veto, against proposals emanating from any other tribune or any magistrate except the Dictator, whose authority overrode all other state officials. The tribunes enjoyed the protection of sacrosanctity, anyone who harmed them being subject to terrible curses, a useful device during the next centuries.

Originally there were only two tribunes, but their number was soon raised. The ancient historians seemed uncertain of the date when the increase in numbers of tribunes took place, and could not even agree about how many tribunes there actually were in this interim stage. There was probably an addition of three tribunes, making five in total, and it probably happened in 471 BC, the traditional date of the second plebeian secession. Information is more definite for the middle of the fifth century BC when the number of tribunes was increased to ten, and remained at that strength throughout the Republic. Tribunes entered office in early December, slightly earlier than the rest of the magistrates whose annual tour of duty began in January.

Naturally some of the patricians were opposed to the institution of the tribunes, epitomized by the probably mythical story of Caius Marcius Coriolanus, the heroic soldier who took his name from his exploits at the siege of the Volscian city of Corioli. The Volsci tried to break out through the siege lines, and Coriolanus drove them back. As a military hero, he would possess some influence, and as a staunch patrician he objected to plebeians in positions of power. He tried to prevent the adoption of the tribunes, allegedly by locking up the grain supply to force the plebs to give up the scheme. The story neatly highlights the ruthlessness of the patricians, and also illustrates how serious were the intentions of the plebs, who were not diverted from the cause despite the threats.

The power of the *tribuni plebis* was accrued only in gradual stages. At first the tribunes were confined to summoning the plebeian assembly, and were excluded from the Senate. In the third century BC they were allowed to listen to senatorial debates, and were eventually granted the right to convoke meetings of the Senate. The office evolved into one of the most useful organs of the state, as the tribunate gradually acquired more influence, but towards the end of the Republic some of the influential and ambitious politicians used unscrupulous methods to buy the co-operation of amenable tribunes to pursue their own political agendas.

The plebs did finally achieve recognition and equality with the patricians but it took a very long time. One slow burning result of plebeian pressure was their admission to the Senate, and to the major magistracies and priesthoods. Originally the plebs were probably not excluded from the Senate but it seems that the patricians made concerted efforts to keep them out of the government, so successful that it took more than a century after the first secession for the plebs to gain access to the consulship.

For a decade, from 376 to 367, the tribunes of the plebs Gaius Licinius Stolo and Lucius Sextius Lateranus campaigned to open up the consulship to plebeians, to ameliorate the problems of debt, and to establish a fairer system of land distribution. In 367 they succeeded in passing their law which achieved most of what they desired. The laws of Rome were always labelled with the family names of the men who succeeded in getting them passed, so this legislation is known as the Licinian-Sextian law.

The next law that dealt with plebeian access to the consulship was passed in 342 BC by the tribune Lucius Genucius. The accounts in the ancient histories, principally the information found on the Roman history of Livy, are at odds with what resulted from the two laws. It was said that the law of 362 stipulated that one of the consuls must be a plebeian, and the law of 342 made provision for both consulships to be held by plebeians. The lists of consuls contradict this assumption, showing that from 362 onwards the patricians still dominated the consulship, but after 342, one of them was consistently a plebeian, so modern historians have reinterpreted the two successive laws. The Licinian-Sextian law most likely allowed plebeians to stand as candidates for the consulship, which did not necessarily mean that any of them would be elected, and the law of Genucius stipulated that one consul should be plebeian every year, because the evidence shows that this is what in fact happened.

THE TWELVE TABLES: THE CODIFICATION OF THE LAW

Another successful outcome of plebeian pressure was the clarification and codification of the law. It was difficult to remain on the right side of the law if no one except a select few knew what the law was. Agitation began in 462 and produced results after a decade. Allegedly the Romans sent an embassy, in reality a working party, to Athens to study the laws of Solon. It has been pointed out that the laws of fifth century Athens had moved on since the time of Solon, but his name perhaps carried weight with the Romans. When they had completed their studies in Athens and other Greek cities, the Romans adopted a novel scheme to institute their own laws. In 451 BC it was agreed to replace the normal system of government with a new one. The consuls and tribunes stepped down, and in their place ten men were elected, to carry out all the usual tasks of day to day government and administration, but also to draw up the law codes, as reflected in their title, *Decemviri legibus scribundis*, literally ten men to write the laws.

The *Decemviri* held office for one year, at the end of which they had drafted several laws, arranged in ten groups, called tables. These were approved and ratified by the whole people in the *comitia centuriata*. Since the ten tables did not embrace all the necessary laws, a second set of *Decemviri* was elected for the year 450 BC to continue the work. A significant factor was that the first group of ten men was made up predominantly, perhaps even totally, of patricians, and the second set comprised a mixture of plebeians and patricians. One man, Appius Claudius, had served with the first ten and canvassed energetically for re-election. He succeeded in being appointed, but there was trouble ahead, and he was one of the causes of it, or was blamed for it after the event. The new *Decemviri* produced two more sets of laws, thus raising the total to the Twelve Tables, by which they are known today. The complete text was inscribed on bronze and displayed in the Forum, but according to Livy the bronzes were destroyed when the Gauls sacked Rome in 390 BC. At any rate, the bronze tablets had already disappeared from view by the later first century BC, but the text itself survived and, according to Cicero, schoolboys had to learn it by heart. Modern scholars have been able to put together some of the laws from the surviving quotations in the ancient literature, but it is not absolutely clear to which table each of the laws belonged. The incomplete text is usually presented nowadays arranged under the twelve headings, following the painstaking study of a nineteenth-century scholar, but new evidence may one day come to light which could alter the allocation of laws to specific tables.

After their achievement in adding the two new tables, the *Decemviri* refused to relinquish their power. Historical fact now shades off into varying degrees of fable, involving a scandal when Appius Claudius tried to rape a young girl called Verginia, the daughter of a centurion in the army. Not content with having assaulted her, Claudius tried to prove that the girl had started life as a slave in his household, but was somehow spirited away as an infant, which meant that she was legally his property. Rather than have his daughter so dishonoured, Verginius killed her, then led the army in a revolt, while the people marched off to the Janiculum Hill, where they remained in protest against such arbitrary treatment of Verginia. The story recalls quite closely the rape of Lucretia by the son of the last Tarquinius, and the parallel may not be wholly coincidental. Tyrannical behaviour quite rightly ends in tears and, when calm and normal government had been restored, Appius Claudius met his just deserts. Verginius accosted him in the Forum, and accused him of breaking one of the laws he had helped to establish, namely the false enslavement of a free person. Claudius was imprisoned, and according to Livy he committed suicide, but Dionysius of Halicarnassus says he was murdered by the reinstated tribunes.

It is not certain whether the *Decemviri* were originally constituted as a permanent body, staffed by annually elected personnel who would permanently replace the consuls and other magistrates. The original intention may have been to suspend normal government on a temporary basis, and appoint the *Decemviri* to carry out the specific task of drafting the laws, so that when this task was completed, the consuls and other magistrates, and the tribunes, would return to office. The chaotic circumstances when the *Decemviri* tried to hang onto power threw into disarray the original plans, whatever they had been. Legislation was required to restore the peace, and to reconstitute the government. Traditionally, it was a series of enactments, known as the Valerio-Horatian laws, that put an end to the powers of the *Decemviri* and reconciled the plebs and patricians, who had temporarily united against a common enemy. As with most aspects of the early Republic, these laws are subject to debate, not least because very similar laws were passed in successive years, by different consuls all named Valerius, so it is almost impossible to disentangle the original legislation of the fifth century from that of later centuries.

EXTERNAL AFFAIRS

From the foundation of the Republic, Rome was embroiled in constant wars, not entirely on an annual basis, but frequently enough to provide them with considerable experience. Although the various military activities are labelled as wars they were not the full scale actions that characterized the later campaigns of the Republic and Empire, and not on the same scale as the wars of the modern world. War in the early Roman Republic was more of a seasonal hazard, or a series of periodic spats. There were casualties on both sides, but often there were no long lasting consequences, and there was not always any wide ranging political aim, consistently pursued.

The most common causes of warfare were territorial. Rome searched for safe boundaries and tried to maintain them – an excuse that would lead eventually to the establishment of the Empire. All wars waged by the Romans were of course perfectly justified, even if they had to enter into sundry contortions of the truth to prove that they were fighting in a just cause. Their enemies no doubt went through the same motions. Rome's neighbours waged war most often because of population pressure and the need for expansion, to find more land in which to settle and grow crops.

The Volsci gradually encroached on the southern areas of Latium for this reason. This is not to imply that all wars were started by migratory tribesmen looking for the ancient equivalent of *Lebensraum*. Some wars were more readily categorized as raids, to run off livestock or steal crops, or simply to loot and pillage. Other wars were fought for political reasons, often over rights of way and monopoly of trade routes, and the commercial advantages that accrued from controlling them. Commercial rights and privileges feature in some of the treaties that were arranged when the wars ended.

The Romans were by no means always the aggressors in the wars of the fifth and fourth centuries BC, nor did they always emerge as the victors. The armies came home with bloody noses more often than the historians liked to admit, but one consistent and stubborn characteristic of the Romans emerged quite early, namely that despite their defeats they did not give in. They lost battles, and sometimes wars, but they did not even consider long-term submission. It sometimes took many years, involving several wars and several generations of citizen-soldiers, to reach a satisfactory conclusion – that is, satisfactory to the Romans – but the Romans never acknowledged that they were beaten and never gave up. The tribes around them were nearly as persistent as the Romans, and kept on trying at irregular intervals to make their point, but in the long run Rome kept on raising more armies, and it was her neighbours who crumbled and finally stopped fighting. Periodically an end to hostilities was declared, alliances were forged and treaties were drawn up, but the terms of the treaties were just as easily broken, often by the Romans themselves if changed circumstances and expediency demanded it. The Romans made common cause with other tribes or cities, and most often these tribes and cities were only too willing to throw in their lot with Rome to unite their forces and fight against their mutual enemies, for instance when the Campanians joined the Romans to counter the threat from the Samnites. After the wars ended and the emergency was over, these arrangements did not always work to the advantage of Rome's partners, who were made aware of their inferior standing. Occasionally Rome's allies reasserted their independence and tried to shake off what they saw as Roman domination, but the result, more often than not, was a reaffirmation and strengthening of that domination

The army that Rome assembled to wage these wars was composed of citizens called up at an annual levy, or *legio*, which means 'the choosing', but the word was also applied to the fighting unit itself, and has descended into modern times as legion. Throughout the Republic, armies had to be gathered in this way by levying troops for specific campaigns. There was no regular standing army as there was in Imperial times, with pay and pensions, and opportunities for promotion. Whenever the army was assembled men who had served as centurions in the last war might find themselves in the ranks again, and then, if they were lucky, they might be promoted during the course of the campaign. There was a property qualification for service in the army, so the poorest men who had very small farms or no property at all were normally excluded from service. Of the eligible male population, it is highly unlikely that every single one of them was recruited when campaigns began, which is why Rome was always able to field yet another army when disasters occurred. Due consideration had to be made for the farming year, to planting and harvest times, and it is probable that in recruiting farmer-soldiers, some able bodied men were left at home to tend the crops and animals, and ensure the food production. Traditionally, the first time that a Roman army was retained under arms beyond the harvest season, and indeed for several years, was at the siege of Veii at the beginning of the fourth century. The state had to introduce payment for the soldiers for the first time to alleviate their problems caused by being under arms for an extended period.

The early Republican army was modelled on the Greek hoplite phalanx. The citizens of the Greek colonies of Italy introduced the system, which was perhaps transmitted to the Romans via the Etruscans, who also adopted the phalanx. This was a heavy-armed infantry army, each soldier carrying a round shield, (*clipeus*) and a long spear. The men lined up in close formation, usually in lines consisting of twelve men, and about eight ranks deep. They overlapped their round shields, and advanced almost as a single unit, bristling with spears, a bit like an ancient forerunner of the tank, or like a roller, which is the literal meaning of phalanx. It was a formidable military machine, but for maximum effectiveness it required the protection and support of cavalry and light-armed troops on the wings. These extra troops would eventually be supplied by the allies of the Romans, since the terms of most alliances included the obligation to raise troops whenever there was a war. One problem that the Romans encountered at the end of the fourth century BC, when they fought in Samnite territory, was that the phalanx was unwieldy in rough terrain, because it was difficult to maintain the vital close formation.

For many years, the annual levy produced only one legion, but by the middle of the fourth century BC, the Romans were often faced with wars on two fronts, and the levy was increased to two legions. By the end of the fourth century, the Romans were regularly raising four legions, and at some point they changed the formation from the phalanx to a looser system based on small sub-divisions of the legion called maniples, which means 'handfuls' of men. The round *clipeus* was abandoned, and an oval shield was substituted, called the *scutum*. It is possible that the soldiers also abandoned the long spears of the phalanx, and started to use javelins instead, but this is a controversial issue. According to Livy each legion of this reformed manipular style was drawn up in three main battle lines, with heavy infantry in the front ranks, assisted by light-armed troops. The front ranks were usually made up of the younger men, and the middle ranks behind them were composed older men with more experience. The veterans and the lighter-armed troops brought up the rear. This is a simplistic outline, giving only the main points, the details of which have been debated by scholars at length and in depth, but in general this is the kind of army employed by the Romans against their neighbours, perhaps from the middle of the fourth century BC.

Almost immediately after the end of the monarchy, the Romans were opposed by a coalition of the Latin cities, in a co-ordinated attempt to put an end to the domination of Rome. Modern scholars label this coalition as the Latin League, and at least one ancient historian refers to it by the Greek term *koinon*, which translates as league, and implies that there was such an association, but it is not certain whether the cities made any formal alliance beyond their shared sense of identity and common heritage. The Latins met each year at the sacred site of Ferentina, south of Aricia, to be distinguished from Ferentinum, several kilometres to the east in the territory of the Hernici. As well as conducting the annual ceremonial, the Latins drew up their army at Ferentina if there was to be a campaign, so they were already accustomed to acting in concert and may not have required any formal alliance or documentation to spur them on to concentrate their efforts against Rome.

Whatever the Latins hoped to achieve, they were seriously disappointed when the Romans defeated them at the battle of Lake Regillus in 499 BC. Some years later in 493 BC, a treaty was arranged by the consul Spurius Cassius. If the Latins had been quiescent for the intervening six years, their subsequent history reveals that they were not yet prepared to acknowledge Rome as the leading state and themselves as subordinate to her. For the Romans, it was imperative to work closely with the Latins and to monitor what was happening in their territory, to prevent the tribes all around Latium from taking over parts of it. What threatened Latium ultimately threatened Rome. The terms of the treaty of 493 BC may have become confused with those of later treaties, but it is likely that the main features were worked out in the fifth century, and perhaps revisited in later agreements. According to Dionysius of Halicarnassus, in 493 BC each side agreed to render assistance if the other was threatened, and just as important, they agreed not to assist enemies of either party. The most important feature for the Romans was the contribution of the Latins to the campaign armies. Allies of Rome could look to the Romans for protection, but reciprocally they were expected to levy troops to fight on Rome's behalf. The number of men to be raised was formally agreed and recorded for each allied state or tribe. Though the military contribution was paramount, the treaty took due notice of civilian affairs. Romans and Latins were granted *conubium*, or the right to intermarry, and *commercium*, which allowed mutual trading and business rights in Rome itself and in the Latin cities. Citizenship was interchangeable. A Roman became a Latin citizen if he resided in a Latin colony, but if he moved back to Rome he resumed his Roman citizenship. A child of a Roman father and a Latin mother was counted a citizen of Rome, and if they were boys they were eligible to serve in the Roman citizen legions.

During the fifth and most of the fourth centuries BC the Romans fought all their immediate neighbours in various campaigns. These wars cannot be documented in detail, in the same way that the campaigns of the later Republic can be described. The surviving accounts of most of the early battles are sketchy and intertwined with legend to such an extent that it is impossible to elucidate what actually happened, save for a few indications of who fought whom and when, what the outcome was, and less often, why they did so, but it is not possible to follow the course of the wars with battle plans, positions of troops, strategic manoeuvres and the like because such information is lacking. Even if a place name is given in any of the sources, the modern location is not always certain, so it is impossible to speculate about the terrain and its influence on the battle.

Rome's neighbours consisted of tribes or cities of varying degrees of sophistication and military prowess. To the south and east of Latium were the Volsci and Aequi, who most often fought independently of each other, but occasionally united to make a concerted effort against Rome if circumstances were favourable. At the beginning of the fifth century the Volsci invaded Latium, sparking off a war which lasted according to traditional dating from 490 to 488 BC. This is the context of the rebellion of Coriolanus, the Roman who had tried to deprive the plebs of their tribunes. He joined the Volsci and fought against Rome, but he was persuaded to withdraw his troops when the Romans sent his mother and his wife to plead with him. He did not come back to Rome and no one knows whether he survived to old age among his adopted people, or was killed by them after the army withdrew. Nor is it known what happened between the Volsci and the Romans.

A few years later the Romans embarked on the first of three wars against the city of Veii, which had been part of the Etruscan sphere of influence since the eighth century BC. Among other grievances, Rome disputed the control of the crossing of the Tiber at Fidenae. The two sides fought each other, on and off, for a long time, culminating in a siege by the Romans which was said to have lasted for ten years. In 396 BC the siege ended in the complete destruction of the city and the absorption of the territory by the Romans. It is significant that the other Etruscan cities did not unite to oppose Rome on behalf of Veii.

In the middle of the fifth century BC the Aequi threatened Rome, at one point surrounding the consul Lucius Minucius in his camp. The army commanded by the other consul was engaged elsewhere, and the situation was desperate, so the Romans pleaded with Lucius Quinctius Cincinnatus to accept the Dictatorship and take the field with another army. According to the legend, Cincinnatus was ploughing on his farm when the senators called on him, but he left this task, took up the Dictatorship, recruited more soldiers, marched to the enemy and defeated them, came home, laid down his office and returned to his farm, all in the breathlessly short time of fifteen days in 458 BC. There seems to have been no conclusive treaty to avert further hostilities, which broke out again on various occasions, until a Roman victory in 431 BC put a temporary end to the endemic fighting. Some time later the Aequi and Volsci pooled their efforts and resources but were defeated once again. A period of relative quiet followed, but the tribes were simply waiting for a more favourable opportunity when Rome was weakened or compromised.

Such an opportunity presented itself after 390 BC, the traditional date according to Varro when the Gauls streamed down from northern Italy and took Rome. The Gallic tribes had settled in the mountains and plains on the south side of the Alps, in an area known as Cisalpine Gaul, literally meaning Gaul on this side of the Alps, or the side nearest the Romans. The Gauls were restless and prone to raiding expeditions to carry off portable wealth and demonstrate their skills as warriors. They were not looking for places to settle, but could cause considerable damage on their way into and out of their raiding zones. The Roman army turned out to try to stop the tribes after they had besieged Clusium. The two sides met at a tributary of the Tiber called the Allia, a name that always recalled utter disaster for the Romans, who turned and fled, scattering all over the area. The road to Rome was open. The Gallic attack on Rome has been played down by modern historians, and indeed it probably attracted heroic hyperbole in later tradition, but the Romans took it seriously enough to evacuate the city, except for a small garrison on the Capitol Hill. There may have been little fighting after the entry into Rome. The Gauls were easily bought off with gold, anxious to return home because they had heard that their own settlements had been attacked. It was not the last Gallic invasion, but it was perhaps the most vivid and traumatic for the Romans, who set up a treasury to finance any future wars against the Gauls. The fund was preserved until the late Republican era, when it was appropriated by Julius Caesar as he was embarking on the civil war with Pompey the Great. Caesar pointed out that since he had spent the last ten years conquering the Gauls, there was no need to maintain the fund any longer.

Taking advantage of what they assumed was Rome's weakened state after the disaster of the Allia, the loss of an army and the sack of Rome, the Aequi, Volsci and Etruscans joined forces to raise rebellion. The wars continued for years, but the uneasy allies were not sufficiently co-ordinated and Rome eventually defeated them one at a time. The Etruscans made peace in 351 BC, while the Volsci held out until 338, when they made an alliance.

In that same year, the Latins were also finally defeated and brought into an alliance, after two attempts at rebellion had been crushed. The treaty of 493 BC had laid down the ground rules of the relationship between the Romans and Latins, ostensibly mutually advantageous to both sides, but with the passage of time, any sense of equality evaporated and Rome began to dominate. The Latins had furnished troops for Rome for a hundred years before the invasion of the Gauls but, although they fought the battles, they did not enjoy the spoils of war or the benefits of peace, and their interests were swept aside in favour of Rome's when treaties were arranged. After 390 BC, the cohesiveness of the Latin League began to dissolve. Rebellion against Rome was fomenting. Some of the Latin cities remained loyal, but the larger and more important ones allied with the Hernici and the Volsci to try to throw off Roman domination. The only result was defeat by Rome and a new treaty in 358 BC, which may have reiterated or been confused with the original treaty of 493. This time, however, there was not even a pretence that Rome was merely the first city among equals.

By 340 BC the Latins had lost patience with an alliance that increasingly relegated them to inferior status. They allied with the Campanians, likewise the victims of unfair treatment by the Romans. Even the cities which had been loyal in the previous rebellion were now increasingly disaffected and joined in the struggle. It took the Romans two years to win the war, but the defeat of the Latins and their allies was total. New treaties were arranged, not with the Latin League as a corporate association, but individually with each city, including the Campanian cities which had joined the Latins. Some cities were incorporated into the Roman state, and the inhabitants became full Romans citizens, with the right to vote and all the legal privileges that Roman citizenship bestowed (*civitas optimo iure*). Other cities that lay in Campania or in the Volscian territory outside the boundaries of Latium, received a half citizenship, without voting rights (*civitas sine suffragio*), and they were expected to contribute troops when called upon as were the other allied communities. Some cities which had fought against Rome were punished, and had to hand over some of their territory to the Romans, but for the most part they retained their own governments, with little interference from the Romans except in cases where their own interests would be compromised. Each city retained its rights of intermarriage and trading with Rome, but not with other cities, and they were forbidden to form any kind of alliance or association with any other community. From then onwards they could direct their internal affairs but not their external policies; they were to have the same friends and enemies as Rome, and to fight in Rome's wars. The Campanian and Latin cities were therefore isolated from each other and from all other Italian cities. They were permitted to form a relationship only with Rome. The Latin League was dead, never to be revived.

THE SAMNITES

While these continuous wars were fought with Rome's immediate neighbours throughout the fifth and fourth centuries, a group of tribes to the south was busily expanding and settling, threatening the Greek coastal cities and the Italian inland settlements. The tribes formed and reformed themselves into different groups as they settled down, taking different names. The Romans knew them as the Samnites, who became their fiercest opponents, and the two sides fought with each other in three wars until the beginning of the third century BC, when the Samnites made peace.

Ironically the Romans began their relationship with the Samnites with an alliance formed in 354 BC. It was a temporary marriage of convenience, which averted hostilities between the Samnites and Rome, and made each party stronger against other tribes, principally the fearsome Gauls. The alliance did not last very long. The first Samnite war began in 343 BC, when the Samnites attacked Capua, whose citizens appealed to Rome for help. At the time, the Latins were disaffected and restive, and Rome needed their manpower, so there was a hasty mobilization while the Romans could still call upon Latin manpower, and the Samnites were defeated in 341. In making peace with them, the Romans handed over to the Samnites some Campanian territory, with scant regard to the wishes or needs of the Campanians themselves, who were supposed to be allies of Rome. Then, when the Latins and Campanians rebelled after this roughshod treatment, Rome enlisted Samnite assistance to help to quell the revolt.

The next war broke out in 326 and rumbled on for two decades, collectively labelled the second Samnite war. It was basically a territorial dispute, with a major squabble over the city of Naples. The Romans accused the Samnites of encouraging the Neapolitans to attack the Campanians, Rome's allies. The Romans had not cared very much when they ceded Campanian territory, but now they were outraged when the city of Naples tried to stake a claim to yet more of it. In 327 the Romans attacked Naples, and the Samnites sent troops to help the Neapolitans, but the city fell to the Romans in 326. From then on there were a series of skirmishes between the Romans and the Samnites, until 321 when the Romans tried to invade Samnium itself. On their way from Campania into Apulia, the Roman army inadvisedly marched through a valley and were ambushed there by the Samnite army. There was no choice except surrender. The Romans were allowed to go free, but only after they had disarmed, shed most of their clothing, and bowed their heads while passing under a makeshift yoke formed from three spears. It was known as the disaster of the Caudine Forks. Until the Romans met the Carthaginians, the Caudine Forks eclipsed the Allia in the annals of spectacular Roman defeats.

The Romans lost some territory to the Samnites, but they were not given to wasting their time in sulking, so they quickly started to wage wars and form alliances in the lands all around the Samnite heartland, gradually creating a Roman-controlled barrier designed to cut off and isolate the Samnites. Protesting, the Samnites invaded Latium in 315 BC. They were victorious against the Romans in that year, but defeated in the next. The Roman victory in 314 BC seems to have stunned the Samnites, affording the Romans the opportunity to continue to strengthen their position, extending their control over much of central Italy in the process. These campaigns were deliberately aggressive, resulting in the annihilation of some tribes and the absorption of their territory. Where they could not annexe, or did not wish to, the Romans made strong alliances. It was clear by now that the Romans were never going to be content with control of the lands bordering Latium. It was time for the tribes and cities which had not yet been assimilated to sink their differences and unite against Rome.

The third Samnite war started in 298 when the Samnites attacked the Lucanians, and Rome came to the assistance of the victims. In 297 the Samnites joined the Etruscans, and in 295 they allied with the Gauls. Before they battled against this alliance, the Romans employed a strategy that was to prove useful later on in the third century BC. By sending a reserve army to attack the Etruscan city of Clusium, they drew the majority of the Etruscan contingent away from the alliance. That left the Samnites and the Gauls, and the Romans met them at the battle of Sentinum. It was a decisive victory for Rome, and probably the first battle which was reliably documented, though the numbers of men given in the ancient sources vary, and are probably greatly exaggerated. The sources for the events of the next five years have not survived, so it is not clear what happened to the Samnites after this military defeat. The Romans probably harassed them, destroyed crops and settlements, until they sued for peace, in 290 BC.

New Ideas

During the wars with their neighbours, the Romans developed and adapted their political and military organization according to circumstances. In the military sphere, the Romans learned from their experience and were willing to make changes to meet their current needs. In the war against Veii, when the Romans besieged the city allegedly for ten years, the army had to be kept in the field for a much longer period than usual. The campaigning season ought to have ended in the autumn or as winter approached. The soldiers would expect to disband and go home for the harvest, but the siege could not be abandoned, so arrangements had to be made to keep the army up to strength, and to ensure that the men and horses did not starve. Traditionally, it was during the siege of Veii that the Romans began to pay their troops, perhaps from the proceeds of a property tax that was levied at about the same time. The connection with the siege of Veii may be apocryphal, and since the Romans had not yet adopted coinage, the payment probably consisted of supplies and equipment rather than money, but it seems clear that at some point at the turn of the fifth and fourth centuries BC the soldiers were no longer expected to serve entirely at their own expense, providing their own equipment and food.

Another innovation concerning the army may have occurred during the wars with the Gauls, or with the Samnites. The Gauls fought in loose open order, relying on the initial overpowering charge to break the enemy ranks, and it required a less rigid formation than the phalanx to oppose them successfully. Similarly, when campaigning in the hills and valleys of Samnite territory, the phalanx was once again at a disadvantage. In these wars, the Romans required some method of hurling missiles against a highly mobile enemy without engaging them in the sort of close battle where the soldiers of the phalanx could use the long spears and considerable weight to overpower the enemy. It was probably these combined experiences that generated the change from the hoplite phalanx to the looser formation of the maniples. Though it is a subject that is fraught with controversy, this may have coincided with the introduction of the *pilum*, the javelin or throwing spear. In the phalanx there would not have been the physical space for the soldiers to throw their spears, but in the looser formation of the maniples, the javelin would be more easily employed, and its use would facilitate attacks on mobile enemies who could not be engaged by the phalanx.

There were also some developments in the political sphere, brought about because of the need for continuity of command, for more personnel to carry out the increasing number of simultaneous tasks, and for government of new territories at a distance from Rome. These innovations included the creation of the pro-magistracy, the development of alliances, and the establishment of colonies.

The creation of the pro-magistracy was a response to specific circumstances, but was far from being a temporary measure, and eventually became a normal procedure of government. Until the late Republic, the two consuls usually spent their year of office at the head of the armies on campaign, and were usually recalled when their consulship expired. On occasion the Senate could vote for an extension of the term of office if it was deemed necessary. The appointment of the new magistrates would still go ahead as planned for the year, while the retiring consul ceased to be one of the eponymous annual magistrates, but was still authorized to act with the powers of a consul. The first authentically recorded instance of this procedure occurred in 326 BC when the Senate voted an extension of command (*prorogatio imperii*) to the consul Quintus Publilius Philo, whose term of office was due to expire at the very moment when he was about to capture the city of Naples. The Romans understood that it would jeopardize the whole enterprise to substitute a new commander who was unknown to the troops, and who was not fully aware of the military situation and would have to be thoroughly briefed. Rather than recall Philo, the Senate granted him the powers of a consul (*imperium pro consule*) without actually re-appointing him consul, so that he could still command the army but was not involved in the current government of Rome. The powers of a praetor could also be extended in the same way, by the grant of *imperium pro praetore*. The establishment of the pro-magistracy was a useful device that separated the annual magisterial office on the one hand and its function and power on the other, and as Rome expanded and took in more and more territory, it had the advantage of increasing the number of available personnel to carry out administrative tasks at Rome, to govern the provinces, and command the armies. In the later Republic the consuls and praetors customarily remained in Rome during the tenure of their office, and then at the end of their term they were usually appointed to another task, designated by the Senate. This was their *provincia*, which originally denoted any tour of duty, including repair of roads, care of the woods and forests, adminstration of the food supply or whatever was deemed the greatest priority. When Rome absorbed territories outside Italy, and required personnel to govern them, the word *provincia* was originally applied to the tour of duty for the governor, and then eventually to the actual territory. Most commonly, as the Republic developed, the retiring consuls and praetors were appointed as governors of the territorial provinces, as proconsuls or propraetors.

In less than thirty years after the conclusion of peace with the Samnites in 290, the Romans very quickly extended their control over the rest of Italy. They had developed useful tools to enable them to do so, and more important, these tools also enabled them to maintain their pre-eminent position. It is one thing to conquer, and quite another to survive long enough to establish successful administrative systems in conquered territory. Roman expansion has been viewed in different lights, depending on the era and context in which various scholars studied the problem. The current distaste for imperialistic dominance, largely based on the experience of horrendous wars of the last hundred years, naturally tends to colour the modern interpretation of the Roman Republic and Empire. The emphasis nowadays is on the less savoury aspects of Rome, on militaristic dominance and oppression, as Roman annexation became a habit, eventually extending beyond Italy and the Mediterranean. But there were benefits as well as obligations in belonging to the Roman commonwealth, and dominance was never total, obliterating all trace of native languages, local laws and government, festivals and religious practices. Treaties of alliance usually preserved local customs, and there was little Roman interference in local government. The allied cities were allowed considerable autonomy, and Romanization was voluntary rather than forcibly imposed. Military needs were always of prime importance to the Romans when entering into alliances or any agreements with other states. Whether the alliances were imposed on defeated cities or tribes, or whether they were formed in peaceful circumstances with an exchange of mutual benefits, all the allies were under obligation to fight for Rome in the event of a war. On the other hand the allied cities or tribes could appeal to Rome for help if they were attacked.

One of the most important methods of controlling and protecting newly acquired territory was the establishment of colonies, which served the purpose of finding settlements and land allotments for surplus population from Rome and eventually from other cities, and also of guarding strategic points and protecting routes, though it has been questioned whether they should be interpreted as military settlements established purely for this purpose. Livy called the early colonies both barriers and gateways. The very early colonies of the late fourth century BC consisted of Roman citizens who retained their full voting rights, as the settlements were planted within Roman territory. In the fifth and fourth centuries Latin colonies were set up on the edges of Latium, and the population was probably drawn from different groups of people, who all became citizens of their particular colonies. The colonies were for the most part autonomous, self governing except for foreign policy and relations with other cities, which was firmly controlled by Rome. Sometime later, the establishment of Latin colonies was extended to other areas outside Latium, but this title does not mean that the settlers were all ethnic Latins. It indicates that they were of Latin status (*ius Latii*), which conferred specific rights and obligations. The main obligation was to provide troops to fight alongside the Roman legions, but there were compensations, in that they were afforded Roman protection if they were threatened, and citizens of Latin colonies were allowed to intermarry with Romans (*conubium*) and to trade with them (*commercium*). If they settled in the city of Rome, Latins acquired Roman citizenship.

Thus there were four different status groups within the Roman system, comprising full citizens with voting rights in Rome, who were allowed

3

Strong Rivals: The Republic Meets Foreign Enemies 290–201 BC

It is of tremendous advantage for modern historians that for the period after the Samnite wars the sources are much more reliable than for the preceding centuries, and the chronology of political and military events, though far from perfect, is not quite as confused. The heroic mythology of the early Republic gives way to more sober history, and properly chronicled events and more sharply defined personalities begin to emerge, probably because the first historian of Rome, Fabius Pictor, could rely upon the living memory of his contemporaries, and perhaps utilize more complete official records.

The Roman world of the third century BC was involved in almost constant warfare, first with neighbouring Italian tribes and then with foreign enemies. The first half of the century was a period of endemic unrest, while the tribes and emergent states in Italy fought each other for a variety of reasons, but mostly because of population pressure and the need for more cultivable land, or for the acquisition of portable wealth. Allegiances changed rapidly in Italy. The Romans and the Italian tribes formed alliances and used the manpower furnished by their allies to combat some of their enemies, and then just as easily they allied with their former enemies and fought against their erstwhile allies instead. These chaotic shifting alliances ceased less than thirty years after the defeat of the Samnites, by which time Rome had finally brought all of central and southern Italy under her control. Scholars estimate that between 338 and 264 BC, Roman territory increased from about five thousand square kilometres to an area more than five times as large. Polybius, writing in the second century BC, was amazed that it had taken such a short time to extend Roman control over the whole peninsula. It is misleading to label the process the unification of Italy, except in the sense of bringing the various tribes under Roman rule. There was no absolute unity or uniformity in Italy, even during the Empire. Romanization was not enforced, and except in so far as Latin was universal for administrative purposes, the allied cities and tribes continued to speak their own languages, to worship their own gods and to carry on their own government within the wider Roman

framework. Ethnic and cultural diversity was never totally stamped out
in Italy.

For nearly fifty years after the victories over the Italians, the Romans
fought major wars against the Carthaginians, the first of which nearly,
but not quite, brought Rome to its knees. The seventeen years of warfare
with Hannibal, on Italian soil, was devastating but did not result in the
annihilation of the Romans, largely because of their own grim resolve
not to give in, and because the extra military manpower furnished by
the Italians enabled the Romans to sustain several catastrophic defeats
and to fight wars simultaneously on more than one front, in Italy, Spain,
Macedonia and Africa. At the end of the third century BC, Rome emerged
stronger than ever, as a dominant power in the Mediterranean world.
The success of the Romans was due to several things, among them the
effectiveness of their political and military institutions, their flexibility in
adapting the old forms to new uses, their intransigent refusal to accept
defeat, their pragmatic and unsentimental ruthlessness on the one hand
and on the other their readiness to share the spoils of war and land with
their allies in return for co-operation in military affairs.

POLITICS IN ROME

Politically the Romans still struggled against the possibility of dominance
by one man. The governing body was still the Senate, where the knowledge,
experience and initiative of individual senators combined for the corporate
benefit of the state, but there were dangers when some senators gained
tremendous power. The main reason why certain families or individuals
started to dominate arose from the fact that the people tended to vote
perpetually for the men in whom they had confidence, especially in times
of crisis, so that those who had won victories or solved social and political
problems proved more popular than others. Accomplishments ih war and
politics tended to run in families, so a *de facto* ruling coterie of influential
clans emerged where the family name alone could ensure success at the
elections.

At the end of the fourth century BC, the senator Appius Claudius had
caused a major disruption to the smooth functioning of the state by trying
to hang onto his powers as censor after his term of office expired. The
censorship was not an annually elected post, and was held for eighteen
months. Nothing at all is known of Appius Claudius before he was made
censor in 312 BC, but he was presumably an illustrious ex-consul, since
the office of censor was the highest and most prestigious in the state,
usually the culmination of a long and successful career. In keeping with
the Roman collegiate system, there were usually two censors, but in the
case of Appius Claudius, the influence of his colleague was nullified. One

of the functions of the office was the reform of the senate, a task which Appius Claudius embarked on with enthusiasm, filling the Senate with men of his own choice, while ousting those of whom he did not approve, and by-passing suitable candidates who might otherwise have become senators. He even brought the sons of freedmen into the Senate. This was shocking enough, but another son of a freedman, who acted as secretary to Claudius, was allowed to hold a magistracy. This went against tradition and offended the upper classes.

With a finger in every pie and possessed of grandiose designs, Appius Claudius instigated massive public works, such as the road and the aqueduct named after him. The Aqua Appia brought water to Rome from the Sabine Hills, and the Via Appia connected the city with Capua. Had there been railways in Rome he would certainly have made the trains run on time. He reformed the voting system to give the poorer people more power, removing them from the single group into which they were all compressed, where their vote counted for very little, and distributing them among all the voting tribes, so that their voting powers counted for more. He appeared to be a man of the people, but he was not trying to institute a democratic form of government because he was not really interested in the welfare of the lower classes, except in so far as their gratitude for the benefits he brought them would engender loyalty to him and buy him votes. His example would be followed by several demagogues in the later Republic. At the end of his term of office, Appius Claudius refused to lay down his powers, extending them for as much as four years according to some sources. His plans for Rome were too ambitious for the constrictions of a single term of office, so he tried to adapt the system to his own needs. Much later, Gaius Julius Caesar would face the same problem of long term plans requiring a corresponding long term continuity of power, and would go about achieving it in similar fashion. Unlike Caesar, however, Appius Claudius evaded assassination, and in his old age he still went on to play a part in the politics and wars of Rome.

In order to combat the accrual of personal power as exemplified by Appius Claudius, laws were passed which clearly illustrate what had been happening in Roman political life. It was made illegal to hold more than one magistracy at a time, and a law was passed to ensure that no one could become consul for a further term until ten years had passed. Although it was possible to extend the powers of the consul after his term of office had ceased, by the procedure known as *prorogatio imperio*, the procedure was used less often, in case certain men adopted the habit of angling for an extension of their powers.

In the second decade of the third century BC, the old rivalry between the plebs and patricians finally petered out. Several plebeian families had already been ennobled and had gained political prestige and powers, and ceased to be representative of the wider cause of the plebs in general, who were perennially oppressed by debts and poverty. At some point between 289 and 286 BC there was some sort of trouble when the plebs went on strike again, the principal cause being the problem of debt. A plebeian called Quintus Hortensius, about whom nothing is known, was made Dictator and empowered to sort out the problems. He passed a law (*lex Hortensia*) which solved the problems and also brought an end to the struggle of the orders between plebs and patricians, but it is not at all certain exactly how this was achieved. The *concilium plebis* was formally recognized but by no means granted sovereign powers. This political assembly perhaps attained greater influence than it had previously enjoyed, but it could not direct policy or make laws. The Senate still governed the state and the magistrates framed all proposals, to which the *concilium plebis* could merely say yes or no. 'Power to the people' never achieved more than this in Rome, despite the machinations of Appius Claudius and the passage of the *lex Hortensia*. Chronic debt remained a problem, and the old division of plebs and patricians was commuted into a similar one between rich and influential and poor and ineffective.

THE CONQUEST OF ITALY

In northern Italy the first signs of trouble in which Rome was involved started when the Gallic tribe of the Senones, who had settled north of Picenum, attacked the city of Arretium (Arezzo). The Romans agreed to relieve the city, but initially met with defeat by the Gauls. True to form, they rallied, assembled another army, and in turn defeated the Senones, severely enough to force them to make peace and cede their territory, which was added to the *Ager Gallicus* in 283.

Other Gallic tribes watched as this occurred, and while they were not altogether sympathetic to the Senones or wished to take up their cause, they realized that the same fate might await them, and determined to resist Rome. The Boii decided to make common cause with the Etruscans, who also wanted to shake off Roman control and welcomed the extra manpower that the Gauls could provide. By 280 they too had been defeated by the Romans, in a battle near Volsinii. The Etruscans were not yet ready to lie down in complete submission, but had their own internal problems, in the form of a dissident populace in several cities struggling against the rule of their aristocrats. The Romans always preferred to deal with elite groups, or ruling classes, and agreed to help the Etruscans reassert aristocratic control. When the disturbances were quelled, the Romans took over some Etruscan territory and planted a colony at Cosa, which was not precisely the result that the Etruscans had wished for. They rebelled, but the only result was the destruction of the city of Volsinii and an end to Etruria as an independent territory in 265.

By this time Roman control of Italy was complete. While the struggle between Etruscans and Romans was playing itself out in the north, trouble had been brewing in the south. The Italian tribes such as the Lucanians and Bruttians were locked into sporadic warfare with the Greek colonies which had been established there for centuries, partly to siphon off surplus population from mainland Greece. Independent to a fault, the Greek cities of southern Italy had not coalesced and had no concept of belonging to an overall Greek community, except perhaps in the cultural sense. They were frequently hard pressed by the Italian tribes, among whom the principal aggressors were most often the fierce Lucanians. In the time-honoured tradition, the usual ploy was to turn to Greece itself for assistance. The King of Sparta, Archidamus, rescued the colonies from the Lucanians, but was unfortunately killed, then it was the turn of King Alexander of Epirus, who defeated both the Lucanians and Bruttians. The trouble was that he did not return to Epirus and leave the newly rescued colonies to themselves, but decided that they would all be better off if they could be welded together with himself as ruler. He was killed in 330 BC. Next, Cleonymus of Sparta was brought in against the Lucanians, and Agathocles of Syracuse fought the Bruttians. Everything unravelled when Agathocles died, and then one of the major Greek colonies, the city of Tarentum took the lead. This was one of the most successful cities, with control of the best harbour in southern Italy and rich agricultural land producing lots of grain in the hinterland. Wealth and status enabled Tarentum to help other cities. The Romans and Tarentines were known to each other, and entered into a treaty probably in the mid-fourth century BC, one of the terms of which was that the Romans should not sail their warships within a certain distance of the harbour of Tarentum.

The Tarentines were not all-powerful, however, and when the city of Thurii was attacked they could not help, so Thurii asked for assistance from the Romans, indicating how far the reputation of Rome had travelled. The Lucanians and Bruttians were duly defeated, and then as a precaution against further attacks, the Romans placed a garrison in Thurii. It may have been sound military sense, but it upset the Tarentines, especially when the Romans started to form alliances with other Greek cities. Next, and even worse, they established a colony in Tarentine territory and, contrary to the terms of the treaty, they sailed their warships into the Gulf of Tarentum. The Tarentines attacked the ships, and threw the garrison out of Thurii. War with the Romans was a daunting prospect, so the Tarentines asked another King of Epirus for help. This was Pyrrhus, an accomplished soldier with a taste for adventure. He arrived in about 281 BC and remained at large in Italy and Sicily for most of the next decade. He came fully equipped with the Macedonian style phalanx, clouds of cavalry and archers, and something the Romans had never seen before, namely elephants trained for battle. When the two armies met at Heraclea, the elephants contributed heavily to the defeat of the Romans, but although beaten the Romans had given a good account of themselves.

Pyrrhus followed up his victory by invading Latium, and sent his envoy Cineas to offer terms. The Senate, spurred on by Appius Claudius who was now old, venerable and blind, rejected the terms because, as Appius reminded the senators, Pyrrhus was unlikely to make a treaty and then cheerfully go home. While he was still in Italy, there could be no peace. Another battle was fought at Asculum in Apulia, and the Romans were defeated again, but they had inflicted tremendous damage on Pyrrhus's army. The king remarked that any more victories like that one, and he would be finished, thus ensuring his lasting fame in the modern phrase 'a Pyrrhic victory'. The Romans had been badly mauled, and it was said that they were considering backing down and accepting peace terms, but were saved by the Carthaginians, who came up with an offer of alliance and cash. The Carthaginians were afraid that Pyrrhus, who had been asked to aid the Sicilian Greeks, would prove extremely detrimental to Carthaginian trading interests if he decided to intervene.

He did. He may have been influenced by his restless quest for adventure, and the more practical consideration that Sicily was a fertile land producing quantities of grain, and possessed good harbours. The Greek cities were constantly menaced by the Mamertines, a group of mercenaries from Campania who had been originally hired by King Agathocles of Syracuse to augment his troops. When the King died, no one was interested in employing the mercenaries, much less paying them, so they turned feral and seized Messana (modern Messina), which they used as a base for expeditions of plunder and pillage of any towns and settlements within their reach.

The Mamertines were not the only threat to the Sicilians, who hoped that Pyrrhus would rid them of the Carthaginians as well. From 278 to the beginning of 275 BC, Pyrrhus took on the dual task and succeeded in ejecting the Carthaginians from the whole island, except for Lilybaeum. The wily Sicilians had no intention of allowing Pyrrhus to become their next overlord, so they said thank you and goodbye and made a separate peace with Carthage. Pyrrhus, now redundant in Sicily, returned to Italy in the spring of 275. The Romans had taken advantage of the respite afforded by Pyrrhus's absence to recoup their losses and raise more troops. The contribution of their allies enabled them to gather sufficient manpower to face Pyrrhus again with more confidence, especially as they had learned a lot from him and put their knowledge to good use. When the armies clashed at Beneventum, the general Manius Curius Dentatus managed to turn the enemy's war elephants back into their own ranks, a significant factor in the defeat of Pyrrhus. The King decided to withdraw altogether, but placed a garrison in Tarentum before he left Italy. His adventuring was ended when he was killed in Greece in 272. The Greek cities were left without a leader, and even Tarentum could not take on the role of protector. The Pyrrhic garrison surrendered to Rome, and Tarentum became an ally like other Greek cities.

Rome was now free to concentrate on tidying up and securing control of southern Italy. Rebellious tribes were subdued, the Samnites gave up lands, colonies were founded, the Lucanians surrendered Paestum, and the Bruttians relinquished their forests. The Romans always recognized and exploited whatever was useful to them, but they also shared some of the benefits with their allies, at least at this stage. With the whole of Italy under Roman control, each city or community in separate alliance and contributing manpower and war material for the protection of the whole, Rome was in an extremely strong position. For the first time since the foundation of the Republic the Romans could imagine themselves on a par with Carthage, Macedonia, Syria and Ptolemaic Egypt. In the course of the next two centuries Rome would absorb them all. The first contest was with Carthage.

THE FIRST PUNIC WAR

Carthage was at least as old as Rome, having been founded probably in the eighth century BC by the Phoenicians, who had reached a more sophisticated and advanced culture than the early Romans. The Phoenicians were seafarers whose trade networks extended beyond the Mediterranean, and their North African colony of Carthage likewise depended on commerce for its livelihood. The Romans called the Phoenicians, including the Carthaginians, the Poeni, hence the wars with Carthage were called the Punic wars, as per the Latin term.

The city of Carthage was administered and organized in similar fashion to Rome, in that the Senate was the governing body, with a smaller group whose task was to prepare business for the meetings, and an assembly of the people who elected the magistrates and the generals. The two chief magistrates were called *suffetes*, who presided over the Senate, and whose responsibilities included all religious, judicial and financial functions of the state. As in Rome, groups of aristocratic families had emerged, regularly squabbling with each other for political pre-eminence, and also, as in Rome, the status of the ruling class was based on wealth, but Carthaginian wealth derived from sea-borne commerce, whereas Roman wealth derived from land and agriculture, which highlights the differences between the two cities. This is not to infer that the Carthaginians did not engage in agriculture, nor that the Romans were strangers to the sea and trading activities. Just as the war with Hannibal was beginning, Gaius

Flaminius passed a law that limited the number of cargo ships owned by Roman senators, so clearly trade was an established part of Roman life by the end of the third century BC. In military affairs, the greater emphasis in Rome was on land-based armies, and in Carthage the emphasis was on naval strength. While Rome levied its own citizens and allies to form their armies, the Carthaginians employed their citizens as crews for their ships and for their armies they bought in mercenaries when necessary, so their troops were composed of Africans, Spaniards, Greeks and some Italians from southern Italy. Provided that they received their pay and fair treatment, these mercenary armies fought very well for Carthage.

Rome and Carthage were already acquainted, allegedly having drawn up their first treaty at the end of the sixth century BC., and their second at some point in the fourth century, but whether this was at the beginning or the end of the century is disputed. In 279 when Pyrrhus was careering around Italy and Sicily, the Carthaginians offered help to Rome, largely because they hoped to draw Pyrrhus away from their commercial interests in Sicily, not being overly concerned about what he might do to the Romans in Italy itself. In all treaties, commercial considerations were of paramount importance to Carthage.

The first clash between the two cities came in 264. It did not start out as a direct confrontation, but Rome answered an appeal from the Mamertines of Messana in Sicily, for help against Hiero, King of Syracuse, who attacked them in 265. The Mamertines had enjoyed nearly twenty years of brigandage against the Greek cities, especially Syracuse, so most of the inhabitants of Sicily no doubt thought that they deserved everything that they got from Hiero. The trouble was that the situation was not as straightforward as it seemed, because the Mamertines had also asked the Carthaginians for help, who had responded by installing a garrison in Messana. The Romans were fully aware of this when they debated whether or not to get involved in the war, because it would mean that they would be fighting not just Hiero, but Carthage too, a much stronger power. From the Roman and the Carthaginian point of view, the conflict was nothing to do with the poor defenceless Mamertines who needed help, but about control of Messana and the Straits named after the city, between Sicily and Italy. The Romans construed the possible Carthaginian seizure of Messana as a threat to the security of Italy, a concept most commonly dismissed by modern scholars as a feeble excuse for Empire building. Another consideration, for Roman senators as for Pyrrhus, was the fact that Sicily was fertile and an abundant source of grain. It may be the case that the Romans were planning ahead, prompted by an acquisitive urge for food and wealth, but sometimes governments do not act according to sober reality, finding themselves overtaken by perceived threat, and so they make pre-emptive strikes on that basis. The Carthaginians may have had no interest whatsoever in an invasion of southern Italy, but they possessed the strongest naval force in the Mediterranean, and if they wished to do so they could make life very difficult for the coastal cities by perpetual hit and run raids. Worse still, if they were to decide that the control of both sides of the Straits of Messana would be beneficial to their trading ventures, and accordingly made a permanent settlement in Italy, the Romans would probably find it more difficult to dislodge them. Better to stop them in their tracks before they even thought of it.

Before the Romans decided to embark on a war outside Italy, the matter was brought before the people's assembly, though it is not specifically recorded which of the assemblies was approached. The people would be primed accordingly, and voted for the war. A levy was called for two legions under one of the consuls, and the army set out for Messana. Part of the force sailed into the harbour there, which encouraged the Mamertines to eject the Carthaginian garrison, because it seemed that an alliance with Rome was now the better option. The war might have ended there, but the Carthaginians asserted themselves and made an alliance with Hiero of Syracuse. Just as Rome was suspicious of the Carthaginian designs on Messana, Carthage was suspicious of Roman intentions in Sicily, especially since Rome had just gobbled up all of southern Italy, converting all the cities and communities into Roman allies.

If the Romans wanted to pursue the war now, it would mean fighting Syracuse and Carthage. Typically they attended to one enemy at a time. In 263 they raised another army and concentrated their efforts on Hiero and the Syracusans, who, after being mauled by the Romans during their first attacks, swiftly decided that they were up against a stronger force than they could muster, and laid down their arms. Hiero allied with Rome against Carthage.

The Romans were now strong enough to challenge Carthage over control of Sicily. They started by attacking Agrigentum, where the Carthaginians had placed a garrison. It fell in 262, and the Romans enslaved the survivors. There could be no clearer indication of Roman intentions to oust the Carthaginians from Sicily, but it was also clear that while Rome was supreme in fighting on land, Carthage was supreme in fighting at sea. The Romans had been aware of the importance of naval power since the end of the fourth century BC, when they had appointed two officials, the *duoviri navales*, to direct operations, but they relied upon their coastal allies, the *socii navales*, to provide ships and crews. The warships that sailed into the Gulf of Tarentum would be provided by the allies, perhaps part of their modest fleet of no more than twenty triremes. In a trireme, each man operated one oar, and the oars were grouped in banks of three. The much more powerful quinquereme had a single bank of oars with five men to each oar, but the Romans had not yet felt the need for these ships. When they met the Carthaginians at sea the Romans changed their minds.

By 260 BC, the Romans felt ready for naval warfare, with a new fleet of a hundred quinqueremes and some twenty triremes. The story goes that they modelled their ships on a captured Carthaginian quinquereme, but the same story is told once again in connection with the blockade of Lilybaeum when the Romans captured the quinquereme of a famous blockade runner. There may have been some characteristics that were new to the Romans, but the shipbuilders of the Italian coasts would be sufficiently well acquainted with warship design to be able to produce the vessels of Rome's first large fleet. The speed and scale of the achievement was truly impressive. A supreme effort was made to build ships and find crews, and by the time they met the Carthaginians at the battle of Mylae in 260 BC, the Romans had assembled their fleet, commanded by the consul Gaius Duilius. They had also invented a grappling hook that allowed them to draw enemy ships closer and then board them, so that they could employ their soldiers as if they were fighting on land. This innovation helped the Romans to win their first naval victory.

Encouraged by their success, the Romans began to over-reach themselves. They decided to carry the war into Africa, and in 256 BC they assembled a very large fleet and thousands of men under the consuls Marcus Atilius Regulus and Manlius Vulso Longus. When the Carthaginian fleet sailed to intercept them, the Romans won another naval victory at the battle of Ecnomus off the Sicilian coast. They lost twenty-four of their own ships, but sank or captured nearly a hundred of the Carthaginian fleet. Regulus now sailed for Africa, where he was so successful at first that the Carthaginians were ready to make peace, but on hearing the terms that were to be imposed on them they decided that they had nothing to lose by continuing the war. They called in the services of Xanthippus from Sparta, who thrashed the Romans and took Regulus prisoner. This was a severe disgrace, which the Romans found hard to accept, entering into legend to explain it away. The strange tale of Regulus emphasizes the stern and virtuous intractability of the Romans. The Carthaginians allegedly sent him back to Rome to deliver their terms, with the solemn promise that if he could not persuade the Romans to make peace, he would return to Carthage for judgement. When he arrived in Rome, Regulus argued against making peace, and dutifully returned to Carthage and execution.

The Roman fleet took a battering from a storm when the remnants of Regulus's troops were rescued from Africa. They lost many ships and what was left of the army, but within a couple of years they were active in Sicily again, with the Carthaginians bottled up in Drepana (modern Trapani) and Lilybaeum, near the modern town of Marsala. The Roman attempts to besiege Lilybaeum and blockade it from the sea dragged on for years, because the Carthaginians could expertly navigate through the shoals outside the harbour and could keep Lilybaeum supplied. The blockade of Drepana fared no better, since the commander, Publius Claudius Pulcher, the son of the infamous Appius Claudius, failed to watch all the entrances to the harbour, so the Carthaginians came out and attacked his fleet from the rear. It was said that Claudius Pulcher brought the defeat on himself, because he had ignored the omens and offended the gods. He was told that the sacred chickens on board ship refused to eat, and he should not engage the enemy, but he declared that they would drink instead and threw them into the sea. He was prosecuted for treason and died shortly afterwards. The situation was made even worse when what remained of the Roman fleet was destroyed in yet another storm.

In 247, when the war had been going on for several years, the Carthaginian general Hamilcar Barca, took over in Sicily and began to turn the tables on the Romans. He occupied the fortress of Eryx, took every opportunity to harass the Roman armies in Sicily and also raided the Italian coast. By 242 BC, the Romans were almost exhausted. They were bankrupt, short of manpower and needed yet another fleet. There were no resources to build one, so the senators decided to use their own funds to pay the bills. When the new ships were ready, the consul Gaius Lutatius Catulus took command.

Catulus attempted to cut the supply lines of the Carthaginian citadels of Drepana, Lilybaeum and Eryx, by blockading them from the sea, but he was wounded and had to relax his attention while he recuperated. He used his recovery period to put into effect two aspects of warfare that the Romans rather neglected, training and intelligence gathering. He set about training his sailors in naval fighting, and found out as much as he could about Carthaginian military and naval dispositions and procedures. Consequently, when the Carthaginians put to sea in spring 241 BC with supplies for their Sicilian garrisons, Catulus was ready for them. Despite the strong March winds which threatened to wreck the Roman fleet, Catulus risked a battle off Aegates (modern Aegusa) not far from Lilybaeum, because he realized that he would never have such an opportunity again. The Romans sank about fifty Carthaginian ships, captured seventy, and took over 1,000 prisoners. The victory finally put an end to the war. It had lasted for twenty-three years.

BETWEEN THE WARS
As part of the peace terms, Rome gained control of Sicily, and a large indemnity was imposed on Carthage that would help the Romans recoup some of the costs of the wars. The Carthaginians were in no condition to argue or carry on hostilities, because they now faced a severe military

problem at home. Their mercenary armies had not been paid and were unlikely to see any cash while Carthage was in such a weak condition and had been deprived of the Sicilian ports so vital to commerce. The mercenaries naturally agitated for fair treatment and finally started a rebellion which the Carthaginian commander Hamilcar Barca took three years to quell. The Romans lent assistance to the Carthaginians to combat the mercenaries. They could have sat back to watch as the Carthaginians went under, but at least Carthage was an organized state and well known to the Romans, whereas if the city was taken over by a band of rampaging, unscrupulous mercenaries, this would require a different approach and probably a fresh war to eradicate them.

At about this time, the Romans were handed Sardinia on a plate. The Carthaginian garrison troops were finding it difficult to keep the natives under control, and were not receiving any help from home. They appealed to Rome for assistance. The Romans politely refused at first but, when the revolt of the Carthaginian mercenaries was over, they changed their minds. The troops sent from Carthage to help the original garrison soon joined with them in asking once more for Roman intervention. This time the Romans accepted the challenge. The Carthaginians attempted to recover control of Sardinia, a natural reaction since Sicily was already lost, but the Romans converted these efforts into an act of aggression against themselves, and declared war on Carthage. Since they were certainly not ready to fight another war with Rome, the Carthaginians backed down. They surrendered Sardinia and Corsica as well, and agreed to pay yet more cash as indemnity. On this occasion, hostilities were averted.

Both the Romans and the Carthaginians were occupied with their own affairs for most of the next two decades. From now onwards the Romans were increasingly drawn into foreign wars in order to protect the interests of weaker states which appealed to them for help against their oppressors, and then against other neighbouring states which felt threatened by Roman interference, even though Rome did not annexe territory at this stage and maintain a permanent presence in lands outside Italy. The first hostilities began after the death of King Agron of the Illyrians, in 231. Agron had formed an alliance with the King of Macedon, and had welded the tribesmen of the Adriatic coast into a nascent state, for which the Roman name, when the area became a province, was Illyricum. After the death of Agron, his widow Queen Teuta pursued his aggressive policy of attacking the cities of the western coast of Greece, and by means of robust piracy and raids she also threatened the Greek colonies of Italy. In the guise of protector of the Greeks, Rome went to war in 229, combining a strong fleet and army to operate on land and sea, to put a stop to Teuta's raids. The Queen was compelled to give up the territories that she had taken over, and the Romans awarded some of them to the rulers who had helped them in the war, such as Demetrius of Pharos, who was confirmed in his own territory and gained more besides.

After about three years of comparative peace, the Romans fought a defensive war with the Gallic tribes who had settled on the south side of the Alps, in the area known as Cisalpine Gaul. Two tribes joined with Rome against a coalition of four other tribes, which included the Boii and the Insubres. The two consuls for 225 each raised an army, one stationed at Ariminum to watch for the Gauls as they came south, and the other sent to Sardinia in case the Carthaginians used the opportunity to regain the island while Rome was preoccupied in the north. The consul at Ariminum heard that the Gauls had by-passed him and gone headlong for Etruria, so he followed as fast as possible, and while the tribesmen were making their way back northwards, laden with booty, the other Roman army from Sardinia disembarked and managed to form up ahead of them. A great battle was fought at Telamon, with the Gauls disastrously trapped between two armies. They gave a good account of themselves and one of the Roman consuls was killed, but in the end the tribesmen were almost wiped out. The Romans spent the next few years campaigning against the Boii and Insubres, and then subduing the inhabitants of the whole area south of the Alps. By 219, only the Ligurians remained outside Roman control in northern Italy.

Just as the wars with the Gauls were ending, trouble broke out again in Illyricum. Demetrius of Pharos proved to be a turncoat, joining forces with Antigonus Doson, the new and vigorous King of Macedon, who embarked on an expansionist policy from 222 BC onwards, managing within a startlingly short space of time to take over nearly the whole of Greece. Sheltering under his alliance with Antigonus, Demetrius attacked some of the communities of Illyricum that had been taken under Rome's wing, and in order to protect them the Romans mobilized for a war, labelled by modern historians the second Illyrian war. There had been no treaties or formal alliances between the Romans and the various cities or communities under Roman protection, and probably no obligation other than a promise to go to war on their behalf, but strong powers just across the Adriatic menaced more than the Illyrian communities, so it was in their own interests that the Romans made war. By 219 BC the threatened cities were liberated, and Demetrius was forced to flee to Macedon, where Antigonus had been succeeded by the new king, Philip V. Having achieved what they set out to do, the Romans went home. They left the situation as it had been before the war and did not annexe Illyrian territory. They made no incursions into Macedon, but Philip V strongly resented their interference, biding his time until he was strong enough to strike back.

While the Romans were engaged in these various wars, the Carthaginians were quiescent in Africa, but were steadily gaining power in Spain. After quelling the revolt of the mercenaries, in 237 BC Hamilcar Barca turned his attention to Carthaginian possessions in Spain, where he hoped to revive the fortunes of his native city and compensate for the loss of Sicily and Sardinia. The Carthaginians had once controlled large areas of Spain, but a combination of opposition from the inhabitants of Marseilles, who were not tolerant of competition in trading ventures, and incursions by the native Iberians, had whittled Carthaginian acquisitions down to a handful of the old Phoenician cities, principally Gades (modern Cadiz), the centre of trade with the west.

Hamilcar has been accused of using Spain as a base for raising and training an army that he intended to use against the Romans in the future, and of instilling into his more famous son Hannibal a deep-rooted loathing of Rome. This is the Roman legendary interpretation to explain their long struggle with Hannibal. After the Carthaginian defeat in 241, Hamilcar may not have harboured any such intention of opening further hostilities with Rome. He required an army to protect the Carthaginian cities against the native Iberians while he exploited the wealth of the country, not least the silver mines which produced vast quantities of precious metal to boost the depleted coffers of Carthage and perhaps his own private funds too. He and his family assumed princely status in Spain and, as long as he did not use his power against Carthage itself, the government there acquiesced. Hamilcar was still bringing the cities of Spain back under Carthaginian control in 229 BC, when he was accidentally drowned while laying siege to one of them. He had three young sons, the eldest of whom was Hannibal, aged about eighteen, not yet old enough or experienced enough to fill his father's place. Instead, Hamilcar's son-in-law Hasdrubal took over, founding another city, New Carthage, or Cartagena, which functioned as a supply base for his troops.

The inhabitants of Massilia were increasingly alarmed at the growing powers of Hamilcar and his successor Hasdrubal, and appealed to Rome. As a result, the Romans sent an embassy and came to an arrangement with Hasdrubal. They proposed that Spain should be divided by the River Ebro, and the Carthaginians should not interfere in the lands to the north of it, but were free to act in the area to the south, despite the fact that the Massilians dwelt there and depended on their trading connections for their livelihood. After promising to help and then ignoring the interests of the Massilians, the Romans went on to make nonsense of the agreement by entering into an alliance, probably without the formality of a treaty, with the city of Saguntum, which had appealed to them for assistance. The city lay south of the Ebro, in Hasdrubal's sphere of influence, so it was clear that the Romans did not feel obliged to obey the rules that they laid down for other people.

If Hasdrubal had lived longer it is possible that he would have found a way of accommodating the Romans, but he was assassinated in 221, and his power passed to his brother-in-law, Hamilcar Barca's eldest son, Hannibal, now in his twenties. When Saguntum, allied to Rome, was attacked by a Spanish tribe allied to Carthage, the scene was set for another conflict between the two great powers, sparked off by their satellites, and cultivated by the reluctance of either of the major powers to compromise. The Romans sent an embassy in 219 BC to protest at the attack on Saguntum. Hannibal referred the matter to Carthage, and during the consequent delay, he mobilized to blockade Saguntum. After eight months the city fell to him. Despite their original protests, the Romans did nothing about it. This encouraged Hannibal to go even further, deliberately crossing the Ebro into the forbidden northern zone. This time the Romans did react. The second Punic war had begun.

THE SECOND PUNIC WAR 218–201 BC

Rome prepared by raising two armies for the consuls of 218, hoping to wage war outside Italy. The consul Publius Cornelius Scipio set off overland for Spain to deal with Hannibal, and the other consul, Tiberius Sempronius Longus embarked for Sicily, a staging post on the way to Africa where he would deal with Carthage. In the event the Roman plans were thwarted before they had been put into practice. Their intention of attacking the Carthaginians on their own territory was a perfectly sound strategy, but Hannibal had the same idea, and had already marched towards Italy before the Romans knew he had mobilized. Scipio heard the news when he arrived at the River Rhône, by which time Hannibal had already crossed the river and was preparing to tackle the Alpine passes. Scipio failed to bring him to battle to stop his progress into Italy, and had to make new plans. He decided not to abandon the Spanish campaign, entrusting the conduct of the war to his younger brother Gnaeus Cornelius Scipio. As consul he had the legal right to bestow praetorian powers on Gnaeus Scipio, so that he could command the armies. The intention was to keep the Carthaginians in check in Spain, and especially to prevent Hannibal's brothers, Hasdrubal and Mago, from raising more troops and bringing them to join Hannibal. The consul then took part of the army intended for Spain, and marched into Italy along the coastal route, chasing after Hannibal and hoping to get there first, but when he arrived he learned that the Carthaginians were through the Alps and had defeated the tribe of the Taurini, around modern Turin. The Gallic tribes of northern Italy who had been recently defeated by the Romans were willing to join Hannibal, so the new recruits for his army made up for the losses in crossing the Alps. Scipio finally engaged him in battle at the Ticinus (now called Ticinio) near Pavia. It was Rome's first defeat, one of several that Hannibal inflicted on them during his fifteen year sojourn in

Italy. The consul Publius was wounded in the battle, allegedly rescued by his young son, also called Publius Cornelius Scipio, who was destined for greater fame in the near future. The Scipios and their followers had to take refuge at Placentia (modern Piacenza), one of the colonies founded after the recent battles against the Gauls.

The consul Tiberius Sempronius Longus hurriedly returned from Sicily, and joined Publius Scipio. They engaged Hannibal again at the Trebia, but lost the battle and a great number of soldiers. As soon as he had recovered from his wounds, Publius Scipio left for Spain to join his brother Gnaeus, where they scored some successes against the Carthaginians over the next few years. In Italy, the new consul for 217, Gaius Flaminius, fared no better against Hannibal. During his earlier career, Flaminius had antagonized many senators. He had been consul in 223, and had commanded the army in the battles against the Gauls, but at most stages of his career he had faced senatorial hostility and manoeuvres to deprive him of office. Fearing that there could be opposition that might deprive him of his command, he left Rome in a great hurry, without observing the proper rituals. His actions approached sacrilege, so he had offended the gods, which is what the Romans said when the news arrived that he had been defeated and killed along with 15,000 men at the battle of Lake Trasimene.

It seemed that no one could stop Hannibal, who had scored a hat-trick in three victories in a very short time. A new strategy was required, since pitched battles were clearly not the answer. After the disaster of Lake Trasimene, the middle-aged Quintus Fabius Maximus was made Dictator. He was elected by the people instead of being more properly appointed by one of the consuls, but Flaminius was dead and the other consul nowhere near Rome, so the Romans compromised and found other legal forms of making him Dictator. The office had not been employed for some time, but these were dangerous times. Two legions were raised, but Fabius used his troops to harass the Carthaginians, keeping them on the move and denying them supplies, refusing to risk a major battle. The Romans nicknamed him the Delayer, *Cunctator* in Latin. His method was correct, but it was a long term plan that would render no rapid results, and it was difficult for the Romans to sit back and take no action when lands around them, especially in Campania, were being devastated, farms destroyed and population killed. Impatience won the day, and the people agitated for the appointment of Fabius's second in command, Publius Minucius Rufus, as a general in his own right. This meant he could command troops, which he immediately committed to battle without proper reconnaissance of the area and Hannibal's dispositions. Fabius had to rescue him.

The consuls for 216, Gaius Terentius Varro and Lucius Aemilius Paullus, reverted to engaging Hannibal in battle. A massive recruitment campaign was undertaken to raise new armies, with which the consuls faced Hannibal at Cannae (modern Canne) in August 216. It was not even ground of their own choosing, and the large armies they commanded did not necessarily afford them superiority. One major defect in the Roman passion for collegiality was that each consul commanded on alternate days, a procedure that allowed each individual to put into operation his own particular plan, whether or not it conflicted with that of the other consul. There was clearly no previously agreed strategy. Aemilius Paullus was the more cautious of the two consuls and would perhaps not have risked battle, but on the fateful day Varro was in command and chose to fight. Hannibal put his lighter armed Spanish troops in the centre, and his more heavily armed African troops on the wings, with instructions that the men in the centre should gradually withdraw after the battle had started, as though they were being steadily beaten back. This drew the Romans forward out of their lines and into the trap. They found themselves enveloped by the soldiers on the wings of Hannibal's army, and the final blow fell when the Roman cavalry units on their own wings were driven off, allowing the Carthaginian horsemen to ride round their rear, enclosing them completely. There was no room to manoeuvre as the Romans were crushed together, so tight that they could not use their weapons. It was said that they fought with their nails and teeth at the end. Nearly the whole army was annihilated, but not quite all the men died. Some of them escaped, and Hannibal took some prisoners, perhaps a few thousand. He tried to persuade the Romans to ransom them, but Roman pride could not countenance this disgrace and they refused.

The battle of Cannae was the greatest disaster that had ever befallen the Romans. Some junior officers such as Publius Cornelius Scipio, the son of the consul, and Fabius Maximus the son of the Dictator, had escaped the slaughter of Cannae and tried to rally the remnants of the troops at Canusium, where they learned that Terentius Varro had survived. The defeated consul sent word to the Senate that his consular colleague Lucius Aemilius Paulus was dead, and that most of the soldiers were killed or captured. Varro had with him about 10,000 men, or the strength of about two legions out of the enormous numbers that had been raised, 80,000 according to some sources, but the figure is disputed. Exact truth as to the numbers that were originally raised could hardly clarify or obscure the fact that Cannae was a disaster of epic proportions. The Roman had lost so many men that it stretched resources to breaking point, and for a short time, Rome was at the mercy of Hannibal's army. But he did not try to take the city. For one thing he had no siege engines and therefore could not conduct an all out siege. He could have tried to blockade the city and starve the Romans out, but if he managed to take Rome he would then have to obliterate it or hold it, and with the small number of troops at his disposal he could not afford to tie any of them down in garrisoning Rome.

His way of war depended on mobility and flexibility. Besides, Rome was by now a cohesive federation so, even if the city fell, he would still not be master of the Romans. He had been in Italy for two years but had not succeeded in detaching Rome's earliest allies. The Gauls of the north and the Bruttians and Apulians of the south, only recently absorbed into the Roman world, were disaffected and therefore sympathetic to him, and he had either conquered or received the submission of other recent allies, but unless he could win over the core of the Roman federation he would have to take each city one at a time.

The Romans held their breath for a while, but then began to repair the damage as far as possible. They recruited and armed 8,000 slaves with the promise of freedom if they fought for Rome, but they did not attempt to meet Hannibal himself in a pitched battle. Instead they concentrated on reconquering their allies who had gone over to the Carthaginians, the most important being Capua, a city almost as large and influential as Rome itself. Its loss was a bitter blow for the Romans. For these campaigns the Romans employed smaller forces, with Fabius Maximus in command of one of them, and generals who would not rush headlong into battle in command of the others.

The war in Italy slowed down to a few comparatively minor actions, while other theatres of war were more lively. Hannibal's victory at Cannae still failed to shake the loyalty of the Latins, but it did encourage other interested parties to make overtures to him. In 215 Philip V of Macedon proposed an alliance, which the Romans discovered when their fleet patrolling the Ionian sea captured a ship with a Carthaginian passenger who carried the text of the treaty. It was vital to stop Philip from arriving in Italy to join Hannibal, so the Roman fleet played its part in patrolling the seas, and supporting the Greeks who were persuaded to ally with Rome and attack Philip on land. The Aetolians, the Spartans and the Pergamenes kept Philip occupied while the Romans attended to other spheres of the war.

As well as fighting in Italy, the Romans had to maintain a military presence in Sardinia, Corsica and Sicily to ward off Carthaginian attempts to reconquer the islands. There was a severe setback in 215–214 when Hiero of Syracuse died and was succeeded by his son Hieronymus, who eventually changed sides and allowed the Carthaginians take over the city. The Roman fleet patrolled the seas around Syracuse but the Romans had to wait until they were in a position to attack in strength on land. The general who finally did take Syracuse, Claudius Marcellus, had been on his way to Sicily as praetor in 216, but was recalled after the disaster at Cannae and spent the next couple of years clearing up, restoring order and retaking Casilinum, one of the cities of Campania which was under Hannibal's control. In 214 he set off once again for Sicily, this time as consul, and in 213 began the siege of Syracuse in earnest. It took him two years to take the city, where Archimedes contributed to the defence by his invention of the 'claw', a war engine imperfectly understood in modern times, but which was said to have lifted the Roman ships out of the water and dunked them back in again. The trick, therefore, would be to keep well away from the sea walls of Syracuse, which is what all defenders of walls ultimately desire. In 211, Syracuse fell to the Romans. Marcellus tried to prevent a massacre of the inhabitants, but during the proceedings, Archimedes was killed allegedly while studying designs for some unknown engine or mathematical problem, which he asked the soldiers not to disturb. Over a hundred years later Marcus Tullius Cicero went to look at his tomb and found it somewhat dilapidated. In Rome, he could scarcely avoid seeing all the art treasures that Marcellus shipped back from Sicily.

Although the war in Sicily was not entirely over when Syracuse fell in 211, it was a step forward, and in the same year the rebellious city of Capua was retaken by the Romans. During the siege of Capua, Hannibal had not attempted to relieve the city by directly attacking the besieging force, but he tried to frighten the Romans into withdrawing their troops by marching to Rome itself. He camped a few miles from the city and then rode up to inspect one of the gates, the Porta Collina. There were skirmishes outside the city walls, but nothing serious occurred and Hannibal went away. According to Livy, he was discouraged because it was clear that the Romans did not intend to recall the army from Capua, nor would they divert the latest levies which were destined for Spain. But the most persuasive news, from Hannibal's point of view, was that the lands around Rome were being sold to raise much needed funds, and somebody had bought the whole area where the Carthaginians were camped, for the normal price.

The recapture of these two major cities of Syracuse and Capua was fortunate, because the Romans were enabled to release seasoned troops for the war in Spain where, after an auspicious start, things were not going well. When Gnaeus Cornelius Scipio took command in 218, he had managed to stabilize the situation north of the Ebro, and then in the following year his brother Publius joined him after he had been wounded at the battle of the Ticinus. It now remained to try to wrest control of the southern areas of Spain from the Carthaginians, who were weakened by the diversion of some of their troops to North Africa, because Carthage was under attack by the Numidian tribesmen under their prince, Syphax. The greatest fear was that the Carthaginians might raise another army and despatch it to Hannibal in Italy, but temporarily this possibility was averted when the Scipio brothers defeated the Carthaginians in a battle in 216 or possibly 215.

The tables were turned when the revolt of Syphax was quelled in Africa and more Carthaginian troops arrived in Spain, assisted by a Numidian cavalry contingent under their chief Masinissa, of whom the Romans would hear much more later on. From 214 the Carthaginian commander was another Hasdrubal, son of Gisco, who brought the Romans to battle in 211. The Scipio brothers had split their forces, and were defeated separately. Both were killed. The Romans were now back to the old status quo, in control of the lands north of the Ebro, where the remains of the army were collected by one of the surviving officers. The Senate appointed the praetor Gaius Claudius Nero to command the northern part of Spain in 211–210. He did not attempt to reconquer of the rest of Spain, probably because he was preoccupied in restoring order, but he was accused of being too cautious and very quickly replaced. He proved his worth three years later, when commanding his consular army in Italy in 207.

The commander who was sent out in place of Nero was Publius Cornelius Scipio, the son of Publius Scipio, and the nephew of Gnaeus Scipio, both of whom had been killed in 211. He was only twenty-five years old and, though he had served in the army with distinction, he had no political experience. He had been aedile, but except for this post he had not held any of the other requisite magistracies that would qualify him for election to the consulship, and in any case he was too young. At the time of his appointment to Spain he was not in any office at all, and therefore ranked as a *privatus*, or private citizen. It was all very irregular. In order to command the armies in Spain, he would need to be elevated to the rank of consul or proconsul, and would require the bestowal of *imperium*, all of which was arranged legally by the *comitia centuriata* where a special law was passed to grant him proconsular powers. The Romans were rapidly becoming expert at getting round their own legislation when necessary, yet still keeping more or less within the law.

Scipio arrived in Spain in 210. His first task was to restore discipline and boost morale, then he spent some time training the troops and gathering information about the country, the geography, the people and the dispositions and habits of the enemy. In this way he learned that at Cartagena, which was protected on the south side by the harbour and on the north side by a lagoon, there was access to the city at low tide when the water level of the lagoon dropped, and it was possible to wade across it to the north wall. In 209 Scipio decided to try to take the city, because it was an important supply base, with a larger harbour than any of the other Carthaginian coastal cities. Besides, it was the point from which Hannibal had begun his march into Italy so it would be a significant gesture to capture the city. Scipio set up a three-pronged attack. The main force approached directly from the camp to the main gate, and the fleet under an officer called Laelius attacked from the harbour. Another smaller force was instructed to cross the lagoon as soon as the water level dropped, and attack the north wall. The defenders there were fewer because the main defensive effort of the Carthaginians was directed to the Roman attacks on the gate and from the harbour, so the Romans were able to surmount the walls facing the lagoon, drive off the opposition and use the wall walk to approach the main gate, which was then attacked from two sides. The city was captured, and shortly afterwards the citadel was surrendered.

When the news of the victory arrived at Rome, it may have lifted spirits somewhat. The burdens of fighting the prolonged war, on several fronts simultaneously, were becoming worryingly severe. Shortage of men and money, and even of food, had to be remedied somehow. In the same year that Scipio set out for Spain, eighteen of the Latin colonies made strenuous efforts to meet their quotas to provide troops and declared that they would be willing to make any sacrifice, but twelve of them declared themselves unable to furnish any more men. The senators contributed from their own funds to provide ships and crews to keep the war effort going, but it was not enough and in 209, in the same year that Cartagena fell, the Romans had to dip into their reserves, built up for three decades from the 5 per cent tax levied on the value of slaves when they were freed. Food supplies were running low because fields and farms had been destroyed, and during the fighting even the ones that were left intact could not be farmed. The harvests from Sicily were not reaching Rome while the war was pursued there, so the Romans purchased grain from Egypt in 210.

The war in Spain was approaching its end. Scipio defeated Hannibal's brother, Hasdrubal Barca, who then set off in 208 with his remaining forces to join Hannibal in Italy. During the early stages of the war, reinforcements for Hannibal spelled disaster for the Romans, but by this time Hannibal's army had dwindled in size and, although he had persuaded several of the anti-Roman cities and Italian tribesmen to join with him, he had not managed to recruit sufficient numbers of them to keep his force up to strength. Scipio therefore allowed Hasdrubal to march away unmolested, and concentrated his energies on the Carthaginian forces that were left in Spain, under Hannibal's youngest brother Mago, who was defeated at the battle of Ilipa in 206. Carthaginian power in Spain was broken for ever and Scipio returned to Rome. In less than a decade, the whole country was annexed and made into two provinces, called Hispania Superior and Ulterior, or Nearer and Further Spain, in 197.

As Hasdrubal was making his way to Italy, Hannibal inflicted another blow on the Romans. At Venusia (modern Venosa) his Numidian cavalry discovered both the consuls for 208, Claudius Marcellus and Crispinus, on an ill-advised reconnaissance, and killed them both. The consuls for 207 raised more men and took command of two armies, Marcus Livius Salinator proceeding northwards to await the arrival of Hasdrubal from Gaul, and Gaius Claudius Nero to Bruttium to face Hannibal, who started off northwards as soon as he heard that Hasdrubal was in Italy. Claudius

Nero shadowed him but did not attack. Then he had an enormous piece of luck when his troops captured messengers with a letter from Hasdrubal, informing Hannibal where their armies should meet in Umbria. Claudius Nero had been censured for inactivity in Spain in 210, but he more than made up for it now, by leaving some troops to watch Hannibal and then hastily setting off with most of his army to march 50 miles a day for five days to join Livius Salinator at his headquarters at Sena Gallica (modern Senigallia) south of Ariminum (modern Rimini). The two consuls caught up with Hasdrubal at the River Metaurus, and wiped out the army, killing Hasdrubal in the process. The energetic Claudius Nero wasted no time in marching back south, setting off that same night. The first news that Hannibal heard of the disaster came when Nero's troops hurled Hasdrubal's head into his camp. Hannibal probably knew now that ultimately his venture could not succeed, but he remained at large in Italy for another three years. The wonder is that he had been able to sustain his army for so long, keeping them enthusiastic enough to continue to follow him, and not letting them starve. His abilities as a commander far outshone that of most of the Romans who faced him, but while he fought against them he also taught them a lot.

Now that Carthage was deprived of Spain and its resources, and had not been able to regain Sardinia or Sicily, the time was ripe for the Romans to strike at Carthage itself. Scipio urged this course of action when he stood for election to the consulship for 205. Fabius Maximus opposed the plan, and the Senate refused to grant him troops or resources, but agreed that he could undertake the expedition provided that he raised an army of volunteers. There was no shortage of men who were anxious to strike a blow against the Carthaginians, and they had great faith in Scipio as a general, so he rapidly raised his army and set sail for Africa from Lilybaeum in 204.

The likely success of the expedition had been underlined, probably in 205 when the Romans consulted the Sibylline Books, a collection of oracles which had been part of Roman religious culture since at least the fifth century BC. Whenever there was a crisis, the Senate could authorize a consultation, and prophecies were usually found that provided the answer to the problem. In this case the prophecy stated that if a foreign enemy invaded Italy he would be defeated if the Romans imported the goddess Cybele and her religious cult into the city. This corroborated a prophecy from the Delphic oracle, so arrangements were set in motion to bring Cybele to Rome. She was an important mother-goddess, from Asia Minor. She was also a nature goddess, and was usually depicted in her chariot drawn by lions, or with lions on either side, or occasionally with a lion sitting on her lap like any domestic cat. Her main attributes were protection of people in wartime, and the cure of diseases. The people of Rome, still threatened by Hannibal on their own ground and with an army about to engage in war in Africa, evidently required reassurance on the grand scale. The Senate obliged by bringing the statue of Cybele from Pessinus in Phrygia in 204, and installing her in the Temple of Victory on the Palatine Hill. It was a good investment. In the following year Hannibal was recalled to Carthage.

When Scipio landed in Africa he was opposed by the Carthaginian army reinforced by their Numidian allies under Syphax. The Romans promptly put the city of Utica under siege and the Carthaginians marched to its relief. Scipio moved off, placed the army in winter quarters and waited. There were discussions between the two armies about making peace, but in spring Scipio went on the offensive and won the battle. Another Carthaginian army was raised with Hasdrubal Gisco and Syphax in command, but when they met the Romans at the battle of the Great Plains they were defeated again. Syphax ran for home but was captured and sent to Italy. Scipio now called in a new ally. While he was still in Spain he had fought against another Numidian chieftain, called Masinissa, who was allied to the Carthaginians at the time, but was won over by Scipio after the victory at Ilipa in 206. This chieftain was set up in the place of Syphax, and as an ally of Rome he brought reinforcements for Scipio's army, principally his cavalry forces.

The Carthaginians made overtures for peace, and during the truce that followed Scipio dictated terms, but both sides knew that if Hannibal was ordered to come home the peace terms would be meaningless. Since this was precisely what Scipio wanted to bring about, he waited and did nothing, certain that Hannibal would be recalled and the war would begin again. Hannibal left Italy in 203, and as soon as he arrived the Carthaginians attacked first, breaking the truce. The story goes that Hannibal asked Scipio to meet him, which he did, in an open space with their respective armies camped at some distance away. They conversed in Greek, but what they talked about is not known, except perhaps the inevitability of the coming battle. The two armies met at Zama in 202, where victory was not a foregone conclusion for Scipio. He ordered the Romans to leave gaps between their ranks and allow the Carthaginian elephants to charge through them, and he placed Masinissa and Laelius in command of the cavalry on the wings. Hannibal stationed his Numidian cavalry opposite Masinissa and the Carthaginian horse opposite Laelius. During the battle the Romans drove all the enemy cavalry off the field, and if they had kept on going in pursuit of the Carthaginians the battle may have turned out very differently. Fortunately for Scipio they stopped, turned around, and charged the rear of Hannibal's army. It was all over for the Carthaginians. Hannibal escaped and turned up later at the court of the Seleucid King Antiochus the Great in Syria.

The Romans were able to dictate peace terms, by which Carthage was disarmed completely. All the war elephants and all the warships except ten triremes were to be given up and, more importantly, the Carthaginians were not to make war on anyone without the approval of Rome. Carthage had to pay another large indemnity, sent hostages to Rome and was reduced to the area of the city itself and the immediately surrounding territory. All other territorial possessions were to be surrendered. As a sort of insurance policy, Masinissa was confirmed as ruler of his own territory on the borders of Carthage.

Scipio was at the zenith of his career and justifiably took the victory title Africanus. His subsequent history was less glamorous and his political enemies, led by Cato the censor, eventually brought him down.

AFTER THE WARS

During the course of the third century BC, Rome had undergone several changes, emerging at the end of the century as the strongest power in the Mediterranean world. The Romans would soon be drawn into the struggles between the states of the Hellenic east, but Greek culture was not entirely alien to them, since they had been exposed to it via the Etruscans for some time, and during the various wars they had met at first hand the Greek colonies of the Italian coasts. After the first Punic war many of the Greeks of southern Italy arrived in Rome, some as slaves of the wealthy Romans. Others became teachers of the sons of the wealthy and found ready acceptance. Greek became a second language to many of the ruling class in Rome and the first historian of Rome, Fabius Pictor, produced his books in Greek. The author of the first play to be performed in Rome, at the end of the first Punic war, was Livius Andronicus from Tarentum. The Greek poet Ennius was brought to Rome in 204 by Cato, and during the war with Hannibal the comedies of Titus Maccius Plautus were performed, based on Greek themes, but Romanised and Latinised for the better appreciation of the audience. Perhaps the most famous was *Miles Gloriosus*, performed in 204 BC. Greek art made its first appearance when Marcellus conveyed to Rome many statues from Sicily. At the beginning of the second century BC, architecture in Rome flourished, greatly influenced by Greek styles.

Roman society had changed too, by the end of the century. There were now considerable numbers of men among the citizen body who had not been born in Rome, nor even in Italy. Some of them perhaps started out as slaves, as for instance when the 8,000 slaves were recruited for the army after the battle of Cannae, with the promise of freedom if they fought well and survived, though of course freedom and citizenship are not the same thing. The city was also packed with refugees from the countryside, where farms and lands had been devastated.

It is to Rome's credit, and a tribute to the loyalty of the Latin allies, that Hannibal was never able to prise them from their allegiance, even when they were exhausted and had seen their lands destroyed. Outside Latium Hannibal captured some of the allied cities by force, and the states or tribes that he did manage to win over were usually those of recent conquest by Rome, on the principle of last in and first out, still discontented with Rome and not yet reconciled to the loss of total independence. These included the Gallic tribes of the north of Italy, and the Bruttians in the south, who presumably thought that Hannibal would defeat the Romans and then they would be free again. The most disappointing defection was that of Capua, which was retaken by the Romans and brutally punished, as was the city of Tarentum. The inhabitants of both cities were either killed or sold as slaves, and the terrible example was noted by other states.

The Roman army and its commanders had learned a great deal from the battles of the third century BC. After the Samnite wars, a more flexible military formation was adopted in place of the rigid phalanx, which had proved unwieldy in hill country. The army was now organized in more manoeuvrable sections called maniples, which literally means 'handfuls' of men. The long spear and the round shield (the *clipeus*) of the phalanx were abandoned, the shield being replaced by an oval version that the Italian allies had been using for some time. It is not certain whether it was at this time that the *pilum* or throwing spear, or more accurately javelin, was introduced in place of the long spear, but significant factors about the new manipular formation include the fact that it was now more convenient to engage the enemy at a distance with some kind of missile, and that in the looser formation the soldiers would have more space to throw a javelin.

It was alleged that the Romans started to follow the example of Pyrrhus in making a fortified camp each night, though it is disputed whether they really had neglected to do this in all their campaigns until this point. There was no standing army until the very end of the Republic, but although the armies were raised each year, or whenever necessary, and disbanded when campaigns were concluded, during the wars of the third century there had been an army in the field almost permanently and a certain professionalism had been built up when men re-enlisted in different armies and fought new campaigns. Some men made a sort of career out of the army, though if they had reached the rank of centurion in one campaign it was no guarantee that they would re-enlist for the next one with the same rank. Continuity of overall command was achieved via the pro-magistracy, but it must be remembered that there was no military academy in Rome where men could learn the skills necessary to lead armies into battle. Although military manuals are not generally known until the Imperial period, there may have been some available instructive literature at this date, but apart from that, commanders were simply expected to know how to wage war, move troops from one place to another, maintain discipline, organize supplies, and deal with sick and wounded On the whole they managed very well in the long run.

Without the contribution of the allies to their armies, the Romans would not have survived, and would probably have been defeated by Hannibal after Cannae. The potential manpower of the Roman armies, consisting of Romans and allied troops, was phenomenal, a fact that was perhaps not realized by Rome's enemies in the first half of the third century BC. This was highlighted when Pyrrhus sent his envoy Cineas to Rome, with an offer of peace. The terms that Pyrrhus offered were rejected because he did not promise to leave Italy, and Cineas, impressed with the numbers of men that the Romans and their allies could muster, reported to Pyrrhus: 'We are fighting a hydra'. According to Polybius, at the time of the war with Hannibal, detailed lists were drawn up of men who were capable of bearing arms. The statistics revealed that the Romans could furnish 250,000 infantry and 23,000 cavalry, while the allies could raise a total somewhat in excess of 450,000 infantry and 47,000 cavalry. The Roman legions bore the brunt of the fighting, but without the allied contingents they would not have been able to sustain the constant warfare that characterized the third century.

The Romans began to attend to their communications throughout Italy before the whole of the peninsula was under their control. At the end of the fourth century BC the Via Appia was built by Appius Claudius as far as Capua, and by 244 BC it had been extended as far as Brundisium (modern Brindisi) on the south coast. The Via Valeria ran across the central Apennines to the Adriatic coast, and in 241 the Via Aurelia, built by Gaius Aurelius Cotta, connected Rome with Cosa, running up the western side of Italy. The roads were needed for the easy movement of troops, but also facilitated commerce. Although Rome's trading ventures have been played down and portrayed as negligible at this period, luxury goods had begun to arrive in the city, probably from Etruscan and Greek sources. Eventually the Romans felt it necessary to pass sumptuary laws to limit the amount of these goods that a family could own. As trade developed and the Romans began to interact with the other states of Italy, and especially with the Greeks of southern Italy and the countries around the Mediterranean, coinage was introduced after the conclusion of the Samnite wars. The Greeks and Carthaginians had been using coins for much longer, but the Romans had not felt the need for coinage, using bronze by weight. One Roman pound was called an *as* (plural *asses*, nothing to do with donkeys). In 289 BC, the Romans established a mint in Rome, or at least it at this date that the first known officials are attested in charge of issuing coins. These were the *tres viri monetales* with their headquarters on the Capitol Hill, near the Temple of Juno Moneta. By the end of the third century the values of bronze and silver coins were rationalized, one silver denarius being worth ten bronze *asses*. Money changers set up businesses in Rome, and Roman coins were equated with international values.

By the end of the third century BC trade had begun to play a larger part in people's lives, with senators taking an active part. In 218 BC Gaius Flaminius passed a law that limited the carrying capacity of cargo ships owned by senators to no more than three hundred amphorae, which served as containers for oil, wine and grain. Clearly the senatorial class had taken to trading ventures eagerly enough.

Administration of the city and the allies had to be adapted to changed circumstances as the third century progressed. Commerce and warfare brought more people to Rome, and brought Romans into contact with foreigners abroad. In 242 BC the Romans appointed a new official, the *praetor inter peregrinos*, literally the praetor over foreigners, whose original duties may have been of a military nature, but by the end of the third century BC his duties concerned disputes between Romans and foreigners, or between two foreigners in the city of Rome. The most important administrative change, with far reaching consequences for the Republic and Empire, was the acquisition of the first provinces and the methods developed to govern them. When the Romans took over Sicily at the end of the first Punic war, they tried to govern by the usual methods that they applied to some of their allies, by fostering relations with the elite ruling class and allowing them to administer the area themselves, within the parameters set by the Romans to satisfy their own requirements. At first the same methods were applied to Sardinia and Corsica when both islands came into their possession, but within a decade or so the Romans realized that direct administration was less cumbersome and gave them what they wanted more easily.

The name that was applied to each of the new territories was *provincia*, which did not originally denote a geographical area. The term derived from the tour of duty that magistrates undertook during or after their term of office, and could embrace all sorts of task such as attending to the roads, the management of forests, or anything that required attention. The government of Sicily, and Sardinia together with Corsica, was regarded as a tour of duty and the same name *provincia* was applied to the task, which eventually became firmly attached to a territory. In order to provide officials to undertake the government of the new provinces, two extra praetors were created in 228 or 227 BC. The consuls could not undertake the government of the provinces along with their other duties, the principal one being command of the armies, and the creation of extra consuls would compromise the collegiate principle as well as establishing too many high-powered individuals. Praetors on the other hand were subordinate to the consuls and could, theoretically at least, be kept in

4

World Power: Rome Begins to Dominate 201–133 BC

The city of Rome, in the second century BC, was becoming more cosmopolitan, comprising an even larger racial intermix than the three main tribes that made up the population of the early city, with definite leanings towards the Hellenistic world, as attested in literature, art and architecture, and even in language, with certain words borrowed from Greek and Latinised. The Romans had broadened their horizons. They had always been aware of the countries around the Mediterranean through diplomacy and trade, but during the half century after the end of the second Punic war, the Romans gradually extended control over many of them.

At first, conquest and absorption was not an established ambition. Despite their reputation for a dynamic acquisitive urge, if not rabid Imperialism, the Romans did not actively seek to annexe territory for about six decades after the defeat of Hannibal. Polybius says that the Romans intended to annexe Greece as soon as the war with Hannibal was over, but if this was true, the Romans took a long time to put their alleged plans into effect. They were occasionally asked to intervene or assist in the affairs of countries outside Italy, to repel an invader or stop the ruler of one state from oppressing another. They usually responded, sometimes after sending someone to investigate the circumstances, gathered an army, fought the battles and then went home. The wars of the third century BC had concerned the west but now, in the second century, Rome was drawn into conflicts to protect states and communities which they called 'friends' in the east. In several cases, protection of friends involved the Romans in further conflicts with the states bordering on the territory of their friends, because these neighbours were upset by what they saw as Roman interference, and potential threats to their own livelihoods.

The Romans had been acquainted with the Greek world for a long time via the Etruscans and the Greek colonies of the coasts of Italy, but now for the first time they met Greeks in the flesh in their homelands, and tried to get along with them. By the second century BC Hellenistic culture, from Hellenes, the name by which the Greeks called themselves, had spread over much of the eastern Mediterranean. After the death of Alexander the Great in 323, the generals of his immediate entourage seized much of the territory that he had conquered and created kingdoms for themselves. Ptolemy took the corpse of Alexander to Egypt and installed it in a splendid tomb in Alexandria. Egypt became a Hellenistic kingdom under a succession of rulers called Ptolemy, until the last of their line, Queen Cleopatra VII, died when Alexandria fell to Octavian in 30. Seleucus, another of Alexander's generals, took over the kingdom of Babylonia, and eventually northern Syria, where he founded the city of Antioch in 300 BC. The Seleucid empire was vast, stretching from modern Turkey to Iran and into central Asia. By the second century BC the area under the control of the descendants of the Seleucids had shrunk, but was still worthy of the label empire, centred on Syria. The Ptolemies and the Seleucids occasionally fought for control of Palestine, but that was not yet a cause for concern to the Romans until they had extended their Empire to include the eastern provinces. These large and powerful kingdoms of Egypt and Syria, together with Macedon, dominated the eastern Mediterranean, surrounded by smaller states whose inhabitants, ever vigilant for encroachment or insult, squabbled with each other. Freedom and independence were jealously guarded, and even when confederacies were formed there was no long-lived leading state which could be said to guide the policies of the confederacy. To become a friend of one state almost automatically meant becoming an enemy of some other state. This lack of unity made it easy for Rome, eventually, to divide and rule in Greece.

For the first half of the second century BC Rome showed no interest in taking over territory across the Adriatic, but tried to impose certain standards of behaviour that were compatible with Roman military and trading interests, and with keeping the peace. Freedom and independence continued unopposed by the Romans, provided that Rome's friends and Rome itself were not threatened in any way. That could be a matter of interpretation, of course, but in general Roman expansionist policies did not begin until after many years of diplomatic and military activity designed to preserve the harmonious relations that Rome desired. From the second half of the second century, specifically after 146, some states lost their independence, passing from semi-free status under Rome's wing, to absorption under Rome's thumb.

The states in the Roman protectorate, such as Illyricum after the first war with Philip of Macedon, were not treated in the same way as the allied cities in Italy, which were bound to Rome by treaties outlining mutual rights and obligations. The connections with the friends of Rome were much less formal, so there was little or no entanglement in the legal niceties of a treaty which would have obliged Rome to intervene if the protected state were attacked. The Romans could monitor the situation and decide whether or not to take up the cause. The promise of assistance was usually honoured, but it remained suitably amorphous, so that it was much easier for the Romans to utilize the member states of the Aetolian confederacy when necessary, and then abandon them when it was felt more prudent to do so, without troubling their collective conscience about it.

THE SECOND MACEDONIAN WAR

While Hannibal was still at large in Italy, the Romans had come into conflict with Philip of Macedon, who had proposed an alliance with the Carthaginians. The enemies of Philip, notably the Aetolians, assisted the Romans, and the first war ended in 205, with lenient terms for Macedon. In 200, war with Philip broke out again, because the King had tried to take over the Illyrians and prise them away from Rome, and was also suspected of aggressive designs on areas further afield. The people of Rhodes, and King Attalus of Pergamum, sent envoys to Rome with rumours of an impending alliance between Philip of Macedon and Antiochus the Great, the ruler of Syria, who were preparing a joint attack on Egypt.

These movements did not comprise a direct threat to Italy, but the Romans sent ambassadors to Philip with the ultimatum that he should not make war on the Greeks or Illyrians. War would be declared if he refused. He did refuse, so war was to follow, but here the senators, who recommended war, came up against an unforeseen problem. The Roman people did not want to campaign in foreign parts on behalf of other states, and said so in the *comitia centuriata*. This public assembly did not possess the authority to formulate policies, but could say yes or no to proposals put to it by the Senate, and it voted a categorical 'no' to a war with Philip of Macedon. The attitude of the people indicates how exhausted the Romans were after the long struggle with Hannibal. They had fought on more than one front for several years during the war with Carthage, perfectly willing to send armies to Spain because there was a threat to Italy if the Carthaginians were allowed to expand their control there, and accrue sufficient wealth and manpower to send assistance to Hannibal. They had condoned the first war against Philip of Macedon to prevent him from allying with Hannibal. This time, however, the trouble did not seem to concern Italy, and the Romans thought that they already had a surplus of widows, fatherless children and grieving parents, far too many to justify going to a peripheral war only a few years after the peace with Carthage.

The Senate, not wishing to overstep the confines of the law by overruling the assembly, revised its presentation and tried again, converting Philip and his ambitions into a direct threat to Rome, and the war into a just one, a ploy that was to be used throughout Rome's history to represent the Romans as the injured party and the enemy as the guilty one. This time the *comitia centuriata* voted 'yes'. In 200 the consul Sulpicius Galba set out to make war on Philip, assisted by the Aetolian confederacy and troops from Pergamum, Rhodes and Athens. Little progress was made at first, until the consul Titus Flamininus took over in 198. Within a short time he had flushed Philip out of Epirus, and arranged a meeting with him proposing terms, but the sticking point was Thessaly, which Philip would not give up, and he still held the fortresses of Corinth, Chalcis and Demetrias. The war started again.

Flamininus's term of office as consul was due to end, and one of the consuls for 197 should have replaced him, but in Rome two tribunes proposed that his command should be extended. This device to extend command, called *prorogatio imperii*, had been used before, exchanging the actual consulship for the powers of a consul. It was a logical step when a commander was in the middle of a war, but the employment of tribunes to propose such measures was to become an over-used political device in the future.

Philip of Macedon and Titus Flamininus faced each other in Thessaly in 197 at the battle of Cynoscephalae, which means Dog's Head, named after the shape of the rocks in the hills where the opponents met. The battle was timely, because Antiochus the Great was marching to assist Philip but had not yet reached him. It was a complete Roman victory, proving the superiority of the looser formation of the Roman army over the compact phalanx of the enemy, which as the Romans themselves had discovered, was formidable on smooth ground but lost cohesion in more broken country. The victory put an end to Philip's ambitions for the time being, and stopped Antiochus in his tracks. Peace was declared, and Flamininus ignored the pleas of the Greeks for revenge on Philip. The terms were crippling enough, entailing surrender of all Philip's territories in Greece and Illyricum, surrender of his warships, and the payment of an indemnity. In 196 Philip became an ally of Rome.

The historian Polybius records the explosion of joy at the Isthmian games in 196 when Flamininus famously explained to the Greeks that henceforth they were free of the domination of Philip of Macedon, and under Roman patronage they were free to govern themselves. Flamininus was immediately mobbed and nearly killed in the enthusiastic reception of his speech. The Roman troops were withdrawn, but it would never be the same again for the Greeks, although they did not yet know that.

While the Romans fought the war with Macedon, other Roman armies were fighting the Gauls in northern Italy, principally the Boii and Insubres, and the Ligurians. From 198 to 191 this war dragged on, and at its conclusion 40,000 Ligurians were transplanted to the south of Italy. Even if the numbers are exaggerated, the fact that there was room for the tribesmen on the devastated lands and abandoned farms of the south, gives some indication of the extent of the devastation that occurred during the war with Hannibal, who based his army there for much of his stay in Italy.

THE AETOLIANS & ANTIOCHUS THE GREAT

Not long after the battle of Cynoscephalae, Antiochus the Great, King of Syria, still hopeful of reconstituting the once extensive empire of the Seleucids, resumed his efforts to expand his territory, this time without an alliance with Philip, but with an even better excuse for invasion because the Aetolians, who were disappointed with the lack of rewards for their assistance to Rome, invited him to Greece as liberator. The Aetolians had hoped for extra territory and financial gains from the war with Philip, and perhaps thought that other Greeks were as disgruntled as they were themselves, but when Antiochus appeared, no one greeted him as liberator. The Romans could not tolerate the presence of Antiochus in Greece and went to war again. The consul Acilius Glabrio won a victory for Rome at Thermopylae in 191, but this did not put an end to the war because Antiochus refused to accept the terms offered him. The next Roman consul sent against him was Lucius Cornelius Scipio, who was in nominal command of the army. The real commander was his more famous brother, Publius Cornelius Scipio Africanus, officially acting in an advisory capacity. Africanus had been consul in 194, and had fought against the Gallic tribes in the following year. In 190 when it was clear that Antiochus had lost a battle but was not yet defeated in the war, Africanus was the logical choice of commander but, since the law dictated that there should be a gap of several years between consulships, Africanus was not eligible for election, and could not command the army. His brother Lucius successfully stood for the consulship instead, and was awarded the command. Ironically, in the entourage of Antiochus there was a famous refugee, Hannibal, who had been exiled from Carthage, so the two generals found themselves ranged opposite each other again, though neither of them was in command of the armies that they accompanied.

The Romans were assisted by troops from Rhodes and Pergamum, and it was Eumenes II, the new King of Pergamum, whose timely action tipped the balance for the Romans at the battle of Magnesia, in Lydia. Eumenes led his horsemen against Antiochus's heavy armoured cavalry and forced them back into their own ranks, then he led another attack on the exposed flank of Antiochus's phalanx. The victory, late in 190 or perhaps in January 189, ended the war. The Romans took the states of Asia Minor into their protection, and rewarded the kingdoms of Rhodes and Pergamum with extra territories from Antiochus's domains. It was said that the Romans also demanded from Antiochus the surrender of Hannibal, but the King would not co-operate, and helped his famous guest to escape.

There were short lived sequels to the war, the first when the Aetolians refused to accept the terms of unconditional surrender, and carried on fighting alone. A Roman army under Fulvius Nobilior besieged and took their fortress of Ambracia, which was surrendered. The Aetolians accepted peace terms and became allies of the Roman people, with the obligation to support the Romans against their enemies. In the following year Prusias, King of Bithynia, where Hannibal had taken refuge, resumed his war on Pergamum, with Hannibal as general. This war had been going on intermittently for several years, whenever there was an opportunity to take territory from Pergamum. In 205 Prusias had invaded when Attalus of Pergamum was in Greece, assisting the Romans against Philip of Macedon. Thwarted on this occasion, seven years later Prusias succeeded in detaching some territory from Attalus's kingdom. After the battle of Magnesia, the Romans instructed Prusias to return the territory that he had gained to the new king, Eumenes. This merely provoked further attacks, with Hannibal aiding Prusias. There was a battle at sea, which Hannibal won, but the Bithynian victories were short-lived. The Romans intervened, winning the war in 182. Eumenes recovered his territory, and the Romans once again demanded the surrender of Hannibal. This time there was no opportunity for escape. The great Carthaginian general took poison.

In Rome, the Scipio brothers, the victors of Magnesia, fared little better. Lucius was accused of accepting bribes from Antiochus, which sounds highly unlikely, and Africanus was also accused of financial skulduggery, the details of which are obscure. The charges were brought by Cato the Censor, who had fought at the battle of Thermopylae, and had been forming an anti-Scipionic party in Rome. It says much for the strength of Cato's following that charges were brought at all, but there was no conviction in the courts. Nonetheless, Africanus left the city for his estates in Campania, and stayed there until his death. Thus both the victor and the vanquished at Zama tasted the bitterness of rejection by their own people, and death in exile from their native cities.

THE THIRD WAR WITH MACEDON

The next few years after the defeat of Antiochus the Great were relatively peaceful except for a revolt in Sardinia, which occupied the Romans from 181 to 176. It was not an unusual pattern after conquest and the creation of a province, when the next generation fought to regain the independence that their parents had lost. The people of Sardinia proved rather exceptional in continuing to resist for the next seventy-five years, and always resorted to banditry, assisted by their mountainous landscape. The Romans clung to the island because it provided grain and minerals.

Developments in Macedonia attracted Roman attention when it became obvious that Philip V was not content with his lot as an ally of Rome. He had been forced to relinquish territory that he claimed after the war with Antiochus, and now held a grudge against Rome for stifling his ambitions. Rome required stability in his kingdom but not development or expansion, so Philip bided his time and concentrated on rearmament and the accrual of wealth. He died before he could put it to use, but his son Perseus continued in the same tradition of covert hostility to Rome. Having succeeded to the wealth and manpower built up by his father, Perseus cultivated the other Greek states who were not happy with the Romans and started to make the ones that were friends of Rome feel very insecure.

It took the Romans until 172 to begin to check him. They had already determined on war, but went through the motions of sending an embassy to make various demands that Perseus could not meet without giving up his autonomy, so war was a foregone conclusion. However, in the eyes of their own people at home and in the eyes of the other Greeks, the Romans had been seen to observe the proper diplomatic forms, somewhat like consultations in the modern world, where meetings are held and closely documented, the people who take part have their say, and then the original plans go ahead anyway.

The war began in 171, but nothing much was achieved until the consul Aemilius Paullus arrived in 168. He already had experience of the problems of the Greek states and their jealousies and rivalries, having been a member of the commission sent out to organize the settlement of the area after the defeat of Antiochus at Magnesia. His first task on arrival was to perk up the army that had been achieving very little for three years, and then he could concentrate on bringing Perseus to battle, which he achieved at Pydna in Macedonia in 168. The Macedonian phalanx at first repulsed the Romans, but in advancing so far the soldiers could not keep close together, and anyway the sun was shining in their eyes and they began to break up. The Romans saw their opportunity and destroyed the phalanx using their short swords. The victory was not a foregone conclusion, and Paullus said afterwards that he always shuddered and broke into a cold sweat whenever he thought of the Macedonian phalanx advancing on his troops.

The Macedonian state was now divided up into four Republics, monitored but not annexed by Rome. A resurgence of power such as Philip and Perseus had achieved could never occur again. Perseus himself was captured and died in Rome as a prisoner, despised and maltreated, to Rome's discredit. Many other prisoners were taken to Rome who had probably had no hand in the war, but who were under suspicion. About 1,000 Achaeans were transported to the city, ostensibly to answer the charges of instigating or engaging in anti-Roman activities. They were not returned to their homelands for some time, so they became in effect hostages to ensure the good behaviour of other Greeks. Fortunately for historians and archaeologists, one of these Achaean captives was the historian Polybius, who was made a client or dependant of Scipio Aemilianus. This Scipio was the natural son of the victor of Pydna, Aemilius Paullus, but as a young child he was adopted by Publius Cornelius Scipio to continue the Scipionic family line. When Polybius wrote his history of Rome, he made all due reference to the Scipio family, especially Africanus, who was Aemilianus's adoptive grandfather.

Rome's relationship with Greece was undergoing a change. The balance of power had shifted when Macedonia was subdued and then broken up, so the Greeks were no longer threatened with domination by the Macedonian kings, but they soon realized that they had exchanged the threat of domination by Macedon for the very real domination by Rome. The Greeks began to murmur, and the Romans grew more and more suspicious. They had been capably and loyally assisted by the Rhodians in the wars against Macedonia, but the Romans chose to forget this when the Rhodians tried to mediate between Perseus and Rome. The Romans took offence and forced the Rhodians to give up territories in Asia Minor, and then added insult to injury by establishing a free port on the island of Delos. Trade was the main support of the Rhodian economy, which was now ruined by Roman intervention. The Romans dealt out similar high-handed treatment to Eumenes of Pergamum, who had also helped them in the war against Perseus, and they attacked the towns of Epirus and enslaved large numbers of the inhabitants. The freedom of the Greeks, declared with pomp and ceremony by Flamininus less than thirty years earlier, was now revealed as an illusion. The Greeks thought that they could continue as before, governing themselves and fighting each other as they wished, in total independence. The Romans interpreted freedom rather differently. It meant dependence on Rome and obedience to Roman wishes, in effect clientship and unconditional loyalty.

The Roman perception of the world that surrounded the Mediterranean was also changing. The victory at Pydna and the subjugation of Macedonia taught the Romans that war could be profitable. They no doubt knew this already, but the wealth that poured into the city from Macedonia made it possible to remit the property tax on Roman citizens in Italy (*tributum civium Romanorum*) from 167 onwards. Within another two decades the Romans started to acquire territories overseas, and revenues flowed into the capital.

SPAIN, AFRICA & GREECE

The inhabitants of the areas recently subjugated by the Romans did not lie down and give in without a struggle. In the two Spanish provinces, rebellions went on for years, hard fought with escalating cruelty on both sides. Several people since the Romans have tried to subdue the Spaniards and found that it is not as easy as it looks, the country itself being a prominent factor in the embarrassment of the aggressors, and the hardiness of the natives being another. Supply of food and war material was always a problem to the Romans in Spain, epitomised by a statement of a much later monarch, Henri IV of France, who said that Spain is a country where large armies starve and small ones are defeated.

The first signs of trouble appeared in both provinces at about the same time. In 155 the Celtiberian tribes in Nearer Spain and the Lusitanians in the Further province raised separate revolts. The Lusitanians were defeated by the praetor Servius Sulpicius Galba in 151, but in pursuing the remnants of the tribes Galba lost many of his troops. In 150 he resorted to treachery, promising a treaty with the tribes and then turning on them. Many were killed, and the rest were sold into slavery. Among those who escaped was a shepherd called Viriathus, or more correctly Viriatus, whose name entered into Roman history because he waged a successful eight-year guerrilla war against the Romans after the massacre in 150. He may have learned, and would perhaps have been surprised, that in the following year a tribune in Rome, supported by Marcus Porcius Cato, had proposed that Galba should be brought to trial for his betrayal of the Lusitanians. But in the end, Viriatus would not have been surprised when the senators closed ranks and Galba escaped condemnation. Such a blatant miscarriage of justice only served to underline the callous attitude of the Romans to the Lusitanian tribesmen. Not much is known of Viriatus between 150 and 147, but by then he had emerged as leader of the Lusitanians, and he managed to weld his own people and the Celtiberians together, operating in guerrilla actions in both Spanish provinces. In 140 he defeated a Roman army under Quintus Fabius Maximus Servilianus, and made peace, but even though the arrangements were ratified by the Roman people, in the following year the Senate reneged on the peace settlement, allowing the new commander Gnaeus Servilius Caepio to resume hostilities. Viriatus was betrayed by one of his own men in the pay of the Romans, and after his death resistance collapsed. The Lusitanians surrendered in 138.

While the wars in Spain were dragging on, the Carthaginians were revitalizing their commerce. It was all they had left since the terms of the peace treaty with Rome at the end of the second Punic war removed their capacity to make war in any part of the world unless the Romans approved. Even though Carthage had been utterly defeated, fear and loathing of their former enemy had not been eradicated from Roman collective consciousness. The recent example of Philip V of Macedonia and his rapid resurgence to political and military power did nothing to allay the suspicion of the Romans that the renewal of Carthaginian trade and the subsequent wealth that it brought could so easily lead to the same result. The alliance between Rome and the Numidian chief Masinissa served to keep Carthage down, since the Numidians constantly raided Carthaginian territory, but by the terms of their treaty the Carthaginians were not allowed to fight back. On several occasions an appeal for assistance was sent from Carthage to Rome, and each time a commission of enquiry was sent to Africa, but ended by condoning Masinissa's actions. In 153 the elderly Marcus Porcius Cato was included in the group of Roman senators who were sent to investigate the latest dispute between Carthage and Masinissa. Cato saw how wealthy and potentially powerful Carthage had become, and on his return to Rome, whenever he spoke in the Senate, no matter what the subject was, he always ended with the words '*Carthago delenda est*', meaning Carthage must be destroyed.

The Carthaginians were in an impossible position, and in 151 or 150 they fought back and attacked Masinissa. Unfortunately they were defeated, and it was more unfortunate still that the Romans interpreted the hostilities as a warlike act. An army was despatched to Africa to remove all Carthaginian war material and siege engines. At first the Carthaginians complied with everything the Romans demanded of them rather than go to war, but they were being deliberately pushed into a corner which, one way or another, involved their annihilation. The Romans had promised to spare the lives of the all the Carthaginians and to allow them to continue to govern themselves, but now came the ultimate demand. The old city of Carthage was to be abandoned, and a new one built at least 10 miles from the coast. A city that relied on trade across the Mediterranean clearly could not survive under those circumstances. The Carthaginians decided that they had nothing to lose, and went to war in 149, the year in which Cato died. They had to manufacture weapons, since the Romans had seized their war equipment. The story goes that the Carthaginian women donated their long hair to make the torsion springs for the catapults, with which the Carthaginians defended their walls. The third Punic war had begun.

One of the officers in the Roman army fighting against the Carthaginians was Scipio Aemilianus. He was not yet politically important but he possessed two powerful names, those of his father Aemilus Paullus and his adoptive family of the Scipios. He was not eligible for any of the higher magistracies, so when he returned from Carthage to Rome his aim was to stand for election as aedile. The Scipio family would be able to muster a large following of clients and friends who could work on the susceptibilities of the Roman populace, who were soon agitating for the election of Aemilianus to the consulship. There was the precedent of Aemilianus's adoptive grandfather, Scipio Africanus, and the added pressure of a war against Carthage that had been started two years before and was not going very well. The Carthaginians were fighting for their lives, and had proved more effective that the Romans anticipated.

Scipio Aemilianus soon gained the upper hand. He defeated a Carthaginian army and put the city of Carthage under siege. The Carthaginians were outnumbered and ran out of food, so the fall of the city was a foregone conclusion, but not before they had made the Romans fight for every building and every inch of ground. Anyone who survived after the Roman victory was enslaved, the city was utterly destroyed and the agricultural land sowed with salt. The days of Roman intervention followed by a peace settlement and the withdrawal of troops were over. The territory formerly ruled by Carthage was annexed and named the province of Africa.

In the same year, 146, the Romans also destroyed Corinth. Two wars in Greece had started almost simultaneously with the Carthaginian war, in 149, when anti-Roman feeling reached a new peak. The Achaeans who had been taken to Rome in 168 after the battle of Pydna were finally allowed to return home in 151. Their opinion of Rome had not improved in the intervening years and their homecoming inflamed the rest of the Achaeans. Before they organized themselves to defy the Romans, a pretender to the Macedonian throne called Andriscus turned up with the claim that he was the son of Perseus, and quickly took over the old kingdom, drawing upon the hatred for the Romans who were seen as oppressors. The first Roman attempts to stop him met with defeat but, in 148 at Pydna, Andriscus was defeated by the praetor Metellus. The previous arrangements whereby Macedonia had been divided into four republics had not prevented the populations from uniting against Rome, so the whole area was annexed.

Watching the developments in Macedonia, and knowing that the Roman forces were spread over a wide area since they were also at war with the Spanish tribes and with the Carthaginians, the members of the Achaean confederacy decided that the Romans would be too preoccupied with other battles to notice if they engaged in military action of their own. They put an end to their dispute with Sparta by attacking, defeating and absorbing the whole state. There was some diplomatic wrangling while the Romans protested and issued warnings, which the Achaeans ignored, and all the time the hatred of Roman domination was spreading to other Greek states. Finally the consul Lucius Mummius was sent out with two legions. The leader of the Achaeans, Critolaus, risked battle and was defeated and killed. The Achaeans tried again and Mummius defeated them a second time at Leucopetra in 146. In the rest of Greece, Metellus, the general who had put down the Macedonian revolt, squashed any remaining embers of rebellion. In order to underline the power of Rome and make an example that would be crystal clear to other cities, Corinth was treated in the same way as Carthage, completely destroyed, looted for its portable wealth and art treasures, and the inhabitants enslaved. The events of the year 146 indicated clearly to the rest of the Mediterranean world that Rome had progressed from disinterested protector of friends to dictator of terms, and brutal oppressor if the terms were not met.

Meanwhile the war in Spain was not yet over. The Celtiberians raised revolt again in 143. Most of the tribesmen surrendered to the consul Quintus Caecilius Metellus when made a sudden attack on them, but the die-hards held out, using the town of Numantia as their stronghold. The Romans sent another commander, Quintus Pompeius Aulus,who blockaded Numantia through the winter and made peace in 140, but typical of the attitude of the Senate to the Spanish tribes, the terms were not ratified and the war continued. The next commander, Gaius Hostilius Mancinus, never reached the stage of making peace, but managed to get himself surrounded, and gave in, surrendering with his army of 20,000 men in 137. One of the officers in his army was Tiberius Sempronius Gracchus, whose father had treated the Spanish tribes well, and was remembered with gratitude. The Numantines would negotiate only with Tiberius, and in the end they let the whole army go free, but without any of their equipment or possessions. In Rome, there was outrage that a Roman army had surrendered. The Senate decreed that Mancinus should be sent back to Numantia and left to the mercy of the rebels, but the rebels were not interested in killing him.

The war against the Celtiberians was becoming an embarrassment, calling for special efforts to bring it to a conclusion. Although the situation was not as dire as the war against Hannibal had been, and there was no direct threat to Rome itself, it was considered that it was time to call in the top man, Scipio Aemilianus, the general who had finished the war against Carthage in 146. He was elected to the consulship for 134, despite the legislation only recently passed to prevent men from holding the office for a second time. When he arrived in Spain he spent some time instilling discipline into the soldiers who were very demoralized, and clearing the camps of all unnecessary personnel, including the slaves of the officers and men, and the camp followers that inevitably clustered around any army. He also recruited local tribesmen to swell the ranks of his army. Then he put Numantia under siege. He built a stone wall and ditch all around the site, with towers at regular intervals, and a series of camps for the soldiers, to the eventual distress of the Numantines and the gratification of archaeologists who have studied the remains of siege works and his camps with their internal layouts, to elucidate how the Roman army operated in the middle of the second century BC. The layout suggests that the army was still organized in manipular formation, not yet by cohorts, which had appeared by Caesar's day.

There were some skirmishes in which the Romans did not always emerge unscathed, but Scipio accomplished his main aims of cutting off the supplies to the Numantines, and detaching the other Spanish tribes from their allegiance and preventing them from rendering assistance. In the end the Numantines were starved out, and sold as slaves, in 133. Peace of a sort came to Spain at last, on Roman terms. A commission of ten senators was sent out to reorganize the whole country.

THE PRICE OF SUCCESS

The wars of the second century BC stretched manpower resources and revealed some problems. Twelve Latin cities had reached the point of exhaustion during the war with Hannibal and had been unable to provide any more recruits, but even after the departure of the Carthaginian army, some of the allies found it difficult to reach their quotas of manpower because many of their menfolk had migrated to Rome. The allied cities themselves agitated for the return of their citizens, and in 187 and 177 some of the Latins who had settled in Rome were sent back to their places of origin. Some men were expelled because they had obtained or claimed Roman citizenship by fraud, which indicates that citizenship was worth having.

In the war with Carthage in the third century BC the Romans had been fighting for survival, and the citizens and allies had responded with a will, but military service in the foreign wars from 200 onwards was not popular. The property qualification for service in the army had to be progressively lowered to find more recruits, but the qualification had been set in the first place to produce men who were wealthy enough to provide their own military equipment. If poorer men were recruited they had to be equipped at state expense, or occasionally by the general who was raising an army. When Scipio took command in Spain he assembled many of his own clients and some volunteers, but no new consular army was raised for the Numantine war. On two occasions, in 151 and 138, the call to arms had been resisted, and the tribunes had lent political support to the resistance. Service in the Roman army, particularly in Spain, had become onerous and unrewarding.

Adult males in Rome and allied cities were eligible for call-up for sixteen years of their lives, and had to serve for six campaigns, after which they were classified as veterans. Although there was no standing army at this period, there was an army in the field somewhere in the Roman world for most of the time, so a sort of professionalism grew out of continued service. Some men made a career out of the army, voluntarily re-enlisting for different campaigns, not necessarily with the rank that they had held in previous campaigns, but with accumulating experience that could be handed on.

A short time after the first provinces were established, the high-handed treatment of the provincials by some of the governors, who regarded their term of office as an opportunity for making their fortunes by fair means or foul, created the need for a legal mechanism to make reparations. The provincials could send delegations to the Senate to complain about a governor's behaviour, and the case would be taken up in Rome. At first such offences were investigated and tried before the people's assembly. In 171 the notorious extortion of money from the inhabitants of the Spanish provinces was the subject of special legal proceedings, but there was no systematic way of dealing with rapacious governors. The problem did not fade away, and extortion grew to such proportions that eventually, in 149, the tribune Lucius Calpurnius Piso passed a law concerning the recovery of money, or the monetary value of goods, that had been illegally extorted from the provinces. As a result of this law a special permanent court was established, the *quaestio de pecuniis repetundis* (the term *repetundae*, always in the plural, means specifically the recovery of extorted money). This court is generally considered to be the first permanent one in Rome, on which other later courts were modelled. It was always accessible, and a coterie of experienced lawyers developed, always on hand to prepare the case for prosecution. Fifty senators formed the jury, with a praetor in charge of proceedings. Taken at face value, the provincials were well protected, but in practice the condemnation of venal governors was rare. The lesser offences were probably ignored by the provincial population, because they were discouraged by the prohibitive expense involved in going to Rome and the time taken to reach a verdict, so it was probably only the worst cases that ever reached the courts. Then there was the solidarity of the senatorial order, and the reluctance of individual senators to pass the verdict of guilty on men whom they knew, and to whom they were probably either indebted or even distantly related by means of dynastic marriages. Besides, each senator might govern a province himself one day, and would probably rely upon making a profit from his tour of duty. It was regarded as a privilege, and some men began to run up debts in campaigning for office, in the hope of being able to settle them if they obtained a province.

One of the most pressing problems of the first half of the second century BC was the question of land. It was a perennial concern, with antecedents in the previous century, and repercussions in the next. The public land (*ager publicus*) had been won by conquest and was theoretically open to all Roman citizens, and after 338 when the Latin League was dissolved, it was available to the Latins as well. There had been disputes from the earliest times about how the land should be used, whether it should be distributed to the poorer classes, or leased to the wealthier citizens who would pay rent, providing an income for the state. With the passage of time there had been successive encroachments on the public lands and large estates had grown up at the expense of the small farmers. Two attempts to limit the size of individual holdings to 500 *iugera* (about 140 hectares or 350 acres) had failed. The first was in 367 when the Licinio-Sextian laws were passed, and the second attempt occurred at some time between 201 and 167, when the limit was once again set at 500 *iugera*, indicating that the previous laws had been ignored and farmers had expanded their holdings. The number of animals that could be grazed by one farmer on the public pasture was limited to 100 cattle, and 500 smaller grazing animals such as sheep and goats. The repetition of these laws illustrates the constant growth of larger holdings encroaching on the public land, often by rich senators whose estates were truly vast.

The land question was bound up with service in the army. The majority of the soldiers were drawn from the small farmers, so if the numbers of farmers declined so did the availability of recruits. When the Romans were fighting their neighbours, raising an army on an annual basis, conducting the campaign and then disbanding the troops so that the soldiers could go home for the harvest, the system worked well enough. It was likely that in those days the levy did not include all the eligible manpower, so that there would be some of the younger men as well as older farmers who remained at home and looked after the farms. The expansion of Rome necessitated foreign wars and longer continuous periods of service, so some of the soldiers would remain under arms for longer, and a greater number of men would be levied at one time, especially when the Romans were hard pressed. For several years, for several reasons, fewer men could stay on the farms.

The decline of the small farms can be attributed to several causes, in addition to the increased exploitation of military manpower. The spread of the *latifundia*, the enormous landed estates of the wealthy, is usually blamed as the chief cause of rural depopulation, but there were other contributory factors. The enforced absence of the soldiers, combined with the death rate during the various wars, and the devastation caused by Hannibal's long sojourn in Italy, meant that some farms were abandoned altogether. The occupants migrated to the towns, and most especially to Rome, where the urban mob swelled in proportion to the decline of the rural population. Many of the soldiers who completed their service with the army came home to find their farms non-existent, run down beyond repair, or purchased by the wealthy landowners whose enormous estates swallowed up the small farms. The introduction of slave labour on the great estates enabled food to be produced more cheaply, and the import of cheap foreign grain and foodstuffs eroded the potential profit from growing crops at home, so even if some of the farmers had managed to hang onto their holdings and make a living, eventually the competition forced them out. These unfortunate people also migrated to Rome, and to the smaller Italian towns and cities.

In 173 the Senate gave one of the consuls the task of investigating the holdings on public and private lands and establishing boundaries between them, because private owners had encroached on public land and now regarded it as their own by right, to pass onto their heirs. The only result of the investigation was that a mere 50,000 *iugera* of public land were purchased from the occupants, and the rest remained in the hands of the wealthy landowners. About thirty years later, the Senate once again started to worry about the decline of the small farmers, the numbers of landless men thronging the city of Rome, and the lack of recruits. It was suggested that the public land should be redistributed to the dispossessed in small allotments, so that the landless men could go back to farming, providing a modest propertied class that would also furnish recruits for the army, and at the same time Rome would be emptied of potential troublemakers. The proposals never came to fruition because redistribution of the land for the dispossessed in Rome entailed the eviction of the men who were already there, the *possessores*, who by now regarded the lands as their own. This was not a recent settlement, since some of the farmers had been farming there for several generations, and any legal requirement that they may have had to pay rent to the state had been lost in the mists of time. But what discouraged the investigators most was the fact that many of the landowners who had taken over public land were senators, well-connected, stupendously wealthy, politically powerful, socially influential and in control of the courts. It was a thorny problem. In 133 Tiberius Sempronius Gracchus entered office as tribune, determined to solve it.

5

Reforming Zeal: The Republic Comes of Age 133–83 BC

The tribunes of the plebs entered office in the December prior to their year of office, before the consuls took up their magistracies in January of the following year. Tiberius Sempronius Gracchus was just one of the tribunes whose tenure began on 10 December 134 for 133. He was to launch proposals for reform which allegedly had been instigated by his observation of the sorry state of the Italian countryside and the farmers who tried to scratch a living from it, all of which he witnessed while he was on his way to the wars in Spain. That was not the only problem that occupied him, for there was much in Rome that was in need of reform by the latter half of the second century BC.

After the wars with the Carthaginians and the Greeks, culminating in the destruction of Carthage and Corinth in 146, Roman attitudes changed. Expansion had not been the main aim of Roman foreign policy until then. Spain was taken from the Carthaginians and the Romans held onto it to keep the Carthaginians out and to exploit the resources of the two newly created Spanish provinces, but there was a considerable price to pay before the whole country was pacified. In the eastern Mediterranean, wars were fought, peace was made, with or without a treaty, and then the soldiers went home. For a short time it was possible to deal with cities, states, tribes or confederacies by playing one off against the other, which obviated the need for direct Roman control until situations got out of hand, then an army would be sent, the problems sorted out, not necessarily to the advantage of the non-Roman participants, and then in most cases the Romans withdrew. After 146, instead of making administrative arrangements and going home, the Romans lost patience and started to annexe territory, administering it from Rome via provincial governors.

As the Romans changed their perceptions of countries outside Italy, and entered on a phase of deliberate expansion, there was also a detectable change in attitudes at home. Selfishness set in, privileges were jealously guarded, and where there had once been willingness to share the benefits of conquest, booty and recently acquired lands, with their allies, the Romans began to ration the rewards and privileges that had hitherto been accorded to the Italians. Although the old struggle between the patricians and the plebs was no longer relevant, there was still no lack of dissension among the Roman populace at all levels. The senatorial class was dominated by a handful of influential families whose members were continually elected to high office, and formed an almost impenetrable network of alliances with other families, by marrying off their sons and daughters in arranged liaisons in order to gain the best possible political and financial advantages. The social and political standing of prominent senators was made all the greater by the client system, whereby vast numbers of people from all walks of life were bound to the head of the family, for mutual support and benefits. Hosts of clients would turn up at the senator's house in the mornings for an audience, probably being set specific tasks for which they were paid in one way or another. A senator might support and finance the careers of aspiring young men in politics or in business, or simply support the heads of poorer families, in return for which these men would become part of the senator's *clientelae*, bound closely to him, and turning out with him in public. A senator's worth was judged by the magnitude of the crowd of clients he could muster when he attended meetings or processed through the Forum.

This network of clients around a senator was augmented or supplemented by another group, or class, of men whom the Romans called *equites*, usually translated into English either in the literal sense of knights because of the connection with horses (from *equus*, plural *equi*, the Latin for horse), or alternatively as the middle classes. Neither of these terms is exact, but there is no suitable equivalent term that conveys the rank and position that these men held. Originally the *equites* were connected to the army, operating as horsemen, as the name suggests. The censors chose a group of young men who would qualify for the gift of the 'public horse', or a mount provided by the state, accompanied by money for the upkeep of the animal. The system survived throughout the Republic, but at the same time the description *equites* began to be applied to a wider group of men, embracing those who served as mounted warriors, and then it was also used to distinguish the class of men who were not senators. So the equestrian order, as it is described in modern books, could include wealthy sons of senators who would eventually enter the Senate, and a whole range of business men, landowners whose wealth derived from agriculture, equestrian tax collectors, merchants and the like. Some of these equestrians were closely bound to senators by dint of running their business enterprises for them. Since senators were forbidden to engage directly in trade, and their ownership of large cargo vessels was severely restricted by a law passed at the end of the third century BC, from this time onwards, if not before, the equestrians stepped in to run the businesses, working for senators as agents or *negotiatores*. With the extension of Roman control over the countries around the Mediterranean, the equestrians also spread into these areas, until there was hardly a city or a port which lacked Roman equestrians engaged in trade or business.

The senators and equestrians derived considerable benefit from the wealth that flowed into Rome as territorial expansion by conquest brought in vast spoils of war and indemnity payments from the defeated states. Some of this timely enrichment of the state was used to finance further wars, but it did not trickle downwards to the benefit of the poorer classes, because prices rose, more food was imported and slaves worked the large estate farms, all of which made it an uphill task for the small farmers to make a living because they did not receive a sufficient return for their produce. The drift to the towns and cities affected the Latins and the Italian allies as well as Rome, but the problem of the urban poor in Rome was endemic, and showed no sign of abating. Dissensions began to widen into conflicts. The senators despised the urban poor and strenuously denied them political power, the urban poor resented the rich land-owning senators, but also despised the allies and objected to any suggestion of allowing them equal rights, and the allies were disaffected with all the Romans because of their increasingly unfair treatment. The Romans did not pay tax after 167, while the allies continued to contribute money and manpower, but after the 170s they no longer shared in the distribution of land and booty even though they had been fighting on Rome's behalf. One of the main strengths of the Roman system of alliances had been the mutual obligations and benefits that both parties shared. Lack of full Roman citizenship had not seemed so disadvantageous when the allies received their rewards, but now there was an imbalance. The Romans were better off, so citizenship with its privileges was more desirable, and in some cases it was deemed worth risking the penalties for claiming it fraudulently.

Politicians could take up any one of the causes of discontent and make mileage out of agitation on behalf of the particular groups who were affected by the problems. The age of dominant political and military personalities began, starting with Tiberius and Gaius Gracchus, followed by Marius, Sulla, Pompey the Great and Julius Caesar. As the problems worsened, in addition to fighting their enemies and sorting out the squabbles between their Greek neighbours, the Romans started to fight each other.

TIBERIUS GRACCHUS

Tiberius Sempronius Gracchus was a member of the plebeian nobility, so his origins entitled him to stand for election as tribune, from which office patricians were excluded. Tiberius was well connected. His father, also called Tiberius Sempronius Gracchus, had been consul twice, always a great distinction in consular families, and had reached the pinnacle of his career when he was made censor in 169. Tiberius junior was born probably in 163, though the date is not certain. His mother was Cornelia, the daughter of Scipio Africanus, the conqueror of Hannibal, and his wife was the daughter of Appius Claudius. With family connections such as these, not many of his contemporaries considered it likely that Tiberius would set out to disrupt the state. Modern historians are divided as to his motives, some saying that he genuinely wanted to improve the welfare of the poorer classes and to solve the problems caused by the drift to the city, while others insist that he was nothing but a demagogue who used his programmes of reforms to further his own career.

His proposals for reform included a law that would redistribute parcels of the public land to the urban poor, by making it illegal for any individual farmer to hold more than 500 *iugera* of such land. Farmers who were already in occupation of the public land could keep this much land rent free, and were allowed an extra 250 *iugera* for each child, up to a maximum of four children, which would provide an estate of 1,500 *iugera*, approximately 900 acres. The rest of the public land was to be allocated to landless farmers in small parcels of 30 *iugera* each, which they were not allowed to sell.

Although the proposed law would entail evictions from the land, Tiberius tried to accommodate the farmers who had been settled there for some time without disrupting them too much, allowing them to remain on the land without paying rent to the state, but many senators had cultivated vast estates, and would have to down-size. Not only that, but the three-man commission that was to be set up to redistribute the land had the last word on which lands were to be given up, and it was possible that the commissioners would earmark some of the most productive acres that would have to be relinquished. Besides, no matter how fertile the land was, all the existing farmers would have put time and money into establishing crops, particularly perhaps olives, which take about ten years to start to yield a profit, and vines. The loss of these crops would rankle, to say the least. Opposition to Tiberius's bill was unavoidable.

Resettlement on the land would alleviate the problems of the urban poor in Rome, but modern scholars have questioned whether the 30 *iugera* allocation would provide a group of farmers with the relevant property qualification to provide recruits for the army, so the only result, not an inconsiderable one, would be to reduce the size of the Roman mob. There were other considerations about reallocating the land. Families who possessed nothing to start with would need gifts or loans to be able to set up. A small plot that could be successfully farmed with only one or two family members would probably not produce enough to make a profit, and would not provide all of the everyday needs of each family, who would need some profit, in whatever form, to exchange for other goods. Another problem was that not all the urban poor would make good farmers, just as the later settlement of time-served veterans on the land failed to solve all their problems, and the drift back to Rome started again. The clause forbidding sale of the 30 *iugera* allotments would not prevent a family from returning to the city, and so the land that had been wrested from previous farmers might be abandoned.

Despite these potential shortcomings, the proposed law was supported by the public, as most land bills were whenever they surfaced in Roman politics. The opposition came from men who might lose lands, and principally from the Senate. Since tribunes possessed the right of *intercessio*, or veto, on proposals of any kind which threatened the interests of the populace, the senators approached one of the other tribunes to ask him to use his veto to block Tiberius's bill. The tribune Marcus Octavius accordingly did so when the bill was presented to the assembly. This was a contradiction of the original purpose of the tribunician veto, since the land law was intended to benefit the people.

Tiberius reacted by bringing the meeting to a close and then trying to persuade Octavius to withdraw his veto. When he met with failure, he proposed that Octavius should be deposed from his office, and he asked the assembly to vote on the issue. It was agreed, and Octavius was physically manhandled and removed from the meeting, despite the fact that tribunes were supposed to be sacrosanct while in office and therefore anyone who injured Octavius was theoretically subject to penalties. Then a new tribune was elected to replace him. The content of the land law now became rather less inflammatory than the methods that Tiberius used to force it through.

The commission of three men to put the land law into effect was allowed to assemble, consisting originally of Tiberius, his brother Gaius Gracchus and his father-in-law Appius Claudius. The personnel changed later on, but the work still went forward, hindered by lack of funds because the Senate refused to allocate them more than a token amount. Tiberius was not defeated on this score, because money was available from a particular bequest to the Romans, which was nothing less than the entire kingdom of the recently deceased King Attalus of Pergamum who died in 133. Tiberius took the matter to the *concilium plebis*, the council of the plebs, to divert some of the money to the land commissioners so that they could carry out their tasks. The cash flow resumed, and the commission's problems were eased, but the senators rounded on Tiberius, accusing him of accepting royal insignia from Pergamum, and intending to make himself king.

Perhaps the matter would have ended there and the land commission would simply have gone about its business, but Tiberius announced that he was going to stand for election as tribune for a second term in 132. A law had been passed in the 180s making it illegal for anyone to seek re-election to the same office until ten years had elapsed, but this may have concerned only the praetorship and consulship. The fact that Tiberius flouted one or two laws did not upset the senators quite so much as the habit of laying everything before the people's assemblies and carrying though his legislation without reference to the Senate. Although the Romans conducted business in the name of the Senate and the People of Rome, it was the Senate that framed and formed policy, not the people. In anticipation of Tiberius's future proposals, the Senate decided to block him before he could start. At the elections, while people were still voting, Tiberius was removed as a candidate. None of this adequately conveys the build up of violent feelings towards him in the Senate.

The next day, Tiberius gathered his considerable crowd of supporters, 3,000 according to some sources, and occupied the Forum in readiness for the meeting of the assembly. Tiberius was now being portrayed as a tyrant. It was no longer a matter of opposition to the policies that he had pushed through, but fear that he might take over the state. One of the senators, Scipio Nasica, who happened to be *pontifex maximus* or chief priest, argued that Tiberius should be killed. The consul, Publius Mucius Scaevola, refused to authorize such a momentous action without a trial, but feelings were running high, and Scipio Nasica won the day, leading the senators out to confront Tiberius and his supporters. In the ensuing riot, worthy of the name battle, Tiberius was killed along with many of his followers. Their corpses were thrown into the Tiber, and therefore denied proper burial. The rest of Tiberius's supporters were rounded up and executed.

What had happened far outclassed the fratricide upon which Rome was founded. The Senate had the power to negotiate, to discuss Tiberius's proposals, to meet him half way and find a suitable compromise, to find some other method of removing the landless men from Rome, such as the foundation of colonies. If no agreement could be reached after sober discussion, the senators had the power to bring Tiberius to court by means of some legal fiction if necessary. No one in Roman politics was ever shy of bringing trumped up charges against a man who was considered to be a troublemaker. Instead the senators chose appalling slaughter in the city itself. Their attendants had brought clubs and weapons with them to the meeting, and the senators themselves picked up pieces of smashed seats and benches and used them on Tiberius's supporters. It would have been small comfort to the bereaved families that an enquiry into the events was set up as soon as everything had calmed down, and Scipio Nasica was quietly packed off to Pergamum at the head of a commission of five senators while the kingdom was taken over in accordance with the will of King Attalus. Nasica never returned to Rome.

Foreign Wars & Roman Expansion 135–121 BC

The absorption of the kingdom of Pergamum was not a simple matter of imposing a Roman administrative system and collecting the taxes. King Eumenes, the predecessor of Attalus, had an illegitimate son called

Aristonicus, who entertained designs on taking over the kingdom for himself. He rallied the people and promised freedom and equality for everyone, and managed to defeat a Roman army that was sent against him, led by Licinius Crassus, who was killed in the battle. The consul for 130, Marcus Perperna, took command and in turn defeated and killed Aristonicus. It took the next four years to pacify and organize the kingdom, which was converted into a new province called Asia, with some of the original territory near the eastern borders given away to local rulers, but these lands were not as fertile as the rest of the province and would not have yielded a great return for the cost of administration. The new province on the shores of the Aegean Sea provided a stepping stone for Rome to monitor events in the east and to expand further if necessary, but above all it was very wealthy, and therefore unfortunately fell victim to greed, as a province where governors and tax collectors could line their pockets, pay all their debts and still come home as rich men.

From 135 to 132 Roman armies were fighting in Sicily, where a serious and well organized slave revolt had started, led by Eunous, a Syrian slave who called himself King Antiochus and set up his capital in the area of Henna. It was estimated that about 70,000 slaves joined the revolt, either under Eunous or in independent actions. Some of Eunous's associates took over Agrigentum, and others captured Tauromenium (modern Taormina), Messana and Catania. The Romans under Calpurnius Piso had to recapture the towns one by one, and it took the best part of three years to do it.

In the north, the people of Massilia were harrassed by the Gallic tribes, principally the Saluvii, and finally appealed to Rome for military assistance, which arrived under the consul Fulvius Flaccus in 125. The campaign was continued under the consul for 124, Gaius Sextius Calvinus, who defeated the Ligurians and took the main Saluvian settlement at Aquae Sextiae (modern Aix-en-Provence), which the Romans fortified and occupied. The route from Italy to the Rhône was now under Roman control, but as usual, when the Romans took over territory, the nearest neighbours felt threatened and made aggressive noises. Roman occupation of Ligurian and Saluvian territory triggered an alliance among the Arverni and Allobroges, settled on each side of the Rhône. The Romans asked them to hand over any Saluvians who had taken refuge with them. The result was war, ending in defeat in 121 of the Allobroges by the proconsul Gnaeus Domitius Ahenobarbus, and of the Arverni by the consul Fabius Maximus. Throughout the hostilities, the Aedui, settled north of the Arverni, remained pro-Roman.

Massilia remained free, but the rest of the territory of southern Gaul from the Alps to the Pyrenees was now under Roman control, as a province called Gallia Transalpina. Travel from Italy into Spain was facilitated by the Via Domitiana, named after its builder Domitius Ahenobarbus. A colony of Roman citizens was founded at Narbo Martius, which became the capital of the province under Augustus when its name was changed to Gallia Narbonensis.

GAIUS GRACCHUS

Ten years would elapse before Tiberius's younger brother Gaius followed in his footsteps and stood for election as tribune for 123. He had been quaestor in Sicily for two years, where he had been overtly resistant to the opportunities for lining his own pockets. Like his brother Tiberius he stood for another term as tribune for 122, but unlike his brother he was elected without opposition. Gaius was a brilliant speaker, convincing and persuasive, and he had some senatorial supporters, one of whom was Fulvius Flaccus who had been consul in 125, and now against all precedent was elected tribune along with Gaius.

As tribune for two years, Gaius Gracchus passed laws that set in motion a series of reforms, but no proper chronology can be established because it is not certain to which year his individual laws belonged, so they are usually all described together. Probably among the first of Gaius's laws was the one aimed principally at Publius Popillius Laenas, who had been responsible for executing Tiberius's supporters. The new law stated that no capital trials should be held unless such proceedings were first approved by the assembly, and anyone who executed or exiled a citizen without such a trial would himself be subject to trial by the assembly. Having established the law, Gaius brought Popillius Laenas to trial and succeeded in exiling him.

Some of Gaius's proposals were probably derived from the unfulfilled plans of Tiberius Gracchus. The work of the original land commission had been allowed to proceed, and since land bills that offered allotments to the poor were always popular, there was probably no shortage of applicants for the allotments. Roman census figures show that the citizen population had risen from 318,828 in 130 to 394,736 five years later. Some scholars consider that the rise in population must be due to settlement on the allotments of public land, but this is difficult to prove or disprove, since the census included Roman citizens of eighteen years and upwards, so in part the increase could have derived from an upsurge in the birth rate and an increase in infant survival.

Gaius made some alterations to the land law via another bill which imposed rents on new allotments, and he removed some of the public land from redistribution. He also developed a programme for founding new colonies, some on lands in Italy including those of Capua and Tarentum, and abroad he proposed the foundation of another colony at Carthage, where the land confiscated by Rome would be allotted to settlers. The colony was to be called Junonia, and 6,000 settlers were allocated 200 *iugera* of land, amounting to about 130 acres.

The establishment of these colonies would help to reduce the numbers of poor in the city of Rome, and for those who remained Gaius passed a law to provide them with cheap grain, which the state would purchase just after the harvests, put into store in warehouses built in the city, and then distribute it every month to the people, who would pay a standard fee that was cheaper than the market price. In theory, riots caused by a shortage of food would be avoided in Rome, and no one should be completely destitute.

Gaius and his late brother Tiberius had pinpointed a number of grievances among the people, and they had also observed or listened to the problems of the soldiers. Recruitment was becoming gradually more difficult because fewer and fewer men possessed the property qualification, even though it had been lowered more than once. With foreign wars taking men far away for long periods, service in the army was unpopular, and Gaius's legislation reveals some of the reasons. It may have been Tiberius who thought of these measures but it was Gaius who enacted them, making it illegal to recruit soldiers of less than seventeen years of age, and removing the requirement for the men to pay for their clothing and equipment issued by the state. This in turn probably indicates that even if the men possessed the relevant property qualification for army service, some of them could not afford to bring their own equipment. Gaius may also have passed a law to reduce the length of military service, though this is not proven.

Extortion of the provincials had scarcely abated, necessitating another law to try to ensure that the men responsible were tried and condemned. Only a few sections of Gaius's law *de repetundis* are known, but it allowed the allies to bring a charge against the men who had stolen money or property. Another of Gaius's concerns was the fact that the jury courts were dominated by the leading senators, who were less likely to condemn one their own order. Gaius disrupted this monopoly by placing the equestrians in charge of the court juries, but the details of how he did this are not clear. The struggle for the control of the courts was a perennial problem and went on for some time, back and forth like a game of tennis. Forty years or so after Gaius Gracchus, Sulla would put the courts back into the hands of senators, and a short time after Sulla's death, Pompey the Great and Crassus were elected consuls and reinstated the equestrians in control of the courts.

So far the legislation of Tiberius and Gaius Gracchus had done very little for Rome's allies, save for the laws outlined above that gave them some redress against extortion. It seems that Gaius had plans for conferring Roman citizenship on all the Latins, and a limited franchise to the Italian allies, perhaps in the form of Latin rights. It was a topical theme, one that inevitably brought trouble in its wake. In 126 the tribune Marcus Junius Pennus passed a law to remove all non-Romans from the city of Rome, which indicated that the grant of citizenship was further away than ever. Exasperated by the refusal of the Romans to grant citizenship to the Latin allies, the inhabitants of Fregellae raised revolt, but the only result was the siege and destruction of the town. The hopes of the allies were revived in the following year. During his consulship in 125, Gaius's supporter Fulvius Flaccus had proposed that citizenship should be given to Latins and the Italian allies, or if the allies did not wish to be incorporated into the Roman state, then they should be given the right of appeal against the actions of Roman magistrates, which to some communities was more important than the right to vote in the Roman elections. The Senate circumvented these suggestions by sending Flaccus off to fight against the Saluvii who threatened Massilia, so the scheme had to be abandoned.

Among the senators and the people of Rome, the thought of enfranchising the Latins and enabling the allies to vote, however greatly their influence was to be limited, always provoked great opposition. There were many more Latins and allies than there were Romans, so senators feared that their own influence would be diluted, and likewise the Roman people did not want the allies to share in their privileges.

After Gaius Gracchus and Fulvius Flaccus left Rome to attend the foundation of the colony at Carthage, the Senate produced a counter-measure of their own, in the form of another tribune, Marcus Livius Drusus. As tribunes, Gaius and Fulvius ought not to have left the city, but perhaps the Senate authorized their absence because it suited them to remove the trouble makers while they rallied. During the interval, the senatorial agent Livius Drusus played to the gallery, dangling fantastic promises before the people of Rome and seducing them away from Gracchus. He proposed the foundation of twelve colonies that would be sufficient to resettle over 30,000 people. With regard to the allies, he avoided the citizenship question, and proposed an alternative that would not offend the jealous Romans, and would keep many of the allies happy. Only three years earlier, Fulvius Flaccus had highlighted the fact that citizenship with full voting rights was not necessarily the main concern for some of the Latins and allies, but avoidance of arbitrary treatment by magistrates, or at least the right of legal redress against such treatment, had more appeal. Livius Drusus latched onto this, proposing that Latins serving in the army under Roman officers should be immune from flogging.

When Gaius and Flaccus returned to Rome, they had lost the support of the people, and their enfranchisement bill came to nothing, either because it was vetoed by Livius Drusus or because the assembly voted against it. But the Italian allies would not forget that they might have come close to a greater equality with the Romans.

Gaius's end was more or less a duplicate of the fate of his brother. He stood for re-election for a third term as tribune in 121. Once again it was not so much a question of what he had done, but what he might achieve in another twelve months. A smear campaign ensured that he was not elected. He probably had no designs on ousting the entire Senate or taking over the state, but his laws were collectively anti-senatorial, so from the senators' point of view he had to be stopped. The opportunity came when Gaius and his followers turned up for the assembly when an important bill was to be presented, and a man was stabbed. Unfortunately he was a member of the staff of the consul Lucius Opimius. The Senate summoned Gaius and his friend Flaccus to appear at a meeting next day, but they stayed away. The consul Opimius was empowered to secure the safety of the state, by decree of the Senate. This procedure was eventually termed *senatus consultum ultimum*, or the last decree, a useful device allowing armed force to be brought in as a last resort. Gaius and Flaccus then went off to the Aventine Hill and armed their entourage, while Opimius gathered an armed band of his own, with some archers from Crete who were staying near Rome. In the ensuing attack Flaccus and Gaius were killed. As with Tiberius's supporters, many of Gaius's followers were executed.

The enormity of what had been done, twice in just over ten years, did not endear the Senate to the people. A new division was created in Roman public life. Henceforth the politicians who worked on behalf of the people, or used the assemblies to further their own careers, were labelled the *populares*, while the groups who sided with and worked via the Senate labelled themselves the *optimates*, or the best men. The two categories were not rigid or permanent. Some men could change camps, and then change back again, according to the political climate they found themselves in and where the best chance of promotion lay. The conflict was to last until the end of the Republic, but unfortunately the violence shown initially by the senators was only the beginning. Worse was to come in Rome.

GAIUS MARIUS

Gaius Marius was elected to his first consulship in 107, during the war with the African ruler Jugurtha, King of Numidia. Marius's entire career derived from success in war, and he was the first man to hold seven consulships in all, an unprecedented number in the Republic. Marius's plebeian ancestors came from Arpinum (modern Arpino) but not one of them was distinguished in any way. Marius was the first man in his family to reach the consulship, so he was a *novus homo*, or a new man in Rome, looked down on by the aristocracy whose illustrious forebears had been elected to the consulship for many generations. Marius's career owed much to the patronage of the Caecilii Metelli, a very distinguished and widespread aristocratic family, but he was a late starter in politics. He had served with Scipio Aemilianus at Numantia in Spain, alongside an ally of the Romans, Jugurtha, the grandson of Masinissa of Numidia. The two were to be opponents in the war in Africa some years later. Having served in the army, Marius turned to politics, backed by the Metelli. He was thirty-four when he was elected to the junior post of quaestor in 123, when Gaius Gracchus was tribune. Marius had been elected tribune himself in 119. In 115 he was one of the praetors in Rome, and then propraetor governing Further Spain. When he returned from his province, he married Julia, sister of Gaius Julius Caesar. In 100 BC Julia and Marius would become the aunt and uncle of the younger Gaius Julius Caesar, who would make more of an impression on Rome than Marius ever did.

When the war with Jugurtha broke out in Africa in 112, an opportunity opened up for Marius to display his military talents. Jugurtha was not in direct line for the succession as King of Numidia, but had been adopted by King Micipsa, the son and successor of Masinissa. Micipsa already had two sons of his own, Hiempsal and Adherbal. When Micipsa died in 118, Jugurtha quickly removed Hiempsal by assassination, but Adherbal escaped from an attack made on him and fled to Rome for help. The Senate decided to split the kingdom into two parts, Jugurtha ruling the western half and Adherbal was given the more fertile eastern half. Within less than six years, Jugurtha turned on Adherbal, despite the advice of the Romans, finally capturing him at Cirta (modern Constantine) and having him murdered, in 112. The Romans became more deeply involved because Jugurtha also massacred the Italian business men and traders who had settled in Cirta. Two consuls fought against Jugurtha without result and eventually Quintus Caecilius Metellus Numidicus was given the command in 109. Marius was made one of his legates, as was Publius Rutilius Rufus, who like Marius had served under Scipio Aemilianus at Numantia. During the African campaign, if not earlier, Rufus and Marius became mortal enemies.

Metellus was successful in two battles and he captured some cities, but these actions did little to bring the war to an end. Marius's ambition probably had not been noticed among the influential Metelli, until he asked for leave from the African campaign to return to Rome in 108 for the consular elections for 107. Metellus was incredulous and advised him to wait, for which perceived insult Marius bore him an eternal grudge. If it was a surprise to Metellus, it was the culmination of carefully laid plans on the part of Marius. For some time he had been preparing the scene in Rome through his followers who were drumming up support for him, which was just as well since he had only six days in Rome to canvass in person. He was duly elected consul, and set about persuading the Senate to remove Metellus from the command of the army in Africa, and to install himself in his place.

When he was confirmed in his command, he began to recruit more soldiers to fill the gaps in the army in Africa. This was not the usual levy to raise new legions, but to augment the troops already there, and the numbers of men were not very large. Marius found the men he wanted by asking for volunteers, and departed from tradition by accepting men with little or no property, known as the *capite censi*, or men who did not possess enough property to qualify for service and who were lumped together in one voting century so that their political power was nullified. Such volunteers had been used before when there were emergencies and a shortage of manpower, and in any case the property qualification had been lowered to the point where the state provided the necessary clothing and equipment, as shown in Gaius Gracchus's legislation relieving the soldiers of the duty of paying for it. There was considerable sense in recruiting able-bodied men who were willing to serve in the army, but it was always considered that men with property would have greater loyalty to the state, and besides they would have something to come home to, whereas men who had no land to farm and no income would require assistance that the state was not willing to give. The most dangerous precedent, one for which Marius is eternally blamed, is that the poorer classes would be more loyal to their commander than the Senate and people of Rome, and when they were discharged they would be dependent on the commander for rewards and settlement. Such a commander, with troops at his beck and call, would then be in a very powerful position, able to dominate the Senate and people by sheer force. Within a very few years after Marius's recruitment campaign, this is exactly what happened, but the blame cannot be laid entirely at his door. The lengthening campaigns in foreign countries, and the need for continuity of command surely contributed to the growth of loyalty of the soldiers to the commanders whom they served for several years, and the unresponsive Senate, which regularly ignored the needs of their returning armies, merely emphasized that loyalty, because the commander was the one person who could arrange for land settlements, reimbursement of some kind, or alternative employment for veterans. If they could not be granted plots of land, the next best thing for soldiers who were to be discharged was another war, preferably one which offered portable wealth and profit.

Marius's quaestor in Africa was Lucius Cornelius Sulla, an impoverished aristocrat of few scruples, decisive, clever, ambitious and ruthless. Though Marius possessed undoubted military talents it was through Sulla's intrigues that the war was finally ended, when he persuaded Jugurtha's father-in-law Bocchus, who was fighting alongside Jugurtha, to hand over the self-made king to the Romans. Bocchus was King of Mauretania, and after his co-operation with the Romans, he was also confirmed as ruler of part of Numidia which Jugurtha had originally ceded to him in return for his help. There was to be no Roman annexation of Numidia, as long as the borders with the province of Africa were secure.

While the war with Jugurtha was going on, a much greater danger to Rome was playing out in the north of Italy. Two Germanic tribes which the Romans called the Cimbri and Teutones had started to move, and their wanderings disturbed other tribes who fought each other and the Romans as well. Great battles were fought by the Roman armies to try to stop the tribesmen from entering Italy, and in each case the Romans were defeated, losing vast numbers of men. In 105, at Arausio (modern Orange), the two Roman commanders allowed their personal animosity to interfere with the campaign. Quintus Servilius Caepio, a blue-blooded aristocrat who had been consul for the previous year, would not co-operate with Gnaeus Mallius Maximus, a *novus homo* like Marius. It was said that this lack of co-operation and co-ordination led to the defeat of the Roman army. The tribesmen killed probably 80,000 men, the worst disaster since Hannibal defeated the Romans at Cannae. This calamity occurred as Marius was winding up his campaign in Africa, before coming home to celebrate his triumph, and even though he was not in Rome to stand for the elections, the people chose him as one of the consuls for 104. This was not strictly legal, but since it was a dire emergency, the illegality was overlooked or reconciled by some means. As soon as he could, Marius marched north, to find that the Cimbri and Teutones had passed through southern France and were heading for Spain. That gave him the time to rest and train his armies. Some of the credit for this is due to Publius Rutilius Rufus, who deserves more recognition for this training and preparation than he has received. Rufus was consul for 105, and had managed to collect the army together and build up morale after the terrible defeat at Arausio. He had started to train the soldiers by means of a physical fitness and arms drill regime that was based on the training programmes of the gladiator schools. According to Sextus Julius Frontinus, the author of *Stratagems*, Marius liked what he saw and adopted the same methods.

There was no sign of the tribesmen for some considerable time, but since the danger was not yet over, the people elected Marius consul for 103 and again for 102, so he was allowed time to reform the organization of the army and develop it into a cohesive and effective fighting force, ready for the return of the Cimbri and Teutones. It is not absolutely certain that all the changes in the army were put into effect by Marius. Even if the reforms were all his own work, they may not have come about all at once, and may not all belong to this period while the Romans waited for the Cimbri and Teutones to reappear, but clearly the two year respite would have offered a great opportunity to rethink the organization and operation of the army, while the soldiers were kept busy with their training and fitness programmes.

It may have been Marius who instigated the change from manipular formation to a different one based on the cohort, the normal organization of the Imperial legions. At Numantia, the layout of Scipio's camps suggests that the manipular formation was still in use, but by Julius Caesar's time, the cohort system had replaced it. The cohort formation was not entirely new, snatched out of thin air according to Marius's imagination. During the war with Hannibal, three maniples had been lumped together to form a cohort, and there is some slight evidence that this had also been done in Spain, but it was not a permanent arrangement, and there may have been variation in the size of the cohort at this early period. Standardization came later. In the fully fledged system, there were ten cohorts to each legion, each comprising six centuries of eighty men, commanded by a centurion. The problem is that no source from any period states how many men there were in a legion, so it is possible that Marius's centuries contained 100 men, which means that each of his legions would be, 6,000 strong, but this must remain in the realm of speculation. Another problem is that there is as yet no evidence of a cohort commander in any of the legions, from Marius's time to the end of the Roman army, so the most important officers in the field were the centurions.

Marius retained the three-line formation of the old style army, with four cohorts in the first line and three cohorts in each of the second and third lines. He is credited with the introduction of the *pilum* with the special softened metal in the shaft, so that when it plunged into an enemy shield, it bent and dropped down, making the shield too unwieldy to use. Since he would be fighting a highly mobile army of tribesmen, Marius aimed at a comparable mobility, stripping down his army to bare essentials, banishing the oppressive clouds of camp followers and hangers-on, and limiting the number of wagons. The soldiers had to carry everything themselves, including their equipment, entrenching tools, rations for at least three days, and pots and pans for cooking. They called themselves Marius's mules, but mostly in good humour and with a sense of pride, not grievance. They shared a strong sense of corporate identity and purpose, enhanced by their new single legionary standard, the eagle, carried by the *aquilifer* in the front rank when the legion marched into battle. When not in use it rested in a shrine, a religious icon of tremendous importance. It was a disgrace to the legion if it was lost in battle. Before Marius adopted this one potent symbol the legions had carried five animal standards. The eagle had always been one of them, but in addition there were the wolf, the boar, the horse and the man with a bull's head. These five symbols are reminiscent of the five classes of the early Roman army, but they possibly indicate even earlier origins deriving from a more primitive tribal era.

The Cimbri and Teutones reappeared in Transalpine Gaul in 102, and Marius marched to intercept them before they could attack Italy. He defeated the Teutones at Aix-en-Provence, and was elected consul for the fifth time for 101. He then had to march to the assistance of his consular colleague, Quintus Lutatius Catulus, whose army had been mauled by the Cimbri and pushed back from the eastern Alps into Italy. Marius finally caught up with the tribesmen at Vercelli, where he defeated them in the high summer of 101.

As the hero and saviour of the Roman people, Marius was elected consul for a sixth term for 100. The unprecedented continuity of annual consulships, rather than an extension of his command with proconsular powers until the tribesmen had been defeated, reflects his popularity in Rome. Somehow the Romans condoned the successive terms of office, circumventing the laws that set a limit of ten years between consulships, and also the legal requirement for the consular candidate to be in Rome in person at the time of the elections. The only other option would have been the appointment of Marius as Dictator, but there was supposed to be a six month limit on the tenure of the office, a feature that was soon to be overturned by Sulla. But the powers of the consuls were more limited than those of the Dictator, and at the time of the emergency the Romans required a trusted army commander, not a politician with supreme power.

During his consulship of 100, Marius fell sharply from his position of saviour and military hero. He was not a successful politician, and because he associated with the wrong sort of people he was almost dragged down with them. Initially his associates appeared to be useful and above board, but it all degenerated into chaos and yet more civil strife. The association stretched back to the African campaign, when the volunteers from Rome fought for Marius against Jugurtha. After their service in the army, they required a reward which would prevent them from drifting back to Rome, penniless and potentially troublesome. The tribune Lucius Appuleius Saturninus had ushered through the necessary legislation to grant allotments of 100 *iugera* to the time-served soldiers in Africa in 103 so, at the successful conclusion of the wars with the Cimbri and Teutones, Marius required the same magic formula that Saturninus had provided for the African veterans, to enable him to settle his soldiers of the recent wars on plots of land. Since Saturninus was tribune for an additional term in 100 when Marius was consul, and Saturninus's friend Gaius Servilius Glaucia was praetor, it seemed like the perfect partnership.

Saturninus proposed bills for the settlement on the land of soldiers and Roman citizens, but included in his proposals much wider implications. The well-worn question of citizenship for the allies was also bound up in his schemes, though not quite so overtly as it was in the programme suggested by Gaius Gracchus. There had been several armies in the field besides Marius's in the north of Italy, notably in Greece and Sicily, so Saturninus included them in his scheme, proposing that lands in those countries should be awarded to the time-served soldiers. Several colonies were to be founded, and land allotments were to be given to Romans citizens in Cisalpine Gaul, but the colonies were presumably not limited to Romans, because there was a clause allowing Marius to bestow citizenship on a limited number of settlers, indicating that some of them at least were intended to be allies. The people of Rome reacted badly to the extension of citizenship to the allies because it threatened their own superior position, and the senators were in agreement with them. The meetings of the assembly did not go well. Saturninus decided to underline his point by bringing in some of Marius's veterans who had a vested interest in seeing the necessary laws passed. They lined the assembly area to keep out hostile voters, and there were some episodes of fisticuffs in which the soldiers were the winners. This in itself was bad enough, but apart from the use of physical force to push through his legislation, Saturninus used moral pressure on the senators by forcing them to swear an oath to uphold the laws that he had passed. They were given five days to do this, and they all did so, grudgingly, except for Quintus Metellus, who packed up and left Rome when Saturninus moved to have him exiled.

Marius was in a difficult position, having attached himself to a monster that he could not control. The use of his soldiers to enforce the passage of laws was something he had probably not foreseen, and it made him doubtful whether the laws passed in this way could be valid. Eventually Saturninus went too far and Marius was thrown into the arms of the Senate. When Saturninus stood for re-election as tribune for 99, he also tried to obtain the consulship for Glaucia. Marius had to make a decision, either to support his erstwhile colleague, or to try to block him. As consul, Marius presided over the elections and he rejected Glaucia as a candidate, so Saturninus proposed a law to overturn this judgement. Meanwhile, his followers turned into vicious thugs and killed one of the other candidates. In the face of complete disorder the Senate passed the last decree to allow the consuls to look to state security. Marius managed to persuade both Saturninus and Glaucia to surrender to him along with several of their entourage. He promised them that there would be no executions, herded them into the Senate House and locked them up. Unfortunately emotions were out of control as they had been in the days of Tiberius and Gaius Gracchus, and someone had the bright idea of entering the Senate through the roof. The mob that had gathered removed the tiles and climbed in. Saturninus, Glaucia and their friends were beaten to death.

The power of the tribunes was escalating out of control, prompting violent reactions in the city. Tiberius and Gaius Gracchus had used the assemblies to pass their laws, deliberately by-passing and undermining the Senate, but they had not forced the senators to swear oaths to uphold their laws, nor had they brought in armed force to persuade the voters to do as they were told. It was very embarrassing for Marius, who left Rome in the year after his consulship, insisting that he was on a religious quest in the east.

THE SOCIAL WAR

The patience of the Italian allies, still waiting for some definite sign that they would be granted Roman citizenship, finally snapped when the tribune Marcus Livius Drusus was killed as he was leaving his house through a crowd of people who had gathered to meet him. Livius Drusus was the son of the man of the same name who had undermined Gaius Gracchus by putting forward wide-ranging proposals about land settlement and the citizenship question. In 91, as tribune, the younger Livius Drusus picked up more or less where his father had left off, by proposing solutions to several problems at once, including the land distribution, the supply of grain to the poor in Rome, the control of the courts and Roman citizenship. His programme included further distribution of public land to poorer citizens, the foundation of colonies to relieve population pressure, the reinstatement of the system that Gracchus had set up for the storage of grain for sale to the poor who remained in Rome and, perhaps the most radical of all, Roman citizenship for the Latins and the Italian allies. This went further than Gracchus had suggested, since in his proposals the Italians would have emerged in a less privileged position than the Latins and the Romans. As for control of the courts, Drusus compromised. The senators should be put back in control of the jury courts, but three hundred equites were to be upgraded to join the Senate.

At first Drusus's proposals seemed reasonable, then after a short interval in which the senators and people could think it through, the objections began. As usual, the distribution of land affected existing landholders, who were understandably unhappy about the possibility of being evicted in favour of the poor. The equites as a class would not be helped by having 300 of their number added to the Senate, and the loss of their control of the courts far outweighed the distinction for the chosen few. As for the allies, they had been watching the proceedings in Rome with interest, but had started to prepare for yet another disappointment by joining forces. Disappointment duly arrived. First the consul Lucius Marcius Philippus successfully countered Drusus's proposals by invalidating them. Then Drusus was assassinated in 91.

The allies not only mobilized, but set up a separate state of their own, based at Corfinium. One of the prime instigators of the revolt was Quintus Poppaedius Silo, a man of the Marsi, a tribe which was one of Rome's early opponents at the beginning of the Republic. Hence the Social war has two alternative names, one derived from the term *socii*, meaning allies, and another the Marsic war, derived from the Marsi.

The rebels renamed the city of Corfinium, calling it Italica, signifying a shared purpose if not total agreement. The new state had a Senate and appointed magistrates. Coinage was issued with their legends in Oscan, the most common language among the Italian allies. All this suggests long term planning, not simply a hasty meeting when Drusus was killed and the citizenship question sank back into obscurity. More important than their organization of a new state, the rebels mustered an army of about 100,000 soldiers willing to fight for their rights. This was not the kind of army that the early Republicans had sometimes faced, but a military force perfectly acquainted with the latest Roman fighting techniques.

This federation of several allied cities was a development that the Romans had probably never anticipated, since each ally was bound to Rome and was forbidden to join with any other state. Fortunately for the Romans, Poppaedius Silo was unable to achieve complete unity among the Italians. The Latins could not be persuaded to join, nor could the Greek states of southern Italy, and among the Italians there were many states which kept clear of the war altogether. Even within the areas where communities joined the Marsi and the new state, some of the populace remained loyal to Rome.

The war began in 90, and the rebel allies scored some successes. They gained control of Campania, Apulia and Lucania. Some of the Etruscan cities had not yet joined the revolt, so some of the rebels aimed for their territory north of Rome, in the hope that the rest of the Etruscans might join them. Hastily the Romans made political moves to stem the rebellion. A law was passed by Lucius Julius Caesar in 90, offering Roman citizenship to the Latins and to allied cities which had not taken part in the fighting. This grant of citizenship had at last been squeezed out of the unwilling Senate and people of Rome, and it meant that the Romans could now rely upon the faithful Latins, the Etruscans, the Umbrians and the Greek states of the south.

Citizenship grants now tumbled out of Rome like confetti. In 89 it was offered to the Italians provided that they applied for it within sixty days, and the communities of Cisalpine Gaul were enfranchised by Gnaeus Pompeius Strabo, who was consul in the same year. He also arranged for the Transpadane Gauls, settled on the north side of the River Po, to receive Latin rights. He was able to bring the war to an end in the north by a combination of diplomacy and fighting, and in southern Italy Lucius Cornelius Sulla mopped up the rebels. The war petered out in 89, except for a few troublesome cities which aimed at the higher goal of freedom from Rome and total autonomy. The city of Nola was one of them, and Sulla put it under siege.

Although some of the hostilities engendered by the Social war rumbled on for a few years, the fighting was much reduced by 88 because the offer of citizenship proved more tempting than continuing to fight and thus the cohesion of the rebels was undermined. Another type of cohesion took its place as those cities which had retained their systems of government under the Roman alliance now started to reorganize themselves along Roman lines. There was no coercion on the part of Rome to put this into effect, but it was encouraged, and the fact that the allies could vote in Rome and stand as candidates for the magistracies no doubt fostered the increasing Romanization of the Italian communities. As Romanization progressed, so did the use of Latin, which gradually took over from other Italian languages, until much later they were reduced to novelties and the preserve of Roman scholars and antiquarians.

THE RISE OF SULLA

Between his service under Marius in Africa and his appearance in the Social war, Lucius Cornelius Sulla had risen to the rank of urban praetor in 97, an office which he was said to have achieved by wholesale bribery of the electorate. As propraetor he had been assigned to the province of Cilicia, but was also entrusted with a diplomatic mission of installing Ariobarzanes as King of Cappadocia, which he achieved without going to war, probably in 95. He returned to Rome in 92, somehow escaping unscathed from a charge of extortion. In 88 after fighting in the Social war as a legate, he was elected consul with Quintus Pompeius Rufus as colleague. The two of them joined their families together when Sulla's daughter Cornelia married the son of Pompeius. In rounding off the Social war, Sulla's army was still engaged in the siege of Nola, but there was a greater command awaiting Sulla. There was to be a war against Mithradates VI, King of Pontus. The Senate had awarded this prestigious appointment to Sulla after Mithradates had started to expand his territory aggressively. He controlled most of the territory around the Black Sea. Since 121 he had ruled the northern part of Cappadocia, and clearly had designs on the rest of it, which he annexed along with Bithynia while the Romans were embroiled in the Social war. Bithynia lay on the borders of the kingdom of Pontus to the east and the Roman province of Asia to the west, which made the Romans nervous and rightly suspicious of what the next moves of Mithradates might be. The King was persuaded to withdraw, but then the Romans, on the same principle that they had adopted with the Numidians and the Carthaginians, encouraged the King of Bithynia to raid Pontus.

Within a very short time in 88, Mithradates took over Bithynia again and then the province of Asia, where he was not altogether unwelcome. The Roman tax gatherers had ruthlessly squeezed money out of the provincials, and Romans and Italians alike were sufficiently hated for the inhabitants of Asia to obey the orders of Mithradates to massacre them all in 88. Then the Italians on the island of Delos were killed by Archelaus, who was going to Athens on behalf of Mithradates. The Athenians had declared for the King of Pontus because they thought that he would rid them of their unpopular government that the Romans had installed. Mithradates had now gained control of most of Greece, and his troops were heading for Macedonia and Thrace. He had to be stopped, and Sulla was the man chosen by the Senate to do it.

At this point, Marius re-entered Roman politics. He teamed up with the tribune Publius Sulpicius Rufus, who was to introduce a bill relating to the recently enfranchised allies. Although the allies were now all citizens, their electoral powers had been curtailed by the expedient of putting them all into a handful of voting tribes, which may have been part of the traditional thirty-five tribes, or newly created extra tribes tacked onto the normal system. By this arrangement the allies would scarcely have a political voice, whereas if they were distributed evenly among all the tribes their influence at the polls would be much greater. It was symptomatic of the jealous attitudes and the resentment of the senators and the people at having to share citizenship with the allies. The situation became a recurrent bone of contention and grist to the mill of the tribunes. The first to take it up was Sulpicius Rufus in 88, immediately after the Social war, with the proposal that the allies should be allocated to all the thirty-five tribes.

The fierce opposition to his bill may have surprised Sulpicius, and he looked round for support. At the same time, Marius required something that only the tribunes could obtain for him, and that was the command against Mithradates. For the second time, Marius allied himself with a tribune. Sulpicius resorted to violence to force through his legislation and tacked on two more bills: one to depose the consul Pompeius Rufus, and the other to switch the command against Mithradates from Sulla to Marius.

Marius presumably did not expect Sulla to lie down and meekly allow his command to be taken from him, but he may have been surprised at Sulla's tactics. At Nola, Sulla commanded an army of six legions, which he was to take to the east for the war against Mithradates. The soldiers were loyal to Sulla and keen to fight in the east, so when officers arrived to take command on behalf of Marius, they did not waste words. They killed them. Sulla then marched on Rome, intending to take over the city. It was an unthinkable enormity to do so. Returning generals were obliged by law to lay down their commands at the boundary of the city, the *pomerium*, and their soldiers were to be dismissed. Crossing the *pomerium* under arms was simply not done. But Sulla did it. Only one of his officers came with him. The rest of them refused to involve themselves in breaking the law or in fighting their fellow Romans.

Marius and Sulpicius were not ready for this development. Sulla had a hard time in entering the city but, despite the resistance by the populace, Marius was defenceless, not having anticipated the need for troops in Rome. Sulpicius, Marius and his son the younger Marius, had to leave the city in a hurry, along with a few of their supporters, because the Senate, cowed by the presence of armed force, acceded to Sulla's wish to have each of them declared *hostis*, which made them all enemies of the state. As outlaws they were denied food and shelter, and anyone could kill them without fear of punishment. With the persuasive influence provided by his army, Sulla annulled all the legislation passed by Sulpicius. He reinstated Pompeius Rufus to the consulship, and awarded himself the command in the war against Mithradates. The cancellation of Sulpicius's laws also meant that there was to be no distribution of the enfranchised allies among the thirty-five voting tribes.

Having obtained all that he wanted for the time being, Sulla removed the army from the city, sending it back to Campania to await departure for the east. Meanwhile, Sulpicius had been killed, and Marius and his son were making their way separately to Africa. There were veterans there who would be grateful to their old commander for arranging their settlement on plots of land. On the way to Africa Marius survived some hair-raising near death experiences which allegedly involved hiding in a marsh and then having to face a would-be executioner, reminding him of who he was and what he had achieved. No one wanted to be responsible for killing Gaius Marius. In view of what happened two years later, it might have been better if someone had despatched him at this juncture, because he would then have died with his reputation intact.

Sulla left Rome in the hands of the new consuls, Lucius Cornelius Cinna and Gnaeus Octavius. They were not partisans of his, but when he asked them not to interfere with his legislation while he was absent, they readily agreed. Once Sulla had safely departed, Cinna then set about doing the exact opposite of what he had promised. He revived the proposals to distribute the allies through all the voting tribes, and met with opposition from his fellow consul and some of the tribunes. In Italy, factional strife began between Marius's supporters and those of Sulla. When Cinna started to gather supporters from among the allies, the Senate declared him *hostis*, so now he had nothing to lose, like Marius, who returned from Africa, joined forces with Cinna and started to recruit soldiers in Etruria. The Samnites, who had not succumbed to the offer of citizenship in the Social War and were still ready to fight, also joined Marius and Cinna. Slaves were recruited with a promise of freedom as a reward. The two outlaws descended on Rome and took the city, at the end of 87. In the disturbances, the consul Octavius was killed. Marius was eager for revenge, and for a short time there was a blood-bath in Rome as his erstwhile opponents were removed. He also had to execute the freed slaves who had helped him to gain entry to the city, because they had gone on a killing spree. This episode tarnished Marius's reputation for ever. It was a sad end to an illustrious career.

Marius and Cinna then set about turning the tables on Sulla. He was declared *hostis*, as they had been, and his laws were repealed. He was deprived of his command and his property was confiscated. Marius was no longer an outlaw. On the first day of January 86, Marius entered on his seventh consulship, and Cinna on his second term, though there can hardly have been a proper election. After only a few days Marius died, and the Romans sighed with relief. The old man had changed from hero to monster, his final acts best forgotten, but in 69 his nephew Gaius Julius Caesar, who had just entered the very junior office of quaestor, arranged a splendid funeral for his aunt Julia, Marius's wife. He carried effigies of Marius in the funeral procession, disobeying one of Sulla's laws designed to prevent such displays. The people cheered the old hero.

Lucius Valerius Flaccus was made consul to fill the gap caused by Marius's death, and was sent to replace Sulla. Cinna could have authorized the distribution of the allies among all the voting tribes but did not do so immediately. The wealthier Italians were enrolled, but the poorer men had to wait until 84 for their turn.

SULLA & THE MITHRADATIC WAR

Sulla's first task was to knock out Athens from the war, so he besieged the city from the autumn of 87 to the spring of 86. He forced his way into the city but lost many of his soldiers in gaining control of the port of Piraeus. Once the city was in Roman hands, Sulla marched to meet the army of Mithradates, who had used the time while the Romans were besieging Athens to move an army into central Greece. Sulla defeated the King's forces in a decisive battle at Chaeronea, and again in a second battle at Orchomenus, but Mithradates would not make peace, because he still controlled the Aegean sea and Sulla had only a few ships.

Lucius Valerius Flaccus arrived in Greece at the head of another army in 86, but he failed to take command of Sulla's troops and headed off to Macedonia and Thrace to follow the land route into the province of Asia, which Mithradates had overrun. Until he had assembled a fleet, Sulla could not cross the sea to enter Asia himself, so he remained in Greece while his quaestor Lucius Licinius Lucullus set about gathering ships. In the meantime, Valerius Flaccus had regained Macedonia and Thrace and had crossed the Bosphorus to enter the kingdom of Bithynia, but then he was killed in a mutiny, perhaps arranged by his legate, Gaius Flavius Fimbria, who took command of the army. By the middle of 85, Fimbria had defeated Mithradates and recovered some territory, but there was no follow-up and no drive into Pontus to annihilate the King. Mithradates sued for peace before he lost yet more territory, and Sulla arranged the peace with the war only half finished, because he needed to return to Rome before he was totally eclipsed. Mithradates emerged relatively unscathed, relinquishing the territory he had overrun but retaining his kingdom intact, and parting with the paltry sum of 3,000 talents and sending eighty of his ships to the Roman fleet. He could go home, lick his wounds and, like Philip of Macedon, build up another army, another fleet and be ready for another excursion into Roman territory within a few years.

Sulla spent the next months restoring order in the province of Asia. The cities that had sided with Mithradates had to pay huge sums of money, 20,000 talents, and he billeted his troops on them to keep order. The cities were already impoverished as a result of the depredations of the Roman tax collectors, followed by the demands of Mithradates. The unfortunate citizens had to borrow the money from the Roman bankers to pay the Roman general. It was not a scheme designed to win hearts and minds in Asia. Leaving a trail of considerable damage behind him, Sulla spent the winter of 84 in Greece.

CINNA & CARBO IN ROME

There is a dearth of information about Cinna's activities during his serial consulships, so it seems as if he entertained no long term plans and instituted no reforms, but merely waited for fate to take him over. He knew that one day Sulla would return to Rome and there would be a day of reckoning, but he left it rather late to make preparations to meet it. In 85 he was consul for the third time, with Gnaeus Papirius Carbo as his colleague, and the two of them engineered their re-election for 84. They had started to raise an army and planned to make war on Sulla in Greece, rather than allow him to return and fight in Italy. Some of the troops had been sent to the Adriatic coast, but they were not entirely converted to the thought of a civil war, and while Cinna was trying to quell a mutiny at Ancona they killed him. Carbo recalled all the troops, determined to make a stand in Italy. Strictly he ought to have arranged for the election of another consul, since a sole consul was contrary to the principle of collegiality, but he decided to carry on alone. He did not want the complication of an election at this stage, especially since the Senate was wavering and had tried to negotiate with Sulla. After the carnage of the last few years nobody wanted a civil war, not even Carbo himself. However, in spring 83 he had no choice. Sulla had landed at Brundisium with five legions.

6

Commanding Generals: The Republic Under Duress 83–48 BC

The Roman Republic was about to experience the first of the civil wars that would finally signify its end and lead to the rise of the Empire. Lucius Cornelius Sulla and Gnaeus Papirius Carbo split the state into two factions, preparing to settle their differences by armed combat. Foreshadowing the later civil war between Pompey the Great and Julius Caesar, the Senate made an attempt to disarm both contenders, but it was too late. There was only a slight chance that a compromise could be reached without fighting, since Sulla was aware that he was highly unlikely to be allowed to develop a political career by simply appearing in Rome as a private citizen and standing for election as consul. He tried to smooth his path by promising to honour the law to distribute the allies throughout the voting tribes, but he excluded the Samnites, who were still rebellious. His views on the question of the allies, and his previous ruthlessness in marching on Rome to gain what he wanted, did nothing to endear the people or the Senate to him, so it was all or nothing and force was the only answer. He had five legions who were trained and experienced, and above all loyal to him as commander. Carbo could muster a greater number of men, but they were not so experienced, and were probably not fully committed to his cause.

CIVIL WAR IN ITALY

Sulla could rely upon three allies who had been lying low during the ascendancy of Marius, Cinna and Carbo. One of these supporters was Marcus Licinius Crassus, who had escaped from the slaughter arranged by Marius and Cinna and had gone to Spain. Another was Quintus Caecilius Metellus Pius, who had chosen self-imposed exile to Africa. Both these men raised armies in the provinces where they had taken refuge, and then joined Sulla. Crassus may have arrived even before Sulla landed in Italy, and Metellus Pius brought his troops to add to Sulla's forces almost as soon as he arrived at Brundisium. Then a younger self-made general arrived, Gnaeus Pompeius, who had raised a legion from his clients on his father's estates in Picenum. He was about twenty-three years old, but master of his own house since the death of his father, Pompeius Strabo, four years earlier. Strabo had fought alongside the consul Octavius in an attempt to stop Marius and Cinna from entering the city, but although he drove their forces back, he seems to have hesitated, and was accused of trying to negotiate with Cinna while at the same time working with Octavius. He may have been trying to save Rome, or simply to save himself, but shortly afterwards he died, probably of the plague which rampaged through his camp. There was no love lost between the populace and Strabo. His body was dragged through the streets by the mob and probably thrown into the Tiber, so he was not granted a proper funeral. The young Pompey escaped the massacre that Marius set in motion in Rome, though his house was trashed by Cinna's gangs, and later on he was prosecuted for misappropriating some of the spoils from Asculum, which his father had besieged during the Social war. Perhaps because of his youth and his attractive appearance, comparable to Alexander the Great, and the good references he was able to drum up, Pompey was acquitted. The fact that he then married the presiding judge's daughter need not signify underhand dealings or corruption. Ironically, one of the men who spoke for Pompey was Gnaeus Papirius Carbo, soon to become an enemy, then a victim of the man he had helped to save. After the court hearing, Pompey disappeared from view, until Sulla came home. Sulla was impressed with him, calling him *Imperator* and standing up when he entered a room. Pompey was sent back to Picenum to raise more troops, and managed to recruit two more legions. As he marched them to rejoin Sulla, three commanders loyal to Carbo and the Marian party attacked him, but he gave them all a surprise by routing them. Pompey was nobody's fool when he was at the head of an army.

Papirius Carbo and his party were also recruiting. The consuls for 83, Lucius Cornelius Scipio and Caius Norbanus, were authorized by the last decree of the Senate (*senatus consultum ultimum*) to raise armies. Sulla tried to negotiate before fighting, which placed him on the moral high ground, but then the war began when he met Norbanus in battle and defeated him. He then marched to the camp of the other consul, Scipio, and for a short time it seemed as though there might still be a chance of peace as the two men agreed to negotiate. Unfortunately, one of Scipio's officers, given the task of informing Norbanus at Capua of the likely truce, attacked and seized the town of Suessa, which Sulla had recently won, and all hope of a negotiated peace evaporated. And it was not Sulla who had struck the first blow.

At this point Metellus Scipio's troops, who had no illusions about who might win this coming war, came over to Sulla, but Metellus could not be persuaded to change camps. Since he had command of all the soldiers, Sulla considered that there was nothing to be gained by killing Metellus, so the consul went free. He raised another army, but these men joined Sulla as well. The other consul, Norbanus, was given a chance to reconsider, but could not be won over and left Capua for Praeneste. There was a lull in the proceedings when Carbo returned to Rome and had himself elected to his third consulship for 82. His colleague was the young Gaius Marius. He was under age, and had not held the required magistracies, but his famous name carried more weight than adherence to the law.

The war affected some of the provinces as well as Italy. Lucius Philippus declared for Sulla and took over Sardinia and killed the governor, and in Africa, the anti-Sullan Fabius Hadrianus was killed in a revolt. Quintus Sertorius, a rugged individualist and dissident in all circumstances, washed his hands of the opponents of Sulla because he considered them incompetent, and set out for Nearer Spain, where he had been appointed propraetorian governor. He remained there for some years, an implacable enemy of Sulla. In Italy the opposing sides waited for spring. Carbo made his headquarters in the north at Ariminum, and Metellus Pius was sent against him, with Pompey following close behind. Sulla himself pursued the young Marius, who attacked him as he was making camp, but was eventually driven off and fled to Praeneste. Sulla left an officer to besiege Praeneste, and sent detachments of his troops by different routes to Rome, which he entered without fighting, because the opponents of Sulla had not bothered to gather defenders. Sulla left some of his veterans to garrison Rome and went in pursuit of Carbo. There was a series of skirmishes, and Pompey distinguished himself by trapping the force of eight legions that Carbo sent to relieve Praeneste. Then a more determined force arrived in the form of the anti-Sullan Samnites led by a warrior called Pontius Telesinus, but all attempts to relieve Praeneste still failed.

The Samnites decided to attack Rome to draw Sulla out. They succeeded. Sulla hastily marched to confront them, and the main battle was fought outside Rome at the Colline Gate. Sulla commanded the troops on his left wing. The enemy almost defeated him and his soldiers ran away despite his appeals, heading for the safety of the city, but they could not enter because the garrison that Sulla had left behind closed the gates, so the soldiers had no choice except to turn and fight harder. They rallied and won a hard fought battle, but the end result still hung in the balance. Then a message arrived from Marcus Licinius Crassus, the commander of the right wing, asking for orders after he had routed and chased off the enemy in a complete victory. Sulla had gained control of the city and won the war in Italy, where only a few towns still held out for another two or three years.

THE DOMINATION OF SULLA

As soon as he entered Rome, Sulla called for a meeting of the Senate, which was held in the Temple of Bellona, where he calmly presented his report on the war against Mithradates, all the time accompanied by the howls and screams of the thousands of prisoners being executed by his soldiers not far from the temple. The message was clear. Sulla had started as he meant to go on.

As a firm adherent of Sulla, the young Pompey, soon to be known as Pompey the Great, rose to fame and fortune as an accomplished general. Sicily and Africa were taken over by Carbo and the Marians, two provinces which supplied grain for Rome, and therefore it was an urgent matter to regain them. Sulla appointed Pompey as commander, and despatched him to deal with his enemies in Sicily. To cement their relationship he offered a marriage alliance with his step-daughter Aemilia, persuading Pompey to divorce his first wife Antistia. A pawn in the political game, as so many Roman women were, Aemilia was pregnant by her husband Marcus Acilius Glabrio. She divorced him, as instructed by Sulla, and miscarried and died in Pompey's house a few months later.

Sulla's intention was to rationalize the career paths of senators and lay down strict rules for progression through the various magistracies, but had to make an exception in Pompey's case, since despite having been an army commander since he was twenty-three years old, the young general had never held any post that had been ratified by the Senate, and had not held any of the junior magistracies. The Senate was easily persuaded to bestow propraetorian powers on Pompey, despite the fact that he had not attained the praetorship. By means of this legal fiction Pompey was now equal in rank to Marcus Veiento Perperna, the current governor of Sicily and a staunch Marian sympathiser.

Pompey rapidly gained control of Sicily. Perperna left the island without a fight and Carbo, who had only just arrived from Africa, was captured and executed. When Sicily was pacified, Pompey was sent to Africa, where he eradicated Sulla's opponents and in pacifying the country he made his own administrative arrangements which included reinstating Hiempsal, the former King of Numidia. For the time being at least Pompey had secured the borders of the province of Africa, and in the process formed personal alliances with foreign dignitaries. It was Pompey's first experience of acting independently of the Senate, employing his considerable talent for administration. It was to become a habit, but his arrangements were not necessarily detrimental to the Roman Empire. After his victories in Sicily and Africa, his soldiers hailed him as *Imperator*, supreme commander, a title that Pompey was careful to refuse with an emotional public demonstration, since it was not wise to give Sulla the impression that he intended to usurp him. The name Magnus, the Great, which the soldiers also bestowed on him, was allowed to stand, and Sulla even addressed Pompey by this name when he returned home demanding permission to hold a triumph. Sulla refused. This is the context of the famous story of

Pompey's outburst, declaring that more people worshipped the rising than the setting sun, revealing his opinion of himself and his aspirations for power in the Roman world. Sulla was uncertain of what he had heard and asked Pompey to repeat the phrase, which he did. After a pregnant pause, Sulla proclaimed 'Let him triumph', probably to the relief of everyone who had heard the exchange.

The unsavoury side of Sulla's domination of Rome had worked itself out while Pompey was absent. Elimination of rivals was Sulla's first act. The proscriptions which he launched were not the last or even the worst that Rome was to see, but the indifference with which he viewed the mayhem and murder definitely does not redound to his credit. Once the names of all Sulla's victims were posted up in Rome, their lives and property were forfeit. The wealthy families were targeted for economic motives, and included senators as well as equites, in order to root out the entire coterie of each extended family and business association. Cash rewards could be claimed for murdering the proscribed men; if the murderers were slaves they missed out on the cash but received their freedom instead. There were great incentives to kill the men on the list, especially since the property of the victims was auctioned off to the highest bidder and the proceeds went to the state. Some men added extra names to the list of the proscribed simply in order to seize their property. Perhaps 500 people were killed, but there may have been many more than that because there are no reliable statistics.

One murder that was related to the proscriptions is well documented. A freedman called Chrysogonus, one of Sulla's henchmen, killed a wealthy man so that he could bid for his property at an auction, inserting his name on the list to make it appear that he had been proscribed by Sulla. Then Chrysogonus accused the son of the murdered man, Sextus Roscius, of committing the crime, and he rigged the auctions so that he obtained the property he wanted at a fraction of its value. Sextus Roscius appeared to be doomed, since his accuser enjoyed the special favour of Sulla, who had now retired but still wielded considerable influence, but the young lawyer Marcus Tullius Cicero took on the defence, laying bare the real facts of the case, and denouncing Chrysogonus. Sextus Roscius was acquitted.

With his potential enemies out of the way and everyone else acutely aware of the consequences of opposition, Sulla embarked on an ambitious project, nothing less than a complete overhaul of the state. For this he required supreme power, unchallenged by other magistrates and especially by tribunes. Towards the end of 82, Sulla was confirmed as Dictator. Special dispensation allowed Sulla to hold the appointment indefinitely. He effected further innovations that were not the norm for the Dictatorship, taking the precaution of having all his past acts ratified and confirmed, and all his future actions authorized. His agenda included strengthening the powers of the Senate, and conversely reducing the powers of the tribunes. Since he had authorized the deaths of a large number of senators, and the surviving descendants of the proscribed were banned from holding office, there were now many gaps in the senatorial ranks. In order to fill these gaps he raised many of his loyal equites to the rank of senator. In effect he doubled the number of senators from 300 to 600, necessitating a corresponding enlargement of the Senate House. The Senate, already pliable and eager to please, was now conveniently made up of men who owed their advancement to him.

The jury courts were returned to senatorial control. Sulla revived the laws that had been designed to regulate the senatorial career path (the *cursus honorum*), preventing anyone from becoming too powerful by holding successive appointments, such as the people had bestowed on Marius, and Cinna had engineered for himself. The number of quaestors was raised to twenty, and this junior magistracy automatically involved entry to the Senate. Thereafter there was a specified progression via the praetorship, and then the consulship. There was an age limit for appointment to each post, so that no one would be able to reach the consulship before the age of forty-two, when hopefully each candidate would be mature and experienced. It was not possible to stand for election to these offices without first having held the previous ones, so the number of eligible candidates for office each year was very restricted.

For several years before Sulla came to power, the tribunate had been a source of embarrassment to the Senate, enhancing the power of the people's assemblies at the expense of the senators. From now on, Sulla intended that only dedicated men would seek to hold office as tribunes, because Sulla banned them from holding any further magistracy. The power of veto does not seem to have been revoked, but the tribunes were reduced to the position they had held in the early days of the Republic, when they could only listen at the door of the Senate and protect the plebs from exploitation or harm. Most significantly the tribunes were no longer allowed to take proposals direct to the assemblies, but had to have them all ratified in advance by the Senate. This had been the main bone of contention in the past, as for instance when Tiberius Gracchus was able to ignore the Senate and have laws passed by the people. Ordinary people did not prosper under Sulla's regime. The grain distribution that Gaius Gracchus had instituted was stopped, and there was massive disruption when the huge numbers of Sulla's veteran soldiers were allocated plots of land all around the city of Rome.

When he considered that his work was finished, Sulla resigned as Dictator at the end of 81. Some years later Gaius Julius Caesar said that Sulla must have been mad to do so. Sulla was consul in 80 with Metellus Pius as colleague, but from then on he wanted to rest and write his memoirs. He was already feeling the effects of the illness that would finally kill him in 78. Within less than ten years after his death, most of his legislation had been abolished.

POMPEY THE GREAT

A short time before Sulla died, Marcus Aemilius Lepidus was elected consul for 78. This was a man who opposed Sulla's policies despite having made his fortune during the proscriptions, and was in turn distrusted by the ex-Dictator. Sulla had made no attempt to strangulate the entire state once the whole of his reforms were in place, so all qualified candidates were allowed to stand for election, without regard for their political views. Lepidus was supported by Pompey, a least at first, but Pompey changed his allegiance when the consul fomented trouble. Lepidus's election manifesto included the restoration of the tribunate to its former position, the revival of the cheap distribution of grain to the people and, more inflammatory, the return to the original owners of lands that had been confiscated during the programme of veteran settlement. This future possibility of repossession brought the discontent about the land distribution to a head in Etruria, where displaced landowners vented their fury on the veterans who had been settled on their farms. Lepidus and his colleague Quintus Lutatius Catulus were both sent to restore order, but Lepidus joined the rebels instead. At this point Pompey the Great, who held no political office and no military command, was empowered to raise an army and turn against Lepidus, who started to march on Rome early in 77. Quintus Lutatius Catulus, already in Etruria with an army, was confirmed in an extended command after his consulship expired, and inflicted the first defeat on Lepidus, then Pompey finished him off near the town of Cosa. Lepidus escaped but died shortly afterwards.

Pompey now had an army and a plan. There was a war in Spain that had been going on since Quintus Sertorius had arrived there and taken over the province. He had been bitterly opposed to the Sullan regime, and was still not reconciled even after Sulla's death. After a few reverses in Spain when he had been forced to flee to Mauretania for a while, Sertorius had gathered a considerable force of die-hard anti-Sullans, one of whom was Marcus Perperna, who had fled from Sicily when the young Pompey arrived to take back the island for Sulla. Sertorius had gained control of both Spanish provinces, and also had a following of native Spanish tribes, so he had carved out a personal Empire for himself that could not be allowed to continue to grow. Quintus Caecilius Metellus Pius had been fighting against Sertorius since he had been consul with Sulla in 80, and may have asked for Pompey to be sent to help him. At least that was probably the story that Pompey favoured. He ought to have disbanded his army after the defeat of Lepidus, but he lingered innocently and delayed, until the Senate gave in and offered him the command in Spain. Pompey's whole career was based on the same ploy. When there was a problem, he bided his time, never clamouring for an appointment to deal with it until it became so severe that the Senate could no longer ignore him. Then he blazed into action and solved it.

In confirming Pompey as additional military commander in Spain, all of Sulla's legislation to regulate senatorial careers was swept under the carpet. Pompey had still not held any magistracy, and was well below the age that Sulla had laid down for holding office, but at the instigation of Lucius Marcius Philippus he was granted proconsular powers. It was perhaps fortunate that neither of the two consuls for that year were eager to take up the command in Spain, so there could be no question of usurping their power, but Philippus made a joke about it, declaring that Pompey was being sent to Spain not with proconsular powers, *pro consule*, but *pro consulibus*, on behalf of the two consuls.

Sertorius was not to be underestimated as a military commander, nor was he likely to capitulate. Pompey had to work very hard in the struggle against him, and in 76 he was defeated when trying to relieve the besieged city of Lauron, which had declared for him and Metellus Pius. Sertorius used the ground to his advantage and trapped part of Pompey's army, while emerging unexpectedly at the rear of the rest of the troops, preventing them from helping the first group, who were slaughtered. The campaign revolved around the availability of supplies, which entailed gaining control of the ports on the east coast of Spain, and detaching Sertorius's allies from him while attracting the tribes who were not well disposed to him. At the end of the campaigning season of 75, Pompey had to write sternly to the Senate, explaining that he had now used up all his own money to pay and supply his troops. In no uncertain terms he demanded help, or he could not be responsible for the results. He had no intention of joining Sertorius or marching across the Alps to take Rome, but he let the senators imagine the worst. Supplies arrived, but late and in niggardly quantities.

More alarmingly, Sertorius approached King Mithradates of Pontus for assistance, in the form of ships and cash. For the Romans, this action put Sertorius beyond the pale. Already in Rome there were hostile feelings towards Mithradates because had resumed his empire-building activities, and reciprocally, Mithradates was angered by the annexation of Bithynia by the Romans when King Nicomedes died. Mithradates did not want the Romans in control of potential bases from which to attack him, and besides he aimed at control of Bithynia for himself. The consuls for 74, Lucius Licinius Lucullus and Marcus Aurelius Cotta, were entrusted with the command against Mithradates. The chronology is not fully established, but Mithradates did respond to Sertorius, sending help probably in 73, and at some point proposing an alliance, asking for officers from Sertorius's army to help train his troops to fight like Romans. Sertorius agreed to this request, but refused to recognize any of the future conquests that Mithradates might achieve.

By this time, Pompey and Metellus had gained some ascendancy over Sertorius, whose allies started to desert him. This may have occurred because Pompey and Metellus transferred their efforts from battles against Sertorius himself to the reduction of the towns and cities that were loyal to him. For the Spanish population, this Roman war, which after all had very little to do with them, had become less attractive. Sertorius was no longer able to fulfil his promises, whatever they were, or to reward them, and the consequences of staying with him to the bitter end were likely to be exactly that: bitter. Then Sertorius was assassinated by Marcus Perperna, and in turn Perperna was soon overwhelmed and captured by Pompey's troops. Pompey executed him, and burned all the correspondence that Perperna handed over to him, rather than go through it all and start a witch hunt in Rome for Sertorius's sympathisers.

Pompey remained in Spain until the end of 72, tidying up loose ends and reducing the few rebellious cities to obedience. The Spanish provinces were pacified and reorganized, in the course of which Pompey was able to swell the ranks of his clients by forging good relations with leading Spaniards. One of these was Lucius Cornelius Balbus, who was granted Roman citizenship and became the close associate and secretary to Julius Caesar. Metellus and Pompey granted citizenship to several Spanish nobles, and had these grants ratified by the Senate.

On the way home, Pompey set up a monument in the Pyrenees, recording his successes in Spain. Then he set off for Italy with his army. His problem of what to do next had been temporarily solved, because the Senate had asked him to help Marcus Licinius Crassus in the war against the army of slaves led by the ex-gladiator, Spartacus. Pompey met about 5,000 of the slaves, the remnants of Spartacus's army who had fled north after Crassus had defeated them in Lucania in 71. Pompey claimed the credit for the victory, though most of the work had been done by Crassus.

The revolt of Spartacus was not the only slave rebellion that the Romans had dealt with, but it was a shock to the system. No one had really expected mere slaves to be able to organize themselves so successfully, much less defeat Roman armies. The episode began when less than 100 gladiators escaped from their training school at Capua in 73. Their leaders were Spartacus, from Thrace, and Crixus, from Gaul. They founded a base camp on the slopes of Mount Vesuvius, where they were joined by thousands of escaped slaves and some poor free men who had little to lose by becoming bandits and rebels. The slaves originally intended to travel northwards out of Italy and go to their various homelands, but after defeating the first Roman army that tried to round them up, they split their forces, Crixus going to the south, where he was eventually defeated, and Spartacus to the north, as far as Cisalpine Gaul, where he won another battle. Then, instead of escaping, Spartacus's group wended its way back southwards. When Crassus was given the command he raised six new legions to add to the four he was given, and moved south. It was not an easy campaign for the Roman forces, but Crassus was finally victorious in a battle fought in Lucania. Spartacus was killed and the captured survivors were crucified on thousands of crosses lining the Via Appia. It was a slow death reserved for slaves, felons and non-Romans. Roman citizens could be executed but not crucified.

Crassus's victory over slaves was not sufficiently honourable to merit a triumphal parade through the streets of Rome, but Pompey was allowed to hold a triumph, ending the parade as was customary at the Temple of Jupiter on the Capitol Hill where he dedicated the spoils of war to the chief god. It was not represented as a triumph over Quintus Sertorius, a Roman citizen, but over Spain. It was a convenient way of celebrating a victory in a civil war with some pretence at good taste. Caesar was to employ the same device at the end of the later civil wars.

In need of further employment, both Pompey and Crassus presented themselves as candidates for the consulship of 70. They were elected with scarcely any opposition, though once again Pompey's candidacy involved some special dispensation from the Senate. Crassus had held the praetorship and had reached the age that Sulla had set down for holding the consulship, but Pompey was not only under age, he was still an equestrian, not yet having become a senator. Since he had not served as quaestor or praetor, the consulship was Pompey's first magistracy, so he had no experience of the Senate. He solved the problem by asking his friend, the polymath Marcus Terentius Varro, to write a book for him explaining senatorial protocol and procedures.

Pompey and Crassus cordially disliked each other but were prepared to co-operate during their term of office. One of their proposals concerned the jury courts, which had been jostled back and forth between senators and equites for many years. The two consuls compromised, creating mixed juries of three groups: senators, equites and a group of men known as the *tribunii aerarii*, whose significance is not understood. Originally they were treasury officials, but the office had gone out of use some time ago. Apart from this, Pompey and Crassus contributed very little to the political history on the year 70, save for the restoration of the tribunate to its former powers, but even here their legislation was not as novel as it might seem, since there had been several successful and some unsuccessful attempts in the past eight years to nibble away at Sulla's laws. Pompey and Crassus merely put the finishing touches to the restoration of tribunician power.

POMPEY'S SPECIAL COMMANDS

For the next three years after the end of their consulships, Crassus and Pompey disappeared from public view. Many retiring consuls went on to govern a province, but that was mundane and not Pompey's style. The only office that might have interested him was a second consulship, but Sulla's legislation forbidding re-election within ten years still stood. Another way of involving himself in politics without standing for election was to canvass on behalf of friends and once they were settled into various offices it was possible to influence policy or legislation, but Pompey was not successful at this aspect of political life. It was not until 67 that he emerged from backstage into the limelight, with an extraordinary command that gave him immense, unprecedented power.

This command was against the pirates who made travel and commerce in the Mediterranean extremely hazardous. The problem had been a long standing perennial one, but up to now only piecemeal efforts had been made to eradicate the pirates. From 104 onwards the corn supply from Sicily and Africa to Rome had been seriously disrupted, resulting in occasional food shortages. In 102 Marcus Antonius, the grandfather of Mark Antony, had been given a command against the pirates, but he enjoyed only partial success and did not entirely eradicate them. Publius Servilius Vatia tried again in 77, taking the war to the coasts of Cilicia where the pirates controlled the inlets and harbours. In defeating the pirates he deprived them of their lands, which denied them their crops, so they turned to piracy again. Three years later in 74, the command was bestowed on Marcus Antonius, the son of the previous commander, and the father of Mark Antony. This time the failure was disastrous. Antonius lost his ships to the Cretan pirates and had to make a treaty. Quintus Metellus took over in 68 and restored control of Crete including the coasts and harbours, but the pirates were still at large, even attacking the harbour at Ostia at the mouth of the Tiber in 67. This was a little too close to home for comfort.

The tribune Aulus Gabinius presented a bill in that same year, but it is not known whether he did so before or after the pirates attacked Ostia. Pompey kept his head down in the background, but the wide ranging scope of the bill strongly suggests that the detailed planning behind it was due to him. An enormous amount of human and financial resources would be required for the task of eradicating the pirates. A fleet of 200 ships was to be assembled, and divided into squadrons under the command of fifteen legates of praetorian rank. It was of paramount importance that one man, of consular rank, directed and co-ordinated the operations. He was to have access to the treasury in Rome, and the resources of the provinces as well, and he was to exercise power over the whole Mediterranean sea with additional authority over the territory up to 50 miles inland in all provinces bordering on the Mediterranean. This amounted to a very large proportion of the resources and territory of the Roman world. No Roman general had ever held such power, although it was not to be permanent. Gabinius suggested that the command should be for three years.

Nobody was specifically named in the bill as supreme commander, but the people knew that Pompey was the man. The Senate knew it too, but objected to placing such enormous power into the hands of one man. The consul Piso was virulently opposed to the bill. He made a stirring speech to the senators, inflaming them so much that they attacked Gabinius, who escaped and made a speech of his own to the people, who then attacked Piso because in his opposition to the bill he ignored the food shortages that afflicted them. The lawyer Hortensius calmed everyone down, but he thought that if the bill was passed it would endanger the state because it gave too much power to one man. Another senator, who was just embarking on his political career, spoke in favour of the bill. This was Gaius Julius Caesar, who had returned from his tour of duty as quaestor, serving under the governor of Further Spain. The ancient sources record that he spoke in favour of one of the bills granting extraordinary powers to Pompey without specifying which one, but it is likely to have been the bill presented by Gabinius, especially since Caesar had first-hand knowledge of the pirates. He had been captured by some of them and ransomed in 75.

One of the main objections to the proposed command, apart from its unprecedentedly large territorial extent, was the fact that so many praetorian legates would report directly to the commander and not to the Senate. Quintus Lutatius Catulus suggested that some of the praetorian commanders should operate independently, which would restore some of the control to the Senate, but it would have been at the expense of co-ordination. The suggestion did not impress the people. Catulus tried to point out the disastrous consequences if the commander of such a vast enterprise should die and leave all his subordinates leaderless. Who would lead them then, he asked. 'You, Catulus!' chorused the people. In the end, after days of political wrangling, the command against the pirates was awarded to Pompey. As soon as he was chosen, the price of corn fell in Rome. He was awarded even more powers than those included in the original bill, including 500 ships instead of the suggested 200, and twenty-four legates (some sources say there were twenty-five) in place of the original fifteen.

Pompey sprang into action and began to appoint his legates and to recruit soldiers and crews. He divided the Mediterranean into thirteen sections with a legate in charge of each one. The rest of his legates were probably given territorial commands but it is not known how or where they operated. It was clear that command of the sea would not be sufficient without the ability to operate against the pirates on land as well, all around the Mediterranean where any of the pirate ships could lurk until the Roman fleets had passed by. Within forty days Pompey cleared the western half of the Mediterranean, and the sea lanes from Sardinia, Sicily and Africa. Then he bottled up the pirates in the eastern Mediterranean. The whole operation had taken less than three months. Instead of executing the pirates, Pompey settled them on lands some distance from the sea, around cities that had declined or had been deserted. The settlements were made without disrupting the original inhabitants, and proved successful in the longer term.

Pompey's campaign was justly famous, a tremendous achievement despite the hyperbole attached to it. The menace to shipping was averted for the time being, but no one could eradicate the pirates for ever, as Pompey would have been the first to admit. He had achieved what he set out to do, but now had his sights set on higher things.

The war against Mithradates VI, King of Pontus, was not going well. Sulla had campaigned against the King and made a treaty in 85, but the war had been inconclusive and the terms were lenient. It suited Sulla to be able to return to Rome before he was completely obliterated and it suited Mithradates to abandon his plans for the time being and prepare for another war at another time. He knew that the Romans would be back at some time, and in fact the governor of the province of Asia, Lucius Lucilius Murena, kept on reminding him by making raids into his territory. There was also a Roman commander in Cilicia, ostensibly to control the pirates, but also ready and able to march against Mithradates if necessary. In 74, Lucius Licinius Lucullus was sent out as governor of both Asia and Cilicia, with the command of five legions.

For the first three years, Lucullus was successful. Mithradates advanced into Bithynia, which had been bequeathed to Rome when King Nicomedes died in 75. Mithradates besieged Cyzicus on the coast of Bithynia, but it had not yet fallen to him when the winter started, so he withdrew. At some point, probably in 73, the Roman officers from Sertorius's army in Spain may have arrived at the court of Mithradates, who promised to send money and supplies to the rebel army, in return for which favour, Sertorius's men would train the eastern troops how to fight the Romans. If the agreement was honoured, the experiment did not help Mithradates. In 72 and 71 Lucullus invaded Mithradates's own kingdom of Pontus. The King fled to Armenia and found refuge in the court of King Tigranes, who was his son-in-law. Lucullus decided to follow him there. The invasion of Armenia was a tremendous undertaking. It was not strictly within Lucullus's remit to attack the kingdom. Initially the Romans achieved a great deal. Lucullus defeated the army of Tigranes, even though it outnumbered his own, then in another battle he defeated the combined forces of Mithradates and

Tigranes, who both fled. This was the turning point. The troops had been fighting non-stop for a long time and they were tired. They did not share Lucullus's enthusiasm for marching further and further into Armenia, especially as winter was approaching, and in Armenia that meant extreme hardship. Lucullus turned around, and on the way back he took the city of Nisibis further south. Within a short time, Mithradates was back in control of Pontus, and Tigranes threatened Cappadocia. The troops began to feel very discontented. They had fought hard, won battles, and now they were as far away from a satisfactory result as they had been at the outset.

At Rome too, faith in Lucullus was waning. For the senators and equestrians, one of Lucullus's most annoying habits was his fair handed treatment of the inhabitants of the population of Asia. He had put a stop to Roman abuses, which upset the tax gatherers, and he had helped to restore the fortunes of the cities which had been impoverished by having to raise the money for indemnity payments after the last Mithradatic war. The people of the province of Asia had set up statues to him and invented a festival called the Lucullea. All this was construed in Rome as damaging Roman and Italian business interests. The province of Asia was detached from his command. Next, he lost Cilicia which was given to the consul Marcius Rex, who would not send any assistance when Mithradates and Tigranes attacked Asia and Cappadocia. The whole of the eastern command was now dismantled and everything was in an almost irretrievable mess.

In 66 the tribune Gaius Manilius proposed that Pompey should take over in the east, to sort out the provinces and take command of the war. Lucullus was left high and dry, and remained an embittered enemy of Pompey for the rest of his life. He had almost defeated Mithradates but everything had been ruined by the machinations of the politicians in Rome. It is perhaps unfair to put all the blame upon Pompey for the downfall of Lucullus, but no one doubted that he wanted the command, or that the campaign against the pirates was just a preliminary. On the other hand, he was the best man for the job, as shown by his eventual success.

Although there was some opposition to Manilius's bill, for the same reasons as before, because it bestowed too much power on one man, this time several senators spoke in favour of it. Marcus Tullius Cicero, who was aiming eventually for the consulship, spoke for it and published his speech afterwards, *De Imperio Gnaei Pompei*. The bill was passed, and when Pompey heard the news he indulged himself in a short melodramatic moment, complaining about how the needs of the state never gave him any rest. Then he contradicted what he had just said by bursting into action. Manilius's law allowed him to take over from the provincial governors of the eastern provinces, to appoint his own legates, to make war as and when he saw fit and to make peace and to conclude treaties. These were not the usual prerogatives of provincial governors or military commanders, but Pompey had clearly put a great deal of planning into his eastern campaign and had worked out what powers he would need to conduct it. One thing he forgot was to follow the example of Sulla and have all his future acts ratified in advance by the Senate, which might have saved him a lot of time and trouble when he returned to Rome.

Pompey commanded a large army consisting of Lucullus's troops, his own soldiers that he had raised for the pirate campaign and allies from local communities all round the Mediterranean. In addition he summoned allied kings to meet him and provide troops. He set up headquarters in Cilicia and made diplomatic arrangements with the surrounding states to ensure the safety of his flanks and rear while he marched against Mithradates. There was a constant rivalry between some of the eastern states that prevented them from uniting, which was advantageous to Rome, but Pompey did not wish to be distracted from his main purpose by being drawn into minor wars between them. Since he would be involved in war not only with Mithradates but also with Tigranes of Armenia, he made efforts to neutralize the Armenians by making overtures to Phraates, the King of Parthia, whose territory bordered on Armenia. If the Parthians could be persuaded to tie down Tigranes while Pompey concentrated on Mithradates, all well and good.

Mithradates was a wily adversary and a born survivor. He avoided pitched battles, hoping to draw Pompey onwards into the mountains where he would not be able to supply his army so easily, then it might be possible to cut his supply lines, bottle him up and starve him into surrender or death. Pompey stopped chasing him and turned off into Lesser Armenia to forage, hoping to lure Mithradates into attacking him, but the plan did not work properly. Later he caught up with Mithradates's army, annihilating about a third of it, but still Mithradates escaped. The old king tried to find refuge with Tigranes again but was forcibly expelled and continued to flee to the north. Pompey turned to Armenia, where he put an end to the revolt of Tigranes junior and reinstated the elder Tigranes on the throne.

It was important to detach as many of Mithradates's allies as possible. In 65 Pompey turned against the Albanians and Iberians who had fought for the King. Pompey eventually came to terms with Osroes, King of the Albanians and Artoces, King of the Iberians. Meanwhile Pompey's legates had been given several tasks, Lucius Afranius was stationed in Armenia and Aulus Gabinius was in Mesopotamia, while others patrolled the coasts and guarded routes. With some of his army Pompey made an excursion towards the Caspian Sea, but turned back before reaching it. Leaving Mithradates to his fate in the north for the time being, Pompey then turned his attention to Syria, Judaea and Nabataea, three kingdoms which were always antagonistic to each other, and where palace revolutions often occurred, substituting one ruler for another, often with the assistance of the other states. A struggle for the throne of Judaea involved Pompey in a minor war in which he captured Jerusalem, and entered the inner sanctuary of the temple, not expecting to find it empty, and perhaps not even fully aware of the enormity of the sacrilege. He set up one of the rival candidates for the throne, but as high priest, not king, so that Judaea remained relatively weak against its neighbours.

At the siege of Jerusalem or perhaps a little earlier, news arrived that Mithradates was dead. His son Pharnaces succeeded him, but had no ambition to continue the war, which could now be finally concluded, and settlement of the whole of the east could begin, with due attention to the delicate balance of power that must be maintained. Pompey spent the winter of 63 to 62 in putting his administrative arrangements in place, generally admitted by modern scholars to be sensible and sound. In the cities with a long history of Greek settlement, it was easy to install the Roman provincial administrative machinery, but in areas such as Pontus there was no infrastructure upon which to build, so Pompey divided the province into eleven districts, each with an administrative centre.

In 62 Pompey returned to Rome. He surprised everyone by disbanding his army, revealing that he had no intention of seizing power in Rome. He had won the war, enriched the treasury by unimaginable amounts, annexed provinces, settled the east and now all he asked was that his arrangements should be ratified by the Senate, and his veterans should be settled on the land. These were perfectly reasonable requests, but his enemies in the Senate were determined not to co-operate. They went through all the details in endless debates, led by Lucius Licinius Lucullus, Quintus Lutatius Catulus and Quintus Metellus. The first two were sworn enemies of Pompey, and he had clashed with Metellus over the control of Crete during the pirate campaign. Another rising politician, Marcus Porcius Cato, lent his considerable talents in oratory to the anti-Pompeian campaign. For some considerable time, Pompey was thwarted at every turn. Rome had changed since he had been away.

ROME DURING POMPEY'S ABSENCE

While Pompey was still in the east, there had been disturbances in Rome, centred on Lucius Sergius Catilina, or Catiline, who was accused of conspiring to overthrow the state. The charge against him was nebulous, and so confused even at the time that it is well nigh impossible to ascertain the truth at a distance of two thousand years. Modern scholars have dismissed most of the stories about Catiline as fabrications. The one man who did firmly believe that Catiline posed a threat was Marcus Tullius Cicero, one of the consuls for 63. Catiline had been a candidate for the consulship for 66 but was not elected, and he was prevented from even standing for election for 65 and 64. In 63 Cicero and Antonius Hybrida were elected and Catiline lost his chance once again. It was said that in desperation he had started to raise troops, and stirred up the people to his side by promising to cancel all debts, which was a common rallying cry in Rome. Towards the end of 63, Catiline went to Etruria, where discontented people of all ranks gathered around him, including veteran soldiers. In Rome, the ringleader was said to be Publius Cornelius Lentulus Sura, stepfather of Mark Antony, who was a teenager in 63. Lentulus was said to have tried to recruit some Gallic tribesmen who were visiting Rome to convert them to the cause, whatever it was, and perhaps provide some cavalry to add to Catiline's army. The Gauls considered the matter, but decided not to get involved, and told their patron in the city what had happened. Cicero was informed and started to gather evidence. Then he pounced, arresting as many suspects as he could, including Lentulus Sura.

This was Cicero's political triumph, saving the state from the conspiracy. The suspects were brought before the Senate, where Cicero demanded the death penalty. He did not suggest a proper trial, possibly because as an experienced lawyer he knew that the men might be acquitted. Julius Caesar, who was now Pontifex Maximus, tried to suggest the milder punishment of closely guarded house arrest in some of the towns of Italy. No one listened to him. Cicero won the day and had all his suspects executed. It was to rebound on him later. And since one of the victims was Mark Antony's stepfather, he had made a mortal enemy.

Pompey was at a disadvantage because he had not been able to exercise a significant influence on Roman politics while he was fighting the war against Mithradates and then attending to the annexation and administration of the eastern provinces, and the alliances with other states. He did manage to secure some of the magistracies for his friends in the year prior to his return to Italy. Metellus Celer and Valerius Flaccus travelled back to Rome for the elections and were both elected praetors for 63, and Titus Ampius Balbus and Titus Labienus were tribunes for the same year. If these men had been sent to prepare the way for Pompey's return, when he would need senatorial co-operation, they achieved little that was noteworthy, except that Labienus and Ampius Balbus proposed that Pompey should be allowed to wear a gold crown at the theatre, and triumphal dress at the games. This was not just an empty gesture. The Romans attached great importance to outward display and marks of merit.

It is just possible that Publius Servilius Rullus, another of the tribunes for 63, was one of Pompey's men. One of the most pressing concerns when the army came home was to find land for the settlement of the retired soldiers, since they did not get pensions, and there was also a backlog of veterans from the war against Sertorius, since the programme designed to deal with them had never been completed. It was always a difficult matter to find land for the soldiers without ejecting people already settled on it, and in 63 Rullus presented a land bill that would have solved several problems at once if it had ever been put into effect. The clauses of the bill had been well thought out, taking into account the high level of debt and unemployment in Rome, and the distress caused by the confiscation of public land whenever redistribution had taken place. Rullus proposed to set up a commission of ten men to deal with all the public land throughout Italy. They were to have praetorian powers for five years, which meant that they would hold *imperium* and would be legally able to command troops. They were not to be responsible to anyone, so they could make decisions without going through the Senate. All this made the senators nervous. The commissioners were to have access to funds to enable them to purchase land, including plots in the provinces. The veterans of Sulla's army were to be allowed to keep their plots, unless they expressed a wish to sell.

There is no firm proof of any relationship between Rullus and Pompey, and some scholars have suggested the complete opposite, that Rullus was in fact an enemy of Pompey, perhaps a front man for Crassus and possibly Julius Caesar, and the bill was designed to embarrass Pompey when he came home because he would have to ask nicely, cap in hand, if the commissioners would help him to settle his veterans. This is the line that Cicero took, and he talked the bill to death, ostensibly on Pompey's behalf. On the other hand, it is possible to interpret Rullus's land bill as solid preparation for the return of Pompey's army from the east, by establishing a well-regulated system of land distribution that would upset as few people as possible and still achieve its aims, while at the same time relieving the urban poor and solving the problem of debts. The bill was not passed, but Caesar would revive parts of it a few years later.

THE RISE OF CAESAR

When Pompey returned to Rome, Gaius Julius Caesar was praetor and soon left the city to govern the province of Further Spain, where he had been quaestor in 69. After conducting a successful campaign against the Lusitanian tribesmen, Caesar had been voted a triumph to celebrate his victory when he returned to Rome in 60. He would have to remain outside Rome until the triumph was held and the troops disbanded, because the law forbade a general to enter the city while in command of an army. This conflicted with Caesar's ambition to stand for the consular elections for the following year. The Senate refused permission for him to stand *in absentia*. Without hesitation, he cancelled the triumph, entered Rome, and was duly elected consul for 59.

Caesar's career up to this point had not been remarkable. As the nephew of Gaius Marius, he was decidedly not a sympathiser of Sulla and his party, but on the other hand he remained aloof from Carbo, so he was not directly involved in the civil war between the two factions. He was only nineteen years old when Sulla came to power, but his lack of years and experience did not make him compliant to Sulla's demand that he should divorce his young wife to sever all connection with the previous regime. Caesar refused to put his wife aside and went into hiding. Unwisely he lingered too long in a marsh where he caught malaria, and was captured, but fortunately he was related through his mother Aurelia to the three Aurelius Cotta brothers, Gaius, Lucius and Marcus, who were followers of Sulla. They spoke up for him, and Sulla relented, allegedly remarking that Caesar should be watched, because he had many Mariuses in him.

Removing himself from Rome, Caesar obtained a post on the staff of the governor of Asia, where he was despatched on a diplomatic mission to King Nicomedes of Bithynia, to collect some ships that had been promised for the Roman fleet. For the rest of his life, Caesar was the butt of scurrilous jokes about Nicomedes, with whom he was widely supposed to have had a homosexual relationship. He went on to serve in a military post in Cilicia, but when he learned of the death of Sulla he returned to Rome. In 73 he was made a priest, *pontifex*, in place of Gaius Aurelius Cotta, who had died. These appointments to the college of fifteen *pontifices* were not elective, but usually passed to a relative of the previous priest. The bestowal of a priesthood was a great honour and usually signified that the chosen man was destined for an important political career. The duties were not onerous and could be combined with other political activities.

Caesar's first meaningful post was obtained in 69 when he served as quaestor in Further Spain, dealing with judgements in the provincial courts and administrative matters. This junior post gave entry to the Senate, thanks to Sulla's legislation, which was not revoked, so after his return to Rome in 68, Caesar could embark on his rise to political fame. It was a slow process. His wife, whom he had refused to divorce, had died just before he left for Spain, leaving him with his daughter and only legitimate child, Julia. In 67 he married Pompeia, no relation to Pompey the Great, but a granddaughter of Sulla. Caesar was not yet a force to be reckoned with in Roman politics, but he appears in the sources from time to time, speaking in favour of the bills to bestow special commands on Pompey, and in 63 he was made high priest.

Unlike Pompey, Caesar's rise to power was not meteoric and did not involve spectacular military commands. He plodded through the relevant magistracies in the proper order, becoming praetor in 62, and governor of Further Spain in 61. When he set out for home in the following year, announcing that he would stand for the consulship for 59, he had made enough of an impression on his rivals for them to realize that he was clever and dangerous and they did not want him in office as consul. They made strenuous efforts to block him, and then when they saw that the Roman people were favourable to him and he would certainly be elected, they resorted to rampant bribery to ensure that a candidate of their own was also elected. Marcus Porcius Cato, normally a strict upholder of the law, condoned the bribery to support his son-in-law Marcus Calpurnius Bibulus, who was voted in as Caesar's consular colleague.

There were now three men who covertly controlled the political scene: Caesar himself as consul, the fabulously wealthy Marcus Licinius Crassus, who supported Caesar largely via ready cash, and Gnaeus Pompeius Magnus, whose long drawn out attempts to have his eastern administration ratified by the Senate, and his veterans settled on the land, drove him into the arms of the other two. This unofficial, non-permanent partnership is labelled by modern historians as the First Triumvirate, but this gives the impression that there was some sort of agreement, an agenda and a set of rules for the three men to work to, which was not the case. Pompey, Caesar and Crassus worked together for their own ends. Pompey required resolution to his political problems, Crassus wanted political esteem and Caesar had the power, for one year, to bring about the necessary legislation. His agenda covered several current problems. The most important was a land bill that would enable Pompey to settle his veteran soldiers, and also alleviate population pressure in Rome without displacing people already settled on the land. All the sticking points of previous bills were to be circumvented, and the expenses that would be incurred in putting the proposals into effect were already covered, since Pompey had filled the treasury with vast wealth from his eastern conquests, some of which could surely be used to settle the soldiers who had enabled him to do so.

There was little in Caesar's bill that was inflammatory, but in the Senate the opponents of Caesar and his proposals, led by Cato, tried to talk the bill to death as they had done with every last detail of Pompey's administrative arrangements for the east. Impatient for quick results, Caesar removed Cato from the Senate and put him in prison. It was perhaps understandable, since Caesar was in a hurry and the bill would ameliorate several problems at once, but to act in such a high-handed manner only proved to his enemies that they had been right to distrust him and his methods, for the opposition was not so much against the land bill, as against Caesar. It was not very long since Tiberius and Gaius Gracchus had tried to instigate reforms involving redistribution of land, and the collective senatorial memory of the threat to their dominance still rankled.

Caesar made one final attempt to have the bill passed by the Senate, in the proper legal manner. He asked the other consul Bibulus what were the main objections to the bill, so that each one could be ironed out in debate, but Bibulus would not co-operate. Then, like the tribunes Tiberius and Gaius Gracchus, Caesar went direct to the people's assembly, with Crassus putting in an appearance alongside him. Pompey made a speech outlining the benefits of the land bill, and hinted that his soldiers would deal with any opponents who tried to sabotage it. There was some rioting in which Bibulus was attacked. He survived, although he was covered in manure for his pains. The bill was passed, despite the intransigence of the Senate. Pompey and Crassus were appointed to the commission of twenty men to carry out the land settlements, and Caesar took the precaution of having all senators swear an oath to support the new law. Cato and his friends refused, but the voice of reason came from Cicero, who could see that there was nothing meaningful to be gained by refusing to uphold it, except to frustrate Caesar.

Disregarding his colleague Bibulus, who had declared that he was watching the skies for omens, which would normally have put an end to all public business, Caesar continued to push through further legislation. All Pompey's arrangements for the eastern provinces and allies were ratified, despite a show of opposition from Lucullus. Yet another law concerning extortion of provincials was passed, the *lex Julia de repetundis*, which remained in force through the Empire. The tax gatherers for the province of Asia were bailed out, having put in a bid for the taxes from which they hoped to make a profit, and then panicking when they found that they had miscalculated and their bid was too high. The King of Egypt, Ptolemy Auletes (literally meaning the flute player), was officially recognized by Rome and his tottering rule was shored up, though he had to pay for the service, and both Caesar and Pompey made a fortune. The Egyptian connection was to play a role later, when Pompey arrived there after his defeat in the civil war, looking for men, money and ships.

The relationship between Pompey and Caesar was cemented by a marriage alliance. When Pompey had returned from the east he had divorced his wife Mucia, the mother of his two sons and his daughter. Since he had not yet remarried, he was the most eligible bachelor in Rome. He married Caesar's only daughter Julia, and the union was generally agreed to be a successful and loving relationship. In the same year, Caesar married Calpurnia, the daughter of Lucius Calpurnius Piso, who was elected consul for 58.

The next item on Caesar's agenda was to obtain a province that would bring him fame, fortune and glory. In an attempt to forestall him before the consular elections in 60, the Senate had fallen back on a law passed by Gaius Gracchus that stipulated that provinces had to be assigned to outgoing magistrates before the elections took place. The Senate allocated the provinces for the outgoing consuls of 59 to make certain that there would be no question of a territorial province for Caesar. He was destined for the mundane task of caretaking woodlands, which would not have satisfied him at all. He overturned this plan and obtained the proconsulship of Gaul, most of which was not yet a Roman province. There were signs of trouble brewing in Gaul because the Aedui, a tribe that was friendly towards Rome, were threatened by another tribe called the Sequani. There was a danger of escalating violence, because other Gallic tribes were being displaced as the Aedui fought their enemies, and the Sequani had allied with the German tribe of the Suebi, enthusiastically led by their chief Ariovistus. There was no immediate threat to Rome, but the memory was still very vivid of the Gallic invasions when the city had been abandoned for some time, and the later migrations of the Cimbri and Teutones, who were finally repulsed by Caesar's uncle Marius.

Caesar obtained his province in stages. The tribune Vatinius passed a law granting Caesar the province of Cisalpine Gaul and Illyricum, with command of three legions. This post was to last for five years, terminating on 1 March 54. The need for continuity and longer than usual commands had been established when Pompey was given three years to eradicate the pirates. The fact that he had achieved his aims in three months instead of three years did not detract from the principle that some problems required more than one proconsular year. Then Caesar also obtained Transalpine Gaul, where Quintus Caecilius Metellus Celer was to have been governor, but he died before taking up his post, so it was awarded to Caesar. Strictly, the territorial extent of Transalpine Gaul was limited to the province formed in 121 to protect the land route from Italy to Spain and the lands belonging to Massilia. The capital was at Narbo (modern Narbonne), reflected in the later name for the province, Gallia Narbonensis. If the meaning of the words Transalpine Gaul was stretched a little, it implied the whole of the country up to the coasts of the Atlantic and what is now the English Channel, giving Caesar free rein to embark on his ten year conquest of Gaul and its conversion into Roman provinces.

Before Caesar left for his new province, he took some pains to protect his legislation from attacks by other politicians, just as Sulla had attempted but failed to do before he left for the east. Part of Caesar's plan included the election of Publius Clodius Pulcher as tribune for 58, despite the fact that he was not of plebeian origin. Caesar and Pompey presided over an adoption ceremony, where an obliging plebeian called Publius Fonteius formally adopted Clodius so that he could legitimately stand for election as tribune.

One of Clodius's first enactments was to outlaw anyone who had executed Roman citizens without trial. This law was aimed at Cicero, who was forced into voluntary exile for a while. Cato was removed for a short time as well. Clodius was responsible for the annexation of Cyprus, which strictly belonged to Egypt, but Ptolemy Auletes was in no position to argue. The new province required a governor and Cato was prevailed upon to take up the appointment. For the benefit of the people Clodius amended Gaius Gracchus's legislation for the distribution of cheap grain, making it entirely free at state expense. He also made it more difficult for anyone to disrupt political proceedings by retiring to observe the skies, as Bibulus had done. He arranged for the two consuls for 58, Caesar's father-in-law Lucius Calpurnius Piso and Pompey's adherent Aulus Gabinius, to govern respectively Macedonia and Syria, each with a five year command. Sulla had tried to limit the duration of provincial government to one year, but it was becoming more common to bestow longer commands on governors of some of the larger or more troublesome provinces, or on commanders who took on special tasks. So far, Clodius's legislation had favoured Caesar, but if he had been primed by Caesar, or had been enacting laws that he thought might please him, he soon veered from this path. He harassed Pompey, nibbling away at some of his eastern arrangements and interfering with the allied states. He even started to agitate against some of Caesar's acts as consul. Clodius's gangs terrorized the streets and Rome was in danger of descending into mob rule.

Pompey retaliated by recruiting two of the tribunes for 57, Titus Annius Milo and Publius Sestius, allowing them to build up rival gangs with which to counter Clodius's men. He began proceedings for the recall of Cicero, who came home in autumn 57. When food shortages became endemic, Pompey was placed in charge of the grain supply for five years, with proconsular powers and permission to appoint fifteen legates. He took his duties very seriously, travelling widely to negotiate with farmers and landowners, merchants and shippers in Italy and the provinces. One of his journeys was the occasion for his most famous pronouncements. When he wanted to set sail even though the captain of his ship warned that the weather was worsening, he said: 'We have to sail. We do not have to live.'

For the last two years, although he was engaged in the conquest of Gaul, Caesar kept a close watch on what was happening in Rome. He had agents there who informed him of what was going on, and who could ensure that some of his own followers obtained magistracies so that at best some of his wishes could be put into effect, or at worst some of his enemies might be prevented from doing him any harm. He did not neglect the military side of his proconsulship. By 56 he had repulsed the Helvetii who had tried to migrate from the Alpine region into Gaul, and had defeated Ariovistus, dispersing the tribesmen of the Suebi, and discouraging the rest of them from crossing the Rhine from Germany. His second campaign was aimed at the Belgae of north-western Gaul, and the tribes which had joined them. This involved almost annihilating the Nervii, a procedure that is justly regarded with distaste by modern historians. For these wide-ranging campaigns he relied on his subordinates who were capable of operating independently as his legates, such as Titus Labienus and Publius Licinius Crassus, the son of Marcus Crassus.

In the spring of 56, Caesar went on a tour of inspection of the provinces under his command, and met Marcus Crassus at Ravenna. In April, he came to Luca (modern Lucca) where he met Pompey and a large congregation of senators. Crassus may have been present as well, but this is not certain. The most important point is that the three men, Caesar, Crassus and Pompey, now dominated Roman politics to the extent that they could decide in advance what was to happen in the political arena for the next few years. They agreed that in order to block the consular candidate Domitius Ahenobarbus, who had announced that he would undo Caesar's legislation, Pompey and Crassus were to be the consuls for 55, which would no doubt be put into effect by the expenditure of large quantities of cash distributed in bribes to the electorate. They could easily afford this sort of massive outlay. Crassus's wealth was legendary. He said that no one could account himself rich unless he could afford to raise, equip and pay an army. Pompey was perhaps even more wealthy, since he had large estates in Picenum, and many contacts and clients in Spain and in the east, where he had lent money and secured profits for himself for the future. For the year following their consulships, Pompey and Crassus would both obtain prestigious commands, and they would see to it that Caesar's Gallic command was prolonged to give him enough time to complete his conquest.

The Republic was not dead, but it was already moribund because, from now onwards, rich men with influence, and more important control of loyal armies, could dominate the political scene and mould it to their own advantage, and sometimes to the advantage of the state. There was much that needed reform, but the intransigence of the Senate and the annual turnover of magistrates meant that any reforms that were agreed upon during a term of office could be annihilated in the following year. In such a political system it was not possible to develop sustainable policies or to implement long-term forward planning. Some of the magistrates who were frustrated simply found ways of beating the system to force through legislation and maintain it afterwards. Sulla had shown the way; Caesar developed it into an art.

As consuls Crassus and Pompey did not engage in far reaching reforms, except to pass laws designed to tidy up electoral procedure, to reduce the disorder that was becoming increasingly common, and to prevent the rampant bribery that attended canvassing for votes. This was somewhat two-faced, since not a little bribery had gone into ensuring their own election.

One success for Pompey concerned the dedication of his stone theatre and temple complex in Rome. He had seen Greek theatres while he was in the east, and determined that Rome should also have a similar cultural centre. It was the first permanent theatre in Rome, in place of the temporary timber structures where performances had been put on in the past, and it had a temple, a meeting house and colonnaded walks complete with sculptures and works of art displayed all around, arranged by Cicero's friend Atticus. It was a Roman version of the modern leisure centre.

The consuls for 54 were Domitius Ahenobarbus and Appius Claudius Pulcher. At some point Pompey's son married Appius's daughter, but there was no solid political alliance, with Appius slavishly following Pompey's agenda. For their proconsulships Pompey was to be governor of both the Spanish provinces for five years, and Crassus was awarded the province of Syria for the same length of time, with an unpublicised but nonetheless well known plan to launch a campaign against Parthia. Crassus raised an army and left Rome, but Pompey remained behind. He was still in charge of the food supply, to which he devoted most of his attention, so he sent two legates, Marcus Petreius and Lucius Afranius to govern Spain on his behalf. This was an important innovation in provincial government, one that Augustus adopted and developed at the beginning of the Empire.

The consul Domitius Ahenobarbus set about bringing down several of Pompey's adherents, who were attacked in the courts. One was Aulus Gabinius, who was the governor of Syria until Crassus took over. He survived the first attacks but was prosecuted when he arrived home in the autumn of 54, for having left his province without permission from the Senate, in order to mount a military expedition to replace Ptolemy Auletes on his throne. Gabinius had succeeded in his mission, with the help of a young cavalry officer, Mark Antony. When Gabinius set off for Rome, Antony travelled to Gaul to join Caesar.

Since Gabinius was Pompey's man, and Pompey had already assisted Ptolemy Auletes, it was assumed that Pompey had ordered the expedition into Egypt. The prosecution of Gabinius was therefore intended to embarrass Pompey. The first charge was for *maiestas*, treason against the Roman people. Gabinius was acquitted, but was then condemned on a different charge, this time for extortion. Cicero failed in his defence of Gabinius and Pompey would not use force to save him. Nor would he resort to armed intervention when the elections were delayed in 54. A personal tragedy laid him low for a while, when his wife Julia died in childbirth. The child died too. Some historians have alleged that this was the start of the rift between Pompey and Caesar, but this is now discounted, since there was no detectable change in their political or personal attitudes towards each other for some years thereafter. Even when the news reached

Rome in 53 that Crassus and most of his army had been wiped out by the Parthians, there was no deterioration in the relationship between Caesar and Pompey. Crassus had been a partner but not a binding force.

Violence in Rome had escalated to such a degree that the elections in 54 were abandoned and it was not until the middle of 53 that consuls for that year were elected. Pompey presided over the proceedings in the midst of rumours that he was to be made Dictator, but he did nothing to stop two men who were inimical towards him, Domitius Calvinus and Marcus Messalla, from becoming consuls for the rest of the year. In 52 the disruption was even worse. The elections that should have been held in 53 for the following years' magistrates had been continually postponed, then in 52 the rival gangs of Clodius, who intended to stand for the praetorship, and Milo who was a consular candidate, clashed at a tavern outside Rome. Clodius was killed. The people of Rome had benefited from Clodius's measures as tribune, and gave him a splendid funeral in the city, which involved turning the Senate House into his pyre.

Having declined to suggest that Pompey should be made Dictator, the Senate now passed the last decree, empowering him to raise troops, in addition to those he already commanded as controller of the food supply. As an acceptable compromise, Bibulus suggested that Pompey should be made sole consul, yet another anomalous appointment in his career. The proposal was accepted and Pompey started energetically tidying up, at first alone, and towards the end of his term with a colleague, his father-in-law Metellus Scipio, whose daughter Cornelia was now Pompey's wife. Milo was brought to trial, and defended unsuccessfully by a nervous Cicero, who was intimidated by Pompey's troops standing all around as he spoke. Pompey had determined to abandon Milo, even though he had once been one of his own men when he needed to use him to check Clodius.

With his usual speed and efficiency Pompey passed laws to curb the violence, prevent bribery at elections, and streamline the proceedings in the jury courts, which were to be limited to three days for the examination of witnesses, and one more day for the final speeches. There were to be 360 jurors, of whom a random eighty-one men would be selected for the final hearing making it impossible for anyone to bribe them all.

Two of Pompey's laws seemed to be directed against Caesar. While he was in Gaul, Caesar as proconsul was immune to any prosecution, but once he gave up his command he would be a private citizen and vulnerable to attack. He had upset enough people to make this a likely occurrence. He may have easily escaped condemnation, but anyone who was undergoing a trial was banned from standing for election. Since he wished to take up a second term as consul as soon as his proconsulship ended, Caesar had asked for permission to stand for election *in absentia* so that he could step directly from one office to another without an interruption, and still be protected from prosecution. This privilege had been refused when he returned from Spain some years before, but this time a law had been passed, known as the law of ten tribunes, allowing him to stand as consular candidate without putting in a personal appearance in Rome. Pompey supported this law and worked hard to push it through, but then he seemed to contradict himself by passing the *lex de iure magistratuum*, stipulating that candidates for any of the magistracies must come to Rome. He added a codicil exempting Caesar from this law, since his case had already been dealt with in a separate law, but in future no one else was to be allowed to emulate him. Interpretations of Pompey's action range from forgetfulness to deceit, but if he had wanted to circumvent the law of ten tribunes he could have simply repealed it. There is no need to interpret this as a breach between Caesar and Pompey in 52.

The next law was designed to impose a gap of five years between a magistracy in Rome and a promagistracy in a province or on a specific task. Both Caesar and Pompey would have to find some way of avoiding prosecution for a period of five years without an appointment, but Pompey had already surmounted this problem by extending his Spanish command for another five years. The law had an unwelcome effect on several men who had never entertained a wish to govern provinces, because there was now a shortage of ex-magistrates who had not held a post for five years. Marcus Tullius Cicero had to leave his beloved Rome to govern Cilicia from the middle of 51 until the summer of 50.

By the time he returned to Rome, there had been a change of attitude towards Caesar. Marcus Marcellus and Servius Sulpicius Rufus were elected consuls for 51, and Marcellus had started to agitate for the recall of Caesar from Gaul. Modern historians are hampered because there is no reliable evidence about the date when Caesar's command was due to end. Crassus and Pompey had been awarded five years in Syria and Spain, with a probable terminal date of 1 March 50, but it is not known if this was also the date when Caesar should lay down his command. Pompey was safe for another five years, and was authorized to remain in Rome while legates governed his provinces. It was beginning to look as though Caesar would not be able to rely on similar privileges. In September 51 Metellus Scipio proposed that any discussion about Caesar's command should be postponed until 1 March 50, which gave Caesar some leeway, but not enough to cover the period of the elections.

The consuls for 50 were no friends of Caesar, and it seemed that the tribune Scribonius Curio would prove to be an even worse enemy, but in the spring he went over to Caesar. The consul Gaius Marcellus opened the debate on Caesar's command by proposing that successors should now be appointed. Curio suggested that the same should apply to Pompey's command in Spain. Pompey proposed an extension of Caesar's command until 13 November 50, but Curio blocked him. It became clear to Pompey that Curio and others were determined to split him from Caesar. In the summer he fell dangerously ill, and was gratified to find that there was widespread rejoicing when he recovered.

In December 50 Gaius Marcellus made two separate proposals: that Caesar should lay down his command and give up his army, and Pompey's command should be terminated. The first was passed and the second was defeated, highlighting the favourable attitude of the Senate to Pompey and their hostility to Caesar. The tribune Curio, whose office was due to end when the incoming tribunes took up office on 10 December, reiterated his consistent proposals that both Caesar and Pompey should lay down their commands at the same time. The vote was overwhelmingly favourable, but Marcellus did not act upon it and dismissed the Senate.

One of the new tribunes for 49 was Mark Antony, who waited only a few days after taking up office on 10 December to make a speech against Pompey in the Senate. Pompey did not retaliate. Cicero thought that Pompey had come to the conclusion that Caesar would obtain what he wanted by force if necessary, but he may have been transposing his own opinions onto Pompey. At the beginning of 49 Caesar sent a letter for the tribunes Antony and Quintus Cassius to relay to the Senate, suggesting that he and Pompey should lay down their commands at the same time, but he included the threat that he would not do so if Pompey retained command of his troops in Spain. Some last minute compromises were proposed. Antony and Cassius vetoed the suggestion that Caesar should give up his command by a certain date. Then it was proposed that Caesar should retain command of Cisalpine Gaul or Illyricum with one legion, but that failed too, despite the fact that the many senators and Pompey himself were in favour of the idea. Soon afterwards the Senate passed the last decree authorizing the magistrates to ensure the safety of the state. Antony and Cassius were prevented from exercising their veto by the threat of violence. Some sources suggest they were physically ejected from the Senate. They left Rome in a hurry with Scribonius Curio to join Caesar in Cisalpine Gaul, where he was poised with his army on the border between his province and Italy, marked by a small river called the Rubicon. It was so geographically insignificant that after two thousand years no one can say exactly where it was, but its political significance was enormous. To cross it at the head of troops was an act of rebellion. By the time Antony and Cassius joined up with Caesar he had crossed it on the night of 10/11 January.

CIVIL WAR

The eventual outbreak of war took everyone by surprise. Neither the Senate nor Pompey was prepared for it, despite the fact that no-one had been able to find any solution to the problem. It was clear that Caesar would never back down unless he could achieve what he wanted, and Pompey was not willing to retire into private life, standing aside while Caesar fulfilled his ambitions. The *optimates* did not want Caesar as consul for a second term, and saw no reason why he should obtain the office by being allowed to break all the rules about standing for office in person and not using wholesale bribery, privileges that were denied to everyone else via Pompey's legislation as sole consul. The *optimates* did not want Pompey in supreme command either, but they thought that they could make use of him. After all, he was the best general they had. They knew that Caesar was determined and ruthless, but they made no preparations to avert disaster when he did the very thing that they feared and invaded Italy.

Pompey already had command of troops, but most of them were in Spain. Some time before the war began he had obtained two legions from Caesar's army on the pretext of beginning a campaign. One of these legions had been originally his own, but Caesar inspired tremendous loyalty in his troops, so after their service in Caesar's army, Pompey's soldiers were no longer trustworthy. Unfortunately, Pompey had overestimated his abilities to raise another army. He had boasted that he only needed to stamp his foot in Italy and troops would spring up, but stamp as he might the men were not forthcoming. To the horror of the senators, he decided to evacuate Rome and establish a base in Greece, where he could train the troops that he did have, and recruit more. It was a strategically correct decision, and Pompey carried out the evacuation of the port of Brundisium with characteristic military aplomb, just as Caesar caught up with him in a rapid march from Rome.

Caesar did not chase after Pompey but returned to the city, observing all the politically correct forms by not crossing the city boundary while still in command of troops, which was a little odd considering that he had just marched into Italy at the head of an army. But it was important to show that he intended no harm and that there were to be no proscriptions such as Sulla and his own uncle Gaius Marius had set in motion. He adopted a studied policy of mildness, his famous *clementia*, which he had demonstrated when he had surrounded the troops led by his avowed enemy Lucius Domitius Ahenobarbus at Corfinium. He let Domitius and his officers go free, to join Pompey if they wished.

In Italy Caesar had the support of many cities and communities, and he worked on the rest, spreading the word that he had no desire to murder people or confiscate property. He was concerned to leave a pacified country behind him when he set off to deal with the Pompeians. He installed his adherents in significant posts: Mark Antony was in charge of Italy, his brother Gaius Antonius was sent to Illyricum and Marcus Aemilius Lepidus was made prefect of the city of Rome. Caesar entrusted the command of Cisalpine Gaul to Marcus Licinius Crassus, the son of the consul who had met his end in Parthia. Scribonius Curio was to command Sardinia, Sicily and Africa, where he could secure the grain supply for Rome. Caesar decided to carry the war to Spain in order to eliminate Pompey's legates and troops there, before facing Pompey himself in Greece. He summed up the situation with the neat phrase that he would deal first with the army with no leader and then the leader with no army.

Caesar made short work of Lucius Afranius and Marcus Petreius, Pompey's legates in Spain. Caesar's troops were experienced and battle hardened, and intensely loyal, and the two Pompeian commanders were no match for him. By August he had accepted their surrender at Ilerda. In Further Spain Marcus Terentius Varro, loyal to Pompey but also a realist, surrendered rather than have his soldiers massacred in an unequal fight.

In Rome, Lepidus had brought about Caesar's appointment as Dictator, which gave him the necessary powers to pass legislation to relieve the chronic debts that always plagued the poorer citizens, and to ensure that food was distributed to them. He held the elections, and was elected consul for 48 with Publius Servilius Isauricus as colleague. Then he laid down his dictatorial powers and embarked for Greece.

Pompey had been granted time to train his army while Caesar was in Spain, but he could not control the senators who were with him, continually exhorting him to this and that activity. When Caesar arrived in Greece he had only half his army, and Mark Antony in charge of the other half still in Italy could not cross to Greece because Marcus Bibulus, the commander of the Pompeian fleet, assiduously patrolled the sea lanes. Pompey had made his base at Dyrrachium where he could be supplied by sea, but if Caesar wished to remain there watching Pompey, he would be forced to forage over a wider and wider area for food and fodder. When Antony managed to evade the Pompeian fleet and landed north of Dyrrachium, Caesar marched to meet him, and Pompey followed but withdrew when he found himself between the two sections of Caesar's army. The opposing forces returned to Dyrrachium, and dug in. Pompey erected a defensive line all round three sides of his camp, with the fourth side open to the sea, and Caesar erected siege works extending round Pompey's lines. At one point Pompey very nearly broke through the siege works, but the attempt failed. So did Caesar's offer of negotiation. The stalemate was ended when Caesar, short of food, moved off towards Thessaly. Pompey broke camp and followed him to a place called Pharsalus. The battle that they fought there was to dictate the future course of Roman history.

7

Civil Wars:
The Rise of Octavian 48–30 BC

Facing Caesar's army at Pharsalus in the summer of 48, Pompey steadfastly refused to engage in a pitched battle, though Caesar tried every day to entice him by drawing up his troops near to Pompey's camp. According to Caesar's account of the civil war, Pompey's resolute refusal of battle nearly succeeded in driving him away in search of food, but on the very day that Caesar had given the order to break camp, Pompey offered battle. The senators who had been eager to risk a battle had probably won the day by persuading Pompey to seek an end to the contest. As soon as he realized that Pompey meant to fight, Caesar halted the withdrawal and ordered his army to form up in the usual three lines, but took the precaution of adding an extra fourth line, which he stationed out of sight. He placed himself and Publius Sulla in command of the cavalry on the right wing because he had observed a build up of strength on the Pompeian left. Mark Antony commanded the Caesarian left wing and Gnaeus Domitius Calvinus the centre.

When the Pompeian cavalry attacked Caesar's right wing, the extra fourth line of Caesarian soldiers, who had been waiting for just such a moment, suddenly appeared and tipped the balance by charging into the cavalry and dispersing them, and then turning on the unprotected Pompeian left flank. Caesar had ordered his men to aim their weapons at the faces of the Pompeian soldiers, which thoroughly demoralized them. They fled for the camp. Some survivors took up a position on high ground where they stayed all night, but surrendered in the morning. Pompey had ridden off the field and escaped. Caesar eventually heard that he was aiming for Cyprus, and guessed that his ultimate destination would be Egypt, where he would try to profit from his connection with Ptolemy Auletes and his heirs, and collect men, money and ships to continue the war.

Caesar sent Mark Antony back to Rome to keep order there, and placed Domitius Calvinus in command of the province of Asia with three legions, made up from the surrendered Pompeian troops. Caesar had won a major battle, but the war was by no means over. Pompey was still free and active, and there were pockets of Pompeian sympathisers distributed in parts of the Roman world, and the Pompeian fleet was still a force to be reckoned with in the Mediterranean. Although Caesar had taken steps to secure Spain after the defeat of the Pompeian generals, his grasp was not as firm as he would have liked. Scribonius Curio had successfully taken over Sardinia and Sicily, but he had been killed when he tried to gain control of the province of Africa. In these two areas, Africa and Spain, the surviving Pompeians would eventually gather.

Instead of pursuing the scattered Pompeian officers and their men, Caesar decided to follow Pompey. If he could capture him it might be possible to bring about a negotiated peace. Caesar had tried to negotiate several times before and during the war and, though it was more than likely that he had done so as a demonstration of his own good faith in contrast to the intransigence of the senators and Pompey himself, there may have been some element of sincerity in his attempts. When he reached Alexandria, however, Pompey was already dead. There was a civil war going on in Egypt between the heirs of Ptolemy Auletes who had recently died. The army of the young Ptolemy XIII was currently in control of Alexandria, and the forces of Cleopatra VII were camped close by, with their sister Arsinoe as an interested onlooker. Their younger brother, who would become Ptolemy XIV, was still a child, and took no part in the war. The advisers of Ptolemy XIII assumed that following closely behind Pompey there would be either Caesar himself or his officers, and they had no wish to become involved in the Roman civil war. The general Achillas allegedly pronounced that 'Dead men don't bite' and so Pompey was killed and beheaded as soon as he landed.

When Caesar arrived in Alexandria he was immediately caught up in the Egyptian civil war. In his account of the civil war Caesar says that he could not leave immediately because of adverse winds which kept his ships in harbour, so he remained in Egypt because he considered that the war between Ptolemy's heirs would affect the Roman people and himself as consul. This altruistic phrase carefully avoids the fact that the Romans were increasingly interested in Egypt, largely because of its wealth, and if Caesar could bring about a peaceful conclusion to the current war and establish one or possibly more of the Ptolemaic heirs on the throne, they would be grateful to him. Another consideration was the fate of the loans he had made to Ptolemy Auletes and the potential loss of his returns on them if anarchy descended on the country.

There was some risk in attempting to end the Egyptian war. Caesar had very few troops, and although he had asked his ally Mithradates King of Pergamum to recruit more soldiers for him in Syria and Cilicia, there would be a delay before they arrived. Consequently Caesar was besieged for a short time in Alexandria by the army of Ptolemy XIII under Achillas. Cleopatra VII was with him in the Royal palace, having arrived there, as the legend says, rolled up in a carpet delivered to Caesar by one of her servants. She is only briefly noted in Caesar's memoir of the events, but it was Cleopatra whom he chose to elevate to the throne of Egypt, and it was Cleopatra who bore him his only acknowledged son, called Ptolemy Caesar and nicknamed Caesarion, or little Caesar.

At some unknown date in the middle of 47, Caesar left Egypt, pausing on the way back to Rome to make war on King Pharnaces, the son of Mithradates VI. Pompey had confirmed him as ruler of the Crimea but he had taken advantage of the preoccupation of the Romans to try to regain the kingdom of Pontus, defeating Caesar's general Domitius Calvinus. Caesar rapidly restored order and left two legions in Pontus, issuing his famous arrogant but amusing statement *veni, vidi, vici* (I came, I saw, I conquered).

He arrived in Rome in midsummer, though it was September by the calendar, which was out of synchronization with the seasons. He was Dictator for the second time, held the elections in which his own men Publius Vatinius and Fufius Calenus were elected consuls, and he promoted several of his adherents to reward them. Among them was his sixteen year old great-nephew Gaius Octavius, who was given the honorary position of *praefectus urbi* during the festival of the *Feriae Latinae*, a very old celebration in memory of the Roman conquest of Alba Longa. All the magistrates left the city to travel to the Alban Mount, leaving the city in the hands of one of the younger members of the upper class families. It was a mark of distinction for the young Octavius, but since he was always ill with some complaint or other, probably no one took much notice of him.

THE WARS IN AFRICA & SPAIN

It was now time to settle the problem of the Pompeians in Africa and Spain. Caesar decided to go to Africa first and started to make preparations for another war. His soldiers chose this moment to dig their heels in. They had been fighting for him for a long time and they were tired, they said, and wanted to be discharged. It was thinly disguised blackmail in the hope of receiving more pay and rewards, but Caesar turned the tables on the men, addressing them as 'Citizens' as though he had already dismissed them, and promising to give them all that they asked for as soon as he had returned from the war in Africa, for which he would employ other troops. The soldiers begged to be allowed to go with him.

The African campaign lasted for a few months and was over by the middle of 46, but it was not a foregone conclusion that Caesar would be victorious. At one point a Caesarian foraging party was attacked by the Pompeian cavalry, and in making for the camp they were attacked again by Marcus Petreius, one of Pompey's generals who had faced Caesar in Spain. Caesar himself had to rally the men in this skirmish, physically manhandling one of the soldiers to explain that the enemy was in the opposite direction to the one in which the men were running.

The Pompeians had taken over the city of Utica, the capital of the province of Africa after Carthage had been destroyed. Cato had taken over from the governor Atius Varus, but he was not chosen as commander of the Pompeian army. Metellus Scipio, Pompey's father-in-law, was appointed instead and Cato acquiesced. Like Pompey himself Scipio refused to engage Caesar in battle, but at Thapsus Caesar managed to lure him into attacking, making it appear that he was in a disadvantageous position, trapped between two Pompeian armies. In the final battle Scipio was defeated, and the Pompeian survivors fled to Utica, where they fought their way into the city by killing many of the inhabitants. Cato stopped the massacre. Many of the Pompeians were eventually hunted down and captured by Caesar's troops, and the rest moved out of Africa to congregate in Spain, supported by the fleet. Cato did not leave Utica, preferring suicide to Caesar's clemency.

Some of Caesar's veteran soldiers were settled in colonies on the African coast, where they served to guard the area against the Pompeian fleet. Their settlement in Africa also absolved Caesar from the obligation of finding lands for all of them in Italy, though there were still many men to settle when he arrived in Rome. He appointed legates to seek out available land that could be purchased and it was paid for from the vast booty from the wars, so no one was evicted and no funds were taken from the state treasury.

Caesar arrived in Rome in July 46. In September he held four separate triumphs, parading through the streets with his captives and the spoils of war, which were traditionally dedicated to Jupiter in the temple on the Capitol Hill. The triumphs were all celebrated over foreign enemies, the Gauls, the Egyptians, Pharnaces and Juba of Numidia, though this last was really over the Pompeians in Africa, who had been assisted by Juba. The leader of the Gauls, Vercingetorix, had been in prison for six years awaiting this event and was killed as soon as the triumph was ended. Cleopatra's sister Arsinoe was marched through the streets, representing the Alexandrian war, but she was spared and sent to Ephesus. The infant son of Juba also featured in the triumph, and was brought up in Rome. He was eventually given Roman citizenship and installed as King of Mauretania. There was no mention of a triumph over Pompey the Great.

There was still a war to be fought against the Pompeians in Spain. Pompey's sons Gnaeus and Sextus had assembled a large army, recruiting soldiers from native Spanish tribes. The memory and reputation of Pompey the Great was still alive in Spain, and he had cultivated many clients in the province. Caesar left Rome towards the end of 46. This final campaign in the prolonged civil war was the most desperate and the most brutal. Caesar besieged Corduba where Sextus Pompey held the town with two legions, but drew off when he saw that he could not take it quickly. He was short of supplies. He transferred the siege to Ategua, full of stores of food and held by the Pompeian Munatius Plancus, whose response to the siege was to murder all the citizens who were sympathetic to Caesar and then throw the bodies over the walls. Caesar hoped to be able to induce Gnaeus Pompey to commit his troops to a battle to relieve the city, but when Gnaeus found he could do nothing to break the deadlock, he marched away. Caesar took Ategua and then chased after Gnaeus and the Pompeians. He caught up with them at a place called Munda, which has not been securely identified, but was probably in the vicinity of Urso, where Caesar later founded a colony. Gnaeus chose his ground well and offered battle, on the day that Caesar had decided to move away, as at Pharsalus. The battle was extremely hard fought on both sides, and Caesar admitted after his victory that he had often struggled to win, but this was the first time he had been forced to fight for his life.

Gnaeus Pompey escaped but was soon captured and, like his father, he was beheaded. His younger brother Sextus left his legions at Corduba and escaped to the coast to join his fleet. Ironically, the son of the man who had suppressed piracy in the Mediterranean became one of the most successful pirates of all time, surviving at sea for the next decade, and a constant irritation to Caesar's successors.

The resistance in Spain did not end after the battle of Munda. Caesar spent several months in pacifying the country, settling veterans, founding colonies, administering justice, adjusting administrative procedures and redefining territorial boundaries. He was joined by his great-nephew Gaius Octavius, who had been invited to accompany Caesar at the beginning of the campaign, but fell ill and could not leave Rome. When he recovered, Octavius made the journey with a few friends and attendants. This was not as simple a task as it may sound and required courage and determination. Caesar was impressed with the boy, with his intelligence, his reserve, and the tactful way he handled deputations from the Spanish communities. Caesar returned to Rome in summer 45, with Octavius travelling in his carriage, until Mark Antony came to meet them, and took Octavius's place. Antony had recently been out of favour with Caesar. After the battle of Pharsalus, when Antony was acting as Caesar's deputy in Rome, he had been somewhat heavy handed in putting down a riot when the populace had been stirred up about the problems of debt. Caesar could not condone his actions, which reflected badly on him as Dictator, so Antony was quietly dropped and he was not asked to take part in the African war, nor did he receive any appointments for 46, in fact he had been overlooked in favour of Marcus Aemilius Lepidus, who was made Caesar's deputy. It was clear on the journey back to Rome that Antony had been forgiven. He was promised the consulship with Caesar as colleague for 44.

CAESAR'S REFORMS

The Republican system demanded considerable repair. From the time of Tiberius and Gaius Gracchus the checks and balances that were originally built into the unwritten constitution had begun to fail, finally descending into chaotic violence. Sulla had shown that the real power lay with the man who could command the personal loyalty of the troops. Soldiers traditionally swore an oath of loyalty to their commanding officers, nearly always the consuls, and through them they owed loyalty to Rome, but personal military power had grown as campaigns lengthened, especially when the wars were fought abroad. Then the troops were not defending the homeland any longer, but fighting on behalf of a commander, who in turn was fighting to support the ideology of Rome, and more than likely to promote himself. As Rome expanded and wars were fought more or less continuously in one part of the world or another, there was a need for more and more troops. The indifference of the Senate to the ultimate fate of their increasingly large number of soldiers threw the two elements together; the commander needed the soldiers to succeed in his tasks and the soldiers needed the commander because he was the one man on whom the veterans placed their hopes for settlement on the land when they were discharged.

On the political scene, internecine strife resulted from the factions that had formed around leading figures, and from the shifting struggles between the *optimates* and the *populares*. Tribunes and other magistrates could be purchased to present the ideas of either of these groups, laws could be passed by the people's assemblies, circumventing the Senate, but then any legislation could be immediately overturned by a new set of magistrates. In this environment, it was impossible to sustain long-term planning or consistent policies. Many Roman politicians were more concerned with their own careers than they were with the government of the city and the provinces, and some of them regarded Rome as the centre of the universe with the provinces as exploitable satellites, places where they would be able to accrue personal wealth, without reference to the fact that they were functioning parts of a homogeneous empire.

By contrast Caesar thought in terms of the whole state embracing Rome itself and the provinces. This is controversial, like almost everything else about Caesar. From his own time to the present day his motives have been questioned. Was his frenetic legislative activity part of a logical long-term plan designed to reshape the government of a single city state into a fully fledged Imperial administration? Or was it piecemeal and haphazard and mostly designed to elevate himself into the sole ruler of Rome and the provinces? In the opinion of the author of this book, Caesar could see clearly what was necessary to improve the government even if he could never make it work perfectly, but he was no longer young and he was in a hurry to force through all the legislation that he envisaged. The laws that he passed were full of common sense measures and not too inflammatory, but his methods were questionable and arrogant. He tried to do too much too soon, and in the end it was not what he did so much as how he did it that turned men against him.

In order to put all his ideas into effect, Caesar required continuous long term power, and he received it legitimately in the form of a Dictatorship for ten years in 46. He was also consul for the third time that year, and again for the fourth time, but without a colleague, for most of 45. He resigned the office before the end of 45, but since he was Dictator this did not represent any loss of power. Besides, some of his associates were made suffect consuls in 45. The *consules suffecti* were additional consuls who took up their office after the elected ones (*consules ordinarii*) resigned their consulships. During the Empire it became more common for the ordinary consuls to resign so that suffect consuls could take their place. The scheme provided the necessary experience and rank for such men to proceed to further appointments. Caesar had also been granted the right to nominate candidates for some magistracies, and he installed some of his friends as provincial governors, but this does not mean that he used them as his deputies, directing their every move. Not all of them turned out to be exemplary role models.

Caesar very rapidly enacted several laws in the intervals between the civil wars. Between 46 and 44 he produced a staggering amount of legislation. He passed laws to alleviate the ever-present problem of debt. He revised the list of people who were eligible for the free corn dole that Clodius had instituted, reducing the number of recipients to 150,000. He reformed the jury courts, which were henceforth to be made up of equal numbers of equestrians and senators. In order to regulate provincial government, he decreed that praetors were to govern for one year and consuls for two, thus preventing anyone from emulating his ten year term as proconsul of Gaul. He abolished the old lunar calendar that required constant adjustments, which had been neglected for the past few years, so that the months no longer matched the seasons. Caesar inserted an extra two months into the year to bring the months into line with the seasons, and then established a new way of reckoning time, based on the Egyptian solar calendar of 365 and one quarter days, rectified by inserting one day every four years. It was not adjusted again until the eighteenth century.

At first there was little active opposition, since many of his adversaries had been removed in the wars, and many people were too weary of the upheavals of the past years to argue. He tried to foster good relations with the Pompeians who had surrendered to him, to win them over without bloodshed, and he extended his good will to the Italians and the provincials. For some time he had promised Roman citizenship to the Transpadane Gauls, and fulfilled this promise as soon as he could. Whether or not it was his main purpose to cultivate the loyalty of people such as these, he was able to extend his client base all over the Empire, just as Pompey had done via his wide-ranging campaigns.

In Rome, Caesar lost some of his popularity by inviting Cleopatra to stay in the capital. She may have arrived in time for his four triumphs in September 46, bringing their son Caesarion with her and her young brother, Ptolemy XIV. She set up her household in Caesar's villa across the Tiber, where Caesar visited her, giving rise to the rumours that he intended to marry her and make her Queen, and himself King of Rome. Many honours had already been voted to him, which he accepted graciously, such as the right to wear triumphal clothing and a laurel wreath on public occasions, very important distinctions in Rome. Up to now he had not shown any definite signs of wanting to become king, but one day a diadem denoting kingship appeared on the head of one of his statues. Two tribunes who may or may not have been guilty of placing the diadem were punished, and the situation was defused, temporarily.

For some years Caesar had been planning new buildings for Rome, financing them with the funds he had gathered while conquering Gaul. As Dictator he embarked on a programme of public works, which beautified the city of Rome and provided employment. The Forum Julii was one of these projects, dedicated in 46. Inside the new Forum there was the temple to Venus that he had vowed to the goddess at the battle of Pharsalus, and opposite the statue of the goddess he placed a gold statue of Cleopatra, which did little to assuage the suspicions that he intended to marry her and make her Queen.

Another project was to rebuild the Senate House that had been burned down in 52. He enlarged the Senate to 900 members, promoting some of the equites to senatorial rank, and admitting men from the Italian towns. These men who were promoted would owe him a debt of gratitude and would support him in the Senate, but then, ironically, there was little very senatorial debate about his measures. Caesar simply informed the senators of his decisions and then passed the laws. As Dictator he was entitled to direct the policies of the state, but it was all very irregular and Cicero complained that government was being carried out from Caesar's house. It was true, because Caesar had a lot to do and had neither time nor patience for strict Republican formalities. Some senators who had not been present at the meetings where the laws were presented found that their signatures had been added to them, as if they had given their consent. It was all too high-handed for strict Republicans, who had hoped for a return to the old way of doing things when the civil wars ended. It is unlikely that Caesar's opponents had ever been prepared to wait for the phase of Caesarian domination to end, hoping that, like Sulla, Caesar would content himself with passing his laws and then resign, but if they had ever thought along such lines they were to be completely disillusioned in February 44. The Senate made Caesar *Dictator perpetuus*, or Dictator for life.

THE IDES OF MARCH 44 BC

Caesar accepted the lifelong Dictatorship on 14 February. He had announced some time ago his intention of mounting a campaign against the Dacians and then the Parthians. Since 53 when Crassus was defeated and killed in Parthia there had been no time for retribution, but now it was possible to think of at least making a show of strength to redress the balance. Some of his contemporaries, followed by some modern historians, have accused Caesar of failing dismally to find a solution to the political disaster into which Rome had sunk, and running away to fight battles that would restore his reputation and glory. Whatever his reasons, Caesar had already prepared for the campaigns, and had sent the young Gaius Octavius to Macedonia to serve with the legions poised to march to the Danube and then to Parthia. He intended to leave quite soon, probably in March. If he went on campaign, and particularly if he was successful, he would return to Rome all powerful, and since he had secured many of the magistracies and a large number of senators, it might not be possible to annul all his legislation while he was away. There were some men who had already begun to think of ridding themselves of Caesar long before the situation reached this critical point. They would have to act soon.

On 15 February 44 the Romans celebrated the festival of the Lupercalia. It was an extremely old fertility rite, in which young men, wearing only a loincloth, ran around the streets of Rome, striking women with goatskin thongs, which was supposed to help them to conceive children, most especially sons who would fight for Rome. This year the consul Mark Antony took part, stripping off and running with the other young men, but carrying a diadem with him. When he reached Caesar's chair, Antony offered him the diadem, the symbol of kingship. Caesar refused it. The crowd roared its approval that he had rejected it. Antony repeated the offer, with the same result. No one can say with certainty how this scenario came about, whether Antony thought it up himself, or whether Caesar was behind it as a means of testing the reaction of the people, or to try to allay suspicion that he wanted to be king. All that it achieved was to deepen the distrust.

It was announced that Caesar was to leave Rome on 18 March. A meeting of the Senate had been called for 15 March, in Pompey's theatre.

On that morning Caesar felt ill, and his wife Calpurnia had a premonition of some disaster, so he very nearly decided not to attend, but his supposed friend Decimus Brutus came to his house and persuaded him to change his mind. The conspirators, comprising seemingly loyal Caesarians as well as pardoned ex-Pompeians, had chosen that date for their liberation of the state, so it would have been somewhat awkward if their victim did not turn up. They called themselves Liberators, and they had high standards. They decided not to kill Antony. Gaius Trebonius distracted him in conversation as he was about to enter the meeting room with Caesar. Inside, twenty-three conspirators met Caesar and all of them struck a blow with their daggers. Caesar fell dead at the base of the statue of Pompey. Senators who had no idea that there had been a plot fled to their homes, as did Mark Antony, where he barricaded himself in and probably waited for an attack. None came.

The incredible truth was that the Liberators had not made any plans except to assassinate Caesar. Once that was achieved they seemed to think that the Republic would bounce back into place, as if nothing had changed. They had not arranged for any of their number to take over and direct operations until everything had calmed down, for that would be to act as tyrannically as Caesar. They had considered the political problem solely from their own point of view as *optimates* and had not thought of what the reaction might be from the people. When they tried to make a speech explaining why they had killed Caesar, the people drove them off and they took refuge on the Capitol Hill. Consequently it was left to Antony to restore order, and it is to his credit that he did so without resorting to bloodshed, or allowing a witch hunt to develop to mow down the Liberators.

Mark Antony & Octavian

Antony and Aemilius Lepidus co-operated to blockade the Capitol and to bring soldiers to the Campus Martius. Antony called a meeting of the Senate for 17 March in the Temple of Tellus, which was conveniently close to his own house. In the meantime he rallied as many of Caesar's supporters as he could, including Caesar's secretary Oppius and his adherent and financier Cornelius Balbus. He also approached Caesar's widow Calpurnia, who gave him all her husband's papers. Faberius, Caesar's private secretary and full of useful information, readily worked with Antony.

The first concern at the meeting of the Senate was to put into effect a general amnesty. Cicero proposed it amid universal acceptance. Then the question of how to deal with the conspirators was considered. A murder had been committed and the perpetrators should be punished, but on the other hand if Caesar really was a tyrant, then the conspirators had performed a singular service to the state and should be rewarded. The problem was that even if Caesar was pronounced a tyrant it was not possible to annul all his acts. Most of the men in office had been placed there by Caesar, future appointments had been arranged in advance, and the provincial governors for the most part owed their position to Caesar. To cancel all this would mean setting up an entirely new government from scratch. His arrangements had to be left as they were. As Cicero wrote despairingly to his friend Atticus, the tyrant was dead, but the tyranny still lived.

On the day following the meeting of the Senate, Caesar's will was read. He had left money to every Roman citizen, and larger sums to some of the men who had killed him. One quarter of his fortune was to be divided equally between his nephews Pinarius and Pedius, but the vast bulk of it went to the youth Gaius Octavius, his great-nephew who was currently in Macedonia. That was not all. There was a codicil to the will, in which Caesar adopted Gaius Octavius as his son. The legality of this has been the cause of much speculation, both ancient and modern. Gaius Octavius was determined to take up his inheritance in full, and eventually he ratified his adoption, so that speculation about whether or not it was legal was squashed.

He arrived in Rome, probably in May 44, already calling himself Gaius Julius Caesar. Strictly he ought to have added Octavianus to the name to signify that he had been adopted from the Octavian family into the Julian clan. Octavian is the name by which historians know him, but he never used it himself. By the time of his arrival, Antony had abolished the Dictatorship, and he had arranged for the chief conspirators Marcus Junius Brutus and Gaius Cassius Longinus to leave Rome, even though they were still in office and ought to have remained in the city. They were given legitimate tasks so that it would not seem like banishment, but Cicero found it very demeaning that his heroes were sent to look after the corn supply in Asia and Sicily. Decimus Brutus was to be governor of Cisalpine Gaul and left to take up his appointment, so three of the conspirators were absent from Rome.

Antony's first meeting with Octavian, as reported by the historian Appian, was not a success, but the speeches invented for them serve to outline their personalities and the political situation. Antony was suspected of mixing up state finances with his own, because he had suddenly been able to pay off his not inconsiderable debts, and perhaps worse, he kept on producing schemes and proposals that he said he had found among Caesar's papers, which gave them slightly more authority than if he had presented them as his own ideas as consul.

The government of the provinces required attention, and the Senate confirmed in office most of the governors appointed by Caesar. Antony had been assigned to Macedonia, as part of Caesar's plan to invade Parthia, but this scheme was now redundant, and Antony preferred to remain within reach of Rome. He decided that as governor of Cisalpine Gaul he would be able to monitor events in the city, so he angled for that province, instead of Macedonia. The problem was that Cisalpine Gaul had been awarded to Decimus Brutus, one of the assassins of Caesar, and he had already taken up his post. For the time being Antony left him in control, but he was just as determined to gain the province eventually for himself. He placed his brother Gaius Antonius in command in Macedonia, with one legion, transferring the other four legions to his own command, ready for action in Cisalpine Gaul. He may have forgotten that Octavian had been with these legions for some time while waiting for Caesar to start his Parthian campaign, which made it easy for the young man to subvert them later on.

Octavian assisted Antony in exchanging his provinces, but in other respects he made life awkward for him. Antony had been careful to emphasize the value of Caesar the politician but had tried to suppress the memory of Caesar the Dictator. Octavian did not subscribe to this subtle distinction, and seized any advantage to proclaim himself as Caesar's heir. When he organized a series of games in honour of Caesar, a comet appeared, which was taken as proof that Caesar had become a god. From then onwards Octavian called himself *divi filius*, the son of a god. It is sometimes hard to remember that Octavian was only eighteen years old when Caesar was assassinated.

Gradually, Antony was portrayed as a potential tyrant. Octavian started to arm himself, gathering Caesar's veterans to protect himself against Antony. Then, listening to Cicero's virulent speeches denouncing Antony, the senators too were convinced of the need to raise troops to guard against his possible take-over of the state. Octavian already commanded troops, and only needed the authorization to use them. Cicero wanted to rid the world of Antony at all costs. He and Octavian made an alliance, and Antony, instead of marching on Rome as Cicero said he would, prudently went to his province of Cisalpine Gaul. He would have to fight Decimus Brutus to gain control of it, and there was no time to lose. He had only one month before his consulship ended, and then the Senate would empower the new consuls to take up arms against him, so he would be fighting on two fronts. He blockaded Decimus Brutus in Mutina (modern Modena).

In the spring of 43, the consul Aulus Hirtius marched northwards, reinforced by Octavian and his troops. Cicero had persuaded the Senate to confer a command on the young man. The other consul Vibius Pansa was on the way from Rome to join them. Antony decided to attack Pansa before the armies could unite. He routed the troops, and Pansa was wounded and died later, but Hirtius arrived before complete victory could be assured, and Antony withdrew. After a second battle at Mutina, Antony had to acknowledge defeat, and set off with his soldiers for Gaul. The governors of Transalpine Gaul and Spain were Caesarians, and might be persuaded to help him.

At Rome, it was considered that Antony was finished, and official thanksgiving was decreed. He was declared *hostis*, an enemy of the state, and Decimus Brutus was ordered to pursue him. Octavian was ordered to help Decimus, but seemed strangely reluctant to march or to relinquish command of any of his troops. Cicero thought that he would be able to use and control Octavian to eliminate Antony, and he made a clever pun about how the young man ought to be praised, honoured and immortalized, in Latin *laudandum adulescentem, ornandum, tollendum*. The word *tollere* can mean to raise up, and also to remove by death. Cicero was clever, but not clever enough to realize that, far from being able to use and then discard Octavian, the supposedly innocent youth had simply been posing as his friend in order to use his political prestige to gain a command. No one seems to have realized that Octavian would never, ever, assist one of the men who had assassinated Caesar, so it was a considerable surprise to Cicero and the Senate when Octavian arrived at Rome with eight legions to ask politely for the consulship.

The Senate was in no position to argue, and so at Octavian became consul, with Caesar's nephew, Quintus Pedius, as colleague. One of Octavian's first acts was to have his adoption by Caesar ratified by law. Confirmed now as Caesar's legitimate heir, Octavian made no secret of the fact that one of his main aims was to condemn all Caesar's assassins. They were all properly tried by court proceedings, even though they were absent. They were all condemned. This meant that they were outside the law, as Antony was. While Octavian marched north to pursue Decimus Brutus, Pedius revoked the law declaring Antony an enemy of the state.

After fleeing from northern Italy, Antony had made spectacular progress. He arrived in Gaul with his army in May 43, and had soon joined with Marcus Aemilius Lepidus. Between them, they commanded ten legions, but potentially they could find themselves fighting against the three legions of Munatius Plancus in Transalpine Gaul, and the two legions of Asinius Pollio in Further Spain. By the end of the summer both these governors had gone over to Antony, leaving Decimus Brutus defenceless against their overwhelming force. When Octavian arrived in northern Italy, he met Antony and Lepidus at Bononia (modern Bologna) and the three of them decided the future of Rome. They were careful to have their association ratified by law. On 27 November 43, the tribune Publius Titius passed the legislation to recognize them as 'three men appointed to reconstitute the Republic' (*tresviri rei publicae constituendae*). This is usually termed by modern historians as the second triumvirate, but officially there had never been a first triumvirate, merely an informal agreement between Pompey, Caesar and Crassus. Antony, Lepidus and Octavian were formally appointed with equal powers to the consuls for five years. They were empowered to make laws, and to nominate magistrates and the governors of provinces. Antony was to govern Cisalpine and Transalpine Gaul, Lepidus was to take control of Gallia Narbonensis and all Spain, Octavian was to control Sardinia, Sicily and Africa. Since they intended to declare war on the Liberators, they would govern their provinces via legates. The eastern provinces were not within their reach, since Brutus and Cassius had seized them and started to raise armies. The war would have to be carried across to the Mediterranean, just as Caesar had made war on Pompey the Great.

Before they could embark on a major war, the three men required the removal of the associates of the self-styled Liberators, and vast quantities of money. They proscribed seventeen men and posted up the lists, but many more names were quickly added and the result was organized mayhem. One of the motives may have been to seize property and therefore wealth, but the prime motive was the eradication of anyone who sympathized with the Liberators. Cicero was one of the first victims. If he had resolutely left Rome to join Brutus and Cassius, he might have survived, but he vacillated and was cut down near one of his villas. In a barbaric act of revenge, Antony had his head and hands nailed to the Rostra in the Forum, where senators stood to make their speeches.

The financial situation was in crisis, since Brutus and Cassius controlled the eastern provinces, so none of the revenues reached Rome. Compared to the east, the western provinces were not so wealthy, and so the heaviest financial burden fell on Italy. As for ready cash, the Triumvirs seized all the personal savings entrusted to the Vestal Virgins, and they revived old taxes and invented new ones, including a tax on wealthy women. This tax met with determined opposition from a deputation led by Hortensia, the daughter of the lawyer Hortensius, accompanied by Octavian's sister and Antony's mother. They protested that women had no voice in politics and therefore they should not be expected to pay for wars unless Rome itself was threatened. The tax was ratified but at a much reduced rate.

Time was of the essence, as the Liberators grew stronger in the east. Brutus captured and eventually killed Antony's brother Gaius, and Cassius reached the province of Syria before the Caesarian governor Dolabella could establish himself there. Cleopatra sent four legions to help Dolabella, but Cassius seized these too. The whole of the east would have to be won back by the Triumvirs. They also had to reckon with the pirate fleet of Sextus Pompey, whose presence in the Mediterranean endangered the corn supply, and hindered the transport of the Triumviral army from Italy to the eastern provinces. Fortunately for the Triumvirs, Sextus Pompey did not unite with the Liberators, but he had gained control of Sicily and early attempts by the Triumvirs to oust him failed dismally.

When the civil war began, Lepidus was left in Rome with some troops in order to keep control and ensure that no one tried to overturn the Triumvirs' legislation. Like Caesar before the campaign against Pompey, Antony did not have enough ships to take his whole army across the sea. Cleopatra sent a fleet from Egypt to aid the Triumvirs, but it was wrecked in a storm. However, the Liberators reacted to the news that she had despatched ships for Antony by sending their own fleet to search for them, which gave the Triumvirs the time they needed to send eight legions under Decidius Saxa and Norbanus Flaccus across the Adriatic to Macedonia. Antony's generals set off eastwards towards Thessalonika, and Brutus and Cassius moved into Thrace and then along the Via Egnatia to meet them. Antony and Octavian took advantage of a brief moment when the enemy fleet drew off and landed at Dyrrachium with the rest of their army. Norbanus and Saxa had established a base at Amphipolis, and Brutus and Cassius had camped to the west of Philippi. Antony marched to Amphipolis, left a garrison there, and took the army to reconnoitre the situation at Philippi. Octavian had to be left behind at Dyrrachium, because he was too ill to travel.

Antony did not attempt to mount a full frontal attack on the camps of Brutus and Cassius, but decided to cut the supply lines by building a causeway across the marsh to the south and come up behind the Liberators. While the work was proceeding, hidden from the Liberators, Octavian arrived, carried in a litter, too ill to ride but determined to be there. The battle of Philippi in late autumn 42 was a prolonged affair. It began with a skirmish when Cassius attacked Antony's troops and then Brutus joined in. The result was a stalemate, when Antony captured Cassius's camp and Brutus captured Octavian's, but did not capture Octavian himself, since he was hiding in the marsh. The stalemate may have persisted for some time but for the fact that Cassius believed that Brutus had been killed, and in despair he committed suicide. Nothing happened for about two weeks, then Brutus offered battle and Antony defeated him. When the body of Brutus was brought to him, he arranged an honourable funeral for him.

Octavian's part in the two battles had not been impressive, and the victory was truly Antony's, but Octavian was far from negligible in the political sphere. They were the two most powerful men of the Triumvirate, Lepidus being gradually eclipsed, but neither Antony nor Octavian could afford to make a separate bid for supremacy. They agreed that Antony would govern the provinces of Gaul via his legates, and also the whole of the east. Octavian would govern Spain, Sardinia, Corsica and Sicily, and Lepidus would control Africa. Octavian would have to fight for Sicily since

Sextus Pompey still controlled the island, and there had been rumours that Lepidus was seeking an alliance with him, so Octavian would have to tread carefully in Rome. His first major task would be to find lands for his discharged veterans, in fulfilment of the promise made to the troops when the Triumvirs had held their meeting at Bononia.

Antony remained in the east, repairing the damage that the Liberators had caused by extracting supplies and money. Some cities had been impoverished, others had tried to resist, but in the end they had all suffered. It was not only the cities of the Roman provinces that had been affected. The fragile relationships with rulers whose kingdoms bordered on the provinces also required attention. Unfortunately the sources do not elucidate Antony's arrangements in the east, as if all his activity had been expunged from the record. Greater emphasis is laid on the fact that he went to Athens for the winter of 42–41. In the spring of 41 he travelled to Ephesus, where he was hailed as the new Dionysus, the god of wine and beneficence, highly appropriate for Antony, who could drink anybody under the table and was ridiculously generous to his friends and acquaintances. The Romans did not approve of treating living persons as if they were divine, but in the east it was quite normal and Pompey had been treated in the same way when he campaigned against Mithradates. Antony's new found divinity would counterbalance Octavian's claims to be the son of the god Caesar.

At Pergamum, Antony met with delegates from the eastern states, and demanded ten years' taxes from communities which had already paid vast sums to the Liberators to support their armies. In response, he was asked if he could arrange a second summer and a second harvest, and in the end he settled for nine years' tax payable over two years. He needed to pay his troops and to supply them, no light task given the number of legions he had at his disposal. The ultimate aim was to mount the campaign against the Parthians that Caesar had planned, but for the time being he concentrated on making friendly overtures to the states which bordered the Parthian Empire.

One state in particular, which could scarcely be said to border on Parthia, was vital to his plans. Egypt was wealthy, possessing all the resources to supply food for the soldiers and to build a fleet of ships. Queen Cleopatra would be at least sympathetic to his needs. She had been placed securely on her throne by Caesar and she had tried to help the Triumvirs by sending soldiers and ships to fight against the Liberators. The question was how to approach her. Antony did not want to go to Egypt because it would place him in a subordinate position, so he sent an envoy to ask Cleopatra to come to meet him at Tarsus, in Cilicia (modern Turkey). She agreed, sailing in her famous Royal barge described by Plutarch at length and in superlative terms. Antony wanted financial assistance for his Parthian campaign. Cleopatra wanted recognition for herself and her son Caesarion as independent rulers of Egypt, and Antony was the man of the moment with all the power of the Roman world at his disposal. The two of them could do good business together, but not on Cilician soil. Cleopatra insisted that while she remained on her barge on the River Cydnus, she was still in Egypt, and Antony must come to her.

This famous meeting started out as a political expedient for both Antony and Cleopatra, but developed into an immortal legend. The historian Appian says that Antony was bowled over and fell in love instantly. This may contain an element of truth, but it was not their first meeting. Antony may have seen the teenage Cleopatra when he was a young cavalry officer in the army that Aulus Gabinius took from Syria to Egypt to stabilize the throne for Ptolemy Auletes. They may not have been formally introduced but Antony would certainly have known of her. When Cleopatra came to Rome as the guest of Caesar, Antony would almost certainly have been properly introduced to her, but she was firmly in Caesar's domain, and therefore out of bounds. Besides, Antony had just married Fulvia, the widow of his friend Curio who had been killed in Africa, and apparently he was in love with his wife. However long it took for Antony to realize Cleopatra's finer points as a woman as well as a political and financial ally, an association developed from the moment when they met at Tarsus. Their relationship transcended any formal alliance. But it played into Octavian's hands, when the time came to use it against Antony.

After their meeting, Antony attended to problems in Syria, and left Decidius Saxa in command when everything was settled. The sources are hostile to Antony and do not allow him any success, even accusing him of creating more problems than he solved, but it is significant that all was calm for some time thereafter. Sailing from Tarsus, Cleopatra returned to Egypt, where Antony joined her for the winter of 41–40. Their relationship as lovers was confirmed when Antony acknowledged as his own the twins that she had borne him, Alexander Helios (named for the sun) and Cleopatra Selene (named for the moon).

In Italy, Octavian was having more trouble than he had anticipated in finding lands for the veteran soldiers. He had begun well, trying to pour oil on troubled waters when the redistribution of land entailed evictions, but he met with active opposition from Lucius Antonius, Antony's brother, and Fulvia, Antony's wife. They said that Antony's veterans were being treated unfairly, but Octavian defused the situation by allowing Antony's men to supervise the proceedings. Lucius then took up the cause of the displaced farmers instead. The end result was a war, in which Lucius was blockaded in Perusia (modern Perugia). In February 40, the town was burned – no one seems to know who was responsible – and Lucius was captured. He was sent to govern Spain, but was accompanied by several of Octavian's supporters to make sure that he acted in accordance with their wishes. Meanwhile, Antony did nothing at all, so that nobody could decide whether he had instigated the whole event, or whether Lucius and Fulvia had acted with misguided zeal on his behalf, but without his knowledge. Seeds of distrust were being sown. Octavian was accumulating ever more power in the west. After the fall of Perusia and the capture of Lucius, many of the Antonians fled, including Antony's wife Fulvia, and his mother, Julia. Fulvia, accompanied by Munatius Plancus, arrived in Greece to meet Antony in Athens, with the news that Plancus's legions had gone over to Octavian. Another blow to Antony was the unexpected death of Fufius Calenus, the governor of Gaul as Antony's legate. Octavian quietly assumed command of Calenus's legions and sent his own man, Salvidienus Rufus, to replace him in Gaul.

Antony did not react immediately. He really needed to go to Italy to meet Octavian, but for the moment he had more pressing local problems to think about, because the Parthians invaded Syria, early in 40, killing the governor Decidius Saxa. Antony delegated his general Ventidius Bassus to restore order in Syria, and then in the autumn of 40 he sailed to Italy. In the meantime, Sextus Pompey had given refuge to Antony's mother as she fled from Octavian, and now Sextus proposed an alliance with Antony, who guardedly said he would agree to it if he could not make peace with Octavian, but if peace was arranged then he would try to reconcile the Senate and people of Rome with Sextus and his men.

Octavian and Antony finally met at Brundisium and settled their differences. War had been narrowly avoided. Antony left his wife Fulvia in Greece, where she died without ever seeing him again. He was accompanied by Domitius Ahenobarbus, originally the commander of the fleet raised by Brutus and Cassius, but now an ally. They found the gates of Brundisium closed against them, and assumed that this was on Octavian's orders. There was some skirmishing as Antony started to besiege the town, but the soldiers on each opposing side were not willing to fight each other. As far as they were concerned the two antagonists were both connected with Caesar and although their own loyalties were divided, the soldiers saw no reason for war. A treaty was made, redefining the division of the Roman world between Antony, who would from now onwards hold the east, relinquishing his command in Gaul, and Octavian, who would control the west. The two men then returned to Rome, where they were met by a relieved population. In order to cement their new alliance, Antony married Octavia, the sister of Octavian, who had been recently widowed. She would become the mother of his two daughters, both called Antonia, the younger of whom would in turn become the mother of three children, the celebrated general Germanicus, the future Emperor Claudius, and Livilla.

The Triumvirs were now in effect whittled down to two, even though Lepidus had not yet been entirely obliterated. One of their major tasks concerned the menace of Sextus Pompey, who had as yet received nothing from the arrangements made at Brundisium, and had reapplied his stranglehold on Rome's corn supply. There were riots in the city. The people implored both Antony and Octavian to put an end to the food shortages. At one point the mob threw stones at Octavian when he tried to speak to the people, and Antony had to rescue him. Neither Octavian nor Antony had enough ships to combat Sextus Pompey, whose crews were by this time far more experienced than any that the Triumvirs could assemble. Negotiation rather than war was the only alternative, so after a false start, the three men met at Misenum on the coast of Italy and another treaty was made in 39. The future now seemed more secure than it had done for some long years, but for a brief moment Antony and Octavian came very close to having their individual futures wiped out at one stroke, when they dined with Pompey on board his ship to celebrate making peace. When the banquet had begun, Pompey's admiral Menas suggested that they should cut the cables and sail away, dumping the two guests overboard when they were far enough out to sea. Fortunately for the Triumvirs, Pompey refused to stoop to such an action.

The terms of the treaty were that Sextus Pompey was to control Sardinia, Corsica and Sicily, which merely ratified the status quo because neither of the Triumvirs could claim complete control of these islands, despite Octavian's attempts to fight for them. In return for the territorial concessions, Sextus Pompey was to guarantee the corn supply for Rome. For the future, he was promised the consulship and control of the Peloponnese. Neither promise was fulfilled.

The Triumvirs had already filled all the main magistracies for 39 through to 36, and now they designated the men who were to hold magistracies for 35 to 31. They declared an amnesty for the men who had taken refuge with Pompey, and some of the magistracies went to them, in multiples in some cases, to reward them and give them administrative experience as well as rank. According to the historian Dio, in 39 there were more than two consuls, and in 38 there were sixty-seven praetors, presumably holding office for a short time and then relinquishing it. As a precaution against opposition, the Triumvirs had all their acts ratified by the Senate, by a law that was retrospective, stretching back to the beginning of the Triumvirate. It was a sort of insurance policy in case anyone took issue with their proceedings from their first meeting onwards. Antony and Octavian were also conscious of the fact that their powers had been granted for five years, and would soon be coming to an end.

In January 38 Octavian made a shrewd, politically motivated move. He had divorced his wife Scribonia in 39, on the day that she gave birth to his daughter Julia, and then after a scarcely suitable interval he married Livia Drusilla, who was well connected and would bring her connections to bear in recruiting allies from among the leading senators. Octavian was not deterred by the fact that Livia was already married to Tiberius Claudius Nero. She was also the mother of a young son, who would become the Emperor Tiberius, and she was pregnant with another child. Since the paternity of these children was not in doubt, and Tiberius Claudius Nero was willing to accommodate Octavian by divorcing his wife, the marriage went ahead and lasted throughout Octavian's lifetime.

Later in the year 38 the prospect of peace was shattered. Sextus Pompey had not received the Peloponnese, so instead of wasting time trying to fight for it he adopted his usual tactics of raiding the ships carrying food supplies to Rome. Octavian's response was to invade Sicily, but he was badly beaten and lost nearly all his ships, the first batch in a battle off Cumae, and most of the surviving vessels in a storm the next day. He was forced to ask Antony for help.

Antony had spent the winter of 39 in Athens, preparing for the Parthian campaign. His general Ventidius had restored order in Syria, and it remained to ensure the loyalty of the kingdoms and tribes of the east before the army set off to make war on the Parthian king, Pacorus. When Octavian's request for assistance arrived, Antony put everything on hold and sailed once again to Brundisium. There was no one there to meet him, so he sailed back, having pointlessly wasted a lot of time. He arrived in Syria in the middle of the summer. Ventidius had fought a battle with the Parthians at Gindarus in northern Syria, in which the Parthian king had been killed. The remnants of the Parthian army had taken refuge with the King of Commagene, Antiochus, at Samosata on the right bank of the River Euphrates. Ventidius marched there and laid siege to the place. Antony took over in autumn 38, and Ventidius returned to Rome to celebrate the triumph that he had undoubtedly earned. It was a personal triumph as well as a public one. The family of Ventidius had been on the losing side in the Social War, and as a child he had been paraded through the streets of Rome in the wake of Pompeius Strabo's triumphal chariot. Now he rode in his own triumphal chariot.

In the autumn of 38, Antony made peace at Samosata and returned to Athens for the winter, intending to resume his preparations for the Parthian campaign in the spring of 37. For the third time he was interrupted. Octavian's efforts against Sextus Pompey had failed once again, so this time Antony assembled 300 ships and sailed with them to Brundisium. According to the ancient sources, for the third time he could not gain entrance to the town, and sailed on to Tarentum, where Octavian met him. Antony gave up 120 ships to help Octavian in the struggle against Sextus Pompey, and received a promise of 20,000 soldiers for the Parthian campaign. The agreement that they made at Tarentum concerned more than just the immediate military needs of each commander. The

Triumvirate had technically ended in 38, five years after it had been formed, but the two men had continued to hold power unchallenged because their own men were holding the most important magistracies and the Senate had been so weakened by the proscriptions that there was hardly anyone left who would argue that in the eyes of the law, neither Octavian nor Antony was entitled to command armies or govern provinces. For the sake of appearances, they renewed their powers for another five years, and the necessary law was passed by the people's assembly in Rome. This removed the likelihood of any challenge to their authority and actions until the end of 33.

Antony now deferred the start of the Parthian campaign until the spring of 36, and wintered in Antioch in Syria, closer to the scene of action than Athens. He left his wife Octavia in Italy, looking after their infant daughter, the elder Antonia. Octavia was pregnant with another child who would be the younger Antonia, and she was also caring for Antony's two sons by Fulvia, Antyllus and Iullus Antonius. She was the perfect Roman mother, modest, forbearing and gentle. The contrast with Antony's immoderate behaviour, especially when he invited Cleopatra to come to Antioch for the winter of 37–36, made it easier for Octavian to blacken Antony's name. The perfect wife Octavia had been repudiated, and it seemed as though Antony had turned his back on Rome. His close association with Cleopatra could be portrayed as treachery.

The Parthian campaign of 36 went badly for Antony, but the naval campaign that Octavian mounted against Sextus Pompey was a resounding success. Octavian's most successful and loyal general, Marcus Vipsanius Agrippa, had spent some time building a new fleet and training the crews in an artifical harbour that he had constructed. Agrippa joined two lakes together by removing the strip of land that separated them, and spent most of the year 37 and the early part of 36 building up the expertise of the sailors and soldiers until they were ready to face Sextus Pompey. Agrippa adapted the grappling iron called the *harpax* that could be catapulted onto enemy ships to draw them close enough to board. He had added protective covering on the ropes that were attached to them so that the enemy could not cut them and break free. This intensive preparation and training eventually paid off, after some reverses on land in Sicily, and an indecisive sea battle off Mylae. Then Agrippa finally brought about the success that Octavian required in September 36, at the naval battle of Naulochus.

The victory elevated Octavian to new heights in Rome, save for an unpleasant episode when the third and forgotten Triumvir, Lepidus, tried to gain control of Sicily. He had gained control of the cities that Sextus Pompey had taken over, but unfortunately Lepidus had failed to realize the persuasive powers of Octavian, the affection that the legions had for him, and the money that he promised them. The soldiers deserted Lepidus, and he had no choice but to surrender. Octavian spared his life, allowed him to retain his office as Pontifex Maximus, and kept him closely watched in Rome for the rest of his life.

Octavian was the man of the hour in Rome, showered with tremendous honours voted to him by the Senate and people, and yet more power, this time that of the tribunes. It is debatable whether he was granted full tribunician power at this time or whether the achieved it by gradual stages, but it was to become the mainstay of his own and all future emperor's imperial power. Tribunes were sacrosanct and could direct and modify all public business. The consulship was an important office which Octavian certainly valued, but he did not hold it on a permanent basis, whereas he never relinquished tribunician power. The problem is that he counted his tribunician years only from 23, not from 36, which seems to indicate that in 36 he had not yet been granted the whole panoply of tribuncian power.

As Octavian went from strength to strength, successfully removing the threat to the grain supply and conveniently close to the Romans so that he was able to mould them into his supporters, Antony remained far distant, achieved little against the Parthians, and was scandalously associated with, perhaps even married to, the Queen of Egypt. The rumour that he may have married Cleopatra probably started in Antioch. The pair were hailed in the east as the embodiment of the Egyptian gods Osiris and Isis, or the Greek deities Dionysus and Aphrodite. All this was very shocking, especially as Romans were forbidden marry foreigners. No one knows for certain whether Antony and Cleopatra had taken part in some sort of ceremony that could be construed as a wedding, but their relationship was consummated while they were at Antioch, and their son Ptolemy Philadelphus was born the following year. If there had been a splendid victory over the Parthians, Antony may have been able to redeem himself, but his timing was not right. In the previous year, the Parthian royal house was in turmoil after the death of Pacorus, and the new king, Phraates, was busily killing off all his relatives who might have been able to challenge him. Antony had more than once delayed the start of his campaign in order to come to the aid of Octavian, and consequently he had lost the chance to exploit the distracting mayhem among the Parthians.

When he finally started the campaign, Antony drew up his army at Zeugma in north-eastern Syria, as if he intended to invade at that point, significantly opposite Carrhae where Crassus had been killed, but instead he made a dash northwards to march through Armenia and Media, hoping that the Parthians would assemble in the wrong place and he could attack them from the north. The plan failed because he was stalled in Media trying to besiege the capital at Phraaspa, and had to retreat, through the horrendous terrain and bitter wintry weather of Armenia. He lost many of his men, and finally left the army with his generals Domitius Ahenobarbus and Canidius, while he travelled ahead to the Syrian coast, sending messengers on ahead to Cleopatra, asking her to meet him with clothing, food and money. She gathered the supplies and set off in person, probably in January, risking her life in an inadvisable winter sea voyage. It may not have been true love, but it was certainly devotion.

There was no question of mounting a campaign against Parthia in 35. The army would have to be rebuilt and he needed money. When his wife Octavia arrived in Athens with supplies, soldiers and cash, Antony did not go to meet her, but simply sent her a message, directing her to send on the money, supplies and troops. He went to Alexandria with Cleopatra. It was not a sound policy. By maltreating his wife he had broken with Octavian, and even worse, he had chosen instead to link himself with the Queen of Egypt and all things eastern. The road to war was open.

CIVIL WAR

It was perhaps not inevitable at this stage that another civil war would break out. Rifts had been healed before, but there was no room for powerful rivals in Octavian's ambition for himself and for Rome. He had already neutralized Lepidus. It would be harder to neutralize Antony, but for the fact that Antony himself gave Octavian so much ready ammunition to fire back at him. In his preoccupation with his tasks in the east, Antony ignored Rome, where he ought to have been exercising the same level of self-advertisement as Octavian. His agents were ineffective, giving Octavian the chance to eclipse him. In 34 Antony was consul, but *in absentia* and only nominally for one day, relinquishing the office in favour of other candidates. He mounted a campaign against Armenia, hoping to consolidate his power in that kingdom so that he could attack Parthia. His conquest of Armenia has been belittled, but it was sound enough, even if not permanent, and Antony issued coinage with the legend *Armenia Devicta*. This was wholly in keeping with the Roman ethos, and it would have greatly assisted Antony's cause if he had celebrated his victory in Rome, dedicating the spoils of war to Jupiter in the temple on the Capitol. Instead Antony chose to celebrate it in Alexandria. He held a parade through the streets of the city, perhaps not intending to make a mockery of the Roman triumph, but it was easy to interpret it as such.

If the street parade had been the end of the matter, the episode might have been forgotten, but the next day Antony sealed his fate with Octavian and Rome. He held another celebration, known as the Donations of Alexandria. Seated on a dais with Cleopatra at his side and their children before them, Antony bestowed on them kingdoms and territories of the east. Alexander Helios was to rule Armenia, Media and Parthia, even though the last two kingdoms were not yet within his gift. Cleopatra Selene was given Cyrenaica and Libya, and Ptolemy Philadelphus, still an infant, was to rule Syria and Cilicia. What was more threatening, from Octavian's point of view, was Antony's proclamation of Caesarion as the true heir of Caesar.

Octavian was engaged in campaigns in Illyricum, to give him military prestige to match Antony's and also to give him legitimate grounds to command armies. He could not yet expect to stir up the populace and the troops to go to war against Antony, most especially since he had announced an end to civil wars when Sextus Pompey had been defeated. On the other hand if he delayed, it was possible that Antony would go on to defeat the Parthians and exact revenge for the death of Crassus. In that case he would be a hero, and there would be no cause to make war on him. Octavian began a political campaign against Antony. He made much of the shameful treatment of Octavia, who had done nothing to warrant desertion, but this was only personal and hardly a basis for war. As consul in 33 Octavian tested public feelings with a speech against Antony, but he shifted most of the opprobrium onto Cleopatra, portraying Antony as her bewitched consort. Cleopatra was foreign and a legitimate enemy. It was rumoured that she went about saying that she would one day issue her orders from the Capitol. Clearly, said Octavian, she harboured an ambition to take over the whole Roman world, and Antony would help her.

In the autumn of 33 Antony abandoned any idea of a Parthian campaign and turned away from the east, focussing on Rome. He started to prepare for war against Octavian, but tried to soothe public feeling in Rome by offering to lay down his triumviral powers if Octavian did the same. The Triumvirate was probably due to end in December 33 anyway, although the date is disputed. If this was so, then in 32 neither Octavian nor Antony was entitled to command armies, but like Pompey and Caesar before them, they were too powerful to be stopped.

The consuls of 32, Sosius and Domitius Ahenobarbus, were both Antony's men, but they were overwhelmed by Octavian's determination to block them. He convened a meeting of the Senate where he arrived with his bodyguard, forcing his way in to seat himself between the two consuls. The illegality of his actions was ignored. He said he had obtained documentary evidence to condemn Antony and would produce it at the next meeting. It precipitated a mass exodus. The consuls and about 300 senators fled to Antony. The Roman world was once again dividing itself into two opposing camps.

About 700 senators remained with Octavian, and some of Antony's men came to Rome, sensing that they might be on the losing side if they stayed in the east. It was said that two of them revealed to Octavian that Antony had lodged his last will and testament with the Vestal Virgins in Rome, so Octavian seized it and read it out at a meeting of the Senate. Antony reaffirmed Caesarion's status as the heir of Caesar, granted legacies to his children by Cleopatra, made his son Antyllus his own personal heir, and finally expressed a wish to be buried in Alexandria with Cleopatra.

Octavian did not advocate war openly, but allowed the indignation of the Senate and people to speak for him. He also took the precaution of having all the inhabitants of Italy swear an oath of allegiance to him, save for the towns such as Bononia where Antony had many clients. It was an unprecedented gesture which gave Octavian the moral support to make war on Cleopatra, and by default on Antony.

The war was fought in Greece. Antony strung his army out to watch the inlets and harbours on the western coast, concentrating on the Gulf of Ambracia, where two projecting peninsulas almost encircled the waters of the gulf. In the spring of 31 Octavian sailed to confront Antony there. Most of Antony's fleet was now bottled up in the gulf. For several months, Octavian's army and Antony's faced each other on the northern and southern sides of the gulf, while Agrippa steadily annihilated Antony's troops on the islands and coasts. The morale of Antony's army sank lower and lower as malaria and dysentery decimated them. Desertions began, and Antony's punishments for indiscipline and betrayal grew more and more severe. Finally, he decided to try to break out with the fleet through the narrow entrance to the gulf, and make for Alexandria, leaving the army under his general Canidius to march overland to Egypt.

The result was the much discussed battle of Actium, often used as a turning point in the civil war and the establishment of Octavian as sole ruler of the Roman world. As a battle it was not deeply significant. Cleopatra escaped carrying the treasury and after desultory fighting Antony followed, transferring from his doomed flagship to a boat and then to Cleopatra's vessel. Most of his ships were captured or sunk. When they arrived in Egypt, Cleopatra entered Alexandria with flags flying as though they had won a great victory, while Antony hid himself away in a hut on the shore.

It was certain that Octavian would follow. He had already purchased the Antonian troops in Greece, except for their commander Canidius, who preferred to join Antony in Egypt. Cleopatra tried to revive Antony, but although he participated in her plans and joined in the drinking revels, he knew he was beaten. Octavian allegedly offered lenient terms for Cleopatra if she would surrender Antony, but she refused. She probably distrusted Octavian, knowing that what he really needed was access to her treasure and the wealth of Egypt. The people were prepared to go to war on her behalf, but she refused to embroil them in death and destruction, knowing that Octavian would have no interest in them beyond gathering their tax payments.

When Octavian appeared in Egypt in 30, Antony took some of his troops to meet him, hopelessly outnumbered. His cavalry routed Octavian's advance guard, and he came back to Alexandria to celebrate, but it was only a matter of time. The soldiers and the fleet went over to Octavian. Antony watched the mass desertion and rode into Alexandria to find that Cleopatra had locked herself into her mausoleum, and was probably already dead. He fell on his sword, but did not die immediately. The story goes that he was hauled up into the mausoleum to die in Cleopatra's arms. It may be true. It may also be true that after a few days, Cleopatra was bitten by the asp hidden in the basket of figs, and died willingly rather than be led as a captive in Octavian's triumph.

Caesarion, the son of Cleopatra and Caesar, had been sent away to try to ensure his safety. He was pursued and killed, as was Antony's son Antyllus. There the vendetta ended. Antony's younger son Iullus Antonius, and the three children of Antony and Cleopatra, were all spared. Octavian was undisputed sole ruler of the Roman world. Arriving at this point had been difficult and protracted; now he needed a legitimate means of staying there.

8

Octavian Augustus: The Republic Becomes an Empire 30 BC–AD 14

There is no firm agreement about the date when the Republic ended and the Empire began, so the choice of 30 BC as the date when the Republican government became Imperial rule is somewhat arbitrary. Various events have been suggested as the turning point: the battle of Actium in 31, the fall of Alexandria in 30, January 27 in Rome when Octavian offered to return the government to the Senate, and the developments of 23 when Octavian-Augustus was ill and forced to think very seriously about the succession. But in reality there was no sharply defined moment of history when everything changed, because it was an evolutionary process rather than a sudden change of tack. What went on before the Empire was formed was similar to what came after, with small adjustments made over a period of time while Octavian consolidated his position.

After the fall of Alexandria in 30, Octavian was the wealthiest, most influential and most important man in the Roman world, and Rome controlled a large extent of territory that included Sicily, Sardinia, Corsica, Spain, Gaul, Illyricum, Macedonia, Achaea, Asia, Bithynia, Syria, Cyrenaica, Crete, Cyprus, Africa and latterly Egypt. This last province provided a large part of Octavian's wealth and from the very beginning it was treated differently from the other provinces. The first governor was Cornelius Gallus, an equestrian, responsible to Octavian, and when the world was more settled and Octavian's position was ratified, that was how it remained, throughout the Empire. The Prefect of Egypt was always an equestrian appointed by the Emperor. No senator was even allowed to set foot in Egypt without Imperial sanction, much less become the governor of such an important province.

The wealth of Egypt enabled Octavian to pay his troops and arrange for the settlement of veterans. Before he marched to Alexandria he had already discharged some veterans and either paid them off or purchased land for them, settling the bill out of his own pocket. He recouped the expense once he gained control of Egypt. It is estimated that at the end of the civil war he commanded sixty legions, having acquired all of Antony's soldiers as well as his own. This was far too many to keep under arms, so he established colonies for veterans in Italy, Gaul and Spain, finally reducing the number of legions to about twenty-eight.

Octavian needed the army to shore up his power, but he could not afford to make a great display of military support. He required legal backing, freely bestowed and not coerced, if he was to remain at the head of state. At the time of his victories over Antony and Cleopatra, he had saved Rome and brought peace, so for the time being he was a hero and was as secure as it was possible to be. Numerous honours were voted to him throughout his career, but as he pointed out in the *Res Gestae*, the memoir that he left recording his achievements, he did not accept all of them, especially if he deemed them inappropriate for his age or experience. These honours formed an important part of his supremacy but did not provide him with the long-term legal basis that he required. He was unassailable in 29, because he was consul for the fifth time. On 1 January of that year all his acts were confirmed by the Senate. As consul, Octavian remained in the east attending to the organization of the provinces, the frontiers and the relationship with the territories that bordered on Roman territory. It was not necessary to undertake a thorough revision of Antony's arrangements for the east, but during the civil war, some cities and kingdoms had supported him, while others had sided with Octavian. Rewards and punishments were decided upon, outstanding debts were collected, or reparations made for those communities which had suffered. An understanding was reached with Parthia, Rome's most powerful neighbour.

Later in the year Octavian returned to Rome and celebrated three triumphs on three separate days, from 13 to 15 August, over Illyricum, where he had waged war largely to keep an army together and rival Antony over Cleopatra, and for the victories at Actium and Alexandria. There was no overt mention of Antony in the triumphs, but his memory was damned, monuments bearing his name obliterated, and his birthday, 14 January, was declared *nefastus*, when no public business could be transacted. For the following year, 28, Octavian entered his sixth consulship with his friend and general Marcus Vipsanius Agrippa. The two men were granted the powers of the censors, and undertook the first census of citizens for twenty-eight years. They also revised the list of senators, rejecting some but also promoting men who were deemed worthy of inclusion. If they lacked the necessary wealth, Octavian provided it. As for himself he was made the leader of the Senate, *princeps senatus*.

All this was very prestigious but not permanent. The consulship was still an annual office and, although he was to be consul for the seventh time for 27, there would surely come a time when he would either have to relinquish the consulship and rely on his moral supremacy, and the tribunician sacrosanctity that had been voted to him, or incur the suspicion that he intended to keep a hold on consular power for ever, and suffer the possible consequences. He had already been offered and had refused the Dictatorship, and now it was no longer appropriate because there was no state of emergency which would justify the appointment. Although he had enjoyed what he called spontaneous universal support when all Italy took the oath to him at the start of the civil war with Antony, there were some dissidents. He could not afford to provide them with any cause to challenge him, and if he continued to rely on the consulship to put forward his ideas for government of Rome and the Empire, his potential enemies would have a greater opportunity to build up a case. It has been suggested that throughout his life opposition to him was minimal, but it may have been a different story if he had not been sensitive to the way in which the Romans conceived of and abhorred the domination of one man.

Embarking on his consulship in 27, Octavian made a speech on 13 January, offering to hand back power to the Senate and people, thereby restoring the Republic. The Senate promptly handed it back. A compromise was arranged. Octavian would govern the provinces of Gaul, Spain, Syria, Cilicia and Cyprus, and Egypt. These provinces were either close to foreign powers and therefore potentially threatened from time to time, or they were areas where internal strife might at some time break out. In either case, they would all require the presence of an army, and Octavian would be the commander of those armies. Government would be carried out via legates personally chosen by Octavian, which gave him the opportunity to appoint men whom he trusted and who would owe their advancement to him. According to the size and importance of the province these governors differed in rank, those with two or more legions being entrusted to ex-consuls, less important provinces to ex-praetors. Whatever their rank, all these legates were titled *legati Augusti propraetore*, expressed on inscriptions in abbreviated form as *leg. Aug. pp.* In the fully evolved system, smaller Imperial provinces with no legion but housing auxiliary troops, would be governed by equestrian prefects, including Egypt. For Octavian, this was power even greater than Pompey had received when he was put in charge of the war against the pirates, but it was not yet permanent, since a prudent time limit of ten years was set on Octavian's command.

The remaining provinces were to be governed by the Senate. All governors of senatorial provinces would be called proconsuls, whether or not they were of praetorian or consular rank, and some of them would command armies. There is some evidence, not without dispute, that Octavian could issue commands to the proconsular governors of senatorial provinces, but the technicalities of how this was done are not established. He may have held legally based consular or proconsular power, or he may simply have maintained an influence over the whole Empire that gave him the moral if not the legal right to interfere in non-Imperial provinces. This summary by no means reflects the amount of scholarly debate that surrounds this topic.

The day after this seminal speech of 13 January was Antony's birthday, which was *nefastus*, precluding the transaction of any public business, and on the day after that there was a religious festival, so it was not until 16 January that the Senate could deliver its vote of thanks. Munatius Plancus suggested that Octavian should now be addressed as Augustus, the name by which he is known to posterity, and which was adopted as a title by succeeding emperors. The name had no connotations of magisterial office or political power, but it was a tremendous honour, connected to *auctoritas*, the full meaning of which is nowhere near properly conveyed by the English translation 'authority'. It suggested power, but was distinct from *potestas*, which contained a more arbitrary element.

Many more honours were voted to Augustus, signifying his supremely elevated position in the Roman world. He accepted them gracefully and took them seriously, including the *corona civica*, or civic crown awarded for saving the lives of citizens. His previous history of eliminating the lives of citizens was tactfully avoided. The honours were important but not guaranteed to preserve power, a point which Augustus was in any case anxious to avoid. He chose to represent himself as first among equals, and eventually adopted the title *Princeps*, for which there was an established precedent when Pompey took the title. Augustus was already *princeps senatus*, or first senator, but *Princeps* was distinct from that, denoting much more.

The first challenge to Augustus's supremacy came in summer 27, when Marcus Licinius Crassus, the grandson of Crassus who was killed in Parthia, claimed the title of *Imperator*, and a triumph for his military success in Moesia. He had personally killed the enemy leader in battle, and also claimed the honour of *spolia opima*, that of dedicating the dead man's weapons and armour to Jupiter. Augustus objected, though on what legal grounds is suspect, and though Crassus held his triumph he was denied the other honours. From then onwards the old Republican tradition of successful generals holding a triumph in Rome was limited to members of Augustus's family, and the adoption of the title *Imperator* by commanders outside the Imperial family, and even sometimes within it, was regarded with suspicion, if not an attempt at usurpation.

The next challenge came in 23. Augustus had left Rome for the provinces in 27 and stayed away for nearly three years. In 24 he arranged the marriage of his daughter Julia with his nephew Marcus Claudius Marcellus, the son of his sister Octavia and her husband Gaius Claudius Marcellus. It was the first attempt to found a dynasty. Then in 23 Augustus fell seriously ill. Never in the best of health, this time it was thought that he might not recover. He gave his signet ring to his trusted friend Marcus Vipsanius Agrippa. Significantly, Agrippa was the only one of Augustus's circle who came near to sharing his power, indicating the high regard that Augustus held for him.

He would have been the only man besides Augustus himself who could have commanded the armies and earned the respect of the Senate, but if Augustus had died at this point, even he may not have been able to establish himself as ruler of the state. Marcellus, Augustus's son-in-law and being obviously groomed for succession, was considered too young and inexperienced, and certainly not yet ready to take on the task.

By the summer of 23, Augustus had recovered, but from that time onwards he relinquished the consulship. This may have come about because he was physically unfit, and because he realized that by this time he did not need the office, or as some of his contemporaries suspected, a conspiracy was discovered. The details are obscure, and no one knows what the so-called conspirators hoped to gain. The main suspects were executed and everything was smoothed over.

The nature of Augustus's power is the subject of debate. In return for the consulship, which he never held again save for those years when he wanted to introduce his grandsons to the business of ruling, he was awarded *imperium proconsulare*, the powers of a proconsul. The disputed factor is whether this *imperium* was equal to all other provincial governors, or whether it exceeded that of the proconsuls and propraetors. In the end the argument is largely academic, since Augustus clearly wielded much more influence than other officials, and was entitled to command all the armies. He would not have wished to advertise this so blatantly, nor would he have wished to use his military power to force through what he wanted to achieve. As a military commander, he could not legally cross the *pomerium*, the city boundary, without laying down his powers, so a special law was passed to exempt him from this inconvenience. At the same time it tacitly proclaimed to all other commanders that the privilege did not extend to them and they had to obey the old law.

TRIBUNICIAN POWER

The mainstay of Augustus's rule, and that of all succeeding emperors, was tribunician power. He had already been granted the sacrosanctity that went with the office, but he may not have achieved the full panoply of tribunician power until later, perhaps in separate stages, or perhaps all at once in 23. Since he was not of plebeian origin, he could not hold the actual post of tribune, but the power and the office were separated so that he could wield the power without being tribune. He bestowed this power on no one else except Agrippa, and later in his reign he granted it to Tiberius. *Tribunicia potestas*, abbreviated on inscriptions to *trib. pot.*, gave him the right to veto any proposals from whatever source, but with the important exception that Augustus was not subject to the veto of other tribunes. He did not use his veto, but the possibility that he could do so if he wished perhaps served to keep the senators compliant, and at the same time reassured the populace that the senators could not oppress them without meeting opposition from Augustus. It was a neat solution to retaining power after he had relinquished the consulship, and it did not require frighteningly novel ideas. Augustus established the basis of Imperial rule, but he did it by embedding it in Republican tradition.

AUGUSTUS'S REFORMS

Once he was assured of supreme, unchallenged, and above all legally established powers, Augustus could attend to the government and administration of the Empire, and the well being of the various classes of people who made up the Empire. Everything about the state required attention: the city of Rome, the provinces and the frontiers, the army, the senators and the equestrian order, the people and religious matters. This is not to imply that Augustus had achieved nothing in these areas since the fall of Alexandria, but he could now make long-term plans, even though he avoided the notion of permanence and still subscribed to annual or periodic renewal of his powers.

In any brief overview of Augustus's achievements from 23 until his death in AD 14, it is easy to convey the impression that from the very beginning he had a fully developed plan for the formation of Imperial government, which he was merely waiting for an opportunity to put into place. He may well have been aware of the broad outlines of what he wanted to do, but there was no unimpeded direct line to the finished product. There were military conquests, taking Roman control up to the Danube area, and there were diplomatic successes, such as the carefully negotiated return of the captured standards of Crassus's army from Parthia in 20, an event which is depicted on the breastplate of the famous statue of Augustus from Prima Porta. But there were setbacks and near disasters as well, and Augustus could not achieve all that he wanted to do without loyal allies. Agrippa worked tirelessly on Augustus's behalf, turning his hand from everything from military conquests in Gaul to beautifying the city of Rome and attending to its water supply and sewage system. Livia's sons, Drusus and Tiberius, spent many years campaigning on the Rhine and Danube, and Tiberius fought long and hard putting down the Pannonian revolt and tidying up after the German revolt of AD 9.

Augustus came to power at a relatively young age and despite his constant ill-health, he lived until his late seventies. The long life that Augustus enjoyed or endured was his greatest asset in reforming the state, because he was allowed the time to work slowly and persuasively rather than hurriedly and arbitrarily imposing his will on a reluctant Senate. Like Julius Caesar, he could discern what was wrong and in need of reform, and could suggest the remedies, but he did not resort to Caesar's dubious methods of forcing ideas through by issuing laws and appending signatures of senators who had not even been present at discussions. After the turmoil of the civil wars, Augustus was careful to keep well within the law, avoiding the concept of permanent or limitless power in the hands of one man, even if it meant that he had to backtrack now and again. *Festina lente*, hurry slowly, was one of Augustus's maxims.

THE SENATE, THE EQUESTRIANS & THE ROMAN PEOPLE

In his dealings with the Senate, Augustus realized that it was necessary for senators to feel that they had some stake in government, otherwise they would either sink into apathy, or erupt in revolt. Gradually, he laid the foundations of a more structured career path for senators, which his successors could develop and refine. Julius Caesar had increased the size of the Senate to 900 members, but Augustus reduced it to a much more manageable figure of 600. Sulla had made the quaestorship an automatic entry to the Senate, and this rule was preserved, but Augustus raised the property qualification for senators from 400,000 sesterces to 1 million sesterces, so only the wealthiest young men, theoretically immune from corrupt practices to gain the office, could hope to become quaestors. Senators were distinguished by the broad purple stripe on their togas, and their sons, who belonged to the equestrian order until they too entered the Senate, were allowed to wear a narrow purple stripe on their togas. Before the age of twenty-five, the sons of senators could seek various junior appointments, which were not rationalized until several decades after Augustus's death. Then they would probably serve as quaestors, then aediles, then praetors, with a gap of some years between posts, so that no one could reach the consulship until he was about thirty-three. This was an improvement on the old Republican system, where men did not normally become consuls until the age of about forty-two. There were various posts for ex-praetors, some of them in the gift of Augustus himself, such as legionary legate, or *legatus Augusti propraetore* or governor of a praetorian Imperial province. There were also posts as governors of the praetorian senatorial provinces, though these carried the title of proconsul. Ex-consuls could look forward to governing an important senatorial province such as Asia or Africa, or an Imperial province. In most cases each man would have to be known to, and trusted by, Augustus.

For the equestrians too, there were opportunities for promotion, especially in Egypt, where Augustus and succeeding Emperors excluded all senators. The legionary commanders in Egypt, and the governors, called prefects, were always equestrians. Augustus also created three more prefectures for equestrians. In 2 BC he transformed his personal bodyguard into the Praetorian Guard, and appointed the first two Praetorian Prefects, who shared the command. Towards the end of his reign he appointed other prefects, of the *annona* or food supply probably in AD 8, and the *vigiles*, the combined police force and fire service, which was formed in AD 6.

For the people of Rome, a secure and constant food supply was one of the most important considerations. The somewhat piecemeal attention that had been given to it in the past was only successful in overcoming short-term problems. There was no continuous policy or relevant personnel dedicated to the food supply. Augustus created a permanent system for its administration, supervised by the equestrian *Praefecti Annonae*, who organized the storage of food from Italy and the provinces and supervised its distribution. Gaius Gracchus had instituted the monthly allocation of grain to the people of Rome at a price below the market value, and the tribune Clodius had removed the charge so that grain could be distributed free to the poor who qualified for the dole. Julius Caesar reduced the number of recipients, and Augustus finally settled on a figure of 200,000.

The phrase 'bread and circuses' has entered modern terminology in connection with conciliating the populace, and Augustus was no exception to the rule. Lavish entertainments had always been laid on by many prominent Romans but, according to Suetonius in his biographies of the first emperors, they were all completely outdone by Augustus, who paid assiduous attention to games and shows, including gladiatorial combats, athletics and sports festivals, and theatrical performances. Like their modern counterparts, the ancient Romans would have loved football, television and opera. These festivals and celebrations served several purposes, not just as entertainment and diversion, but also in fostering unity, and a sense of a brilliant past and a brilliant destiny. Sometimes festivals were of a religious nature, such as the Secular Games in 17 BC, hailed as the beginning of a new era. The shadow of the civil wars of the last few decades was obliterated by the promise of peace and prosperity.

THE PROPAGANDA MACHINE & THE IMPERIAL CULT

Outward display, literature and art were all commandeered in Augustus's scheme, not just in Rome, but all over the Empire. The representation of Augustus himself as ruler has been thoroughly investigated by more than one modern author. Coin portraits and sculptures were widely distributed throughout the Roman world as part of the positive propaganda concerned with Augustus as saviour. It was an integral part of this propaganda that he was always presented as a youthful figure, despite the fact that he lived to a ripe old age. If he had allowed himself to be portrayed as an older man his credibility may have been destroyed, so even on coins issued late in his reign he appeared as he had always done. In the ancient Roman world there was nothing like the glaring searchlight of newspaper and television media attention, where he could not have avoided the visible evidence that he was ageing.

Augustus controlled his own publicity department via the visual imagery that was produced, and also in literature. Leading Republican Romans often gathered around them literary circles and some like Pompey the Great became the patrons of various writers and artists. Through his equestrian friend Maecenas, who likewise gathered around him poets and literary men, Augustus utilized the system for the benefit of himself and Rome, employing several writers, among them poets such as Horace (Quintus Horatius Flaccus) and Virgil (Publius Vergilius Maro) to celebrate Rome and its past. Both these men were Italians rather than native Romans, demonstrating the social mobility that had begun in the later Republic and which Caesar and Augustus promoted. Publius Vergilius Maro, more commonly called in modern times Virgil with an 'i' instead of an 'e', was a native of Mantua, and was the elder of these two poets, born in 70 BC. His *Eclogues* and *Georgics* venerate the rustic life, and his great work, the *Aeneid*, celebrates the greatness of Rome, linking the city with ancient Troy. Aeneas and his son Anchises escape the fall of Troy and make their way to Italy, encountering various obstacles on the way, like the Greek hero Odysseus in Homer's *Iliad*. Although the work looks back towards a historical perspective, it is not an accurate portrayal of the foundation of Rome, but refers to the new Augustan age. In the sixth book, Aeneas visits the realm of the dead, where the future of Rome is told to him.

Horace was born in 65 BC in Venusia (modern Venosa) in Apulia, the son of a freedman who had amassed a fortune sufficient to provide Horace with a typical upper class Roman education in Rome and Athens. Horace was on the wrong side in the civil war between the forces of Brutus and Cassius and those of Antony and Octavian, but escaped unscathed, and was recruited by Maecenas before Octavian and Antony went to war with each other. Horace celebrates the rule of Augustus bringing peace and well-being, but not with the customary sickening flamboyancy of overt panegyrics.

The Imperial cult of emperor worship had several different roots that Augustus joined together to produce a system which demonstrated certain unifying elements, but varied in practice and method in different parts of the Empire. There were precedents when Pompey was treated as a living god in the east, and Julius Caesar was deified after his death. As Caesar's heir Octavian-Augustus presented himself as the son of a god. In Rome and the west, the worship of a living person was not the norm, but in the east it was customary. Soon after the battle of Actium, Octavian-Augustus allowed the Greeks to worship himself and the goddess Roma, but Roman citizens who may have been uncomfortable with this worshipped instead the deified Caesar and Rome. In the west, the Imperial cult was established some time later. It started in Spain where altars to Augustus were set up from about the year 25 BC. The cult spread to Gaul, then to Germany, appearing in Italy after the dedication of the temple to Mars Ultor, Mars the Avenger, in 2 BC. The cult was not imposed on any community, but its development relied on local initiatives that were then endorsed and encouraged. Sacred altars were established at Lyons for the Three Gauls, and another for the tribe of the Ubii on the Rhine, at a place which was called literally the altar of the Ubii, *Ara Ubiorum*. Later a colony was founded there by the Emperor Claudius, and the place was renamed *Colonia Claudia Ara Agrippinensium*. The modern name for the city simply commemorates the first element of the title, *Colonia*, as the city of Cologne. There were no temples at Lyons and Cologne, only the altars, where priests called *sacerdotes* officiated at the ceremonies dedicated to Augustus and Rome. The Imperial cult provided another unifying influence, but since it took some time to become embedded in provincial life and administration it was probably of more benefit to the successors of Augustus than to Augustus himself.

THE ARMY & THE FRONTIERS

Although there had been several armies in the field on a more or less permanent basis during the period of the civil wars, there was no standing army before the reign of Augustus. After the battle of Actium and the fall of Alexandria, the major task facing Octavian-Augustus was to reduce the numerous armies to a manageable size, which entailed the discharge of time served soldiers and settling veterans on the land or pensioning them off. When this process was complete there were about twenty-eight legions still in existence.

There was a need for legions and auxiliary troops to keep the peace in the provinces, and to protect the frontiers where Rome met tribes and communities not yet absorbed into the Empire. A more pressing requirement for troops, but not one which was overtly proclaimed, was to provide support for Octavian's regime, and for all succeeding Emperors. When Octavian made the gesture to return the government of Rome and the Empire to the Senate in 27 BC he emerged as governor of most of the provinces which contained armies, with only a few areas where senatorial governors could command troops. Since the appointment of the legates of legions and the commanders of the auxiliary units remained within the gift of Augustus, and since he could also intervene in senatorial provinces, the loyalty of all troops was directed to him. It became the norm to swear an oath of allegiance to the Emperor on enlistment, and to renew it annually at a parade on the reigning Emperor's birthday.

Once Augustus was secure as supreme commander, he could begin to rationalize the organization of the army. This process was extended over a number of years and did not spring fully fledged from a couple of all-embracing decrees passed in any particular year, so what is described here is the evolved form of the army, developed from the foundation created by Augustus. Each legion was given a number and a name, but some of them already possessed such forms of identity, for instance V *Macedonica* had been formed during the latter days of the Republic, and V *Alaudae*, 'the Larks', was one of Caesar's legions, and neither of them wished to give up their numbers and names. There was therefore some duplication of numbers, with the result that although there were twenty-eight Augustan legions they were not labelled from I through to XXVIII.

Pay and length of service was eventually standardized, in stages from13 BC onwards. The Republican soldiers were eligible for service for a period of sixteen years or sixteen campaigns, so Augustus used the same principle to set the terms of service for the legionaries of the standing, professional Roman army, who were under arms for twenty years, that is for sixteen years and then as veterans in reserve for another four years. They were paid 225 denarii per annum, in three instalments, with deductions for food, clothing, the burial club and savings. At the end of their service, they were given pensions instead of lands, from a military treasury (*aerarium militare*) that was set up by Augustus in AD 6, financed initially by 170 million sesterces from his own funds and thereafter from taxation, in this case a 1 per cent tax on sales at auctions, and 5 per cent on inheritances. From AD 14 when Augustus died there was finally an end to the redistribution of lands on which to settle discharged veterans, which had plagued the Republic every time a victorious general returned home. Provided with their pensions, some of the veterans set up businesses, or bought farms on their own initiative. The scheme was designed to prevent crowds of penniless and aimless veterans from wandering around the countryside and endangering the public in Italy and the provinces.

The command structure was adapted to the needs of a permanent army, stationed sometimes far from Rome. The legionary legates of Caesar's day were commanders appointed by him on a more or less temporary basis according to the current location and the nature of the campaign. Augustus appointed legionary legates, usually senators who had served as praetors in Rome, and who would be over thirty years old. They would stay in their posts for a few years and then move on. Next in rank was the *tribunus laticlavius*, literally the broad stripe tribune, another man of senatorial rank, but younger and less experienced than the legate. Continuity was provided by the next most senior officer, the *praefectus castrorum*, or the prefect of the camp, who would be a professional soldier and would have served in the legions for a long time. Prior to this post he had usually been promoted to senior centurion, the *primus pilus*, literally 'the first spear'. Ranking above the senior centurion were the five equestrian officers serving as tribunes, distinct from the senatorial tribune, and designated *tribuni angusticlavii*, or narrow stripe tribunes. Commonly described as the backbone of the army were the sixty centurions commanding the sixty centuries, containing not one hundred men as the title suggests, but eighty men. These were grouped together into ten cohorts, six centuries in each, but there is no evidence that there was ever a cohort commander in the legions, so the centurions were the men upon whom the senior officers depended.

The legionaries were all Roman citizens, but at this period this did not mean that they all came from Rome itself. As time went on citizenship was extended to individuals and communities throughout the Empire, and until the third century at least there seems to have been no lack of them to fill the gaps in the legions, which were filled mostly by volunteers, although in especially stressful times the Romans had to resort to conscription.

The auxiliary troops of the Imperial army were not Roman citizens. Their organization was based on the Republican system of recruiting soldiers from among Rome's allies. If campaigns were fought in foreign countries, the same principle was applied, and troops were provided by rulers or states who were attached to Rome. These men would fight under their own officers, and would go home when the wars ended. At Augustus's death in AD 14 the *auxilia* was not fully established, so it was left to his successors to complete what he had begun. In the evolved system, the auxiliary troops consisted of cavalry units called *alae*, and infantry units called cohorts, each 500 or 1,000 strong, and mixed units combining some mounted men and some foot soldiers, called *cohortes equitatae*. The commanders of these units would follow a prescribed career path, beginning with about three years as an infantry cohort commander and working up to the command of a cavalry unit of 500 men. There were only a few 1,000 strong cavalry units and no province had more than one; the commander of these units was an important officer who could expect to go on to further military commands and civilian posts.

The auxiliaries may have been paid at the same rate as the legionaries, though this is very much discussed by modern scholars. They served for 25 years, and on discharge they received pensions and Roman citizenship, which at first was extended to their children, even though they were not supposed to marry while serving in the army. Later on, these privileges were reduced.

The legions and the auxiliary troops were stationed in the provinces where internal policing was necessary, or where the frontiers required vigilance and sometimes armed combat. In the Augustan period, the camps and forts where the armies were housed were not of a permanent nature and had not yet attained the regular layouts of the later Imperial era. When wars broke out troops could be moved to the war zone, and extra troops could be recruited, for instance in AD 6 when the Pannonian revolt

1. The timeless symbol of Rome: the She-Wolf who rescued the twins Romulus and Remus. This is a copy in the EUR Museo della Civiltà Romana; the original is in the Palazzo dei Conservatori on the Capitoline Hill in Rome, complete with the rotund twins who were added *c.*1510 by Pallaiuolo. This famous bro nze sculpture dates from the fifth century BC, made by an Etruscan artist who was influenced by the Greeks. No one knows where the wolf was located until the tenth century AD, when she was given a home in the Lateran Palace. She was brought from there to the Capitol in 1471.

2. The Pons Fabricius, the bridge spanning the gap between the Campus Martius on the left bank of the Tiber, and the north-eastern side of the Tiber island. This bridge is the most ancient of all the bridges still in use in Rome. It dates from 62 BC, probably replacing an earlier timber bridge. Its builder was Lucius Fabricius, who recorded his work by means of two inscriptions, one on each side of the bridge. There was a tremendous flood in 23 BC, which may be the reason why the consuls of 21 BC examined the structure, declaring it to be safe, and recording their results in another inscription.

3. The Forum Romanum, viewed from the Palatine Hill. The arch of Severus stands in the centre of the photo and to its right the oblong, unadorned brick building is the Senate House. In 52 BC the earlier Senate House was burned down when the Roman people were rather too zealous in giving their benefactor Publius Clodius a good funeral. Julius Caesar planned a new building as part of his whole new Forum complex, which was completed by Augustus. The present building is a restored version of the Senate House of the late third century, when many buildings were repaired or rebuilt after a fire. The new building followed the same the ground plan of its predecessor, save for the brick buttresses projecting from the long sides.

4. The Temple of Hercules in the Forum Boarium, the Cattle Market, near the Tiber. Its dedication to Hercules is not proven, and because of its round shape the temple is often attributed to the goddess Vesta. It dates probably from the later second century BC, and was repaired in the first century AD.

5. The Forum Romanum viewed through the arch of Severus, looking towards the Palatine Hill. Next to the free standing column can be seen the ruins of the Rostra, where politicians made speeches to the people. Beyond that are the remains of the circular white Temple of Vesta.

Right: 6. The famous statue of Augustus from Prima Porta in Italy, now in the Vatican Museum. In 20 BC Augustus arranged for the return by the Parthians of the Roman standards captured from the army of Marcus Licinius Crassus in 53 BC. It was a diplomatic coup of the highest order, achieved without going to war, and Augustus had the event commemorated on the breastplate of his statue.

Below: 7. View of the Flavian amphitheatre in Rome, better known as the Colosseum, the largest amphitheatre in the Roman Empire. The columns in the foreground belong to the Temple of Venus and Rome, built by the Emperor Hadrian. The Colosseum takes its name from the colossal statue of Nero which was demolished to make way for the new amphitheatre. In AD 70 the new Emperor Vespasian began to build this vast monument, still under construction when he died in AD 79. By then it was three storeys high, and the Emperor Titus added the fourth storey, formally opening the building in AD 80. It was repaired several times in the third, fourth, and fifth centuries, revealing its importance to the Roman people and successive emperors. The photo shows a section of the outer wall on the left, still at its original height, and the ruined interior wall. There was an earthquake in 1349, when portions of the outer wall tumbled down, the stones providing a quarry for other building works in Rome.

8. The arch of Titus at the end of the Forum Romanum, where the road from the Colosseum joins the Via Sacra coming down from the Palatine Hill. It was built to commemorate the conquest of Judaea and the capture of Jerusalem in AD 70 by Vespasian's son Titus, who was emperor from AD 79 to 81. Titus died before the arch was finished and the inscription records him as Divus, divine, after his deification by his brother Domitian, who succeeded him in AD 81 and dedicated the arch, probably in the following year. Since the arch once formed part of the medieval defences of Rome, it suffered considerable damage, but it was taken apart and sensitively restored in the nineteenth century.

9. The old-style facade of the Pantheon in Rome, still showing the inscription recording the building erected by Augustus's friend Marcus Vipsanius Agrippa. Behind the classic portico with its eight granite columns is the Rotunda, built by the Emperor Hadrian and his architects. It is a circular building with a hemispherical, coffered dome, an architectural and engineering achievement that would tax even modern builders with their more advanced equipment and materials. The name Pantheon indicates that the temple was dedicated to all the gods. In the middle ages it was used as a Christian church.

10. Hadrian's mausoleum on the bank of the Tiber in Rome. Like the mausoleum of Augustus, it would probably have been surrounded by a columned arcade, and topped with a conical roof. The foundation stones were laid in the AD 120s, but the building was not completed until AD 139, by Antoninus Pius, a year after Hadrian's death. The ashes of Hadrian and his wife Sabina, and those of most of the families of Antoninus Pius and Septimius Severus were housed in this mausoleum, but no trace of them has survived. The Emperor Aurelian incorporated the mausoleum into the city walls of the late third century. The modern name of the monument, Castel Sant'Angelo, derives from medieval times, when the mausoleum was used as a fortress and prison, and a papal refuge. It is linked to the Vatican by a corridor built in the thirteenth century.

11. A well-preserved section of Hadrian's Wall at Walltown Crags in Northumberland, England. The Emperor visited Britain in AD 122 and perhaps surveyed the route of the wall himself, as part of his policy of calling a halt to further expansion and attending to the consolidation and protection of the parts of the Empire that could be feasibly held. The new British frontier was 80 Roman miles long, running from Bowness on Solway in the west, to Wallsend on the River Tyne in the east. For much of its central sector it followed the north-facing heights of the geological feature known as the Whin Sill across the Pennines. It took several years to build, and was subject to changes of plan, the final form comprising seventeen forts, fortlets known as milecastles (a modern term invented for the buildings) situated 1 Roman mile apart, and two towers, or turrets between each milecastle. It has been labelled 'overkill' by modern historians.

12. Preserved remains of one of the milecastles on Hadrian's Wall, at Cawfields in Northumberland. There were two gates, one on the north side through the Wall and one on the south. On either side of the central road connecting the gates, there were usually barrack blocks, and the full complement of the fortlet was probably one century of eighty soldiers. When the Antonine Wall was built further north in Scotland, by Hadrian's successor Antoninus Pius, some of the forts and the milecastles soon went out of use as fully occupied garrison posts. They were not fully reoccupied when the frontier was once again brought back to the line of Hadrian's Wall. Some of the milecastles were used for metal working or other occupations.

13. The Hadrianic frontier in Germany was built of timber, of which there was a plentiful supply, unlike the north of Britain, where stone was plentiful but trees were scarce. This is a reconstructed section of the frontier in Germany, showing what the palisade may have looked like, with a ditch in front of it. There was a series of small forts, called *Kleinkastelle* in German, approximating to the milecastles of Hadrian's Wall, situated just behind the palisade. There were also watch towers at short intervals to guard the frontier – see the photo of the reconstructed stone-built watchtower of the German frontier.

14. Reconstructed stone-built watchtower of the German frontier. Earlier timber towers running along the line of part of the German frontier may have been built in Flavian times by Vespasian or Domitian, but it was Hadrian who consolidated the frontier and marked it by a continuous palisade with watchtowers like this one accompanying it.

Above: 15. The arch of Septimius Severus in the Forum Romanum in Rome, with its inscription recording his victories and titles, and those of his son Caracalla. The inscription states that the arch was set up by the Senate and People of Rome on the occasion of the restoration of the Republic, not literally, since the emperors still ruled, but the civil wars with the two usurpers Clodius Albinus and Pescennius Niger had been won by Severus. The panels over the smaller flanking arches, two on each side, all very much worn away, represent significant events of the Emperor's campaigns. The two panels on the side shown here, facing away from the Forum Romanum, portray scenes from the Parthian war, specifically the attack on the city of Seleucia and the capture of Ctesiphon.

Right: 16. One of the towers of the gate at the legionary fortress of Castra Regina (modern Regensburg) in Germany, which was strongly fortified after the destruction caused by the Marcomanni in the late 160s AD. A building inscription dated to AD 179 records the construction of defences with gates and towers (*vallum cum portis et turribus*). The gateway resembles the Porta Nigra at Trier which also dates to the late second century, and as at Trier, the Regensburg gate would originally have had two towers flanking two arches. The gate survived because it was incorporated into the Bishop's Palace at Regensburg.

17. Provincial towns also started to think about building walls in the later second century. At Caerwent (Venta Silurum, capital of the Silures) in Wales, earthwork fortifications may have been erected in the second century, replaced in stone in the more turbulent late third century, when other towns in Britain were being fortified. This is the best preserved of several projecting interval towers of the south wall of Caerwent. The towers were probably added after the walls had been built, most likely in the mid-fourth century.

18. Part of the defences of Senlis in France. The walls and towers are very similar to those at Beauvais, Soissons and Amiens, indicating that there may have been a corporate programme of fortification in Roman Gaul, most likely under the Emperor Probus who reigned from AD 276 to 282. The invasions of Franks and Alamanni in the AD 260s had caused tremendous destruction, and the Emperor Aurelian and then Probus made strenuous efforts to repair the damage. The projecting drum towers at Senlis were spaced 30 metres apart, with the bases of each tower filled up solid to the level of the wall walk, so that it would have been very difficult to break through. Sixteen of the original twenty-eight towers survive. The two depicted here were incorporated into the twelfth-century Royal Palace, and one tower had a fourteenth-century oratory added to it.
Photo J.T. Taylor.

Right: 19. Late Roman tower at Comagena (modern Tulln) in Austria, a rectangular fort on the right bank of the Danube, named after its garrison, the *ala I Commagenorum*. The first fort on this site was probably founded by Domitian, with earth and timber ramparts, which were rebuilt in stone by Trajan. It was partially destroyed on two occasions in the third century, and again in the second half of the fourth century. In the late Roman period several forts on the Danube had projecting drum towers added to the walls, but it is rare that they survive to this height. It is known as the *Salzturm*,

Below: 20. The Great Court or peristyle in Diocletian's Palace, Split. The arch supported by four granite columns marked the division between the private and public areas. This was the main reception area, a rectangle flanked by columns leading up to the arch, where Diocletian and his officials would make their public entrances. The court was built in the florid eastern style customary in Syria and Asia Minor, where many of the workmen came from.

21. Head from the colossal marble statue of the Emperor Constantine, on display in the courtyard of the Palazzo dei Conservatori in Rome. The statue was once housed in the western apse of the Basilica of Maxentius in the Forum Romanum. The Basilica was completed by Constantine himself. He may have been originally portrayed wearing an oak wreath, as suggested by the alterations to his hairline visible on the carved head. He radiates calm and confidence, with his gaze fixed on otherworldly concerns. The statue was about 10 metres high, but not much of it survives – apart from the head seen here, the remains of one arm, one foot, the right hand and a knee are also on display.

22. The arch of Constantine viewed from an upper storey of the Colosseum. Like the arch of Severus in the Forum Romanum it has a central arch flanked by two smaller ones. It was dedicated in AD 315 on the tenth anniversary of Constantine's reign, and celebrates the defeat of Maxentius at the battle of the Milvian Bridge in AD 312, though the inscription in the top central panel merely mentions the defeat of the tyrant, without naming Maxentius. Some of the relief sculpture dates from Constantine's day, but much of the arch was assembled from reused panels and roundels from other monuments, traditionally from the reigns of Trajan, Hadrian and Marcus Aurelius, with the original emperor re-carved to look like Constantine.

23. The Basilica of Maxentius, running along the right side of the Via Sacra as it descends from the Palatine Hill into the Forum Romanum in Rome. It was begun in AD 307, and completed by Constantine after AD 313. In style it departed from the usual aisled basilica design, and resembles the various monumental bath buildings in construction. Only half of the building survives, the other section having been destroyed probably in the ninth century when there was a serious earthquake.

24. The Basilica at Trier (ancient Augusta Treverorum) in Germany, built by Constantine on the site of an older palace, which may have been the headquarters of the procurator of the provinces of Belgica and Upper and Lower Germany. When Trier became one of the provincial Imperial capitals, a new administrative building was needed, where the emperor held court and gave audiences. It was to be on the grand scale, very imposing, tailored to fit Constantine's self-image, and it is the largest surviving late Roman building of its type. In the twelfth century the ruined hall became the residence of the archbishops of Trier, and it was restored to its former glory in the nineteenth century, when it was converted into a church. Photo J.T. Taylor.

25. Cavalry soldiers usually opted for large imposing tombstones, sometimes showing the horseman riding over a stylized long-haired barbarian. Others like Longinus Biarta, depicted here, represented themselves enjoying the afterlife in the top panel (not shown here) and as cavalryman in the lower panel. There is considerable detail in this relief sculpture. Longinus is probably exercising his horse, with all its trappings, on a long rein, with his shield slung over the saddle, which is clearly displayed. It used to be thought that the Romans did not use saddles, but enough evidence has now been assembled to be certain that they did. There were no stirrups, but the horns of the saddle kept the rider in place. This tombstone from Cologne is very similar to other two-part tombstones, in particular the one for Marcus Aurelius Durises from Mainz, which is also divided into two panels, showing the horse in the lower one in very similar pose to that of Longinus. Perhaps there was a pattern book of designs to choose from.

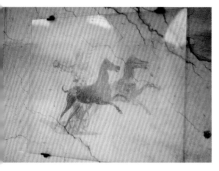

26. Wall painting of a charioteer in Ostia, one of a pair still in situ on the first floor corridor walls of the apartment block which is named after them, the House of the Charioteers.

27. Finely detailed black and white mosaics adorn many of the floors of buildings in Ostia. The artist was obviously familiar with elephants.

28. A street scene in Ostia in Italy, showing the multi-storey apartment blocks, some of which are preserved up to the second or even third level. According to legend, Ostia at the mouth of the Tiber was founded by King Ancus Martius, or Marcius, to provide a harbour for Rome. The town was fortified in the fourth century BC, temples and houses began to appear in the third century and by the first century BC the warehouses, for which Ostia is famous, had been established. Claudius built the harbour north-west of the town, and Trajan enlarged it, so Ostia functioned for a long time as the port for Rome, and much of the food supply was brought in through the town.

29. The peristyle and garden of the House of the Vettii at Pompeii. It was owned by two brothers, Aulus Vettius Restitutus and Aulus Vettius Conviva, who redecorated the house after the earthquake in AD 62, making it famous for its wall paintings in Pompeian Fourth Style. Photo J.T. Taylor.

30. The House of the Faun at Pompeii, arguably the most famous and one of the most sumptuous houses of the city, if not of the Roman world. The house was originally a modest Samnite dwelling, converted into a large mansion in the second century BC. The dancing faun stood in the larger of the two *atria*, which led into the dining room, and then into one of the two peristyles, a rectangular enclosed garden surrounded by an arcade supported by columns which can be seen in the photo. The house is renowned for its art work, wall paintings and mosaics, one of which is the famous mosaic showing Alexander in battle against Darius, King of the Persians. It is now in the National Museum of Naples.

31. A *thermopolium* at Herculaneum, an equivalent of a fast food cafeteria and wine bar, of which there were several extant examples at Pompeii and Herculaneum. The shop counters were usually arranged in an L shape, or like this one round three sides, equipped with sunken terracotta pots called *dolia* from which a variety of hot and cold food was served. Some establishments had rooms where customers could sit down to eat and drink. Photo J.T. Taylor.

32. The arch at the ancient town of Glanum in France, possibly dating to the end of the reign of Augustus. It is not well preserved, having lost the upper sections. The carved figures show captured arms and armour, and Gaul personified as a woman, in submissive pose. Photo J.T. Taylor.

33. The Roman aqueduct at Segovia, Spain. The people and the cars provide the scale for this truly massive piece of architectural engineering. Photo J.T. Taylor.

34. The north facade of the Porte de Mars at Reims (ancient Durocortorum) in France, the largest arch in the Roman world. The arch was incorporated into the Roman city defences, and used as the north gateway. The other three gates have disappeared. In medieval times the Porte de Mars was covered in earth to form the base of a castle, only being rediscovered in the seventeenth century. As a result of its mistreatment it has lost its upper storey, and the carvings are extremely worn, but the sculpture is important for the so-called reaper relief on the inside of the central arch. This depicts a reaping machine, a wheeled vehicle with long teeth at the front, pushed by a horse and guided by a man. The teeth ripped through the crop and pulled off the heads, which were collected in a basket. Considerable doubt attached to the interpretation of this carving, but it corresponds to a description of such a machine written by Pliny. Doubt was dispelled when another relief was discovered in Belgium, showing the same kind of reaper. Photo J.T. Taylor.

35. Amphitheatre at the *canabae legionis*, or civil settlement outside the legionary fortress at Carnuntum on the Danube in Austria, between the modern towns of Petronell and Bad-Deutsch Altenburg. It was excavated in the nineteenth century and there are sufficient remains to identify the entrances and seating. There was also an amphitheatre for the legion outside the fortress, but nothing can be seen of it today.

36. Remains of the amphitheatre at Salona (modern Solin), near Split in the former Yugoslavia. The remains have been robbed and consequently are not as substantial as those at Trier, but the circuit is almost complete, save for the encroachment made by a road and some modern buildings on the west side. Salona was the most important city on the province of Dalmatia. It was a Greek foundation, taken over by the Romans in the first century BC.

37. Most cities and larger towns possessed a theatre for the performance of plays and entertainments. Theatres were usually built on the Greek pattern, the seating arranged in a semi-circle facing the stage, which had a straight rear wall. This is the theatre at Orange (ancient Arausio) in France, dating from the first century BC. All that remains of the rear wall is the stone work, but originally there would have been rows of columns forming the *frons scenae*, usually laid out as a street scene with houses or other buildings. The action of the plays was normally set out of doors. Photo J.T. Taylor.

began on the Danube, conscription was applied in Italy, and the future Emperor Tiberius gathered a large army, including legions brought in from the east, to put the rebellion down.

Though the Roman world had boundaries in Republican times and in Augustus's day, there was no concept of frontiers in the form of running barriers dividing Roman controlled territory from other lands ruled by client kings allied to Rome, or where Rome perhaps influenced but did not direct affairs. That came later under the Emperor Hadrian. In the first days of the Empire the Romans subscribed to the theory of constant expansion, *imperium sine fine* or power without end, in both the territorial and the temporal sense. Towards the end of his reign Augustus abandoned this idea. In AD 9 the German tribes beyond the Rhine, seemingly pacified and ready for Roman settlement and consolidation, suddenly erupted under their leader Arminius, who had served in the Roman army and therefore understood the way in which the military men functioned. He trapped and annihilated three Roman legions, and the Romans pulled back to the Rhine. Augustus advised his successor Tiberius not to try to expand the Empire beyond its current boundaries. Later emperors ignored the advice and added territories here and there, sometimes for reasons of defence, or for economic gain, or both.

THE SUCCESSION

There was a continuous problem about the succession and what would happen to the Empire after Augustus's death. As sole ruler of the state, Augustus did not accept power on a permanent basis. Instead it was renewed in five or ten year batches, neatly avoiding the hated concept of kingship or the domination of one man. In 13 BC his powers were bestowed on him once again for another term of five years, expiring in 8 BC, when he would be fifty-five years old. He was the only man in the Roman world with the relevant political and military experience to govern, and above all he was the man who had earned the faith and support of the Roman people. He tried to ensure that his chosen heirs also earned the same support, demonstrating that they were worthy of the power to govern.

The major problem that he had to overcome was that the hereditary principle had not yet been applied to the government of Rome. Possessions, legal status and even personal influence could be passed down to heirs, but not political power. It was therefore a matter of introducing a successor and ensuring that the Senate and people of Rome, and above all the army, accepted the chosen heir. Augustus's dilemma was that all his designated heirs died young, giving rise to the suspicion expressed in some ancient sources, and utilized to great effect by Robert Graves in *I, Claudius*, that Livia had poisoned or otherwise despatched them all in favour of her own son Tiberius. A contributory factor to the demise of Augustus's heirs, with or without interference from Livia, is that in a country with a hot summer climate, no refrigerators, but a lot of mosquitoes, death at a relatively young age was not uncommon in Roman families. Despite the fact that Graeco-Roman medical science was relatively advanced, doctors could not always combat food poisoning, malaria, contagious diseases, or accidents, none of which have ever been known to respect youth.

Augustus's first choice of heir, his nephew Marcellus, died late in 23, leaving Augustus's daughter Julia a widow. She was then married off to Marcus Vipsanius Agrippa, and together they produced three daughters and two sons, Gaius and Lucius, who were adopted by Augustus and groomed for succession. They were introduced at an early age into public life, under his supervision. Augustus had not held the consulship for some time but he entered on his twelfth term of office when Gaius was consul in 5 BC. Three years later in 2 BC he took up his thirteenth consulship with Lucius as colleague. The boys were gradually given more responsibilities, and were accorded certain honours, but nothing too much or unsuitable for their abilities or experience.

Unfortunately Lucius, the younger of the two boys, died in AD 2, and Gaius died two years later. In AD 4, Tiberius, who was back in Rome after his self-imposed exile in Rhodes, but without any particular office, was brought back into the government, receiving tribunician power for ten years. In the summer of that year, Augustus adopted as his own sons Tiberius and Agrippa Postumus, the son of Marcus Vipsanius Agrippa and Augustus's daughter Julia. Agrippa Postumus was so named because he had been born after the death of his father in 12 BC, and he was almost alone in the world, since his mother Julia had been banished in 2 BC after a notorious sexual scandal.

In his turn Tiberius adopted his nephew Germanicus, the son of his brother Drusus, who had died in Germany in 9 BC. There were now potentially four successors to Augustus: Tiberius and Agrippa Postumus in the first rank, and Germanicus and Tiberius's own son Drusus, in the second rank. Of them all Tiberius was the man who was most experienced, and Germanicus was the man who was the most popular. Once again the succession did not go according to plan. Agrippa Postumus was allegedly involved in a plot and banished in AD 7.

On his way to Capri in AD 14, Augustus fell ill. He reached Nola, where he owned property, and prepared for the end, gathering his friends around his bed to ask if they had enjoyed the performance. On 19 August the greatest showman and most astute psychologist of the Roman world died, to take his place among the gods of the Roman world shortly afterwards when he was deified. His adopted son Tiberius reluctantly inherited the government of the Empire.

9

Julio-Claudians:
Tiberius to Nero AD 14–68

THE EMPEROR TIBERIUS AD 14–37

Tiberius was an outsider, being of purely Claudian stock, while Augustus, Caligula, Claudius and Nero could trace their ancestry through both Claudian and Julian bloodlines. Although Tiberius had been associated with Augustus since childhood, and eventually marked out for the succession after all the other candidates had died, he was very reluctant to take on the task. He was in his mid fifties, not experienced in politics or the social life of Rome, but he knew enough of the world to realize that governing the Empire was going to be difficult. He had no precedents to fall back on, since hereditary succession had not yet been fully established, and though Augustus had reigned for such a long time that the Republic was all but forgotten, it lived on as an ideal in the minds of some men.

Tiberius's reluctance to take on the government of the Empire was variously interpreted, as were most of his actions. It seemed that he was simply being coy about it so that the Senate would implore him to take command, or that he was trying to imitate Augustus in 27 BC. There may have been no subterfuge at all. Tiberius could never dissemble as Augustus did, nor hide his true feelings. His sense of responsibility ensured that he did become Emperor, but he did not accept with a good grace and smiling countenance, and thereby crystallized his reputation for churlishness. It did not help that one of the first actions of his reign was the execution of Agrippa Postumus, banished some years before by Augustus. It may have been Augustus himself who ordered Postumus's death, but the bad odour attached itself to Tiberius.

For many years Tiberius had been absent from Rome, usually with the army. He was in Armenia in 20 BC when the Parthians ousted the Roman candidate for the throne, and from 15 until 6 BC he was almost continually on campaign, in Raetia and Noricum north of the Alps, in Illyricum and Germany. When these campaigns ended he took himself to Rhodes, allegedly because he felt overshadowed by the promotion of Gaius and Lucius Caesar. He was also unhappy in his marriage, which had been forced on him by Augustus. When Marcus Vipsanius Agrippa died, his widow Julia, Augustus's daughter, was thus eligible to marry again. She and Tiberius were treated as pawns in Augustus's scheme to provide for the succession, so they were thrown together in a marriage that neither of them desired or enjoyed. If they had liked each other, the dynastic problems might have been overcome, but they most definitely did not like each other, and the only offspring born of the ill-fated marriage did not survive. What made it worse for Tiberius was his enforced estrangement from his beloved wife Vipsania, the daughter of Agrippa. This marriage had been very happy and at the time of the divorce Tiberius's son Drusus was still an infant. If Tiberius was as embittered as the ancient historians said he was, this was one of the reasons.

Modern historians have reinstated Tiberius by concentrating less on his sensational idiosyncracies and more on the political and military history of his reign. When Augustus died, the Roman world was leaderless, potentially ripe for another power struggle and civil war. The historian Velleius Paterculus comments on the narrow margin between the preservation of stability and the possible descent into chaos. But there was no war, no chaos and no opposition from the Senate, the Praetorian Guard or the people. Everyone kept their heads, in both the figurative and physical senses.

Tiberius, a soldier and commander, had a firm grasp of the realities of power. Immediately after the death of Augustus, Tiberius made sure of the Praetorians by paying them a donative, and secured the loyalty of the armies in the provinces by administering the oath that had been established by Augustus. He adopted the name Augustus but refused the title *Imperator* and *Pater Patriae*. These were highly honorific titles but they gave him no real political power. That was provided by his proconsular *imperium* and his tribunician power, which he eventually accepted for life. In this he departed from Augustan precedent, by not choosing to set a temporal limit on these powers. Perhaps he considered that after only a five or ten year term he would not be given a second chance.

Although Tiberius did not cultivate the populace by putting on frequent shows and games, or even attending them when they were organized, there was no serious discontent with the new emperor among the people of Rome or the provinces. It was a different case with the soldiers. They took the oath of loyalty, but they thought less about political matters than they did about their conditions of service and their pay, and the armies on the Rhine and in Pannonia seized the opportunity to make their grievances known. Their actions have been termed as revolts, but setting up a usurper was not the prime concern of the armies. They wanted a pay rise, and proper dismissal when they had served their full terms. Tiberius despatched his son Drusus to the troops in Pannonia, and his adopted son Germanicus to Germany. Drusus, aided by Lucius Aelius Sejanus took a firm hand and quelled Pannonian troops. But Germanicus adopted a softer approach and promised to meet most of the soldiers' demands. He was probably genuinely sympathetic. The story goes that one soldier grabbed Germanicus's hand and thrust it into his mouth, to demonstrate that he was old and toothless and ready for demobilization.

Some suspicion attached to Germanicus's actions, because he could so easily have exploited the unrest among the soldiers and turned it into a bid for supreme power. Instead he gave the soldiers something to do by mounting a campaign across the Rhine, which achieved little but incidentally discovered the remains of the legions which had been annihilated by Arminius in AD 9.

In his dealings with the Senate, Tiberius was conciliatory. The election of the chief magistrates was taken from the people and given to the Senate, so there was some semblance of choice rather than mere confirmation of Imperial wishes. Tiberius tried to foster true debate and individual thought, but it was probably too late for that. With Augustus, senators knew the rules and where they stood, but with Tiberius they were uncertain. He took part in senatorial proceedings but only succeeded in making the senators ill at ease, as he did when he sat in on court hearings. In encouraging senatorial participation in government, Tiberius did not wish to dominate, even to the point of accepting opinions contrary to his own, but since did not always make his wishes clear, and worse still was sometimes inconsistent, the senators lost confidence and became either apathetic or far too familiar with the Emperor who insisted that he was only the first among equals. Augustus had managed to play the part while still making it clear where the boundaries lay, but Tiberius seemed to give out contradictory messages, treat me as one of yourselves, he seemed to be saying, and then, if anyone did so, he disliked the closeness. The relationship between the senators and the Emperor gradually soured, irretrievably. Trials for treason, *maiestas*, increased in number, informers multiplied, and freedom of action became more and more constrained, because there were no hard and fast rules as to what constituted treason.

As his reign progressed Tiberius himself became more embittered. He had always tried to avoid public life and the Imperial court, and all his successes had been achieved far from Rome, on the frontiers and with the army. His military and administrative skills were never fully appreciated, and he had not promoted himself in Rome among the senatorial class or the people. He had not been first choice of successor to Augustus and, when he finally became emperor, he was almost at the age when he should have been able to look forward to retirement, but was then thrust into another job for which he had neither aptitude nor experience. For nearly ten years his rule was balanced and fair. The provinces benefited from his rule because he recognized efficient and honest governors and left them in their posts for several years. The continuity enabled the provincials to flourish under governors who did not use extortion to make themselves wealthy, but in the longer term the policy stultified the careers of equestrians and senators alike, since the normal tour of duty consisted of only one or two years in a province followed by appointments to military commands or civil posts in Rome. In this way many men gained a varied experience of government and a coterie of available manpower was built up.

There were few signs of unrest in Rome or Italy, save for the discovery of a conspiracy hatched by Scribonius Libo in 16, and two rebellions in the provinces, in Africa under Tacfarinas, and in Gaul under Florus and Sacrovir. These were all suppressed without calamity. More troublesome were the actions of Tiberius's nephew and adopted son Germanicus, who campaigned in Germany in 15 and 16, without achieving very much except for instigating an inordinate loyal following among the soldiers. His popularity made Tiberius suspicious of his possible designs on the Empire, a situation which Germanicus did nothing to remedy when he was sent to the east, where Parthian interests in Armenia were escalating. Germanicus succeeded in coming to an agreement with the Parthian king, Artabanus, but then he exceeded his brief by travelling to Egypt, where he behaved as if he were Emperor, commendably sorting out various problems. The problem was that Germanicus had not asked permission to go to Egypt, and it was in direct contravention of Augustus's ruling that no senator should enter the province without Imperial permission. Germanicus was a little too arrogant for Tiberius's taste, so when he died suddenly in Syria, in 19, it was rumoured that the Emperor had arranged for his removal. There was further scandal attached to the case, since Tiberius had appointed as governor of Syria an experienced and trusted colleague, Gnaeus Calpurnius Piso, perhaps to watch over Germanicus, possibly to report on his actions. Piso had quarrelled with Germanicus, and tried to stir up the troops against him. Germanicus ordered him to leave Syria. Piso said that he left of his own accord but, before he had departed from the east, unwelcome news reached him that Germanicus was dead. Not only that but, before he died, Germanicus said that Piso had poisoned him. Piso rushed back to Syria and attempted to take over the province again without checking first with the Emperor. It looked suspiciously like a military coup, and Piso also made the mistake of allowing Agrippina, the widow of Germanicus, to return to Rome with her family and friends, where they built up a case against him.

The unfortunate Piso was put on trial when he was recalled to Rome. He was cleared of the poisoning charge, but it was certain that he would be condemned for interfering with the loyalty of the army and forcing his way back as governor of Syria. He killed himself before a verdict was given. It was not this charge that interested most people. Scandalmongers said that Tiberius had used Piso to get rid of Germanicus, and had then abandoned him to the courts. The rumours went on to insist that all this was done to promote Tiberius's own son Drusus. Modern scholars discount this theory, but in Tiberius's own lifetime the scandal persisted. Four years later, Drusus also died. The death of his son marked a turning point in Tiberius's life. He did not recruit or actively promote a successor for over a decade.

Drusus's death also marked the rise to prominence of Lucius Aelius Sejanus. He was the son of Lucius Seius Strabo, who had been Praetorian Prefect under Augustus. On his accession in 14, Tiberius promoted Sejanus as his father's colleague as Praetorian Prefect, and in 17 he made Seius Strabo Prefect of Egypt. He did not bring in a colleague for Sejanus, who was now sole commander of the guard. The Praetorians were stationed in different parts of Italy at the time, but Sejanus soon made plans to concentrate them in a camp just on the outskirts of Rome. Tiberius's son Drusus had foreseen the immense accretion of power that Sejanus would enjoy if the guardsmen were brought to Rome, and had not been in favour of the idea, but after his death, Tiberius presumably acquiesced and the Praetorian Camp was built near the Porta Viminalis.

Sejanus harboured ambitions of his own, aiming for connections with the Imperial family. He sought permission to marry Drusus's widow Livilla, but Tiberius refused him. Undeterred, Sejanus started a campaign to eliminate Agrippina, the widow of Germanicus. She was openly inimical to Tiberius and rather free with her opinions, doing herself no favours in the long run. Concentrating at first on Agrippina's supporters, Sejanus used the loose definitions of treason to bring various people to trial. He was patient, and it took him a few years to bring about the banishment of Agrippina and her elder son Nero in 29, and the imprisonment of her younger son Drusus the following year. Only Gaius, the youngest son of Germanicus and Agrippina, was left unmolested.

By this time Tiberius had removed himself from Rome and gone to live on the island of Capri. He had promoted Sejanus and still trusted him, all the more so because Sejanus had saved his life by throwing himself across the Emperor to protect him from a fall of rocks. So for a while the Praetorian Prefect had an almost free hand in Rome. Tiberius had not relinquished control altogether. He attended to government and administration from Capri, but he was perhaps not kept fully informed of the growing power of Sejanus, who was elected consul for the year 31, with Tiberius as colleague, and was to have proconsular power bestowed on him. At this point, it is said that Tiberius was alerted to Sejanus's ambitions by his sister-in-law Antonia, the widow of his brother Drusus, and the mother of Germanicus. She does not seem to have been personally threatened by Sejanus, but she suspected that he was about to remove

Gaius, and possibly Tiberius's grandson Gemellus, until only Tiberius himself barred his path to supreme power. It is not certain whether Sejanus really plotted against Tiberius, but he was certainly aiming for shared power. History may have been different if Sejanus had been allowed to eliminate Gaius, who became the notorious Emperor Caligula, but he was stopped in his tracks when Tiberius appointed Naevius Sutorius Macro as Praetorian Prefect, with instructions to replace Sejanus. It was almost comic in the way in which it was done. Macro handed Sejanus a letter from the Emperor, and since he was expecting to be granted proconsular power, Sejanus had no reason to believe that half way through the letter would suddenly turn into an accusation and denouncement. His fall from power was immediate. Everyone melted away, and he was executed that same day. His followers and his young children were also despatched.

Tiberius now knew that he could trust nobody. One unfortunate result of his isolation was that he began to fear that his governors and military commanders might turn against him and use the armies to raise rebellion, a feature of Roman government that was to come to prominence in the next three decades. Wearily but conscientiously Tiberius continued to administer the Empire after the suppression of Sejanus. He was not out of touch with current affairs, and in 33 when there was a financial crisis, he gave 100 million sesterces to the state treasury, at 0 per cent interest, to improve monetary circulation. People of the early twenty-first century will recognize a distant echo.

In 35, he decided to name his heirs. There were only two possibilities from the Julio-Claudian house, his grandson Tiberius Gemellus and Gaius Caligula, the son of Germanicus. Despite the nomination of successors, Tiberius did not promote Gaius, the elder of the two boys, perhaps recognizing his unsuitability for holding office. He may have promoted Gemellus if he had been older. Unfortunately, he was not granted the time to train either of his heirs. He fell ill in 37 and decided to go back to Rome, but he died at Misenum. He was seventy-eight years old and had led an arduous life. There was probably no need for Gaius, who was with him, to smother him, as rumour would have it. Two days later, supported by the Praetorian Prefect Macro, Gaius became emperor. Tiberius, unlike his adopted father, was not deified after his death.

GAIUS, OR CALIGULA AD 37–41

Gaius's father Germanicus usually took his family with him when he was with the army, and had a miniature uniform made for his youngest son, complete with a pair of boots (*caligae*) like the soldiers wore, so Gaius was soon called Little Boots, Caligula, and the name stuck. On his accession, which was seemingly unopposed, Gaius was the darling of the people and the army. He started well, abolishing the notorious treason trials and conciliating the nobility, allowing the Senate to make decisions, and entertaining the populace via a series of games and shows.

Aged twenty-five when he succeeded Tiberius, Gaius had not held any important offices and had little experience of government. He had been quaestor in 33, a junior post which would not have afforded much training as Emperor. His whole life up to now had been bizarre. His father Germanicus died when Gaius was only a child, and his domineering and outspoken mother Agrippina was not exactly well-disposed to the Emperor Tiberius, who was suspected of some subterfuge in arranging for Germanicus's death. The followers of the family and then the family members themselves were persecuted by Sejanus, who removed Agrippina and her eldest son by having them banished, and shortly afterwards he imprisoned her younger son Drusus. Since it seemed at the time that Tiberius probably condoned these acts, the teenaged Gaius would hardly feel secure. Clearly he was next in the firing line, but before Sejanus could act, Tiberius engineered his downfall and replaced him with the new Praetorian Prefect, Macro. Then Gaius was invited to Capri, where the septuagenarian Tiberius made him and his cousin Gemellus his joint heirs. It was an unsettling beginning, but at first Gaius seemed to have emerged unscathed.

Turning to the Julio-Claudian family, Gaius adopted Gemellus, marking him out as his intended successor, and bestowed the consulship on his uncle Claudius, who had played little part in public life, ignored by the Imperial household because of his physical infirmities, his stammer, his lameness and his alleged tendency to drool. To strengthen the alliance, Claudius married his third wife, Messalina, whose paternal and maternal ancestor was Augustus himself. There was no sign as yet of the despotic, megalomaniac, absolutist emperor that Gaius would become.

After a serious illness in 37, not properly documented, the monster of the ancient sources emerged. Excuses have been made for Gaius's increasingly absurd behaviour on account of this unexplained illness. It has been claimed that Gaius had a nervous breakdown, or that he had suffered brain fever. The debate is insoluble, and hostile portraits in the ancient sources partly obscure the reasons for his subsequent actions. He quickly executed Gemellus and the Praetorian Prefect Macro, reinstated the treason trials, and reduced the Senate to a nonentity by taking total control of the government. His policies, as described in the sources, are not consistent. He annexed Mauretania and deposed the client king, Ptolemy, and he mounted a military expedition to the Rhine, where the Germanic tribes were engaged in raiding. The campaign may have been in response to a plot hatched by Aemilius Lepidus, who had married Gaius's sister Drusilla, and after her death had started an affair with Agrippina, Gaius's other sister. If Lepidus managed to stir up the Rhine legions and get the commanders on his side, he could launch a coup against the Emperor, but the plot was suppressed, with the help of two competent military men, the future emperors Sulpicius Galba and Flavius Vespasianus. It was said that Gaius also planned an invasion of Britain but it never took place. Allegedly he reached the coast of Gaul and made his soldiers collect seashells. Various explanations have been advanced for this strange tale. It is possible that the soldiers refused to embark, as they did later when Claudius mounted the invasion of Britain. Gaius may have suddenly become alarmed about leaving Italy where more plots could be formed against him, and the story about the seashells may have arisen from confusion over terminology. The word *musculi* denotes shells, but it is also the term used for military siege equipment, which would have to be carted back to the legionary bases.

In the east, Gaius managed to undo Augustus's carefully strengthened borders with Parthia, by interfering with the provinces and client kingdoms. As a result the Parthians gained a preponderant influence in Armenia, always a bone of contention between the two empires. In Judaea, Gaius favoured his friend Herod Agrippa by placing him in control of the territories ruled by his relatives, and he caused further resentment by making it clear that he intended to have a statue of himself as a living god placed in all synagogues, including the temple at Jerusalem. Before the order could be put into effect, the Praetorians assassinated the living god.

By the end of his reign, the darling of the people had upset virtually everyone from all walks of life. He had tried to keep the Praetorians well-disposed by a cash payment on his accession and by various favours thereafter, but in the end even the guardsmen lost patience with him, possibly forming an alliance with some senators who wished to be rid of Gaius. The men who killed the Emperor were Praetorians, and it was also a group of Praetorians who found Claudius hiding behind a curtain in the Imperial palace, and dragged him out, not to assassinate him, but to declare him emperor.

CLAUDIUS AD 41–54

On his accession Claudius was fifty-one years old, and had always been considered the least likely candidate for Imperial rule, because of his physical infirmities and his supposed weakness of intellect. But Claudius was nobody's fool. He devoted himself to academic study, kept a low profile, and survived intact through the reigns of Augustus, Tiberius and Gaius Caligula. His father was Tiberius's brother, Drusus, and his mother was Antonia, the younger daughter of Mark Antony and Octavia, Augustus's sister. Claudius had witnessed the death of all his close relatives. His father died after an accident in Germany when Claudius was less than

one year old. His brother Germanicus died under suspicious circumstances
in Syria. Germanicus's wife Agrippina, from then on hostile to Tiberius,
paid for her attitude when Sejanus banished her. Claudius's sister Livia
Julia, or Livilla, was accused of having an affair with Sejanus, and of
arranging the death of her husband, Drusus, the son of Tiberius. She was
executed and her memory was damned. Antonia, Claudius's mother, was
instrumental in the downfall of Sejanus, since she was respected by her
brother-in-law Tiberius, who listened to her when she came to warn him
of the rising ambition of the Praetorian Prefect, who had asked permission
to marry Livilla and been refused in 25. When Gaius Caligula became
emperor, he first bestowed various honours on Antonia, who had brought
him up after the death of Germanicus, but only a few weeks into his reign
he tired of her and drove her to suicide. From 37 onwards Claudius trod
very carefully. He was made consul with Gaius as colleague, but this would
not guarantee his future security. Tiberius had intended that Gaius and his
own grandson Tiberius Gemellus should be his co-heirs, but Gemellus was
soon murdered, leaving Claudius no doubt very wary.

When Gaius was assassinated, Claudius could not be certain whether
the plotters had decided to despatch him as well. As a member of the Julio-
Claudian house, which had provided two emperors of dubious character,
he may have been tarred with the same brush. The senators were ready
to reinstate the Republic, but could only acquiesce when the Praetorians
declared Claudius emperor. All the emperors depended on the armed forces
to gain and retain power, but Claudius was the first who was so blatantly
indebted to the Praetorians, and to keep them well-disposed he paid huge
donatives to each man, setting a dangerous precedent for the future. He
took the name Caesar, which was eventually transformed into a title, to
connect himself with the Julian family. He courted the favour of the Senate,
treating all senators respectfully, trying to encourage them to take a more
active part in government, asking their advice and sometimes following
it. He was not altogether successful in reviving the Senate. Two reigns
had begun well and ended badly, and at this stage there was no reason to
believe that Claudius would be any different. He put an end to the treason
trials, abolished some of the taxes that Gaius had established to fill his
depleted coffers, and provided the people with games and shows. Tiberius
had started out with liberal views, but had ended by reintroducing treason
trials and becoming more estranged from the Senate and people. Gaius
had displayed a very short-lived leniency, and had become unpredictable
and vindictive. Claudius's benevolent attitude was not wholly trusted, and
eventually there were executions, about thirty-five senators and many
more equites who were perhaps their clients or supporters. There was an
attempt at rebellion, led by Furius Camillus Scribonianus, the commander
of the army in Dalmatia, but fortunately the soldiers were not interested in

fighting and dying for him, being happy to accept Claudius, who attended to their needs and gave them things to do.

Since he was not a military man, Claudius relied upon his generals. When rebellion broke out in Mauretania, he sent Suetonius Paullinus and Hosidius Geta to suppress it. The country had been annexed by Gaius, after he had deposed King Ptolemy. It was not unusual for the inhabitants of new provinces to try to shake off Roman rule, but the country was quickly pacified and Claudius created two provinces, Mauretania Tingitana and Mauretania Caesariensis. Romanization in the two provinces never proceeded rapidly, but the Mauri, or Moors, provided excellent cavalry for the Roman army.

For the first time since Augustus had advised against extending the Empire, Claudius embarked on just such a policy. He reversed Gaius's policy and converted Judaea into a province as it had once been, annexed Lycia together with Pamphylia, and annexed Thrace. His most famous achievement was the conquest of Britain. Julius Caesar had invaded the island in 55 and 54 BC, but had not attempted to conquer and annexe it. Augustus had refused to contemplate such a task even when approached by a British king seeking Roman assistance in regaining his throne. Gaius had started the project, using the same excuse that one of the tribal rulers needed help, but never finished it. In 43, Claudius authorized the invasion.

The British tribes knew all about the Romans and had been trading with them for years. British rulers often squabbled with each other, and deposed kings knew where to go for help. The King of the Atrebates, Verica, had been expelled by the brothers Caratacus and Togodumnus, and his kingdom had been absorbed into theirs as part of their aggressive expansion policies. Verica fled to Rome and the two brothers demanded his return. The Romans of the Republic had been in this position before, several times, and the intervention usually resulted in annexation. Claudius decided to take up the challenge. Besides, Britain was a stronghold of the Druids, and Claudius was determined to suppress the cult. He assembled four legions, three from the Rhine and one from Pannonia, and placed Aulus Plautius Silvanus in command. The Romans made steady progress, until it was considered safe for the Emperor himself to visit the new province, bringing with him some war elephants to impress the natives. The conquest was by no means complete when Claudius died, but despite various reversals, successive emperors tenaciously held onto Britain, until Honorius withdrew the troops in 410.

The annexation of new territories greatly enhanced Claudius's reputation, earning him the respect of the Senate and the people, and several acclamations as *Imperator* from the army, assiduously numbered by the emperors and utilized on inscriptions as part of their titles. Claudius achieved twenty-seven acclamations in all, and was proud of his military reputation, even though it was achieved via his generals. The work of Aulus Plautius in Britain was continued by Publius Ostorius Scapula and Aulus Didius Gallus, and on the Rhine, Domitius Corbulo strengthened the Rhine frontier.

After annexation, Claudius did not simply exploit the new provinces. He took great care of the whole Empire, fostering Romanization where there was a willing population, extending Roman citizenship and Latin rights to various communities, founding Roman colonies (*coloniae*) and building roads. He admitted some of the enfranchised Gallic nobility to the Senate, not without some disapproval from existing senators, among whom a joke circulated that they would refuse to show the new Gallic senators the way to the Senate House. Such snobbery persisted, but Claudius laid the foundations of a more cosmopolitan senatorial order, in which the provincials gradually played a greater part, without obliterating the Roman and Italian senatorial class.

With an energy and enthusiasm that belied his age and his semi-obscure background, Claudius launched into every detail of administration. He centralized and expanded the administrative machinery, by dividing its functions into groups and placing a secretary over each. These were mostly freedmen, though some equestrians were given posts in the central administration. Finances were looked after by Pallas, the freedman secretary *a rationibus*, correspondence by the *ab epistulis*, a post held by Narcissus. The library and archives were supervised by *a studiis*, legal matters and petitions by *a cognitionibus* and *a libellis*. This is the product of an analytical mind anxious to bring everything under control, and Claudius's system endured. The Emperor also improved the water supply for the city of Rome, extended the boundary (*pomerium*) and improved communications in Italy by building roads to the coast and to the Alps. He built a new harbour at Ostia, the port of Rome, and tried to increase trade and to improve agriculture.

In his personal life Claudius was less successful. His marriage to Messalina ended in scandal and her execution, and his subsequent choice of spouse led to his own death. He married the younger Agrippina, daughter of Germanicus and Agrippina the elder, hence Claudius's niece. It was not a love match, but might have secured the succession if only Agrippina's ambition and the character of her son Lucius had been more moderate. Lucius was Agrippina's son by her first husband, Gnaeus Domitius Ahenobarbus, and on his adoption he took the name Nero Claudius Caesar. He was quickly betrothed to Claudius's daughter Octavia, and rapidly began to eclipse Claudius's son Britannicus who was much younger than Nero. Agrippina, inordinately ambitious for power, was instrumental in the rise of her son, through whom she hoped to rule the whole Roman world.

Claudius promoted Nero as Augustus would have done, designating him consul for the year 58, by which time he would perhaps have been considered mature enough, and appointing him as city prefect. In 53 he married Octavia, and in the following year, when Nero was sixteen and his acceptance as heir to the throne was secured, Claudius died. He was probably poisoned by Agrippina, who could not afford to wait for her husband to expire naturally, in case that took a long time, allowing Nero to extricate himself from her control. Without protest from the Praetorians, the Senate, the people or the army, Nero became emperor on 13 October, 54.

Nero AD 54–68

The three most important individuals who guided the young Emperor were his mother Agrippina, the Praetorian Prefect Sextus Afranius Burrus, and Lucius Annaeus Seneca, who had been brought back to Rome from exile by Claudius to be tutor to Nero and Britannicus. Agrippina's power was greater than any of the Imperial women had so far enjoyed. Coins were issued with her head on the obverse, whereas Imperial women were normally depicted on the reverse, subordinate to the emperor.

The first task was to ensure the loyalty of the Praetorians by distributing cash to each man. The people would be similarly tamed via cash payments, and kept entertained with the usual games and shows. But first Nero must be made secure closer to home. There were some immediate changes of personnel. Claudius's freedman secretary Narcissus was executed, and Pallas was removed from his post, even though he was favourable to Agrippina, and perhaps had been her lover when she was making her way into Imperial power. Britannicus, Claudius's son, was poisoned in 55, and some years later in 62, Nero's wife Octavia was also killed. No one rose up to avenge Claudius's children. With all potential rivals removed in the first years of Nero's reign, Agrippina tried to control her son, but was eventually removed from the palace in 56, leaving Nero in the hands of Burrus and Seneca, whose influence was effective, sound and beneficial for the Empire until 62. They allowed Nero to imagine that all the ideas for government sprang from him, while he pursued his interests in art and literature.

Inevitably, as he grew older Nero began to demand greater independence. The most important obstacle to achieving it was his mother, so he planned to have her permanently removed by scuttling the boat in which she was to make a journey, but although it sank she managed to reach the shore at Baiae. If she thought that she had been the victim of an accident she was quickly made aware of the truth. On Nero's orders, the Prefect of the Fleet at Misenum sent some sailors to kill her. Nero lay low for a while, but when he realized that there was to be no retribution, save for a dent in his popularity, he also realized that he could do as he wished.

In 62 the Praetorian Prefect Burrus died, thus removing one of the better influences on Nero's behaviour. He chose two new Praetorian Prefects, promoting the Prefect of the *Vigiles*, Ofonius Tigellinus, and the Prefect of the Annona, Faenius Rufus. These men were no friends of Seneca, and he chose to recede out of the limelight and pursue his private studies. Nero then turned on his wife. He divorced and then murdered Octavia, which highly displeased the populace. But once again, only Nero's image suffered. There was nothing anyone could do about his actions. Autocratic rule began again in Rome.

Distant relatives of the Imperial family were singled out and removed. In 62 Nero murdered a grandson of Tiberius called Rubellius Plautus, and the son-in-law of Claudius, Cornelius Sulla. In 64, Didius Junius Silanus was driven to suicide because he was descended from Augustus. Just as previous emperors had done, Nero revived the treason laws. On the whole Nero ignored and despised the Senate, but he clearly did not ignore individuals. Senators began to fear wider persecutions. Having alienated the senatorial class, Nero also succeeded in alienating the populace in Rome. The fire that destroyed much of the city in 64 did nothing to enhance his reputation, since it was rumoured that he had started it deliberately, even though he was not in the city at the time, and made strenuous efforts to bring the fire under control, and he also relieved the people who had lost their homes and livelihoods. If his actions had ended there he may have been able to raise his reputation by several notches, but he blamed the Christians for starting the fire and embarked on religious persecution, possibly confined to the city and not spreading all over the Empire. In this the people were mostly supportive, since the Christians were not popular. Then it was made clear that Nero was not going to rebuild housing and restore the city, but he was going to flatten several acres of what was left and build an unimaginably large palace complex, the famous *Domus Aurea*, so that he could be properly housed at last.

In the provinces, Nero relied upon his generals as Claudius had done, but did not treat them so well. The British rebellion of Boudicca in 60 cost many lives and was only put down after tremendous destruction of the three main cities that had been founded at Colchester (Camulodunum), where a colony had been established for veterans of the Twentieth legion, and St Albans (Verulamium) and London (Londinium). The general Suetonius Paullinus, diverted from his attack on the Druid stronghold in Anglesey, hurried to London, but then abandoned the south and withdrew to assemble his troops somewhere in the Midlands to meet Boudicca head-on. He won the battle but re-establishing control of the province and pacifying it took much longer. Suetonius was recalled because he treated the natives too harshly, and more lenient governors were sent out, whose background was not military but administrative and legal. This is probably the work of Seneca and Burrus, who were still able to influence the young Emperor at the time.

At the very beginning of Nero's reign the Parthians had overrun Armenia. Gaius Domitius Corbulo, who had successfully pacified the Rhine frontier under Claudius, was sent out to drive the Parthians back. He did so, campaigning in the difficult terrain of Armenia for several years. He was made governor of Syria in 60 and for the next few years he kept the eastern part of the Roman world secure. He commanded a large territory and large armies, until Nero realized that such a powerful general represented a threat, and drove him to suicide in 67. In the previous year, the Jewish revolt had begun in Judaea, necessitating Roman intervention. Nero appointed Gaius Licinius Mucianus as governor of Syria, and gave the command in Judaea to Titus Flavius Vespasianus, allegedly as punishment for dozing off while the Emperor recited poetry on his tour of Greece. But Vespasian was a tried and tested soldier who had commanded a legion in the invasion of Britain, and had served as governor of Africa. The world was soon to hear more of Mucianus and Vespasian.

Towards the end of his reign, Nero had offended and frightened most of the classes of Roman society. Like Gaius Caligula he had emptied the treasury and began to have wealthy men murdered so that he could take over their property. A plot was formed to remove him in 65, and replace him with a senator called Gaius Calpurnius Piso, but it was discovered and the ringleaders were executed. The Praetorian Prefect Tigellinus set up a secret service to watch people, and another reign of terror began. It was aimed principally at the nobility, but in reality no one was safe. Meanwhile, Nero proclaimed himself a living god, and toured Greece where he entered literary and artistic competitions and was awarded all the prizes, some of which he received without having even entered the competition. It could not continue in this vein.

The protest began in spring 68 with a short-lived revolt in Gaul led by Gaius Julius Vindex, the governor of a Gallic province, but it is not certain which one. The governor of Upper Germany, Lucius Verginius Rufus, quelled the rebellion, but made it clear that he did not want to be emperor himself, and declared his loyalty to the Senate, not to Nero. At the same time in Spain, Servius Sulpicius Galba at first supported Vindex, then struck out on his own with the intention of replacing Nero. One of his supporters in Rome, Nymphidius Sabinus, acting on Galba's behalf, offered 30,000 sesterces to each Praetorian guardsman. It was now too late for Nero to act, even if he had possessed the means to do anything. He had alienated everyone and had not cultivated the soldiers. On 9 June 68 he committed suicide, with a little help from his friends, and Galba found that he had bought the Empire.

During the years from the fall of Alexandria to the death of Nero, the administrative systems of the Empire, and the organization of the army, were gradually adapted and developed. The Imperial government did not spring fully fledged from Augustus's head, nor did he start out in 30 BC with a master plan that he intended to put into effect. He felt his way slowly to avoid controversy, adapted to circumstances, and sometimes had to backtrack and start again. When he died, the machinery of government was not finalized. Tiberius and Claudius were the men who refined and shaped the system, and their successors adapted it as circumstances changed.

Ruling the Roman world without the benefit of modern communications defies the imagination. Many different lands and peoples made up the Roman Empire. Economically and administratively the various nationalities were part of a unified whole but they were not entirely subsumed by Romanization, which was not actively enforced but encouraged where the provincials expressed an interest. The administration of such a large and diverse territory was tidied up by Claudius, whose system survived, with adjustments, until the fourth century.

As the Empire grew, one factor that provided a measure of cohesion was the Imperial cult. The Romans subscribed readily enough to the concept of deification of prominent men after their deaths, but the evolved form of the Imperial cult included worship of both the deceased members of the Imperial families, and the spirit (*numen* or *genius*) of living ones. This bestowed on the emperors a sacrosanctity that was to play a large part in Imperial rule in the third century.

Under Augustus, a limited social mobility had begun, cutting across the snobbery of the Roman upper classes by allowing men from humble backgrounds to become senators, with access to the higher offices of state. The composition of the Senate changed as successive emperors allowed Italian equestrians, then provincials to enter its ranks. The process continued throughout the history of the Empire, but although the elevation of provincials was an honour, the power of the Senate declined because even the most conciliatory emperors could not allow the Senate to direct policy. All the Julio-Claudians began by establishing good relations with the senators, and then to varying degrees soured the relationship by either ignoring them, or actively persecuting them.

In the provinces there was a gradual extension of citizenship or Latin rights, a policy that had been in existence since Augustus's day, but was usually limited to deserving individuals or members of local government. Claudius extended citizenship to whole peoples, providing a pattern for future emperors to follow. The Republican attitude towards the provinces as territories to be exploited was replaced by integration. Tiberius was concerned to alleviate tax burdens, because he realized that squeezing the provincials dry was not conducive to long-term, steady profits.

10

Expanding Empire:
Pushing the Boundaries AD 69–117

GALBA AD 68–69 & OTHO AD 69

Servius Sulpicius Galba was in his seventies when he was declared emperor, a member of the senatorial aristocracy, but not related in any way to the Julio-Claudian family. He adopted the name Caesar in order to engender loyalty among the armies, since the soldiers were loyal to the Julian house, and the name, which eventually became a title, established Galba as the successor of Nero. The adoption of the name pacified the armies for a while, and Galba's pretence that he was acting on behalf of the Senate served to mollify the senators, who recognized him as emperor and conferred Imperial powers upon him. He arrived in Rome in the autumn of 68 with his supporters. One of these was Marcus Salvius Otho, who had been governor of Lusitania for the last ten years. Nero had sent him there in order to steal his wife Poppaea, whom he married as soon as she was divorced, and it seemed that the lady herself was not unwilling.

Galba made several mistakes. He encountered feeble opposition from Clodius Macer in Africa, but with only one legion Macer had no real chance of prevailing against the troops of Galba, who easily arranged his assassination. He also persuaded Fabius Valens, a legionary commander, to murder the governor of Lower Germany, Fonteius Capito. Galba replaced him with one of his supporters, Aulus Vitellius, an appointment that was to contribute to the chaos of the year 69, called the 'Year of Four Emperors'.

Galba eradicated Nero's soldiers and supporters in Rome, instead of trying to win them over or to buy them, but his stern principles would not allow him to pay money for loyalty. This was perhaps the biggest mistake of all, because he also reneged on his offer of 30,000 sesterces for each of the Praetorians, who never received anything from him, and therefore conceived of him as untrustworthy. Perhaps it would not have been so irritating if he had not rewarded his supporters from Gaul, but he was so obviously partisan, conferring appointments on his own followers, that he alienated many men who might otherwise have helped him.

At the beginning of 69, news arrived of the discontent of the armies, in particular the legions of Upper Germany, who refused to take the oath of loyalty to the Emperor. Then the troops of Lower Germany declared for the new governor Vitellius. He accepted their proclamation and made plans to march on Rome. Fabius Valens and Aulus Caecina Alienus, recently appointed legionary legate in Upper Germany, joined with Vitellius.

In Rome, Galba tried to strengthen his regime by adopting an heir, choosing Lucius Calpurnius Piso, who had little claim to fame save for the fact that he was the brother of a man who had plotted against Nero. The choice was unfortunate, because Otho had assisted Galba from the beginning and had expected that if a successor was to be named, then it should have been himself. Otho did not find it difficult to win over the Praetorians, who made him emperor and murdered Galba. Otho took the name Caesar as Galba had done, but he had more credibility as the successor of the Julians than Galba had enjoyed. Unfortunately his reign was to be very short. He had the support of several legions, on the Danube and in the east, but they were nowhere near Rome, so even if they set off to help him they would not arrive for some considerable time. Consequently he was vastly outnumbered by Vitellius's troops.

Vitellius was approaching Italy, marching a little more slowly behind two advance columns under Valens and Caecina who crossed the Alps via the Mont Genevre and St Bernard passes. Otho tried to prevent Valens and Caecina from crossing the River Po, having vacillated too long to send troops to block the passes. Between Cremona and Bedriacum, Otho's generals Suetonius Paullinus and Celsus, with very few troops, almost stopped Caecina, but ultimately failed. Suetonius advised Otho not to engage the enemy until more soldiers had arrived from Dalmatia, but Otho was concerned that the Vitellians would also build up more support and more military strength, so risked fighting near Cremona. He was defeated. He said that he did not wish to involve everyone in civil war, told his supporters to declare for Vitellius, and committed suicide.

VITELLIUS AD 69

The Senate acknowledged and conferred powers on Vitellius, who was still in Gaul. He prudently sent many of his troops back to their bases, but when he eventually arrived in Rome he was dressed like a conquering hero, at the head of 60,000 troops. The soldiers ran riot in the city. It was disquieting to find that Vitellius had no control over them, and nor did anyone else. The Praetorians were all dismissed and replaced with Vitellius's German troops. It did not bode well for the future, but it did provide the excuse for the governors of Judaea and Syria to start their campaign to rescue Rome from Vitellius, which was their official party line after the event.

Nero had appointed Mucianus as governor of Syria and Vespasian as governor of Judaea, where the Jewish revolt was still not quelled. The two men corresponded with each other via Vespasian's son Titus. They did not reveal their hand until July, but the supposedly spontaneous acclamation of Vespasian as emperor presumably required quite a lot of intrigue and forward planning. When they heard of Nero's death and the proclamation of Galba, Vespasian and Mucianus would have to decide what to do. Even if they disapproved of what was happening in Rome, it would not be wise to ask the soldiers to withhold the oath of allegiance to whoever was emperor since it would signal rebellion. So they played the game until they were ready, and at the beginning of July the troops in Egypt, Judaea and Syria in quick succession declared for Vespasian.

When the news of the events in the eastern provinces reached Rome, Vespasian's brother Flavius Sabinus, and his younger son Domitian, aged about eighteen, were in some danger. Sabinus had been city prefect under Nero. Galba removed him from office. Unlike other associates of Nero his life was spared, possibly because his brother Vespasian was in command of legions in Judaea, and it was not prudent to irritate such commanders. Otho reinstated Sabinus, who retained his office and kept order in the city until Vitellius arrived in the summer. Now, with Vespasian as rival emperor, Vitellius put Sabinus and Domitian under house arrest.

Meanwhile, the Flavian troops began to move towards Rome. Mucianus set off on the overland route from Syria, preceded by the legions of Pannonia under Antonius Primus, who was closer to Italy. At Cremona, Primus met Vitellius's troops commanded by Caecina, who tried to negotiate, possibly to ingratiate himself with the side that looked most likely to win. Caecina's own soldiers arrested him, and the second battle of Cremona was fought and won by Antonius Primus. Unfortunately Primus was either unwilling or unable to prevent his army from sacking the town. Had he stopped the carnage, he may have fared better under Vespasian. As Primus's troops approached Rome, Vitellius abdicated, and Sabinus celebrated a peaceful outcome, prematurely, as it turned out. It soon became obvious that Vitellius could not persuade his adherents to lie down meekly and accept Vespasian as emperor. They vented their anger and disappointment on the Flavian party, and soon Sabinus and his friends fled to the Capitol Hill, barricading themselves in by using anything they could find, including some statues, to block access. Sabinus sent for Domitian, but not long after he had arrived, the Vitellians stormed the temporary stronghold. Sabinus was killed, but Domitian escaped, allegedly by mingling with a procession of priests of Isis, and then perhaps by hiding at a friend's house.

Fortunately, Antonius Primus arrived in time to prevent a witch hunt, but his soldiers ran riot just as Vitellius's troops had done when they arrived in the city. This outrage, combined with the sack of Cremona, cast an unfavourable light on Vespasian, who wished for a squeaky clean beginning for his reign. Antonius Primus had done more than anyone to help the Flavians to gain power, but he was sacrificed for the sake of appearances, eventually retiring to Gaul. When Mucianus arrived in Rome, he could take the credit for restoring order, all part of the Flavian mythology established after the event and disseminated by the literary work of Flavius Josephus, who was at first one of the leaders of the Jewish revolt, and afterwards a partisan of Vespasian and Titus.

Vespasian AD 69–79

The Senate accepted Vespasian's rule, making the new Emperor and his son Titus consuls, and Domitian urban praetor with consular powers. Vespasian himself did not set out from the east until peace was restored in Rome. He had halted operations against the Jews after Nero's suicide, waiting to see what would happen next. He put Titus in charge of the mopping up in Judaea, and arrived in Rome probably at the end of the year 70, though different dates are favoured by different authors.

A law was passed conferring Imperial powers on Vespasian (*lex de Imperio Vespasiani*). In accordance with normal custom, Vespasian would have dated the beginning of his reign, his *dies imperii*, from the date when the law was passed, but being too honest and too realistic about the way in which he had become emperor, he dated his reign from the beginning of July when the troops in Alexandria had acclaimed him. Some of the text of this law survives on a bronze tablet from Rome. There is debate about the lost portions and the nature of the law in general. The Senate traditionally formulated the law to confer power on the Emperors, and the people's assembly passed it. It is not certain whether the law concerning Vespasian was based on the exact texts of previous bestowals of Imperial powers, or whether it was amended because this was a special case. Some scholars have suggested that after the disastrous reign of Nero there was an attempt to limit the powers accorded to Vespasian. This seems unlikely. Vespasian would know perfectly well what was normally entailed in the conferment of power, and would not countenance any curtailment or restrictions. He required all the support that he could summon for his reign, especially the law which made it legal. He was the first emperor who was not remotely related to the Julio-Claudians. He was an Italian, or more precisely a Sabine born in the town of Reate. He was most definitely not a member of the Roman senatorial aristocracy. Worse still, in the eyes of this clique of aristocrats, he was the first of his equestrian family to be made a senator. His brother Sabinus had become a senator long before Vespasian, who initially seemed reluctant to improve upon his equestrian status. It was said that for a few years he had bought and sold mules for a living. He was therefore not the sort of man who would inspire loyalty among the senators. But his track record as a military man was secure. In the invasion of Britain under Claudius he had been a legionary commander and had stormed the British hill fort of Maiden Castle in Dorset, and he had served in Germany and Thrace. His appointment to the command in Judaea may have been partly as a punishment for not enthusing about Nero's literary prowess, but it was a sound choice.

The suppression of the Jewish revolt was the task of Vespasian's son Titus. He took Jerusalem in 70, destroying the Temple and subduing all but a few of the rebels, who held out for a few more years. The most famous episode of these years is the siege and eventual fall of Masada, where nearly 400 Jews killed themselves in 73 rather than submit to the Romans. Another revolt, contemporary with the rebellion in Judaea, occurred in Gaul and Germany, led by Julius Civilis a Batavian who had served in the Roman army and been given Roman citizenship. At the beginning of the revolt he declared that he was a supporter of Vespasian, but it quickly became a fully fledged rebellion against Roman rule. Most, but not all, of the Germanic tribes of the Rhineland joined Civilis, but of the Gallic tribes, several refused to rally to his standard and remained loyal to Rome. Civilis had the advantage that the Rhine legions were very much under strength, since many men had accompanied Vitellius to Rome, so the Roman commanders had to disperse their few remaining troops to deal with attacks from the rebels. The situation deteriorated rapidly, several Roman forts were destroyed, the colonies of Cologne and Trier were captured, and as a result of these successes, more of the Gauls came over to Civilis. When Mucianus reached Rome and restored order, he gathered some of the troops that Vitellius had brought with him, and sent them back to the Rhine, commanded by Petillius Cerialis. Two more legions, one from Britain and one from Spain joined Cerialis, who concentrated on the recovery of the Rhine, while at the same time Annius Gallus with four legions operated against the tribe of the Lingones. Between them the two commanders suppressed the revolt, but the number of troops that had been assembled for the task indicates how serious the rebellion was. Civilis surrendered to Cerialis, and Vespasian strengthened the Rhine garrison.

As a prime consideration Vespasian needed to consolidate his power and to ensure that he would retain it. As Galba and Otho had done, he adopted the name Caesar, but went one stage further by also incorporating the titles Imperator and Augustus into his name. His official nomenclature was *Imperator Caesar Vespasianus Augustus*, which set the pattern for future emperors. The use of *Imperator* as a name is to be distinguished from the victory titles accrued via (allegedly) spontaneous acclamations by the troops, which were so assiduously collected and numbered by the non-military Claudius, and later by Domitian, who did much more than just accompanying his armies on campaign. All the emperors displayed on inscriptions and in official correspondence the number of times they had been saluted as Imperator, as well as using the term as part of their names.

Since the support of the military was essential to all emperors, Vespasian reconstituted the Praetorian Guard that Vitellius had dismissed, and to make doubly sure of its loyalty he made Titus Praetorian Prefect, keeping the important posts within the family. The Praetorians could make or break emperors, but so could the armies in the provinces, as Vespasian was only too well aware. The historian Tacitus would describe laconically how the secret of empire was revealed during the civil disturbances of 68 to 69, and emperors could be made in places far from Rome itself. The armies, therefore, had to be befriended and fostered. When Julius Civilis led the revolt in Gaul, it showed how nationalist feelings still predominated even after more than a century of Roman rule. Civilis was a dangerous enemy. Having served as a commander of an auxiliary unit in the Roman army, he was fully conversant with Roman military methods and how to combat them. The auxiliary troops of Republican times had been allowed to fight under their own commanders and were often disbanded when the wars ended. The same situation pertained under Augustus and the early emperors, but now the *auxilia* had to be reorganized, and made a regular part of the standing army established by Augustus. As the Empire expanded, the troops moved further away from Rome towards the edges of Roman territory. Auxiliary troops fighting close to home under their own tribal leaders could be potentially dangerous, and yet the extra manpower and expertise could not be discarded altogether. From Vespasian onwards, auxiliaries were raised from tribes around the Empire but were sent far away from their homes, and were commanded by Roman officers. After they had completed their term of service of twenty-five years, they were given pensions and also Roman citizenship, a privilege well worth having, as shown by the fact that there were several false claims on record, usually punishable by death.

Vespasian ignored the example of Augustus, who had not monopolized the consulship after he had established himself. Vespasian and both his sons were consuls many times. The succession was secured and made crystal clear. 'Either my sons shall succeed me, or no one' said the new Emperor, and set about elevating Titus, with Domitian in second place but still given some powers. In 71 he bestowed proconsular and tribunician power on Titus. Two years later, Vespasian and Titus assumed the office of censor, reviewing the Senate and bringing in new men from Italy and some of the provinces, mostly in the west. So many men had been killed in the 'Year of Four Emperors' that there were several vacancies to be filled.

As Claudius had recognized, the days of an exclusively Roman Senate and jealously guarded Roman citizenship were over. The Empire would be made stronger if it became a commonwealth, with shared citizenship sensibly bestowed, and the expansion of social mobility with attainable goals in government and the army. Probably in connection with the census, a survey of agricultural land and produce was carried out, so that tax could be properly assessed and collected, with the incidental result that a transparent record of such assessments would leave no opportunity for cheating the provincials.

The provinces were encouraged, but not forced, to urbanize and Romanize. Colonies were founded, cities were granted municipal status, Latin rights were conferred on many communities in Spain, which was ready for demilitarization. Boundaries were adjusted and new territory taken in. In the east, the main focus was always on the activities of the Parthians, especially their interest in the kingdom of Armenia. Vespasian strengthened the territories bordering on the Parthian Empire, and those on the western borders of Armenia. He placed troops in Cappadocia, and annexed Commagene, which was administered as part of Syria, where the number of troops was increased. After Petillius Cerialis, who may have been Vespasian's son-in-law, had suppressed the revolt of Civilis, he was sent to Britain in 71. The rebellion of Boudicca in 60 had put an end to further expansion for several years, and governors had been chosen whose experience was in civil and juridical adminstration rather than in military matters. The governors concentrated on the repair of the damage and fostering better relations with the Britons. Vespasian reversed the policy of non-expansion, sending troops northwards into Brigantia, covering what is now Lancashire, Cumbria and much of Yorkshire. There was a valid excuse that made this a legitimate exercise. For many years the kingdom of Brigantia had been ruled by its queen Cartimandua, who was loyal to the Romans, but dissension within her kingdom had started before Boudicca's rebellion. Cartimandua's estranged husband Venutius had been building up his anti-Roman party for some time, and was finally strong enough to force his wife out of the kingdom. Appeals to Rome from British kings were not unusual, but were not always answered. In this case, the presence of a hostile king on the northern borders of the province of Britain could not be tolerated. Cerialis's campaigns are not well documented either in ancient literature or by archaeological methods, since it is difficult to put a precise enough date on the camps and forts that are known in the areas where he campaigned. The sites could have been established by Cerialis or by his successors, or could have been used more than once. Cerialis's exploits were considered satisfactory by Vespasian, who recalled him probably in 74. He was succeeded by Sextus Julius Frontinus, who turned aside from the north to concentrate on the integration of Wales, and then by Gnaeus Julius Agricola, whose exploits were recorded by his son-in-law, the historian Tacitus, and tend to overshadow the achievements of the previous governors. He was still in command, conquering northern Britain, when Vespasian died.

The decade of Vespasian's reign was mostly peaceful. Apart from the wars in Britain, and after the suppression of the Jews, there was no serious trouble in the Empire. It was mostly the philosophers, the Stoics and Cynics, who objected to Vespasian. Some of them were die-hard Republicans longing for a return to a mythically perfect form of rule that they had never experienced except in history books, elaborated by imagination and wishful thinking. Others would have tolerated kings if only they had been chosen from the best educated men of the aristocracy, and not from a recent member of the equestrian class who had once sold mules and relied upon the army to shore up his rule. At least Vespasian did not try to dissemble about his origins or the source of his power. There was a continual needling and mostly verbal opposition to Imperial rule in general and Vespasian in particular from Helvidius Priscus, whose family and friends had tried the same opposition to Nero and paid the penalty for it. Perhaps if Priscus had evolved a coherent policy, or formulated a list of demands for better government, or even tried to engage the Emperor in discussion, he may have been treated leniently and possibly scored some successes, but his policy seemed to have been one of random broadsides whenever there was an opportunity, and puerile rudeness combined with obstruction. Vespasian held out for a long time, but in the end the only way to stop the insults and pointless challenges was to execute a few of the perpetrators. The historian Suetonius hints darkly at genuine conspiracies, without giving any details, but it is known that two men were punished in 79 for plotting. Caecina, who had been defeated by Antonius Primus at Cremona, was executed, and a senator, Eprius Marcellus, committed suicide. These blots on Vespasian's reign hardly compare with the terrors of Caligula or Nero.

At the beginning of his reign, Vespasian found the treasury empty, and set about refilling it. Caligula's extravagances had been repaired by Claudius but all the profits that had accrued were frittered away by Nero after he had detached himself from the influence of his advisers. The census that Vespasian conducted and the survey of agricultural lands and produce informed him of the tax potential of the whole Empire, and he immediately began to collect revenues. While he toured Greece, Nero had granted tax immunity to the whole of Achaea, but Vespasian reversed the decision. He also invented new taxes, the most infamous being the tax on urine that the fullers collected outside their establishments. The ammonia content was the main agent in cleaning cloth. Titus protested but had to give in when Vespasian handed him some coins and asked if he could smell anything.

In concert with raising revenues, Vespasian put a brake on unnecessary expenditure. He spent money on worthy causes, such as road building in the provinces, and repair of damages caused by the civil war. In Rome, the buildings on the Capitol Hill had been destroyed or damaged when the Vitellians attacked the Flavians, so restoration of this symbolic site began when Mucianus arrived, presumably endorsed by Vespasian. The spoils taken from Judaea, when the Jewish revolt was crushed, financed the building of the Colosseum, the colloquial name for the Flavian amphitheatre, derived from its location, near the colossal statue of Nero that had stood in the grounds of his notorious Golden House.

By the end of his reign, the treasury was in good health, and he left a flourishing empire after the years of peace. Vespasian died in 79, in his seventieth year, at his home town of Reate in the Sabine country. He asked to be helped to his feet so that he might die upright, and famously joked 'Dear me, I seem to be turning into a god'. He was right of course, since he was deified after his death. The succession was assured. Titus had shared all the major offices with Vespasian and had carried out much of the administrative work of the Empire. He succeeded his father unopposed.

TITUS AD 79–81

The Emperor Titus, who ruled for only one year and two months, is difficult to assess. As a young man he was not popular with either the senators or the populace, but by the time of his accession he had learned how to win friends and influence people. According to the ancient sources he was generous to a fault, providing games and entertainments for the people and distributing lavish presents at most of them. He said that he considered the day lost if he had not been able to give gifts. He dedicated the Colosseum, and put on games for 100 days, and when he opened the new baths on part of the site of the Golden House, he organized gladiatorial shows to celebrate the event.

Two major disasters occurred while Titus was emperor, first the terrible eruption of Vesuvius that obliterated Pompeii and Herculaneum in 79, and then the fire in Rome in 80. Even these served to emphasize Titus's generosity, since he responded by providing men and money to help the victims. After the fire in Rome he sold much of his own property to contribute to the relief fund. Apart from these disasters, Titus's reign was depicted as a golden age. He had been the full partner of Vespasian and was therefore tried and tested before he came to power, but there was some opposition to his rule, mostly from the senatorial class who at the very least felt cheated of a share in government by Titus's continued monopolization of the consulship. Nevertheless no one was executed, there were no treason trials, and informers were driven out of the city.

It may have continued in this way if Titus had lived longer, but it is worth pointing out that if Caligula's and Nero's reigns had lasted for only two years, they too may have been considered generous and enlightened rulers. Another consideration is that the ancient authors would not be reluctant to praise his virtues and to laud his short reign as a sharp contrast to that of his universally detested brother Domitian, who succeeded him when Titus died of an unknown illness in September 81. He was deified by Domitian, about a month later.

DOMITIAN AD 81–96

After Titus's death several stories circulated that Domitian had killed him, or at least hastened his demise, but the variety of methods that he was alleged to have used to despatch Titus give the lie to the tale, all supposition and no substance. Such rumours did not impede the succession. The troops hailed him as Imperator on the day of Titus's death, and on the following day the Senate confirmed Domitian as emperor, with the title Augustus. Within a few days of his accession, Domitian awarded the title Augusta to his wife, Domitia, the daughter of Domitius Corbulo. The precedent had been set by Augustus, who awarded the title to his wife Livia, and the next Imperial lady to receive it was Antonia, who was granted the title posthumously by her son Claudius. She had been awarded it by Caligula, but refused to accept it from his hands. Agrippina took the title as part of her plan to dominate the Roman world through her son Nero. From Domitian's reign onwards it became more common for the wives of emperors to take the title.

During his reign Domitian's titles proliferated. The preamble cited him as *Imperator Caesar divi Vespasiani filius Domitianus Augustus*, indicating that he was the son of the divine Vespasian, with the same titles as his father. Domitian was also *Pater Patriae* (father of his country, a highly honorific appellation) and Pontifex Maximus. More important, tribunician power was granted to him, and he commanded all the armies, with all military and civil appointment within his gift. His rule was assured, but to make certain he followed his father's example, and was also consul for ten years of his fifteen-year reign. He usually stepped down after a few months, giving the opportunity for other men to become suffect consuls and thereby gain experience of government, but during his tenure of the office, Domitian could put administrative measures into effect.

Like other emperors who ended badly, Domitian was said to have begun well. The documentary sources are universally hostile, but Suetonius, who wrote during Hadrian's reign, reports in three separate passages that Domitian's earlier behaviour contrasted sharply with that of his later years. At first he was generous like his brother, fair minded and just. Significantly, Suetonius says that Domitian's cruelty began after the suppression of the revolt of Saturninus in 89.

Domitian was a perfectionist, who would in modern parlance be labelled a control freak. His rule was autocratic, but at least at first it arose from his desire to attend to the smallest detail of government, concerned to oversee everything and do it properly. His administration was sound and sensible. The provinces were governed well, and he seems to have tried to curb extortion, with genuine motives, but he perhaps drove it underground instead. After Domitian's death, his successor Nerva could find very little among his enactments to repeal. His silver coinage was the most pure in content of any that had gone before or was issued afterwards. His buildings had to be magnificent, two examples being the *Domus Augustana*, his palace on the Palatine Hill in Rome, and his villa at Alba, where several centuries later, the summer residence of the Popes was built. The ambition to do nothing sordid or shabby extended to the way in which Domitian represented himself. Probably in 86, he decided that his title should be *dominus et deus*, lord and god. The first part of this title was just about acceptable. Pliny addressed Trajan as *dominus* without hesitation. It is the equivalent of 'master' as workers would address their employers, except that it was interpreted as an indication of how Domitian viewed everyone from the senators to the lowliest slaves. The populace had no trouble in acclaiming Domitian and Domitia as *domino et dominae* on feast days. *Deus* on the other hand, was more suspect. Domitian was the focus of the Imperial cult, but worship of the emperors was directed at their spirit, or *genius* rather than the mortal man. It was said that Domitian demanded obeisance as well, prefiguring the third century emperors who distanced themselves from their subjects in the same way.

At the beginning of his reign Domitian treated the senators with fairness but also with indifference. He tried to pre-empt potential opposition by a studied policy of conciliation, appointing the son of Helvidius Priscus, who had been a thorn in Vespasian's side, to the consulship, to show that there were no hard feelings. He held ten consulships himself but did not restrict access to his own extended family, allowing non-Flavians to take up the office. He continued his father's policy of promoting equestrians, appointing more and more of them to administrative posts, sometimes at the expense of freedmen, who had monopolized Claudius's centralized civil service. At least one equestrian, Lucius Julius Ursus was promoted to the Senate, and then the consulship, after serving as Praetorian Prefect. Another was temporarily appointed to take charge of a proconsular province when the governor was executed for reasons unknown.

The populace were kept entertained by the usual shows and games. On one memorable occasion the Colosseum was flooded to stage a naval battle. But although he attended all the shows, Domitian incurred the displeasure of the audience because he attended to his correspondence while supposedly watching the action. He courted popularity as many emperors did by distributing cash gifts (*congiaria*) to celebrate special occasions, in this case his victories over the German tribe of the Chatti, and the Dacians and the Sarmatians.

At the end of 82 Domitian started to overhaul the mint in Rome. As a committed perfectionist he issued silver coinage of a very high standard, but unfortunately had to devalue it later in his reign. In 83 he awarded a 33 per cent pay rise to the soldiers. It was long overdue, and also very unpopular with everyone except the armies. At some point in 82 or 83 he dismissed the freedman Tiberius Julius who had served under Vespasian and Titus as financial secretary, or *a rationibus*. It is not know who replaced him, or whether this was the first appointment of an equestrian to the post. The freedman Abascantus, secretary *ab epistulis*, whose name is known from the work of the poet Statius, was also dismissed and replaced by an equestrian, Titinius Capito. The rumour grew up that Domitian could not tolerate any of the staff who had worked under Titus and Vespasian, but it is more likely that he considered each case individually and appointed men he thought best suited to the task.

The way in which local government worked in the provinces is illustrated by three municipal charters from towns in Spain, all dated to Domitian's reign. The charters were modelled on the city of Rome, documenting in detail the rights and duties of municipal officials and the ordinary people. It is clear that the municipal authorities were allowed considerable freedom of action in governing their towns, hardly supporting the image of Domitian as oppressor. He continued the work that Vespasian had begun with regard to the provinces, but perhaps with a sense of detachment rather than a genuinely benevolent attitude. He responded to crises and specific needs. When he considered that the food supply was deficient in cereals, he tried to promote the production of grain by issuing an edict that forbade the planting of new vines in Italy, and removed half of the plantations in the rest of the Empire. The law has attracted much speculation as to Domitian's motives, but it probably was a sincere attempt to increase cereal production. In the end it was not practicable, and had to be withdrawn.

The reigns of Vespasian and Titus were not noted for military activity, except for the ongoing campaigns in northern Britain, but under Domitian there were additional actions on the Rhine and Danube. The general who was responsible for the conquest of northern England and most of Scotland was Gnaeus Julius Agricola, who took over from Cerialis and Frontinus and built on their work. He was unusual in that he had served in Britain twice already, as military tribune at the time of the rebellion of Boudicca, as legionary legate of the Twentieth legion, and now as governor of the province, probably from 78 to 84, though these opening and closing dates are much disputed. Most military officers served in different provinces as they were rising to prominence, rather than in the same one at different times. Agricola's career was also unusual in that he was governor of Britain for seven years instead of the more normal three of four. His campaigns on behalf of the Flavian emperors were described by the historian Tacitus, and there are several archaeological remains that illustrate the conquest, but unfortunately it is not so easy to marry up the literature with the archaeology. For the reign of Domitian, the most important question is when and why Agricola's conquests were given up, probably only two or three years after he had fought the final battle, completed the conquest, and left the province to his successor. Tacitus describes the withdrawal of troops with great bitterness, but it is possible that Domitian had good reasons to do so.

Perhaps in 82 or more likely 83, Domitian started a campaign in Germany against the tribesmen of the Chatti, who lived beyond the Rhine. The dates are disputed and the reasons for the war are not clear. The Chatti may have been raiding the province from their homelands, but this is not documented. They were formidable enemies. According to Tacitus, who would never have credited Domitian with a genuine achievement, the Chatti differed from other tribes in that they were united and organized, and could form plans and carry them out, unlike some other tribes. In the words of Tacitus, 'other Germans go to battle, the Chatti make war'.

Domitian raised a new legion called *I Minervia* in honour of his favourite goddess Minerva. This legion probably replaced *XXI Rapax* at Bonn, which accompanied Domitian on campaign, along with detachments from the four legions of Upper Germany. The army may have penetrated far into Chattan territory. The author Julius Frontinus, who had been governor of Britain before Agricola, says that Domitian covered 120 Roman miles on this campaign, which was once taken to mean that he established the frontier line of watchtowers and small forts enclosing the Taunus and Wetterau region of Germany. However, this frontier is probably Vespasian's, developed by Domitian, so Frontinus perhaps meant that Domitian penetrated for a considerable distance into Chattan territory. There is insufficient information to be sure when and in what manner this war ended. Domitian celebrated a triumph in 83, issued a *congiarium* to the populace of Rome in 84, and by 85 he had been acclaimed *Imperator* for the fifth time, but none of these events can be securely related to the Chattan war.

Shortly after the problems on the Rhine were solved, another war broke out on the Danube frontier. Probably in the winter of 85/86, though the date is uncertain, the Dacians crossed the river, defeated the Roman army in Moesia and killed the governor Oppius Sabinus. There may be a connection with the abandonment of Agricola's conquests in Britain and the outbreak of this war, when Domitian needed troops and may have taken some from the British garrison. Coin evidence indicates that Roman troops were in Scotland long enough to receive issues of bronze coins of 86 in their pay, but there are no examples of issues of 87 from the same sites. This suggests that troops were suddenly withdrawn from the newly established forts in Scotland, perhaps because detachments were assembled for Domitian's war, either to strengthen the Rhine frontier while troops from there went to Dacia, or to go direct to the Danube. Despite the expenditure of much ink or keyboard skills, no such connection between the Dacian war and Britain has been conclusively demonstrated to the satisfaction of all parties.

Dacian territory corresponds roughly to modern Romania, with the Carpathian mountains as their stronghold. The Dacians were fearsome fighters, led by Decebalus, who had been building up a power base for some time. He had perhaps removed the original chief Diurpaneus, who seems to have started the war. These Dacian leaders were not the first to unify the tribesmen. In the reign of Augustus, the Dacians were potentially just as troublesome, under their chief Burebista. Other tribes from the vast territory beyond the Danube had successfully attacked Roman territory and been repulsed, the Roxolani in 67, and the Sarmatians in 69, taking advantage of the turmoil of the civil war in Rome. Mucianus repelled them on his journey from Syria to Italy. In the following year they attacked again, defeating the Romans and killing the governor of Moesia, Fonteius Agrippa. Vespasian sent out a new governor, Rubrius Gallus, who restored order, and strengthened the frontier according to Vespasian's orders. Domitian's problems on the Danube were therefore not new.

The reasons why the Dacians invaded are unknown. There may have been pressure from other tribes, or a shortage of lands, or they may have become alarmed at Domitian's success against the Chatti, and decided to attack before the Romans attacked them. Domitian responded as rapidly as possible, collecting an army with the Praetorian Prefect Cornelius Fuscus in command, and set off with the troops to the Danube. Little is known about the progress of the war, but between February and September 86 Domitian was hailed as *Imperator* by the troops three times, making his total up to fourteen. Victories of some kind are indicated, but probably in the following year, Cornelius Fuscus mounted what should have been a punitive expedition across the Danube and was defeated and killed. There seems to have been a hiatus while Domitian collected another army, and devoted some time to thorough preparation and reconnaissance. He may also have divided Moesia into two provinces at this time, called Moesia Superior and Moesia Inferior. The governors of these two provinces, Funisulanus Vettonianus and Curiatius Maternus, were both rewarded by Domitian, perhaps for work in stabilizing the frontier. The result of the long preparation was a victory at a site called Tapae, under Tettius Julianus, dated without conclusive proof to 88. There is no record of a peace treaty or even a proper conclusion to the war. When he was assassinated, Domitian was preparing for another Danube campaign, indicating that Decebalus had not been subdued. The Dacians may have been bought off with cash payments, since in January 89 Domitian was faced with a rebellion by the Roman commander in Upper Germany, Lucius Antonius Saturninus.

Saturninus could call upon four legions, two based at Mainz, and one each at Vindonissa (modern Windisch) and one at Argentorate (modern Strasburg). His aims are not clear, but his discontent coupled with the precedent of Vitellius's march on Rome twenty years before may have spurred him on to attempt to usurp Domitian. On his way from Rome to Mainz, Domitian summoned the single legion from Spain, *VII Gemina*, which was commanded by Marcus Ulpius Trajanus, the future Emperor Trajan. Before they reached Mainz, the commander in Lower Germany, Aulus Buccius Lappius Maximus, had attacked and defeated Saturninus. His legions received the honorary title *pia fidelis Domitiana*, but the latter part of this title was dropped after Domitian's assassination.

Retribution was swift and gruesome. Partisans of Saturninus were hunted down and killed, and although no senators were punished because there was no proof that any of them had been involved, Domitian was probably left wondering about how many of them knew about the plot. Suetonius says that Domitian became more suspicious and cruel after the revolt, which may well be true. The Emperor had tried somewhat dispassionately to foster good relations with the Senate, but he had felt quite secure with the army, and now that was shattered. From now onwards, there were to be no double legionary fortresses such as that at Mainz, because too many soldiers stationed in one place would be useful to future usurpers. Domitian also restricted the amount of money that could be held in the soldiers' savings accounts in the fort headquarters to 1,000 sesterces, because Saturninus had used all the cash at the fortresses to finance the rebellion.

As soon as the rebellion been put down, news arrived of trouble in Pannonia, where Domitian arrived probably in the spring of 89. The tribes of the Marcomanni and Quadi constituted the main threat to Roman security, but the official excuse for the war against them was that they had not sent help for the campaign against the Dacians. At about this time, Domitian made a treaty with the Dacians, which he does not seem to have arranged before withdrawing from their territory after the battle at Tapae. By the terms of this treaty, Dacia became a client state of Rome. Client kings received the title *Rex sociusque amicus*, friend and ally of the Roman people. The Dacians received subsidies and Roman assistance to build forts to defend themselves against other tribes. The payment of subsidies was a system of external control that the Romans had used before and would use throughout their history, in order to keep the leader of a tribe well disposed to Rome, and willing to control his own people. The system was employed to good effect later, in the second century, by the Emperor Hadrian to ensure peace beyond the frontiers. It was never a popular scheme with the Senate and people of Rome because it looked like tribute from a weaker state to a stronger one, and in Domitian's case the terms of the treaty caused enormous discontent, most especially because of the assistance in fort building. When the next war was waged by the Emperor Trajan, the forts had to be taken and destroyed.

One of the terms of the treaty allowed the Romans to march through Dacian territory to attack the Marcomanni and Quadi. Little is known about the course of the war against these tribes, except that the number of legions in Pannonia was increased from two to four, while no other province held more than three. Furthermore, although Domitian held a triumph at the end of 89 over the Dacians, and the Chatti, which really meant Saturninus, he held none over the Marcommani. The Danube wars were not finished, and broke out again in 92. This time, Domitian may have been engaged on two fronts, fighting the Sarmatians as well as the Marcomanni, but the evidence used to support this theory, documenting awards to military officers for their exploits in a war against Germans and Sarmatians, is not securely dated to Domitian's reign.

At the end of the war of 92 on the Danube, the Empire was predominantly peaceful. Domitian attended to the defence of the provinces, continuing Vespasian's and Titus's work. He did not annexe Dacia after the Danube campaigns and made no attempt to regain Scotland after the troops were withdrawn. The eastern provinces were quiet for the time being, since the Parthians were not aggressive, perhaps because there were now six legions to defend the frontier, one in Judaea, two in Cappadocia and three in Syria. In the west, the Rhine ceased to be the main theatre of war, while on the Danube the numbers of troops increased to meet an escalating threat. After the assassination of Domitian this threat was ultimately left to Trajan to deal with.

Most of the disturbance was now focused on Rome itself, where the reign of terror had begun. In 91, Domitian had executed Cornelia, a Vestal Virgin who had been found guilty of immoral relations with more than one man. The ancient penalty for Vestal Virgins who reneged on their vow of chastity was to be buried alive, and Domitian insisted on the strict application of the law. Allegedly it was Cornelia's second offence, so Domitian could not afford to acquit her when she merited punishment, but the barbarity of the punishment was held against him. A series of executions took place in 93, beginning with Herennius Senecio, the author of a work praising Helvidius Priscus, Vespasian's opponent. Arulenus Rusticus was next, for writing about Thrasea Paetus, related to Priscus and another opponent of Imperial rule. The younger Helvidius had written a play parodying Domitian's household, so despite having promoted him to the consulship, Domitian executed him too. The episode was particularly sordid because the senators, eager to exonerate themselves perhaps, manhandled Priscus to prison. All these victims were Stoics, related to each other by marriage ties, and the women of their families were exiled.

More senators were executed in the following years, for reasons that may be deliberately obscured in the sources, to portray them as the unpredictable whims of an unhinged tyrant. Acilius Glabrio was forced to fight in the arena, on account of his impiety, and Domitian's cousin Titus Flavius Clemens was executed for atheism. Salvius Cocceianus unwisely celebrated the birthday of his kinsman Otho, the emperor of 69, and was therefore executed for having designs on usurping the throne. Pompusianus was despatched because he read the speeches of famous generals, and went about carrying a map of the world. There were more examples, but the point has been made that executions became more and more commonplace, for improbable reasons. The victims may have been involved in plots against Domitian, but the number of executions could only foment more plots as senators and equites feared for their lives.

Domitian used to say that no one would believe him if he said men were plotting against him until he was dead. The tragedy is that when the final conspiracy was formed it started not among the senators but very close to home. It was the members of his own household staff who killed him, allegedly with the consent of his wife Domitia. No senators were ever proven to have been part of the conspiracy but the alacrity with which the aged senator Marcus Cocceius Nerva was proclaimed emperor suggests that at least some leading men were informed of the plot and were ready and waiting to act once the assassination had occurred.

Domitian was forty-five years old when he was killed on 18 September 96. He was almost universally detested, except for the populace of Rome, who remained largely indifferent. Only the Praetorians mourned his loss. His memory was damned, and the historian Tacitus made sure that he remained so for all time.

NERVA AD 96–98

The accession of the Emperor Nerva was accomplished without a hitch, so smoothly in fact that it is assumed that he must have been a party to the assassination plot and had been waiting in the wings for his stage entrance. He was not the designated heir of the previous emperor, and he was the first to be chosen by the senators and not by the army, so he had to ensure that the soldiers accepted him. The Praetorians were courted by him but eventually forced him to execute the assassins of Domitian, some considerable time after the murder had taken place.

In reviewing Domitian's administration and legislation, Nerva left most of it intact, but repealed certain harmless acts with exaggerated fuss. For the Roman populace and the troops, there were cash gifts, and the burdens of the poor were partly relieved by tax exemptions and land distributions, partly funded by a sale of Nerva's own property. Poor families in Italy were assisted by a new scheme, the *alimenta*, a three-way arrangement where the state lent to several small farmers a percentage of the value of their lands, which acted as security. Interest rates were very low, and the payments were directed to the local municipality instead of to Rome, so that the money could be used to make grants to support and feed young children until they reached puberty. Trajan took on the scheme and developed it.

Since he had no heirs and was already past middle age, Nerva looked around for an acceptable successor, and chose Marcus Ulpius Trajanus, a military officer who had served under Domitian and supported him at the time of Saturninus's revolt in 89. Nerva formally adopted him, and appointed him as governor of Upper Germany. Imperial powers were conferred on Trajan before he succeeded, so there could be no doubt as to who the next emperor should be, when Nerva died at the beginning of 98.

TRAJAN AD 98–117

The Emperor Trajan was the first provincial to become emperor. He was born *c.*53 at Italica, in Spain, and his family owed its success to Vespasian, who had made Trajan's father a senator. Vespasian was not a Roman aristocrat, but an Italian, and Trajan was not even an Italian, which demonstrates the expansion of Roman citizenship and social mobility in Italy and the Empire. In only a few generations from the time of Augustus, first the Italians and then provincials were admitted to the consulship, and within a short time they could also aspire to Imperial rule.

When Nerva died, Trajan was governor of Upper Germany, but he already possessed full Imperial powers. He wrote to the Senate, but did not come to the city. Instead he marched from the Rhine to the Danube, where the tribesmen threatened the province of Pannonia, and in Dacia, Decebalus was once again building up his power base. The new emperor remained in the Danube provinces until autumn 99, possibly strengthening frontier defences and reconnoitring the area, and gathering intelligence. It does not seem that he fought important battles or advanced into non-Roman territory, but Domitian had been preparing for another Danube campaign when he was assassinated, so there was some unfinished business with the tribes, but Trajan did not make a move for another two years.

He made a good impression when he returned to Rome by entering modestly on foot instead of riding at the head of troops. He was immensely popular with the regular army, so he could afford the gesture of ejecting the Praetorians who had executed Domitian's assassins. His cash gift to the guardsmen was much less than other emperors had paid but there were no repercussions. He spent two years in Rome attending to all sectors of society, not simply to court popularity, although that was one of the effects, but to show concern for the well-being of Romans, Italians and provincials. In 99 when he arrived from the Danube he gave 300 sesterces each to the Roman people, which was not unusual, but he also added more names to the lists for the free corn dole.

In 101 he embarked on the first of his Dacian wars. The years from his inspection tour in 99 had probably been spent in preparing for this war, which was a popular move, especially since he concentrated on the disgraceful treaty that Domitian had made, involving payments to the Dacians and technical assistance from Roman engineers. It is possible that Domitian himself intended to reverse this policy as soon as he was able, or there was a reasonable excuse, but it was Trajan who did so, and took the credit for it. The cause of the war is not known. There does not seem to have been an invasion of Roman territory, so it is possible that Decebalus was keeping within the terms of the treaty. But the Romans did not trust him, and they were eager to see Domitian's arrangements overturned.

Preparations for the advance into Dacia included repairing the road originally built by Tiberius on the Roman side of the Danube, near an awe-inspiring gorge called the Iron Gates. Trajan assembled a huge army of at least nine legions, or large detachments from them, since some soldiers were probably left behind as small garrisons, and a number of auxiliary units, and crossed the Danube into Dacian territory. There was a battle at Tapae, where Domitian's general Tettius Julianus first defeated Decebalus. This time there was no satisfactory conclusion, and Trajan decided to spend the winter on the Roman side of the Danube. He was attacked by the Roxolani but the Romans beat them off.

The second year of the campaign was more successful. The Romans struck at the heart of Dacian territory and fought so hard that Decebalus was forced to submit. According to the terms of a treaty that was imposed on him, Decebalus surrendered his war equipment, and promised military assistance for the Romans. It was common for defeated tribes to provide troops for the Roman army, which at one and the same time reinforced the troops of the province to which they were sent and reduced the available manpower of the tribes.

Trajan did not annexe Dacian territory, though he left some troops north of the Danube, and the Roman army of Moesia and Pannonia would monitor events. It took three years for Decebalus to rearm. When he was ready he attacked the Iazyges, who were allies of Rome, defeated and expelled Trajan's garrisons and then erupted into Moesia, in 105. Other tribes joined him. Trajan arrived as quickly as possible, and had to spend time in winning back the loyalty of these tribes so that he could advance without fear of being cut off. In 106 he built a stone bridge with a wooden superstructure across the Danube and entered Dacian territory. After fierce fighting the Romans captured the Dacian capital at Sarmizegethusa. Decebalus was nearly taken but committed suicide. Resistance collapsed, and this time Dacia was annexed and placed under a consular governor with two legions and auxiliary troops. The new province was bordered on the west by the River Tisza, on the east by the River Aluta, and on the south by the Danube. The annexation enabled the Romans to protect the Danube more easily from incursions from the north.

The victories were marked by three monuments at Adamklissi, a circular mausoleum or Tropaeum, and an altar recording the first Dacian war, and another circular mausoleum for the second war. Both campaigns were recorded in pictorial detail on the carved reliefs spiralling up Trajan's column in Rome. It had been well worth the effort. The Carpathians were rich in minerals, with lucrative iron mines, but better still they were virtually overflowing with gold and silver. Trajan held the victory title Dacicus, possibly after the first war, but this honorary description, and his unofficial title Optimus Princeps which was awarded to him early in his reign, were more than justified by the successful outcome of the second war, which so enriched the Roman state. The precious metals brought back to Rome were measured in hundreds of tons.

While the second Dacian war was in progress, the client king of Arabia Petraea, died in 105. It was Pompey who made the territory a client kingdom, and it had remained so ever since, but now the location of the country, neighbouring Syria and the Parthian Empire, made it strategically important, so instead of installing another king, Trajan ordered the governor of Syria, Aulus Cornelius Palma, to send troops in. The southern part of the kingdom formed the new province of Arabia, with a new capital at Bostra, which became the headquarters of a legion from the Syrian garrison. Trajan's newly raised legion, II *Traiana*, was sent to Syria to replace it. The northern part of Arabia was attached to Syria itself. The extra legion in the east would help to protect the frontier and strengthen the army if there were to be a campaign against Parthia.

Trajan now spent some years in Rome, where he embarked on a building programme that included the Forum that bears his name, with rows of shops, a law court, and two libraries, one for Latin works and one for Greek. The column recording the Dacian wars stood inside the new forum. Trajan's Baths were founded in the city, and he built another theatre. Roads and bridges were built to facilitate communications in Italy, the harbour at Ostia was improved and building work was carried out at other ports. The *alimenta* scheme that Nerva had established was developed, and in Rome children were added to the list of those eligible for the corn dole to ease the burdens of the poor.

In the provinces, the financial situation in some of the towns had deteriorated. As some of the leading men had become senators and took a more active part in the government of the Empire, the towns from which they were drawn began to suffer a decline in manpower, and in consequence were deprived of the skills and wealth of these men who would normally have devoted all their energies to government at home. The problem was made worse when the remaining town councillors embarked on ambitious plans to outdo each other, and other communities, in embellishing their towns and providing entertainments. Provincial governors could not direct affairs in the cities which had been proclaimed free and autonomous, and normally the emperors did not interfere with the administration of towns in the senatorial provinces, but Trajan reviewed the problems and swept all custom aside. He appointed *curatores* to take over financial affairs in some towns. The first known example is Caere in Italy, in 113, and perhaps the best known example of the direction of affairs in a whole province is Bithynia, where the Younger Pliny was sent out as governor under Trajan's watchful eye. The letters that Pliny wrote about everyday details, and Trajan's short, sometimes monosyllabic replies, bring history and administration alive.

The years of peace were ended in 113. The Parthians under Chosroes began to stir, and trouble arose as always over Armenia. Chosroes placed one of his nephews on the Armenian throne, which was interpreted as an act of war. Chosroes tried to negotiate and was refused. Trajan assembled an army and advanced to Armenia in 114. He decided against trying to control it by means of friendly kings, and annexed the whole country, but this did not solve the problem entirely. As with all Roman annexations, the border shifted to neighbouring territory, in this case to Mesopotamia, and if Armenia was to be controlled and protected, the package had to include Mesopotamia as well. About eighty years later, Severus encountered the same problem. After spending the winter at Antioch, Trajan advanced into Parthia from Zeugma, summoning troops from his allies and trying to detach the allies of the Persians from Chosroes. He overran the upper reaches of the River Euphrates and northern Mesopotamia, and then retired to winter quarters at Antioch. The next campaign took him to the Parthian capital at Ctesiphon, in 116. He annexed more territory as the new province of Parthia, and dealt with the rest of the vast Parthian Empire by fostering dissension among the claimants to the throne, bestowing the crown on yet another of Chosroes' nephews.

The annexation of such large territories was too much, too soon. There was no consolidation, and not enough manpower to garrison and administer the provinces. It all began to fall apart almost immediately. A widespread rebellion of the Jews over much of the east caused disruption and tied down Roman troops in Mesopotamia, Africa, Egypt and Cyprus, and in 117 there was trouble in Dacia as well. Quadratus Bassus, the governor of Syria, was sent to deal with it, and in his place Trajan appointed his relative and close associate, Publius Aelius Hadrianus, who had accompanied him in the Dacian wars, and to the east, though it is not known in what capacity.

When all was reasonably quiet in the east, but not pacified, Trajan decided to return to Rome. He never arrived, suffering a stroke at Selinus in Cilicia. His wife Plotina and the Praetorian Prefect Acilius Attianus were with him. He died after a few days, probably on 8 August. The short interval would allow some time for Plotina and Attianus to inform Hadrian, in Syria, and to decide what to do. Trajan had obviously groomed Hadrian for the succession, appointing him to important posts and advancing his career, but he had not formally adopted him or specifically named him as the next emperor. Hadrian therefore succeeded Trajan with only the sworn testimony of Plotina and Attianus that he had been adopted and named as heir on Trajan's deathbed. Fortunately the troops in Syria readily accepted him, and he counted his *dies imperii* as 8 August, but it was not an auspicious beginning.

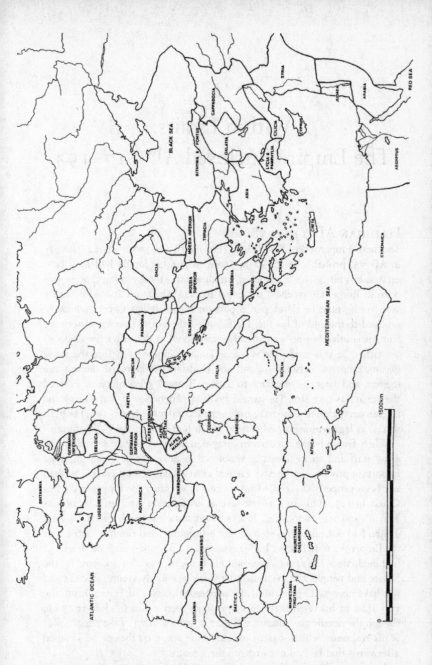

Map 1. Map of the provinces of the Roman Empire in the second century, at its largest extent after the conquests of the Emperor Trajan. When Hadrian succeeded he abandoned some of the recently conquered territory and devoted his energies to consolidation and protection of the Empire.

11

Within Limits:
The Empire Enclosed AD 117–193

HADRIAN AD 117–138

The new Emperor Publius Aelius Hadrianus, was born on 24 January in AD 76, probably at Italica in Spain, where his family had long held estates. His birthplace is disputed, an alternative theory being that he was born in Rome. He received the usual Roman education and while still a very young man he developed a passion for all things Greek, which he retained to the end of his life. He followed the normal career pattern for Roman youths, but he was already exceptional in that after the death of his father, he was made the ward of Trajan, some time before the latter became emperor. Between 95 and 100 Hadrian served as tribune in three legions, and after his marriage to Sabina, Trajan's great-niece, he entered the Senate as quaestor. He gained his first experience of war during the Dacian campaign of 101–102, and in the second war of 105–106, Hadrian served as legate of *legio I Minervia*, which had been raised by Domitian.

When Trajan began his eastern campaign in 113, Hadrian served on the army staff and was eventually appointed as governor of Syria, the most important province in the east. He was clearly favoured by Trajan, but had not been properly designated his successor, so when the Emperor died in Cilicia in 117, Hadrian was not sure of his position until his adoption as Trajan's son was announced. It all seemed somewhat ambiguous, because Trajan had not taken this step during his lifetime, and rumours arose that the Emperor's wife Plotina had engineered the adoption after her husband had died. Since the armies accepted Hadrian, he was also accepted by the Senate and people, but even then, he was not entirely secure, since he did not have universal approval as the adopted successor of Trajan. From the very start of his reign there seems to have been a plot to eliminate him, though the details are obscure. All that is really known of the alleged plot is his response, which was to execute four senators, though he claimed afterwards that he had not ordered their deaths.

Arriving in Rome in the summer of 118, Hadrian spent a short time in the city, arranging a triumph to celebrate Trajan's victories, which may have seemed hypocritical to some senators in view of the fact that Hadrian abandoned some of his predecessor's territorial gains. In 121 the Emperor set off on the first of his many travels through the Empire, beginning with the Rhineland, and then journeying to Britain in 122. From then until 127 he travelled in Gaul, Spain, Greece, Asia and Sicily. In 128 after a brief stay in Rome he went to Africa, where he reviewed the troops and made a speech in praise of them, which has been preserved on an inscription. He spent more time out of Rome than in it, but he took many officials with him and attended to the government of the Empire while travelling. He was the first emperor to take an interest in the provinces and the troops, and in the lives of ordinary people, but even this beneficent attitude did little to increase his popularity.

Hadrian had an innate desire to tidy things up, to codify and put everything in order. Attending to the law, he tried to alleviate the burdens of the Roman citizens in Italy who had to come to Rome if they wanted to present appeals. Hadrian divided Italy into four regions and appointed four ex-consulars to hear the cases in each area, but it seemed as though he regarded Italy as just another province and the scheme was abandoned after his death. His more lasting achievement was in private law, which was dealt with by the *praetor urbanus*, each of whom issued the praetor's edict on taking up office. The edict was substantially the same as that of the preceding praetor, but changes could be made to it as the praetors dealt with new cases. Hadrian asked the jurist Salvius Julianus to codify the existing laws, and the result was the *Edictum Perpetuum*, a permanent set of laws, which henceforth could be altered only by the Emperor or the Senate.

Hadrian's interest in the arts extended to buildings, and in Rome itself he was responsible for the massive Temple of Venus and Rome which now faces the Colosseum, and for the unique Pantheon, on the site of a temple that was first built by Marcus Vipsanius Agrippa. The Pantheon still bears Agrippa's name, not that of Hadrian. Another celebrated building is Hadrian's villa at Tivoli, where he could retreat and devote himself to private study on the few occasions when he was not travelling.

His personal life was not happy. He was estranged from his wife Sabina, and had no children, and his passionate attachment to the youth Antinous detracted from his image. Like Augustus, he was unfortunate in his first choice of heir. He adopted Lucius Ceionius Commodus, who took the name of Lucius Aelius Caesar. This man was intended to be the next emperor but he died before Hadrian, who then adopted Titus Aurelius Fulvius Boionius Antoninus, better known as Antoninus Pius. The adoption was carried out on condition that Antoninus in turn adopted the seven-year-old Lucius Verus, the son of Lucius Ceionius Commodus, and the teenager Marcus Annius Verus, who became the Emperor Marcus Aurelius.

The Frontiers of the Roman Empire

Hadrian's most enduring contribution to the Roman Empire is the creation of the frontier systems. During the reign of Trajan the Roman Empire had reached its greatest extent. With his death in 117 the period of aggressive, or accidental, expansion came to an end. Whenever the Romans had acquired new conquests they inevitably came into contact with new neighbours, who could be compliant or aggressive, according to their perceptions of the Romans. In the prevailing opinion of the Romans, whatever the mood of their neighbours, there was always an imperative for the defence of their boundaries, which sometimes led to new wars and new conquests and then new boundaries. Militaristic imperialism, trading considerations, and the search for precious metals, also played their part in expansion and annexation, but on some occasions Rome's remorseless empire-building can be classified under the heading of the search for viable and safe boundaries.

The Empire that Trajan bequeathed to his successor Hadrian was the product of several centuries of territorial expansion. This expansion had necessitated the continual evolution of the administrative system that had been designed originally to deal with a city state. Roman provincial government and military organization had been modified and adapted to cope with the steady addition of new territories. On the whole this had been a largely successful enterprise, since the Romans were comfortable with improvization, adaptation and change when necessary. After the death of Emperor Trajan, who had expanded the Empire and earned considerable popularity for doing so, Hadrian reversed this policy, calling a halt to endless conquest. One of his first decisions was to give up the recent conquests north of the Danube, and he abandoned Trajan's schemes for a war with the Parthians. It would have been unnecessarily costly in terms of manpower and cash, and another reason for turning his back on an eastern campaign was his immediate need to consolidate his power in Rome and the Empire. The execution of the four senators at the outset of his reign was an inauspicious time, and if he had then gone to Parthia to carry out the war that Trajan had planned it would probably have been a suicidal act.

His policy of ending imperial expansion made him extremely unpopular with almost everyone, because it went against the Roman ethos of *imperium sine fine*, power without end. If Rome did not continually extend her control of new lands and new peoples, the senators would be deprived of opportunity to govern and possibly exploit new provinces, the military men would be deprived of glory, and traders would be deprived of profit. Hadrian probably thought that the costs of administration and defence of a constantly expanding Empire would outstrip the resources of the Empire as a whole.

Initially, the abandonment of Trajan's conquests may not have been viewed with alarm, since it was not irreversible, but Hadrian made it clear that this was not a temporary withdrawal from the land beyond Dacia and from a potential eastern war, but a permanent state of affairs. He set about the creation of clearly marked boundaries, enclosing the Empire, and ending the expansion into areas beyond the frontiers. He wanted to consolidate within these boundaries the territory that he thought Rome could successfully administer.

From the mid-second century onwards, parts of the Empire were protected by physical barriers such as the appropriately named Hadrian's Wall in Britain, or the timber palisade in Germany. In Raetia there was another stone wall, not as massive as the one in Britain, and in parts of Africa stone walls were built to guard the agricultural lands and guide the pastoral tribes with their flocks and herds onto the designated paths. If there was no physical barrier, the Roman provinces were enclosed within plainly marked and protected boundaries which divided Roman territory from that of the various non-Roman peoples.

The purpose of the frontiers and how they worked are subject to scholarly debate. Were the frontiers designed to stop all movement, or were they designed to channel the movement of people, to watch and guard, and probably collect tolls at the same time? There is no surviving ancient record of what the frontiers were intended to do. Only the historian Eutropius, writing in the late Empire, touches on the subject by informing his readers that Hadrian built a wall in Britain to divide the Romans from the barbarians, which is not very helpful to military strategists, archaeologists or modern historians. The purpose and function of the frontiers may have been slightly different in each province, perhaps adapted to local circumstances, and the Romans may have operated in different ways at different times in the frontier zones, responding to perceived threats. Some modern historians have labelled Roman frontiers as ultimate failures, but it does not seem that the Romans thought of them in that way. Antoninus Pius, Marcus Aurelius, Septimius Severus, Diocletian, Constantine and Valentinian all repaired frontier works, or established new ones on much the same pattern as before.

There were some later adjustments, and on occasions there were campaigns that went beyond the frontiers. Antoninus Pius made some territorial advances in Britain and in Germany, but he did not depart from the established Hadrianic pattern of a running barrier with forts strung out along them. As far as the Romans were concerned the system worked and the frontiers were neither destroyed nor breached until the onslaughts of the mid-third century. Even then, the damage was repaired and the frontiers were put back into commission.

The establishment of the frontiers does not mean that the Romans would henceforth have absolutely nothing to do with the people on the other side of the boundaries. Diplomatic relations still continued, trading was allowed in both directions across the frontiers, though usually at specified locations, and client states were designated as friends of Rome. In some cases, especially on the northern frontier beyond the Rhine and Danube, the Romans promoted and supported a tribal chief and the elite groups by means of gifts and subsidies, in return for which the local ruler would keep his people in order and friendly to Rome. Gift exchange was an established native custom for most tribes, but after Hadrian's reign gift giving was not always viewed sympathetically at Rome, sometimes falling into the category of bribes to buy peace. One of the greatest advantages of friendly relations with the tribesmen was the provision of recruits for the army. The soldiers from the Germanic tribes proved loyal to Rome and served her well, and in the straitened circumstances of the third century, the Romans would probably have been overwhelmed if they had been unable to tap into this huge resource of manpower.

For most of the time while Hadrian was emperor there was peace, in that there were no major wars such as those that had characterised the reign of Trajan. There were localized rebellions, which were put down with relatively little trouble, except for the Jewish revolts, one at the beginning of Hadrian's reign, and another more serious one from 132 to 135 under the leader Bar Kochba. The death toll on both sides was high, and the Roman victory was bitter. From 70 onwards the province of Judaea had been governed by a praetorian legate who also commanded the legion, but after the suppression of the Bar Kochba revolt the province lost its Jewish identity and was more tightly controlled, being renamed Syria Palaestina and assigned to a consular governor. The Jews were denied entry to Jerusalem. To this day, the Jews refer to Hadrian by a scatological term.

ANTONINUS PIUS AD 138–161

Hadrian died in July 138, and was succeeded by Antoninus Pius, who was immediately presented with a problem. The Senate expressed its collective dislike of Hadrian by refusing to deify him, and proposing that all his acts should be nullified. As the new emperor pointed out, if this proposal was achieved, then he would not be emperor. The Senate backed down, deified Hadrian and awarded Antoninus the name Pius, for his delicate dealings with his predecessor's memory. The Roman Empire entered into one of the most prolonged periods of peace that it had ever known, labelled as a true golden age, in contrast to the turmoil that began shortly afterwards.

Hadrian's work in pacifying, protecting, and integrating the peoples of the Empire was one of the most important contributory factors to this peaceful and prosperous reign. There were no serious wars, only some minor actions in the provinces of Dacia, Mauretania and Numidia. The frontiers that Hadrian had established were extended, in Germany by an eastward advance for a few miles, and in Britain by a considerable drive northwards into Scotland, to the narrow gap between the Firth of Forth and the River Clyde. In each case a new frontier line was drawn, almost exactly like the lines that had just been abandoned. No new system was invented to guard the frontiers, and in Britain the advance northwards from Hadrian's Wall was very short lived, so that the Hadrianic system was quickly reconstituted.

For the twenty-three years of Antoninus's reign, there were no spectacular trials, no treasonable actions, no executions, no financial crises and no scandals, the lack of which leaves the historians, both ancient and modern, with very little to say about the period. Unfortunately, this golden age was about to become, in the words of Cassius Dio, one of iron and rust.

MARCUS AURELIUS AD 161–180

When Antoninus Pius died in 161, the two boys who had been adopted as his sons, Lucius Verus and Marcus Aurelius, both succeeded him, without faction or personal rivalry. They shared power equally, both adopting the title Augustus. Sharing power in this way was not a new idea. In the first century, Titus had been given the title Augustus along with his father Vespasian. In 166, Marcus Aurelius's two young sons, Commodus and Annius Verus, were both granted the title Caesar, and from the second century onwards this title was used to designate the junior partners, who were the designated successors to Imperial rule.

The reign of Marcus Aurelius was beset by various problems. Not long after his accession, Armenia came under threat from the Parthians. The control of Armenia was always a bone of contention between the two Empires, so Rome prepared for war. Lucius Verus campaigned against the Parthian regime for four years from 162 to 166, reliant upon his military officers for eventual success. Almost immediately after the conclusion of peace in the east, bands of tribesmen from across the Danube invaded the Roman Empire in 166 or 167. Marcus Aurelius and Lucius Verus marched to repel the invasion.

The tribes of the Marcomanni, Quadi, Sarmatae or Sarmatians, and the Iazyges entered Dacia, and crossed the Danube into Pannonia. The Romans had already met the Marcomanni and Quadi in the first century. During the reign of Augustus, one of the prominent men among the Marcomanni, Maroboduus, united the tribesmen and promoted himself as their leader. When he was toppled by another tribesman called Catvalda, Maroboduus was brought to Italy by Tiberius and settled near Ravenna where he remained for the rest of his life. The Marcomanni were subsequently threatened by another tribe, so the Romans allowed them to migrate and settle on the north bank of the Danube. From then onwards until their eruption across the Danube in the 160s, nothing much was heard of the Marcomanni.

The Sarmatians and Iazyges were descended from the same nomadic roots, originally located on the lower reaches of the Danube, but they moved westwards through Dacia and settled again on the Hungarian plain. Emperor Domitian launched a campaign against them in 89, and they were sufficiently pacified for Trajan to convert them into allies of Rome. In the 160s they joined with the Marcomanni to attack the Roman provinces. At one point the tribes even penetrated Italy, reaching Aquileia, which was uncomfortably close to Rome. The Romans would probably not need to read their history books to remember the invasions of the Cimbri and Teutones during the Republic, and the efforts that were necessary to repel them.

The tribesmen were not always intent on destruction and hit and run raids. Many of them wanted to settle within the Roman Empire, and Marcus accommodated them, finding lands for some of the tribes in Dacia, Pannonia and Moesia, perhaps even in Italy itself. This was neither the first nor the last such settlement as more and more tribes approached the Roman world, fleeing from fiercer tribes who flushed them out of their homes, or seeking more fertile lands on which to settle. Once they were inside the Empire these tribes often provided recruits for the Roman army.

Campaigning against the tribes who did not want to settle or were denied access to the Empire, Marcus adopted a policy of continual harassment, not allowing them to stay in one place, breaking up gatherings but preventing free movement, and restricting the places where the tribesmen could conduct their trading activities with the Roman Empire. This last measure probably hit hard, because the leaders of the tribes were often dependent upon receiving goods from the Roman world and being able to trade their own produce, so that they could control the flow of wealth to their own men and thereby remain in their eminent position as leaders. The importance of trading rights to the tribesmen is disputed, because there is no evidence for an abundance of Roman artefacts that found their way into the territory beyond the frontiers, or *barbaricum* as the Romans called it. But the withdrawal of trading rights was employed by more than one emperor in connection with tribal wars, so the Romans presumably knew that it had an adverse effect.

The wars against the northern tribes began in 166 and lasted until Marcus's death in 180, with a short respite of about three years from 173 to 176. The ultimate aim of Marcus's wars with the tribes, apart from driving them out of Italy, was perhaps to defeat them decisively and then to annexe and garrison their territory. According to the historian

Cassius Dio, he planned to create two provinces called Sarmatia and Marcomannia, but whether this is true or false has been debated. If there was such a plan, it was never realized.

After the death of Lucius Verus in 169, Marcus fought most of these northern wars alone as sole emperor, while also combating other problems that threatened the Empire. Verus had most probably been a victim of the plague of unknown origin, which had first broken out in the early 160s. It killed hundreds of civilians and soldiers. State bankruptcy was another threat to stability. In a noble gesture, and to set an example, Marcus sold the Palace furniture and his personal goods.

Another unexpected threat to the regime broke out in 175. While Marcus was fighting in the north, his friend Avidius Cassius, who was governor of the province of Asia, raised revolt. There are conflicting accounts of the reasons behind the rebellion. It was said that he was wrongly informed that the Emperor had died, and in order to preserve the Empire he organized a take-over, which was of necessity termed a revolt. Other rumours blamed Marcus's wife Faustina for encouraging Avidius, because she was afraid that her husband, who was beginning to show signs of serious illness, might die, and she wished to find a champion who would ensure the succession of her son Commodus. Whatever his reasons, Avidius was declared emperor. He governed Egypt, where he could control most of Rome's corn supply, and most of the eastern provinces declared for him. After three months and six days his rule was ended and he was killed. It was a bitter personal blow for Marcus, all the more tragic since Avidius was his friend.

In governing the Roman Empire, Marcus Aurelius preserved much of the established practice of his predecessors, continuing to develop practices which had already been established, but he also initiated a new order. Social distinctions began to be crystallized, but the snobbery of the Republic and early Empire was relaxed. Augustus had inaugurated a limited social mobility that was fostered by the Flavians and by Hadrian, and Marcus finally separated social rank from noble birth. He judged people by their abilities, and appointed them to situations where their talents could be utilized to the greatest effect. Henceforth rank was bound up with the civilian or military posts held by each individual, but in order to avoid upsetting the old order he often elevated men of proven competence to the necessary social status normally associated with the appointments. He promoted non-senators by adlecting them to the Senate, sometimes providing them with the necessary funds so that they qualified for the rank. He appointed some of them to legionary commands, and in some cases to the consulship.

Marcus's relationship with the Senate was cordial and benign. He listened to the opinions of his senators, and discussed his policies with them. The equestrians were reorganized on a hierarchical basis, with superlative labels for each stage in a man's advancement from *egregius*, to *perfectissimus*, and then to *eminentissimus*. More administrative posts were created for equestrians, especially procuratorial offices. The Imperial civil service was expanded; the finance minister, *a rationibus*, was given a higher salary and an assistant. The *consilium principis*, previously an advisory body, was granted official status, and its members received the title *consiliaris*. The city prefect was given wider juridical powers, and the Praetorian Prefects were made responsible for keeping order in Italy.

Perhaps the most far-reaching development was Marcus's increased employment of military officers in ordinary or extraordinary commands, without regard to their personal origins or status. The close interest that he maintained suggests that he noted men of tried and tested expertise. High appointments were theoretically open to everyone, ranging from the sons of freedmen, through provincials to equestrians, who might begin their careers in the army, and then progress to even higher appointments through the equestrian and senatorial posts to which Marcus promoted them. Avidius Cassius was one of the men whose career was assisted by Marcus's liberal policies. His ancestors were enfranchised provincials, but it was no barrier to his promotion as governor of Asia. Publius Helvius Pertinax, whose father was a freedman, rose from the ranks of the army, achieving the consulship in 175. A well-documented extraordinary career is that of Marcus Valerius Maximianus, an equestrian promoted by Marcus Aurelius to the Senate with the rank of praetor, and then given legionary commands in Pannonia, Dacia and Moesia. During the Danubian wars, Maximianus was very active in a variety of special roles, including command of a fleet operating on the Danube to bring supplies to the Pannonian armies.

Maximianus's career, documented on several inscriptions, is indicative of Marcus's policies of creating special commands in wartime, allowing some of his commanders to act independently. Marcus Aurelius, the emperor who appreciated the benefits of peace and prosperity, was forced to spend most of his time fighting wars, and in the absence of a permanent staff such as those of more modern armies, he established a corps of military men with wide experience and specialist knowledge. The urgency of the almost constant wars of the later years of the second century meant that these men were engaged almost exclusively in military service, with only brief experience of civilian government posts. In the early Empire, military and civil careers were closely intertwined, but there was a gradual separation, more noticeable under Hadrian, but perhaps beginning under the Flavian emperors. The process was given greater prominence during the Danubian wars of Marcus Aurelius. Professionalism and specialization developed in the army, making it a more efficient tool, but on the other hand it gave the military officers a strong influence over large armies, whose loyalties to their commanders could be exploited. The legionary legates were closer and more real to the soldiers than the emperor, and more importantly they were the men who could offer immediate benefits, like ready money and the promise of more of it in the future.

This was the dilemma of the later Roman Empire. If defence of the Roman world was to be effective, the frontier armies were obviously essential, and it was also essential that they should contain large numbers of professional and well-trained soldiers, who should be commanded by experienced officers. As shown by the revolt of Avidius Cassius, this combination could be very dangerous if either the soldiers or the generals, or both parties, conceived a desire for mastery of the Roman world. This problem was never satisfactorily solved. Whenever the all-important succession was in dispute, it was the army and its commanders who decided who should rule, the secret of Empire, as the historian Tacitus called it, but it had never really been a secret. The endemic warfare of Marcus Aurelius's reign, too extensive to be overseen by one man, gave the Emperor no choice but to entrust various military commanders with great powers, setting a precedent for the future. Combined with the sporadic movements of the tribesmen north of the Rhine and Danube, trying to enter the Empire for raids or for permanent settlement, and the problems of the succession, the seeds of the third century crisis had already been sown.

COMMODUS AD 180–193

Marcus Aurelius died in 180, at Vindobona (modern Vienna), before the Danube wars were concluded. Though Marcus had started out with a colleague of equal rank, and two designated successors, Lucius Verus and Marcus's own young son Annius Verus, had both died, so in 180 there was only his son Commodus, who had been elevated to the rank of Caesar as a boy, and was made Augustus, sharing power with his father, as soon as he had reached the age of sixteen. It was the only way to avoid jealous rivalries and even civil war when one emperor died and another was to take his place. Commodus had the enormous advantage of being the undoubted heir, and as Augustus since 176 he was accepted as the next emperor. The succession of Commodus was the first true hereditary succession since Vespasian bequeathed the Empire to his sons Titus and Domitian.

After the death of his father, Commodus brought the wars with the Danube tribes to an end by diplomatic means. The peace was a long lasting arrangement, despite the fact that Commodus was severely criticised for not carrying on fighting and annihilating the enemy. It is possible that just before his death Marcus Aurelius had already come to the conclusion that he should make peace, abandoning his alleged plans for total conquest and the creation of new provinces. The treaty that Commodus arranged with the Marcomanni and Quadi contained the useful provision that the tribesmen should immediately furnish an enormous batch of recruits for the Roman army. This method of recruitment became more common as time went on. The Marcomanni and Quadi kept the peace and honoured the terms of their treaty with Commodus, even after his death. The major problem in the Danube area arose from small scale raids, which Commodus dealt with by policing rather than campaigning. Several inscriptions record the construction of watchtowers to control the movements of robbers (*latrones*). The towers would be garrisoned by soldiers from the Roman army, backed up by more troops if trouble broke out.

In theory, Commodus had every chance of becoming a philosopher emperor like his father. He had been groomed for succession since his childhood, and Marcus Aurelius was the first emperor since Flavian times to have a son of his own for whom the succession was hereditary and absolutely unequivocal. Marcus has been blamed for allowing Commodus to succeed him, but if he had recognized his son's potential defects and had designated someone else while Commodus was growing up, it is possible that the Roman world would have divided into factions promoting their own candidates and the civil war of 193 would have broken out in 180 instead. There were alternatives to succession by natural or adoptive heirs, ranging from bribery and corruption, through the acclamation of a candidate by strong-willed soldiery, to full scale civil war. The third century was to become familiar with all of these methods of Imperial succession.

The reign of Commodus began reasonably well. There was no serious neglect of the frontiers or the army, and the provinces did not suffer under his rule. But he descended into farce and finally into terror, ending with his assassination by the Praetorian Prefect and the palace chamberlain. Commodus had been given every opportunity to learn how to govern, and he inherited Marcus's circle of advisers with considerable cumulative experience, but he soon removed them all, promoting in their places men like Perennis and then Cleander, his personal favourites. By the end of his reign he had alienated almost everyone and there were grave problems.

In 190, Commodus's favourite, Marcus Aurelius Cleander, was the most influential man in Rome. He had started out as a slave, but had been freed by the Emperor Marcus Aurelius and as was customary he had taken the name of the citizen who had manumitted him. His status as Imperial freedman gave him access to the court and Imperial family. He was made chamberlain to Commodus, and gained even more power and influence when Perennis, the more important of the two Praetorian Prefects, was executed. Cleander somehow managed to subordinate the two succeeding

Praetorian Prefects to himself and rapidly became the fount of all power. Commodus made him his security chief, with a new title '*a pugione*' or 'the dagger', indicating his position of supremacy. He was privy to the Emperor's plans and policies, and he had the power to elevate and promote people to various appointments, but on the other hand with complete control over men and their careers, he could thwart people and even remove them. Everyone had to go through Cleander's efficient filter system, before he could even hope to rise to any significant post.

Eventually Cleander went too far, having alienated too many people, with the inevitable result that even well-balanced, sane men who normally distanced themselves from politics and government were by now amenable to Cleander's elimination. He was made the scapegoat for a food shortage, and when the Roman mob indulged in riots, Commodus panicked. He realized that not even Cleander could solve the problem this time, so he executed him. Towards the end of his reign, Commodus had become completely detached from the needs of the Empire and his behaviour was increasingly bizarre. It began to seem that he must be unhinged. He had ignored the advice of his counsellors, allowing his subordinates to gain too much influence over him, and made no efforts to diminish the increasing power of his favourites. He had failed to realize, or did not care, that the emperor must be the sole source of power and patronage, and that if any of his subordinates took his place in the dispensation of appointments and rewards, he would be seriously undermined. He had not achieved the fine balance that was necessary in dealing with his court circle, his military officers, the senators and the people. Of necessity the emperor had to be sensitive in the control of his close associates, preventing them from accruing too much power without stifling all hope of promotion.

Commodus was nervous in the years following the death of Cleander and became highly unpredictable. Life under Commodus was similar to that during the later years of Domitian. No one felt safe. Senators and equites alike felt threatened. The Praetorian Prefects, Regillus and Julius Julianus, were successively removed, after the latter had enjoyed a brief period as sole Prefect. A series of murders began. The senators were not just fearful for themselves but for their entire circles of *clientelae*, drawn from all ranks from the city and from the rural population, from Italy and the provinces. An individual senator could wield considerable and widespread influence, and to eradicate this influence and avoid the possibility that any one of them might try to gain control of the Empire, it was necessary to eradicate the entire circle of each senatorial victim. This may be what Cassius Dio implies when he says that many other people were killed as well as senators, even including women.

The activities of the Emperor became more and more outrageous. Identifying himself with Hercules, he devoted himself to gladiatorial pursuits, delighting in displaying his talents in public performances. At the end of his reign these gladiatorial shows were compulsory viewing. Senators were not given the option of boycotting them. They were even obliged to chant in unison, hailing Commodus as Lord, First Among Men, Victorious and so on. At one performance, Commodus cut off the head of an ostrich, waving it at the senators as if to suggest that he could just as easily cut off the heads of everyone else. Dio describes how he took refuge in chewing laurel leaves so as to disguise the fact that he was laughing – a potentially fatal reaction if the Emperor happened to see it.

This ridiculous state of affairs was lightened a little by the appointment of Aemilius Laetus as one of the Praetorian Prefects. Laetus was a native of North Africa, and had promoted the careers of some of his fellow countrymen to posts on the northern frontiers. One of these was Septimius Severus, who was made governor of Upper Pannonia in 191. He had no experience of the Rhine and Danube areas, nor of the government of a fairly large province with an army, but in Roman tradition, he took on the task without any previous training.

It was a time of great insecurity for everyone, and it was clear that sooner or later the reign of Commodus would end, probably with bloodshed. Severus was ambitious, and even if he had not planned to become emperor at this stage he would at least have given some thought as to how he might survive in a change of regime. Severus's career had begun at the age of twenty-eight, when he entered the Senate in the reign of Marcus Aurelius. He had risen slowly, taking up the normal appointments one after another. He was quaestor in Rome in 170, and had then served in Baetica, Sardinia and Africa. He was legionary legate of *IV Scythicae* in Syria, with Helvius Pertinax as governor. From 186–189 he governed Gallia Lugdunensis. His knowledge of the Empire was reasonably wide, but his career was not spectacular, and he had not seen much military action. He reached the consulship in 190 at the age of forty-five. It was not such a signal honour, since there were twenty-five consuls in that same year, giving each man about one month's experience of the office and its duties. These suffect consulships were sometimes awarded when the Emperor wished to honour some of his supporters, or when there too few candidates for the proconsular offices, so some men were promoted so that they could acquire some experience and the appropriate rank. Severus's appointment, was probably purchased from Cleander. According to Dio he was only one among many who were appointed in this fashion. In view of the events of the very near future, it is not important how Severus became consul. Poised in Upper Pannonia, Severus waited and watched. The garrison of his province comprised three legions, and the route into Italy was quite short

Sooner or later Commodus was sure to meet an untimely end. His sister had already been involved in a plot to remove him. It is not known how far in advance the Praetorian Prefect Laetus planned the assassination of Commodus, nor if he confided in anyone except perhaps a few accomplices. On New Year's Eve, 192, he and the palace chamberlain Eclectus murdered the Emperor, and shortly afterwards Publius Helvius Pertinax was proclaimed in his place. It is not certain that Pertinax was party to the plot. Dio and Herodian insist that the assassination was an *ad hoc* decision as Laetus seized his chance, and Pertinax was taken completely by surprise when he was declared emperor.

PERTINAX AD 193

Pertinax was sixty-seven years old, a man of wide experience. He started life as the son of a slave, and began his career in the army. In Marcus's reign he had been elevated first to equestrian rank and then adlected into the Senate. He had been governor of Lower Moesia, Upper Moesia, Dacia and Syria. He was a sterling example of the social mobility that had begun with the reign of Augustus. In the early years of the Empire, it had been possible to rise from lowly origins to consul within three generations, but Pertinax rose from the humblest rank to emperor in one lifetime. The Senate accepted him without demur, voting him all the usual titles, including *Pater Patriae*, 'father of his country', and his wife and son were respectively offered the titles Augusta and Caesar, but Pertinax rejected these honours on their behalf. He persuaded the senators to spare the life of Laetus. Although he had worked on behalf of Commodus as Praetorian Prefect, this did not mean that he supported the Emperor and all his actions, as demonstrated by the fact that he had killed him.

Winning over the Praetorian Guard was not quite so straightforward. Pertinax was a strict disciplinarian, noted for his severe punishment of the soldiers in Britain when they had proclaimed him emperor, which was potentially a death sentence even if the chosen man decided to march on Rome and topple the incumbent ruler. Now, ironically, he was positively encouraging the Praetorians to do under coercion the very thing that he had previously punished the British soldiers for doing voluntarily. The Praetorians were given a payment of 12,000 *sesterces* per man, which they accepted but at the ceremony where they were supposed to take the oath of loyalty to Pertinax, some of the soldiers decided that a senator called Triarius Maternus suited them rather better, but their attempt to create a new emperor failed, largely because their chosen candidate fled, minus his clothes.

Pertinax set about tidying up the Imperial household, selling all the slaves whom he considered to be superfluous, and banishing the many hangers-on, but according to Herodian a few concubines soon found their way back into the palace. In the Senate, Pertinax reinstated the men who had been exiled or had fled, and he assisted the families of those who had been condemned or killed. His major problem was lack of funds, but somehow he found the cash to pay the donatives to placate the Praetorians and the Roman mob. He turned his attention to the coinage. It had been debased in 190–2, so Pertinax brought the silver standard of the *denarius* back to the level it had enjoyed in the days of Vespasian. He reduced customs dues to try to boost commercial activity, and he tried to promote agriculture by granting titles of ownership to waste lands with ten years' tax exemption. There may be some confusion in the sources, since Hadrian's laws on waste lands were still in operation, but it is also possible that Pertinax hoped to speed things up. He did not rule for long enough for any judgement to be made about the likely success of his measures and his intentions, but Herodian thought that given time he would have changed the administration for the better, instituting 'sound and orderly government'.

Pertinax was not given time. Laetus instigated his murder after only eighty-seven days as emperor. In this instance there was no immediately obvious successor who could take up the reins of state. Pertinax had not chosen anyone as his successor and Laetus clearly did not want to be emperor himself. Not even the Praetorians, whose commanders and officers had from time to time gained a preponderant influence in political events, took the initiative in raising an emperor of their own choice. Instead they waited to see who would pay the most cash, standing by while Flavius Sulpicianus, Pertinax's father-in-law and currently Prefect of the City, tried to outbid Didius Julianus for the purchase of the Empire, but he was unsuccessful. Finally Julianus bought the Empire for the price of 25,000 *sesterces* per Praetorian Guardsman, and became the Emperor of Rome himself for a short time.

As soon as the news of the death of Pertinax reached the frontiers, the armies and their generals were ready. Early in April, Severus was proclaimed emperor by his troops at Carnuntum on the Danube. There were two other rival candidates, Pescennius Niger in Syria and Clodius Albinus in Britain. They were situated at opposite ends of the Empire, and appropriately named for the opposite ends of the spectrum, black (*niger*) and white (*albus*). Niger was proclaimed at some time before the end of May 193, while Clodius Albinus may have entered the scene somewhat later. The chronology is not established, but it does not really matter who was proclaimed before anyone else. They were bound to fight each other in a contest involving civil war. Severus decided to ignore the threats from the eastern and western contenders, and went straight to Rome to secure his position there. He had the shortest distance to travel to the capital city and took advantage of it. The proclamation of Severus as emperor cannot have been as spontaneous as it sounds, nor can it have depended entirely on opportunism. Though he was not in a position to predict exactly what would happen in Rome, Severus could still have prepared the ground very generally, by establishing a large and loyal *clientelae*, by sounding out likely contacts outside his own group of clients, and creating networks of influential people ranging from army officers, wealthy senators and equites, down to the most lowly individual with specialized knowledge or particular talents. His marriage to Julia Domna, his second wife, had been carefully arranged, not simply because her horoscope contained the brilliant news that she was to be the wife of an emperor, but also because her eastern connections were important, bringing more influential and wealthy people into Severus's circle. Networks had to be very wide, spread over as much of the Empire as possible, as well as in Rome itself, providing eyes and ears for political and military developments. Information about who was friend or foe was absolutely vital in a regime like that of Commodus, simply as a survival tool, but the network could be turned to good use when the time came. No one could predict the precise moment and consequently no one would know who would be where and in what post when the crisis came, but it was obvious that there would be a crisis, because there was no designated heir, and Commodus's behaviour was less and less conducive to longevity. It was highly likely that at some point the Empire was going to need an emperor quite suddenly, and Severus had probably thought about it long before Laetus chose and then eliminated Pertinax.

Money was the most important tool for would-be emperors. Influential and wealthy connections were essential to provide rapid access to cash. Money could buy the army and other people, at least temporarily. The next most important considerations would be to cultivate the soldiers and monitor their moods, and to investigate the opinions of the other provincial governors. Severus would need to know whether there was support for him. He did not want to be forced into a premature civil war before he had even crossed the Alps. Prepared and waiting, Severus was probably quite ready to take over as emperor when Commodus was murdered at the beginning of 193, but the transition between old and new emperor was rapid, leaving no room for Severus to act before the accession of Pertinax. He was fortunate that he did not act too soon and then find himself in opposition to the new emperor. Severus swore allegiance to Pertinax, then waited upon events.

According to the *Historia Augusta*, the legions of the Rhine and Danube declared for Severus, encouraged by their generals, and when he established himself as emperor in Rome Severus issued coins specifically honouring many of these legions by their individual names. The evidence is not conclusive but it will bear the interpretation that Severus had thoroughly prepared the ground long before his acclamation. His investment paid off because sometime later, when civil war began in the west, the governor of Lower Germany, Virius Lupus, stood firm for Severus and opposed Clodius Albinus when the latter reached Gaul.

Since Pertinax had promised a brighter future for the Empire and it had looked as though he might have been able to stabilize the government if he had survived long enough, Severus chose to enter Rome as his avenger. He adopted his predecessor's name to demonstrate solidarity and continuity with the regime. His first coins bore the name Imperator Caesar Lucius Septimius Pertinax Augustus. It was important to disassociate himself from Commodus, but in the stance that he took as the avenger of Pertinax he was able to present himself the role of selfless leader doing his duty to the state, rather than as an opportunistic general racing to the top. Later, when he was more secure, he was forced to change his attitude towards Commodus, because he wanted to establish a firmer basis for his power by connecting himself with the house of Marcus Aurelius and Antoninus Pius.

Severus would have to overcome three potential opponents when he arrived in Rome, in the form of the legitimate Emperor Didius Julianus, the Praetorians and the Senate. It would probably be possible to deal with them separately. Julianus took hasty steps to defend himself as soon as he knew that Severus was approaching Italy. He executed Laetus and persuaded the Senate to declare Severus a public enemy (*hostis*), but the Praetorians pre-empted both Julianus and the Senate by opening up negotiations with Severus. The Senate quickly sacrificed Julianus, condemning him to death and declaring Severus emperor.

The Praetorians were eliminated before Severus entered Rome. He took them by surprise by summoning them to a meeting where they found themselves surrounded by his legions. He dismissed them all with dishonour. Since they had been the first to negotiate with him, they probably expected to be rewarded, but Severus knew how extremely fickle they were, and in any case he did not want to be placed in the dubious position of owing his power to them. He mastered them from the start. When he was ready he created a new and larger Guard, recruited from the legions and not just from Italians. The Praetorians had become very arrogant and had started to terrorize people, shamelessly abusing their privileges. The demise of the Praetorians was not regretted, except that the historian Dio accused Severus of filling Italy with unemployed Italians and disgruntled ex-guardsmen who continued to terrorize people.

The new emperor treated the Senate with studied respect. He brought his troops to Rome ready for battle, but he changed into civilian dress when he crossed the city boundary. He promised to rule like Marcus Aurelius, and guaranteed never to put any senator to death without first bringing him to trial by his peers in the Senate. He distributed cash to the soldiers and the Roman populace. Civil war was postponed for a while. Clodius Albinus was offered the title of Caesar, designating him as the next emperor. It has been questioned whether Albinus believed that Severus's offer was genuine. He must have known that Severus had two sons, but he may have reasoned that they were very young, and did not represent a threat.

Clodius Albinus is presented by the historians as somewhat naive, which was perhaps inevitable since he was ultimately defeated. If he had been the victor in the civil wars, he would probably have earned a reputation for crafty and calculated planning, waiting until the right moment had come before committing himself to battle. In reality he may have had much more common sense and been much more prescient than he has been depicted. He may have played the game as well as he could, accepting the name of Caesar gracefully, pretending to acquiesce in the arrangement while all along he was simply stalling for extra time to prepare. There was more than one choice of action. He could have given in without a fight, abdicating and perhaps being lynched by his own legions. He could have remained in Britain at the head of his own small Empire as Carausius did a century later, or he could meet Severus somewhere in Gaul or Germany and hope to defeat him there. If he made no move at all he could be sure that Severus would eventually come after him, so he could not sit still, but on the other hand he was handicapped by having to leave at least some form of secure garrison behind him in Britain before he could begin to ferry troops onto the continent. Far from being the dupe of Severus, it is just as likely that Clodius Albinus was grateful to have reached what he may have regarded as a temporary stay of execution and breathed a sigh of relief, knowing that Niger was to be the first to receive Severus's attentions.

12

Military Rule:
Emperors & Usurpers AD 193–260

SEVERUS AD 193–211

In the course of the third century, from the reign of Severus onwards, the Empire progressed from the Principate, a modern term derived from Augustus's use of the title *princeps*, into the Dominate, based on the title *dominus*, signifying lordship. Severus introduced into the Roman world the concept of the divinity and sacrosanctity of the Imperial household, the *domus divina*. It also signified the start of a more overtly autocratic rule.

THE ELIMINATION OF NIGER & ALBINUS

Niger was in a strong position. He could draw upon the considerable resources of the eastern provinces, where he had powerful adherents. The proconsul of Asia, Asellius Aemilianus, had declared for him, and had occupied Byzantium. Niger also controlled Egypt and could withhold the corn supply to Rome. If he was allowed to do so, food shortages would quickly diminish Severus's popularity, so speed was essential in challenging him. Severus ordered the troops in Africa to watch the western border of Egypt, and prevent the legion there (*II Traiana*) from sending help to Niger. Late in 193, having consolidated his position in Rome, Severus was ready. He travelled overland via Pannonia and Moesia, ordering the troops in Moesia to set off ahead of him. His general Candidus defeated Niger's ally Aemilianus at Cyzicus, but the elimination of Aemilianus did not bring about the surrender of Byzantium. The city was put under siege.

Niger withdrew into Syria, but because he seemed unable to stop Severus's advance some cities turned against him, wishing to be on the right side at the end of the war. Laodicea was probably the first city to break away, spurred on by jealousy of its main rival, Antioch, where Niger set up his .headquarters. By the spring of 194, the war was over. Niger fled, but was overtaken and killed. Severus sent his head to Byzantium to demonstrate that there was now no leader to rally behind, but the city still refused to surrender until the end of 195. Severus destroyed it to set an example to other rebellious cities, but Byzantium was far too important for Roman emperors to lose, so it was rebuilt.

Laodicea, Tyre and other cities which had declared for Severus were rewarded, but those which had sided with Niger were heavily fined, especially Antioch. Niger's adherents, embracing senators, equestrians, officers and soldiers alike, were severely punished. They found refuge in Parthia, working as engineers, builders and arms manufacturers. When he discovered this, Severus stopped the punishments and concentrated instead on restoring Roman control and influence on the eastern frontier. The Parthian King Vologaeses, had been sympathetic to Niger, and the city of Hatra had helped him. There was rebellion against Roman control in Osroene and Mesopotamia, and the city of Nisibis, which had been in Roman hands since the expedition of Lucius Verus in the 160s, was besieged, but held out for Severus. Order was quickly restored. Severus converted Osroene into a province in charge of a procurator, and he rewarded Nisibis by elevating the city to the rank and privileged status of a *colonia*, or colony. It may have been at this point when Severus divided the province of Syria into two unequal parts and renamed them, the larger northern part being Syria Coele with two legions, and the smaller southern province being Syria Phoenice, with one legion. From now on, no governor would command more than two legions, reducing the chances of rebellion backed by an army.

Severus initially adopted the victory titles *Parthicus Arabicus* and *Parthicus Adiabenicus* after the defeat of Niger, but when he moved against Albinus in the west he dropped the *Parthicus* title, because of its suggestion of a Parthian victory. He wanted to ensure that he did not provoke the King of Parthia unnecessarily, and took what steps he could to secure the eastern frontier, so that he could then march to Gaul. Albinus had by now gained support in the Senate. The chronology of the breakdown of relations is not crystal clear, so it is not certain who made the first hostile move. Severus portrayed Albinus as the instigator of the war, because in 195 or 196 he declared himself Augustus, which was a direct challenge to the legitimate emperor. Severus responded by making it clear that Albinus was not destined to succeed him. He fabricated his own descent from the respected Marcus Aurelius, and solved the problem of Commodus, whose memory had been damned, by asking the Senate to overturn this decision and deify Commodus. This pacified the army, since they had no quarrel with Commodus. Severus raised his eldest son Septimius Bassianus to the rank of Caesar, renaming him Marcus Aurelius Antoninus, better known as Caracalla, a nickname derived from the Gallic hooded cloak that he habitually wore. Being groomed for succession, Caracalla was given the unequivocal title *Imperator destinatus*. Severus did not promote his younger son Geta as rapidly, but he intended that his sons should succeed him.

Albinus moved troops into Gaul and established himself at Lugdunum (modern Lyons), where he began to issue coins in his own name as Augustus. He brought troops from Britain, and recruited more in Gaul. *Cohors XIII Urbana* from Lyons joined him, but the Rhine legions refused to help. Albinus presumably did not remove all the troops from Britain, probably ensuring the protection of the cities and coasts, in case he was driven back to the island. However, there are some indications that he effected a large scale evacuation of Hadrian's Wall. Archaeological evidence reveals that the Wall garrisons of the late second century were completely changed by the third century.

In order to prevent Albinus from invading Italy from his base in Gaul, Severus garrisoned the Alpine passes, but there was no invasion. The governor of Gallia Lugdunensis left the province rather than join Albinus, and Virius Lupus, the governor of Lower Germany, attempted to stand against him. The city of Trier also held out, and perhaps other cities followed suit. The issue was decided at the battle of Lyons in February 197. Albinus conveniently committed suicide, and infamously, Severus allowed his troops to sack Lyons. The city never fully recovered. The episode demonstrated how easily a Roman army would turn against other Roman troops or against a Roman city, and it highlighted the overwhelming power of the army in co-operation with the emperor. The mutual dependence of the soldiers upon the emperor for their pay and perks, and of the emperor on the soldiers for their corporate support had never been so blatant as it was under Severus.

At some unknown date, Severus divided Britain into two separate provinces, just as he dealt with Syria, and for the same reasons, to prevent any other governor from gaining access to large numbers of troops. This division may have occurred when troops were sent back to the province after the defeat of Albinus, but some scholars prefer a later date, perhaps after Caracalla's settlement in 208, or even at some time after 213.

In the aftermath of the civil wars there was a reshuffling of personnel in provincial and central government posts, and in the army. Severus chose his provincial governors and army commanders very carefully, especially since he planned to leave Rome to attend to the unfinished work on the eastern frontier. The centre of government was wherever he was himself, but if he could trust his provincial governors and military officers in the rest of the Roman world, so much the better.

THE ARMY

Attention to the army was a hallmark of Severus's reign. Probably in 197 he put into effect his army reforms, in particular his pay rise for the soldiers. It created great disapproval, because most Romans wanted defence at an impossibly cheap price. The last army pay rise had been granted over a century earlier by Domitian, so it was well overdue, as was the recognition of the soldiers as people, with the right to marry and reasonable prospects of promotion, which is what Severus gave them. Marriages had been forbidden to soldiers, but liaisons with local women near the camps had always occurred, so the new legislation merely acknowledged the existing situation.

Severus relied upon his government officials and the army to keep a firm grasp on Rome and Italy. He had reconstituted the Praetorian Guard, larger now than in previous reigns, and he also installed a new legion at Alba (modern Albano), not far from Rome. This was *legio II Parthica*, raised at an unknown date, but it was stationed in Italy when Severus went on campaign against the Parthians. The units of the new Praetorian Guard, combined with the new legion, provided Severus with about 30,000 men, all under his immediate control.

THE PROMOTION OF THE EQUESTRIANS

Severus opened up promotion for soldiers from the ranks, and created more military commands and governmental posts for the equestrians, continuing a trend already set in motion by previous emperors. The three new legions that he raised, all named *Parthica*, were commanded by equestrians instead of senators, and he appointed more equestrians as the governors of the new eastern provinces created after the Parthian campaigns. The equestrian class in general experienced a whole new impetus under Severus. It is not valid to speak of a senatorial decline, but the influence of the senators remained static, because Severus curbed its influence.

Severus held the purse strings of the whole Empire, he was the commander in chief of the armed forces, and was the source of all patronage and advancement. He appointed his loyal supporters to key posts. From *c.*196 Cornelius Anullinus, one of his close associates, was city prefect. The Emperor's personal friend and fellow countryman from Africa, Caius Fulvius Plautianus, was prefect of the *vigiles* from 193 to 196, and in 197 he was appointed commander of the Praetorian Guard, rapidly becoming the most infamous Praetorian Prefect since Sejanus, eliminating his colleague and enjoying sole command of the Praetorian Guard for the rest of his career.

THE PARTHIAN CAMPAIGN

Severus set off for the Parthian campaign in early summer 197. From the Roman point of view there was a pressing need to attack Parthia, since

King Vologaeses had occupied Mesopotamia and laid siege to Nisibis. The city was ably defended by Laetus (not the man who assassinated Commodus). Despite the initial aggression of Vologaeses, the Parthian Royal House was weak and split into factions, which could only assist the advance of Severus's army. Vologaeses retreated as Severus aimed for the Euphrates valley, encountering no resistance at Seleucia or Babylon, and only a slight problem at the Parthian capital Ctesiphon, which he sacked.

The campaign had been a demonstration of strength to deter the Parthians from interfering in Roman administrative arrangements on her eastern borders. There was no intention of remaining in Parthian territory, and in 198 Severus set off for Rome. The army was in high spirits, acclaiming him Imperator for the tenth and eleventh time, and proclaiming Caracalla joint Augustus with his father, while Severus's younger son Geta was made Caesar.

The only resistance that Severus experienced during this expedition came from the city of Hatra, which he besieged unsuccessfully in 198 and again in 199. In order to consolidate his demonstration against Parthia, he encased the upper Euphrates in Roman provinces. In 195 he had created the new province of Osroene, and now he adopted a scheme originally proposed by Trajan but abandoned by Hadrian, of annexing Mesopotamia in 198. He installed an equestrian prefect as governor, with the capital at Nisibis and a garrison comprised of two newly raised legions, *I* and *III Parthica*, both of which were commanded by equestrians. The approaches to Syria Phoenice and Arabia were protected from Parthian attack by the Palmyrene militia, who patrolled the eastern desert on the Emperor's behalf. But the annexation of Mesopotamia as a Roman province was costly, a constant thorn in the side of the Parthian kings, and the cause of future confrontations.

Severus returned home via a tour of Mesopotamia, Syria, Palestine, Arabia and Egypt. Entering Rome as conquering hero, Severus celebrated a triumph in which his sons Caracalla and Geta played a prominent part. He also celebrated his ten year rule, his *Decennalia*, with appropriate pomp and ceremony, and distributions of cash to the people of Rome. The most durable evidence of his military achievements is the arch named after him in the Forum in Rome, close by the Senate House.

THE FRONTIERS OF AFRICA

After a short stay in Rome, Severus and his family, including the Praetorian Prefect Plautianus, embarked on a voyage to Africa, the Emperor's native land, where his generals had extended the frontiers, taking in more territory, rationalizing boundaries, protecting routes, and building new forts. Hadrian had done much to rationalize and stabilize the frontiers of

Africa. In Numidia he had moved *III Augusta* from its base at Ammaedara to a new fortress at Lambaesis, and he had constructed watchtowers and small posts on the frontiers of Mauretania Caesariensis and Tingitana, but there was no unbroken running barrier like those in Britain and Germany. Commodus continued the frontier work by building outposts to give advance warning of raids.

Severus extended Roman territory in Africa, through his governors and generals, in particular Quintus Anicius Faustus, a native of Africa, and legate of *legio III Augusta* at Lambaesis from 197 to 201. In Mauretania Caesariensis Severus took in more territory, creating a new frontier commemorated on inscriptions as the *nova praetentura*, begun in 198 by Octavius Pudens, another African. This extension of the Empire earned for Severus the title of *propagator imperii*, attested on several inscriptions in Africa.

The Downfall of Plautianus

In 204 Severus celebrated the Secular Games. The ceremony was rooted in the Roman past, combining religious ceremonial with games and festivals, occurring once every 110 years, so that no one ever witnessed more than one celebration in a lifetime, or *saeculum*. Severus marked the occasion on his coinage, and put his whole family on display at all the ceremonies. The *domus divina*, attested on inscriptions, denoting the Imperial household as an entity, sacrosanct and unassailable, was now firmly established in Roman consciousness.

The Praetorian Prefect Plautianus had built up a vast accretion of power and his unashamed exploitation of it had made him more feared and detested than either Sejanus or Cleander. Plautianus's daughter Plautilla had been betrothed to Caracalla since 201, so the Praetorian Prefect was a member of the Imperial household. His name appears on several inscriptions alongside those of Severus and Caracalla. He treated Julia Domna with contempt, and towards the end of the second Parthian campaign he began to eliminate men of good reputation and distinguished service, such as Quintus Aemilius Saturninus, his colleague as Praetorian Prefect, and Laetus, who had been with Severus since 193, and Tiberius Claudius Candidus, the first officer to see action against Niger's troops. For a while, Plautianus was unassailable, because Severus was oblivious of the enormities, but the Emperor was finally made aware of what was happening by his brother Septimius Geta, who denounced Plautianus on his deathbed. Caracalla took the initiative, persuading his father that Plautianus had hatched a plot to remove the entire Imperial household. On 22 January 205, Plautianus was killed. Two Praetorian Prefects were appointed in his place, Quintus Maecius Laetus, who had been prefect of Egypt 200–3, and Aemilius Papinianus, an Imperial secretary with a good reputation as a jurist.

THE EXPEDITION TO BRITAIN

The situation in Britain after the defeat of Albinus is variously depicted, ranging from one of extreme gravity to perfectly normal routine. Successive governors, Virius Lupus, Valerius Pudens and Alfenus Senecio, had carried out rebuilding and repairs to several forts in the north, but this does not mean that the repairs were necessary because of destruction by British tribesmen. According to Cassius Dio, the governor Virius Lupus was forced to buy peace from the Maeatae, who lived 'near the wall that cuts the island in half', by which it is normally assumed that he meant the more northerly Antonine Wall. Beyond the Maeatae there were the Caledonians. Both tribes were hardy and hostile, and moreover they were not subject to Rome. No one since Julius Agricola had succeeded in the conquest of Scotland, and Dio affirms that Severus now intended to conquer the whole island.

The Imperial armies, including troops from the Rhine and Danube armies, possibly *II Parthica* from Italy and detachments from the Praetorian Guard, arrived in Britain in 208 and Severus set up his headquarters at York. He brought his two sons with him to give them experience, and he was accompanied by his *comites* and chosen officials, since he governed the whole Empire from his British base.

The archaeological traces of Severus's two campaigns in northern Britain are slightly more useful than the ancient literary evidence. Severan supply bases have been identified at Arbeia (modern South Shields), at Corbridge, and at Cramond on the Forth. At Carpow on the Tay, Severus established a legionary base, where tiles of *VI Victrix* have been found. Two lines of marching camps have been traced in the north leading into Scotland, usually identified as those used by Severus's army. There were two campaigns, the first in 208–9 led by Severus himself and the second in 210 led by Caracalla alone.

Severus's younger son Geta was left behind in York, perhaps compensated when he was finally made Augustus, the colleague of his father and brother. The Imperial family did not enjoy harmonious relations. Caracalla had an obvious wish to rid himself of his brother and it may also be true that he tried to kill Severus while they rode out together to meet the Caledonians to arrange a truce. There was hardly any need to kill him, since Severus was already ill. In February 211, on the brink of preparing a third campaign, he died at York. On his deathbed he told his sons not to disagree with each other, to pay the soldiers, and to despise everyone else.

Caracalla may have mounted a third British campaign in 211, before he concluded peace and returned to Rome. The frontier remained stable for the next eighty-five years, so whatever arrangements he made presumably had some worth. Severus may have already divided Britain into two provinces, but some scholars suggest that it was Caracalla's work, after his father's death. At about this time, Caracalla readjusted the boundaries of the two Pannonian provinces, so that there were two legions in each, as part of a consistent policy to reduce the number of legions at the disposal of any provincial governor.

CARACALLA AD 211–217

Very soon after returning to Rome, Caracalla murdered Geta, perhaps at the beginning of 212. He then took refuge in the Praetorian camp claiming that he had killed Geta in self defence. The soldiers were far from happy to forget that they had sworn allegiance to Geta, but cash payments helped them to edit him out of their collective memory. Caracalla eradicated all his brother's supporters, killing a large number of people, including the Praetorian Prefect, Papinianus. All over the Empire, orders went out to chisel Geta's name out of inscriptions, and to destroy his portraits and statues. Even papyrus records were edited for any reference to Geta.

UNIVERSAL CITIZENSHIP

The most famous administrative measure of Caracalla's reign, giving rise to endless discussion, is the *Constitutio Antoniniana*, traditionally dated to 212. By this edict, Roman citizenship was granted to all free born inhabitants of the Empire, and since it was usual to take the name of the man who enfranchised new citizens, after 212 there were a great preponderance of men and women all over the Empire with the family name Aurelius, from Caracalla's official name Marcus Aurelius Antoninus. The levelling effect of the *Constitutio* theoretically subjected all free peoples of the Empire to Roman law, though in practice local customs remained intact. Financially it broadened the base of the inheritance tax, paid by all citizens.

Though the act could be said to degrade Roman citizenship, in reality it had already lost its status. After 212 a new elite evolved. Instead of Romans and provincials, or citizens and non-citizens, the yardstick shifted to a distinction between upper and lower classes. The new groups were labelled *honestiores* and *humiliores*, beginning as a social distinction but soon crystallized in law. *Honestiores* were possessed of greater legal privileges than *humiliores*, for whom punishments were much more severe.

THE RHINE & DANUBE FRONTIERS

For several years there had been no serious trouble in the north, but in 212–213 Upper Germany was threatened by invasions of tribesmen, labelled by the ancient sources as the Alamanni, though the use of the name in this context may be anachronistic. The term simply means 'all men', denoting a federation of different tribes who chose to adopt a non-ethnic name for themselves, though it is unlikely that the federation had been formed as early as 213.

Caracalla responded to the danger by conducting a campaign for which he appears to have prepared very thoroughly. In Raetia considerable numbers of new milestones indicate that the network of roads was repaired and increased; troops were collected from various sources, including detachments from *II Adiutrix* from Upper Pannonia and from *II Traiana* from Egypt. The campaign is not well-documented, but Caracalla's frontier policy probably combined open warfare and demonstrations of strength, possibly followed by the payment of subsidies to the tribes to keep them quiet. In other cases he may have played one tribe against another to divert their attention from Roman territory. Whatever his methods, they brought peace for two decades thereafter. Caracalla took the title *Germanicus Maximus*, and received his third acclamation as Imperator.

THE EAST

As a dedicated admirer of Alexander the Great, Caracalla was drawn to the east, whether or not there was a need for Roman intervention. The opportunity was timely since the Parthian Royal House was still disunited, Vologaeses V and his brother Artabanus being at odds with each other. Preparing for the eastern campaign, Caracalla took over the kingdom of Edessa, which he made into a colony, intending to use it as a military base. He tried and failed to take over the kingdom of Armenia.

He marched to the east by way of the Danube provinces, attending to affairs in Dacia, making some sort of alliance and probably raising troops there, arriving in Macedonia towards the end of 214. Vologaeses diplomatically avoided all action which would put him in the wrong with regard to the Roman Emperor, so Caracalla was hard pressed to find any reason to make war. He was temporarily distracted by trouble in Alexandria, where there were serious problems, demanding the Imperial presence. Leaving the Parthian campaign to his general Theocritus, who was sent to attack Armenia, Caracalla went to Alexandria where he is credited with killing many people in 215–6. At the end of 216 he returned to the east, where the situation had changed. Theocritus's expedition had been disastrous, and Vologaeses had been replaced by his more energetic brother Artabanus V. Roman ascendancy was no longer assured. Instead of mounting a quick campaign, Caracalla tried to negotiate a marriage between his daughter and the son of Artabanus, but the offer was refused. The troops resented this ineffective inaction. Rumours began to circulate, foremost among them the prophecy that the Praetorian Prefect Macrinus would succeed Caracalla. The Emperor heard of it, and Macrinus began to fear for his life. At least, that was his story after he had murdered Caracalla, early in April 217.

MACRINUS AD 217–218

The Praetorian Prefect Marcus Opellius Macrinus was the first non-senator to become emperor. He was a native of Mauretania who had survived the fall of his patron, the infamous Plautianus. He started out with three disadvantages: he was not of the correct social class, he owed his elevation to the army, and he was not in Rome when he became emperor. The rise of Macrinus ought to have created waves in the Senate and throughout the Roman world, but the senators were so relieved to be rid of Caracalla that they did not care at first that the new emperor was not of the relevant social rank.

Macrinus took the name of Severus to imbue his reign with some continuity with the previous regime. In a letter to the Senate, Macrinus announced his adoption of the Severan name and gave himself the additional titles of Pius Felix Augustus. It would have been more fitting to wait for the Senate to bestow these titles upon him, but Macrinus chose to act on his own authority. On the subject of Caracalla, everyone proceeded with circumspection. The Senate did not dare to vote for damnation of Caracalla's memory because of their fear of the soldiers, who had supported him, so Macrinus neither declared him an enemy of Rome, nor did he deify him. The episode illustrates the divergent interests of the civil population and the military, and the fact that the preponderant influence lay with the soldiers.

In keeping with Imperial practice, Macrinus was consul in 218, with Oclatinius Adventus as his colleague, but this appointment caused resentment, since Adventus's origins were even lower than those of Macrinus himself. He was an uneducated ex-mercenary who had been a member of the *frumentarii* or secret police. Macrinus made him city prefect, but replaced him soon afterwards by Marius Maximus, perhaps because of public disapproval, but more likely because Adventus was an old man who had seen long service. Other appointments of Macrinus were criticised, because he employed non-senators in positions of responsibility which more usually went to consulars, choosing suitable men for the tasks he gave them, regardless of social standing or rank. He removed Caracalla's adherents Sabinus and Castinus from their posts as governors of Pannonia and Dacia, and installed in their stead his own men Marcius Agrippa, a slave who had been convicted and banished, and Deccius Triccianus, once a door-keeper to the governor of Pannonia, rising to commander of *II Parthica* and then to provincial governor.

Macrinus inherited the Parthian war from Caracalla. Taking advantage of the preoccupation of the Roman high command, King Artabanus had seized the chance to launch an offensive against Mesopotamia. Macrinus prepared for a counter offensive, but the war was ended by negotiation. He bought peace from Artabanus, and readjusted some territorial boundaries. Despite his appointment as Praetorian Prefect, Macrinus was not a military man, but an experienced jurist, and an administrator with a wide knowledge of how the Empire functioned, and realistic about his own capabilities in conducting a war in the east. Sufficiently satisfied with the outcome of the eastern campaign, he awarded himself the title *Parthicus Maximus* in his report to the Senate.

In attempting to provide for the future succession, Macrinus bestowed on his young son Diadumenianus the name Antoninus and the title Caesar, confirmed by the Senate. In deference to the army, he finally deified Caracalla. The army was essential as the main prop for his regime, but he needed to strike a balance. Macrinus tried to curb the expenses of the army, without unduly offending the troops. While he did not attempt to withdraw any privileges, he did not celebrate the Parthian victory by gifts to the soldiers, and worse still, he reverted to the Severan rates of pay, ignoring the rise that Caracalla had awarded the army, a measure which may have pleased the Senate and people but certainly did not please the soldiers, who were accustomed to the lavish rewards given them by Caracalla. The discontented troops began to murmur.

Macrinus made a fatal mistake in failing to disperse individual army units in winter quarters. By allowing them to stay together, he made it easier for them to foment rebellion, so when relatives of the Severan family made their move, the ground had been well prepared. The Empress Julia Domna did not long survive her son Caracalla, but she had a sister, Julia Maesa, whose ambitions were no less ardent than her own. Julia Maesa's two daughters, Julia Soaemias and Julia Mammaea, each had a young son, and Maesa was determined that her elder grandson should be emperor. She persuaded the soldiers that Caracalla was the true father of Soaemias's son Varius Avitus Bassianus, and on 16 May 218 the army declared the boy Emperor, with the name Marcus Aurelius Antoninus, nicknamed Elagabalus, after his devotion to the eastern god of the same name.

ELAGABALUS AD 218–222

Macrinus persuaded the Senate to declare Elagabalus a usurper and enemy of the state, and elevated his son Diadumenianus to the rank of Augustus, but the troops deserted them and both were killed. Elagabalus entered Antioch early in June, paying the soldiers 2,000 *sesterces* each to persuade them not to sack the city. He wrote to the Senate as emperor, styling himself Imperator Caesar Antoninus, grandson of Severus. At the end of September 219, Elagabalus arrived in Rome, bringing with him the strange and passionate cult of the god after which he was named. As priest of this cult Elagabalus would not be persuaded to wear suitable Roman clothing, and had ordered a painting of himself in his priestly robes to be sent on ahead to Rome and placed in the Senate House, so that everyone would become accustomed to seeing him. Despite these visual aids, the Senate and people of Rome had no inkling of the character of the new emperor, nor of the overpowering influence of the Syrian princesses.

Probably before he arrived in Rome, Elagabalus embarked on the usual round of reshuffling military and government officials, disposing of Macrinus's followers and installing his own. Publius Valerius Comazon was made Praetorian Prefect, though he had absolutely no experience. He rose even higher, quite rapidly attaining the rank of consul. He held the post of city prefect three times, which was considered positively scandalous for an equestrian who had once been condemned to the galleys. Significantly, Claudius Attalus, the senator responsible for condemning him to the galleys, did not long survive Comazon's appointment as Praetorian Prefect. Other victims were despatched as quickly, and the Senate obligingly condemned them after Elagabalus had killed them.

For the reign of Elagabalus the focus of the ancient sources is the scandals in Rome, with the result that knowledge of what was happening in the provinces is not elucidated. The enormities of the reign hold all the attention. It was not so much Elagabalus's outrageous sexual behaviour that caused offence as the fact that he was strongly influenced, to the exclusion of all else, by the unsuitable men with whom he associated, and he was unable or unwilling to shake off the controlling authority of his mother Julia Soaemias. His grandmother Julia Maesa failed to control him, but soon found a way of supplanting him by her other grandson, Gessius Bassianus Alexianus, the son of Julia Mammaea. She arranged his formal adoption by Elagabalus, who was only a few years older than his cousin. The Senate ratified the adoption, fully aware of the ridiculousness of it all. Alexianus was renamed Severus Alexander, and was made consul in 221. Before long, Elagabalus was intriguing against his cousin, but found that Alexander was too well protected by his grandmother and the Praetorians. The end was not far off. On 6 March 222 the soldiers killed Elagabalus, his mother, and many of his adherents, including Fulvius the city prefect. Once again Comazon, the only one of Elagabalus's court to survive, filled this sudden vacancy for his third term as city prefect. Marcus Aurelius Severus Alexander, still a teenager, was declared emperor.

Severus Alexander AD 222–235

Reforms and reparations were badly needed. One of the first Imperial appointments was Domitius Ulpianus, or Ulpian, as sole Praetorian Prefect, unencumbered by a colleague throughout his short-lived appointment. He was a jurist, not a soldier, but at this moment administrators and legal experts were required to a greater extent than soldiers. Ulpian was part of Julia Maesa's circle, perhaps with long established connections with the Severan dynasty. He had been *praefectus annonae* at the beginning of 222, becoming Praetorian Prefect in December of the same year. His achievements were worthy, but unfortunately he was murdered, perhaps in the spring of 223, but some sources give the date 228.

Throughout the reign of Severus Alexander, the Syrian princesses Julia Maesa and Julia Mammaea were the guiding forces in the government. Mammaea was honoured with several titles which gave her no actual political powers but extended her influence. In particular she took on the role that Julia Domna had held with regard to the army, with the title *mater castrorum*, or mother of the camp. Not content with that alone, eventually she was known as *mater Augusti et castrorum et senatus atque patriae*, indicating that her influence if not her authority extended over most aspects of Roman life, including the senate. This sort of influence worked through connections and favours, not via political procedures, but it was just as effective. The Syrian princesses took care to surround the young Emperor with the best qualified advisers, choosing sixteen of the noblest senators to guide him, acting as part of his council, or *consilium*.

Fortunately for the young Emperor and his advisers that there was a peaceful interlude from 222 until 230, during which the policy of expansion and aggressive warfare was dormant, taking second place to restructuring the government. The eight or nine years before war broke out in the east enabled a new aristocracy to establish itself, and some of the old Severan notables re-emerged during the 220s, infiltrating government posts and the Imperial court.

The Rise of the Sassanid Persians

While the Romans had been concentrating on their internal problems, the Parthian Royal House was under threat from a powerful new lord, nominally a vassal of Artabanus V. This was Ardashir, or Artaxerxes, son of Sasan, of Iranian lineage. In 224 the Sassanid Persian dynasty with Ardashir at its head supplanted that of the Parthian Artabanus, after the latter was defeated and killed on the battlefield of Hormizdagan. Within a few years, Ardashir had begun to expand his empire to incorporate the states around the old Parthian kingdom. This naturally brought him into contact with Roman frontier territories. The first news of trouble on the eastern frontier reached Rome probably in 229 when the Persian king attacked Hatra. By 230 Severus Alexander was preparing for an eastern expedition, recruiting soldiers in Italy and the provinces. He left Rome in spring 231.

There was trouble among the troops when Severus Alexander arrived in the east. The Mesopotamian legions had murdered the governor Flavius Heracleo, and the Egyptian troops among Alexander's army were restless. These problems were dealt with before the campaign began. Coins were issued with the legends *Fides militum* and *Fides exercitus* proclaiming the loyalty of the army, but it was more an indication of wishful thinking than reality. Using Antioch as a base, Alexander attacked in three columns, leading the central one himself, while the others marched to the north and south, one to Armenia and then into Media, and the other towards the Persian city of Ctesiphon. The results were mixed, with huge losses on both sides, but especially to the Roman troops when they marched back through the hostile terrain of Armenia. Alexander was blamed for his slow advance and lack of support for the other two columns, and at some point there was an attempted usurpation by a certain Uranius, who was quickly suppressed.

Alexander's achievements were perhaps not as abysmal as they have been painted. The Persians remained quiet after the campaigns, not causing any serious trouble until the 240s under Ardashir's successor Shapur I. While he was still in Antioch, Alexander received news of disturbances on the Rhine and Danube. There had been attacks on the frontiers at several points, in Upper Germany, and in Raetia. Without concluding an official peace with Ardashir, Alexander returned to Rome at the end of 232. He held a triumph, and then began preparations for the war on the northern frontiers. He took with him troops which had fought in Mesopotamia, such as the archers from Osroene and the units of Moors. As part of the preparations he placed an experienced officer in command of the recruits. This was a soldier of Thracian origin who had risen from the ranks, Caius Julius Verus Maximinus, who would be responsible for training the troops for the coming campaign.

The destruction of several forts along the Taunus-Wetterau frontier in Germany has been dated to 233 or thereabouts, suggesting that this area was where the German tribes concentrated their attacks, an assumption corroborated by the fact that Severus Alexander chose Mainz as his base, launching an offensive in 234 against a new federation of Germanic tribes who were by now calling themselves the Alamanni. Alexander won a victory, but instead of pursuing the enemy and eradicating them, he began to negotiate, offering money and perhaps food and supplies. He may have assessed the situation correctly, analysing what this was that the tribesmen needed, preferring to give it to them before they came to take it, but the troops saw it differently. The Emperor's policy caused much resentment. In spring 235, Severus Alexander and his mother were murdered, and the Pannonian soldiers proclaimed as Emperor Caius Julius Verus Maximinus, nicknamed Thrax, the Thracian.

MAXIMINUS THRAX AD 235–238

Maximinus was better known to the troops than Severus Alexander, with a proven military record. He was the first soldier-emperor to rise from the ranks, only a few decades after Septimius Severus had broadened the base of recruitment and facilitated promotions for outstanding soldiers and junior officers. Maximinus Thrax was perceived by the Senate as a barbarian, but nevertheless the senators passed the necessary decrees investing Maximinus with Imperial powers.

The new Emperor did not disappoint his supporters, immediately continuing the war against the Germanic tribes, but even in the Rhine and Danube armies, not everyone was unanimous in support of his rule. Severus Alexander's Osroenian archers set up their own emperor, a man called Quartinus, and a group of officers declared for a senator called Magnus. Neither group was successful.

Maximinus developed a healthy distrust of everyone, especially senators. His very young son was quickly declared Caesar. The immediate entourage of Severus Alexander was removed, but without wholesale murder. Some men were relegated to lower grade posts, such as the equestrian Timesitheus, one of the close associates of Alexander, who was sent out of the way to a provincial command.

By the end of 235, Maximinus was calling himself *Germanicus Maximus*, and in 236 he had transferred the army to Pannonia, basing himself at Sirmium to fight against the Sarmatians and Dacians. Inscriptions from Pannonia refer to soldiers killed in a Dacian war in the reign of Maximinus. Occupied with these northern wars, Maximinus did not enter Rome to reaffirm his rule and try to win at least some members of the Senate to his side. Instead he ignored the Senate and concentrated wholly on the frontiers, consuming vast amounts of money to pay the soldiers. The usual taxes did not prove sufficient for his needs, but to be fair to him, income had not matched expenditure for some considerable time.

Perhaps he could have limited the financial damage caused by his taxation policies, but in concentrating on the matter in hand he did not seem to care about other sectors of the community, laying himself open to charges of cruelty, greed and corruption. He complicated matters by giving the soldiers a pay rise, never a popular move because the inhabitants of Rome, secure now for many years, did not experience at first hand the threats to their frontiers and probably did not worry about it very much until there was a sudden scare, as in the reign of Marcus Aurelius when the Germans reached Aquileia in the north of Italy. To the Romans of Italy and the more peaceful provinces, the army was far away, full of semi-barbarous men who were troublesome and greedy. It was no longer a case of their own young men marching bravely away to fight in defence of the Empire, then coming home as heroic corpses or victorious heroes. When the Empire was smaller, the army was a part of the state, consisting of neighbours and friends, but now it was literally a foreign body, and despite the work that the soldiers did, the army was not appreciated, particularly when money was wrested from unwilling hands to pay for its services.

The financial dilemma had important consequences, provincial in origin but affecting the whole Empire. Some of the wealthy nobles in Africa rebelled against the extraordinarily harsh tax collections, killing the Roman procurator in Thysdrus (modern El Djem), and then realizing that in order to prevent Imperial retribution they would need an emperor of their own. The proconsul Marcus Antonius Gordianus Sempronianus was persuaded to take on the task, but since he was in his eighties, he immediately shared power with his son of the same name, both of them known to modern audiences as Gordian I and II.

GORDIAN I & GORDIAN II AD 238

From now onwards it is virtually impossible to establish the precise chronology of the virtually simultaneous events on the northern frontiers, in Africa and in Rome. At the beginning of April 238 the Senate confirmed the Gordians in power. In Rome the Praetorian Prefect Vitalianus, loyal to Maximinus, was killed by agents of the Gordians, and the city prefect Sabinus was killed during a riot. In Africa, the two Gordians were quickly routed and killed by the governor of Numidia, Capellianus, who was loyal to Maximinus, and who was fortunately not interested in seizing power for himself. The Empire was now officially leaderless.

Maximinus, outlawed by the Senate, gathered his troops and marched towards Italy. Another emperor had to be found, but the Senate compromised by electing two of them, Marcus Clodius Pupienus Maximus and Decimus Caelius Calvinus Balbinus, as if the new emperors were regarded as consuls, each checking and balancing the other. When the people and the soldiers of the Praetorian Guard agitated in favour of the thirteen-year-old Marcus Antonius Gordianus, the nephew of Gordian II, the Senate recognized the boy as Caesar, conceding that he would be the successor of the two senatorial emperors.

As Maximinus approached Italy, Balbinus remained in Rome, while Pupienus marched north to meet the outlawed emperor, and won a victory of sorts. Maximinus's army, besieging Aquileia, was disaffected, because food supplies were low and morale was even lower. Eventually the soldiers of *II Parthica*, thinking of the safety of their families at Alba, not far from Rome, decided to kill Maximinus and his son. Pupienus took over all the troops, keeping the German contingents as his bodyguard. He sent the others back to their bases and returned to Rome. His employment of German guards made the Praetorians uneasy, in case he planned to dismiss them and install the German units instead. In the event, the experiment with two equal emperors failed because of mutual jealousies and their inability to win over the Praetorian Guard, who brutally tortured and then murdered both Pupienus and Balbinus, and declared Gordian III Emperor.

Gordian III AD 238–244

The main sources for the history of Rome now expire altogether or lose themselves in fantasy, so only an outline can be given of the events of the next few years. Besides the soldiers, the nobles also rallied to Gordian, as did the populace, possibly because his accession brought a temporary peace after a long period of unrest, and measures were taken to put right the several wrongs that had plagued the state since the reign of Caracalla. Attempts were made to improve the finances of the inhabitants of the Empire without compromising the state treasury. The ranks of the sycophants and informers were considerably thinned, and control of the army was tightened up. *Legio III Augusta* in Africa was disbanded for its part in the defeat and deaths of the first two Gordians, but without the legion to keep order and to take charge of defence, trouble broke out afresh in Africa. The governor of Mauretania, Caesariensis, had to restore order.

Gordian III was a teenager, hardly of an age to rule by himself. By 241, the most important man in his entourage was Timesitheus, who was appointed Praetorian Prefect and to all practical intents and purposes directed policy and military matters. The Imperial peace did not last long over the whole Empire. Internal as well as external troubles beset the provinces. In some areas there was dissension between the civilian population and the soldiers, as the famous inscription from the Thracian village of Skaptopara (in Bulgaria) demonstrates. In 238 the villagers petitioned Gordian III to protect them against the depredations of the soldiers of the nearby garrisons, who descended upon them demanding *hospitium* (in Greek *xenia* or *xeinie*), literally 'hospitality' but implying much more than that. It was not exactly an illegal procedure, having its roots in Republican and early Imperial practice when soldiers were quartered not in barracks but in official lodging houses, but in the case of Skaptopara it descended into blatant exploitation, because the soldiers took whatever they wanted without paying for it. Gordian referred the villagers to the provincial governor. The complaints of the inhabitants of Skaptopara may have been symptomatic of similar problems elsewhere.

Externally, there were ominous signs of disturbance in the Empire. In the west, coin hoards deposited in the years 238–244 indicate some kind of trouble, usually interpreted as unrest originating from incursions of tribesmen from beyond the Rhine. It seems that there was some destruction in north-west Gaul, and in some parts of Germany, where coins and other objects were buried between 241–244 at Kösching and Gunzenhausen, and the fort at Künzing was destroyed. Further east, Pannonia was quiet and untroubled, but in Moesia and Dacia the Carpi and the Goths had erupted into Roman territory. The Emperors Pupienus and Balbinus sent the general Menophilus to restore order in 238. He brought the tribes to terms and arranged a treaty, which was more favourable to the Goths, who received subsidies, than to the Carpi, who did not. It may have been a deliberate ploy to set one tribe against another.

In 239 the Persian King Ardashir took advantage of his enemy's preoccupation, attacking Dura Europos on the Euphrates, and possibly capturing Hatra. He overran the greater part of Mesopotamia, threatening Syria. A gap in the coinage of Antioch from 240–241 implies that he may have attacked or even taken the city. In 241 in Rome, preparations for war were begun. In the same year, Timesitheus became Praetorian Prefect, and his daughter was married to Gordian III.

Before Timesitheus could begin the war with Ardashir, he was forced to attend to the Goths and Germans in Illyricum. After a short war against them in 242, Timesitheus concluded peace, probably recruiting defeated tribesmen for the eastern campaign. He and Gordian III arrived in the east probably in the last months of 242, thus delaying the start of the Persian campaign until the spring of 243. By now Ardashir had raised his son Shapur as his colleague, and the latter may have taken over Edessa. Timesitheus wrested Osroene from Persian control, and after a battle at Rhesaena the Persians left Nisibis and Singara, but at this high point of the war Timesitheus died. The Romans did not recover from the blow, though Gordian III and the Praetorian Prefect Marcus Julius Verus Philippus (Philip the Arab), followed the original plan and marched to Ctesiphon. Events are now clouded in obscurity. From unknown causes, Gordian III died. Philip was blamed for his death, but there are four different versions in the ancient sources for Gordian's demise, so it seems that even the historians were not sure of the facts.

Philip the Arab AD 244–249

Philip was declared emperor by the troops. He said that Gordian's death was from natural causes, and treated the dead emperor with the greatest respect, transporting his ashes to Rome, insisting upon his deification, and negotiating carefully with the Senate, gaining recognition as emperor in the process. Meanwhile he had to extricate the army from the clutches of the Persians. He negotiated peace, by means of an indemnity to the Persians of 500,000 denarii, and giving up control of Armenia. He retained control of Osroene and Mesopotamia. Philip issued coins proclaiming that he had made peace with the Persians (*pax fundata cum Persis*) but the fact that he had bought his way out of a tricky situation was not well received at Rome, so despite his proud statement on his coinage, he is accused of hastening back to Rome without settling the east. The accusation is unfair since Philip placed his brother Priscus in command as equestrian prefect of Mesopotamia. Documents show that Priscus was also governor of Syria, and an inscription reveals that he held the title *rector Orientis*. This does not signify an actual office, but it does indicate that he held wide ranging powers over the eastern provinces.

When he arrived in Rome, Philip made his son Caesar, and later he elevated him to Augustus in 247. The Emperor's wife, Otacilia Severa, was named Augusta. As a further insurance policy for his regime Philip deified his father Marinus, even though he had never been emperor. This was an unprecedented measure, but it was perhaps less artificial than trying to claim descent from any of the previous emperors, none of whom had been particularly admirable or worthy as ancestors.

Philip enjoyed good relations with the Senate, and from the outset of his reign he reaffirmed the old Roman virtues and traditions. From 246–7 he fought the Carpi and Quadi on the Danube, taking the titles *Germanicus* and *Carpicus Maximus*. In 248, back in Rome, he celebrated the Secular Games, always a significant festival for the Romans, marking their development and power over the centuries, but this time the celebrations even more meaningful, since it was the first millennium of Rome, an occasion worthy of celebration, highlighting the fact that Rome if not the Empire had existed for 1,000 years. There were theatrical and musical events, spectacles in the Circus and the amphitheatre, literary and artistic displays. Strictly, the Secular Games were not due to take place for over sixty years, but the ritual religious purifications associated with the Games were probably felt by some to be long overdue.

As part of his dealings with the Goths, Philip stopped paying their subsidies in 248, with the result that by 249 the tribes had formed a coalition, united in adversity to Rome. They invaded Moesia and Thrace, and laid siege to the city of Marcianopolis. Two revolts also broke out among the Roman army commanders in the north and the east. One of the usurpers, Pacatianus, had been given an extended command over Pannonia and Moesia, though it is not specified exactly where his authority lay. His command is symptomatic of the need to combine the armies of more than one province in order to defend large areas, because the enemies of Rome now ranged far and wide, moved rapidly and could not be dealt with by one provincial governor acting alone and keeping within his own defined territory. The corollary to this requirement was that usurpation was rendered more feasible when such commands over large areas and large numbers of soldiers were instituted. Pacatianus issued coins during his brief reign, as did Jotapianus, the other usurper who was declared emperor in the east, in 248 or 249.

Philip lost his nerve and offered to resign, but the Senate made a show of solidarity, shored up by a senator called Caius Messius Quintus Decius, who declared that the revolts would be short lived. He must have sounded confident and convincing, since Philip entrusted to him the defence of Moesia and the Balkans, and the command against Pacatianus. The results were mixed. Decius put down the revolt but was declared emperor by his troops. Civil war followed, despite Decius's attempts to avert disaster and come to terms with Philip. Two Roman armies, one from Rome and the other from the Danube, converged on northern Italy. The location of the final battle is disputed, but wherever it was fought, Decius was the victor and Philip was killed. Complications about the succession were avoided when Philip's eleven year old son was murdered by the Praetorians in Rome.

DECIUS AD 249–251

Decius was confirmed as emperor towards the end of 249. He started off by attempting to reunify the Roman Empire. As one of the means of doing so he reaffirmed the old Roman religion, not just reinvigorating the cult practices and rituals, but also attending to the restoration of the temple buildings and their internal and external decorative elements. An inscription from Cosa bestows on him the title of *restitutor sacrorum*. As a consequence of his policies he outlawed the cults that he saw as most threatening to unity, chiefly Christianity. Philip had been tolerant towards the Christians, earning himself a reputation in the process, completely unfounded, that he was the first Christian emperor. His reign was the calm before the storm, and the new persecution surprised the Christian community. It came in the form of an order to sacrifice to the gods of the Empire, rigorously enforced throughout the Roman world. Compliant participants were issued with a certificate to prove that they had obeyed the order. Many people crumbled in the face of the authorities and did as they were told, but perhaps some of the Christians rendered unto Caesar what was his due, privately continuing undeterred in their Christian beliefs. The edict had the advantage of singling out those who were not prepared to conform, and executions followed. The Pope Fabian was among the first to be killed, on 20 January 250. Other trials and executions took place all over the Empire; some people ran away and found refuge in lonely places. The trials embraced not just the lowly adherents, but was aimed at the chief officials of the Church, so the name of Decius has been preserved as the arch-tyrant in the works of the later Christian authors, whose writings have lost nothing in the way of umbrage with the passage of time.

For the persecuted Christians it was seen as divine retribution when the Carpi attacked Dacia and the Goths invaded Moesia in 250. Decius was granted the name of Trajan by the Senate when he became emperor, so the parallel with the erstwhile conqueror of Dacia will have been apparent to anyone with a sense of history when he cleared the Carpi from the Roman province, earning himself the title *restitutor Daciarum*. His campaign had begun well, but he faced a more resolute enemy in the Gothic leader Cniva in Moesia and Thrace. The Goths made camp in front of Nicopolis, and whilst they could not be said to be experts in siege tactics, they had learned a lot on their travels, and they later succeeded in taking Philippopolis. Decius could not dislodge them, so he waited for them to move off in search of food. Meanwhile he made his son Herennius Etruscus, who was already Caesar, his colleague in his regime; his younger son Hostilianus was in Rome with a respected senator, Publius Licinius Valerianus (the future Emperor Valerian) in charge of the civil administration while Decius himself led the army. The presence of a respected senator delegated by the Emperor did not prevent the Roman mob from raising a candidate of their own, Julius Valens Licinianus, to replace Decius, whose name they removed from inscriptions in the city.

Decius was probably too embroiled in the struggle in the Danube provinces to notice that he had been usurped. In 251 the Goths began to move northwards, so Decius followed, fighting battles but unable to bring them to final confrontation until he reached the Dobrudja. He risked battle at Abrittus (modern Razgrad in Bulgaria) and was killed. His dynasty did not survive, since his son Herennius Etruscus may have been killed in one of the earlier skirmishes. There was now a power vacuum which the legions were not slow to fill, declaring for the governor of Moesia, Caius Vibius Afinius Trebonianus Gallus.

TREBONIANUS GALLUS AD 251–253

It was rumoured that Gallus had stood by while Decius fought, or even that he had actually betrayed the Emperor and had gone over to the Goths. When he made peace with the Goths it certainly seemed that he favoured them. He resumed their subsidy payments and allowed them to go free, taking their booty and prisoners with them. He did not feel strong enough to defeat them decisively, and he needed to go to Rome to establish himself in power. He eventually adopted Decius's younger son Hostilianus and raised him alongside his own son Volusianus, making them Caesars and then Augusti.

The most immediate crisis was the plague of 252–3. Hostilianus succumbed to it, leaving Volusianus and his father as emperors. Gallus was powerless to raise morale. Making little progress against the Goths, it also seemed that Gallus could not solve the problems of actual or potential invasions from across the Danube and that he was not prepared to deal with the threat to the eastern provinces, where the Persian King Shapur I took Nisibis. Gallus may have made preparations to conduct a campaign from Antioch, where the mint began to issue a large quantity of *antoniniani*, the coins used to pay the soldiers, as if in preparation for a gathering of troops. But Shapur moved more quickly than the Romans, and captured Antioch, where the Roman coinage was interrupted in 263. In these circumstances the inhabitants of the affected provinces naturally look to someone in the immediate vicinity who can help them without delay. The usurper Uranius Antoninus, Priest-King of Emesa, seized power to organize defence against the Persians.

THE REVOLT OF AEMILIUS AEMILIANUS

The Danube frontier was hardly less pressured, so there the troops chose the governor of Lower Moesia, Aemilius Aemilianus, as emperor. He put an end to the subsidies to the Goths and defeated them in battle. Aemilianus realized that his claims would be received in a much better light if he adopted a respectful attitude towards the Senate. Regardless of the fact that Trebonianus Gallus was the legitimate emperor, he sent a letter to Rome suggesting a division of responsibilities. The Senate should exercise supreme power, and he would be the general in chief commanding the Danube and the east.

Gallus sent his general Valerian with the Rhine legions against Aemilianus who was marching on Rome, but the legions proclaimed Valerian as emperor. Valerian perhaps reasoned that he might as well fight on his own behalf, instead of trying to support an emperor who seemed to be rapidly losing control of the Empire. The soldiers killed Gallus and Volusianus, and soon afterwards Aemilianus was eliminated by his troops, leaving Valerian as sole emperor. He set about confirming his power immediately. The Senate bestowed the title Caesar on his adult son Publius Licinius Gallienus. When Valerian arrived in Rome he made Gallienus his colleague as Augustus. Now at last there were two emperors who would be able to deal with the problems in the two halves of the Empire at the same time, Gallienus taking the west and Valerian going to the east as soon as he could, to combat the Persian menace.

THE JOINT RULE OF VALERIAN & GALLIENUS AD 253–260

In 253 Shapur I turned his full attention on Armenia, killing King Chosroes, whose son Tiridates fled, leaving Armenia wide open to Persian domination. The Romans soon recovered their losses. On his arrival in the east Valerian set up headquarters at Antioch and started rebuilding the city. The mint reopened, and damage to the surrounding Syrian territories was repaired. From 253 to 255 the situation in the threatened provinces of both east and west slowly improved. Gallienus celebrated victories over the Germans in Illyricum. By 256 it seemed that Rome was in the ascendancy again, until the new threat from the Franks broke out in Gaul and Germany. Gallienus left the Danube provinces, installing his son Valerian the younger at Viminacium as Caesar, while he established his headquarters on the Rhine frontier at Cologne. He opened a mint there, which soon began to issue coins naming Gallienus as *restitutor Galliarum*, the restorer of the Gallic provinces.

In May 258 Valerian arrived in Antioch, while at the same time Gallienus was threatened by a usurper called Ingenuus, whose troops had proclaimed him emperor in Illyricum. It is probable that Gallienus's son, the younger Valerian, was killed in this revolt. Personal disaster was followed by Imperial crisis, on three fronts if not four. Valerian was fully occupied in the east fighting against Shapur I, and Gallienus was re-establishing his authority over Illyricum, but now there were more invasions by the Goths threatening the Black Sea coastal cities, and the Alamanni were restless on the frontiers of Germany and Raetia. The defence of all the western provinces at the same time was impossible. Gallienus had placed his younger son Saloninus at Cologne as the new Caesar, while he returned to northern Italy and set up his headquarters at Milan, where he established a mint. Disasters piled up one on top of another. In the summer of 260, Shapur captured Emperor Valerian, perhaps by treachery. The Persians were now free to dominate the entire east, because there was no one to stop them. Usurpers appeared in several places, because in the absence of Imperial troops, self-help on the frontiers had become the only alternative. At Carnuntum the soldiers chose Regalianus to lead them against the Iazyges and Roxolani. In the east Callistus (also called Ballista in some sources) and Macrianus took charge of the remnants of Valerian's defeated army. Neither Macrianus nor Callistus declared themselves emperors, but Macrianus proclaimed his two sons, Titus Fulvius Junius Macrianus and Titus Fulvius Junius Quietus, as Augusti. In Gaul the governor Postumus was declared emperor. An inscription found at Augsburg shows that the domain of Postumus extended over Raetia as well as the Rhine frontier and the Gallic provinces; Britain was with him and Spain came over to him later.

Emperor Gallienus was backed into a corner in Milan, with only a fraction of the armies of the Empire at his disposal. With these troops and reduced resources he faced multiple problems. There were three usurpers in different parts of the Empire, in command of sizeable armies. The Persians were at liberty to raid the whole of the east, and for the first time in Roman history an emperor had not only failed to check them but had been ignominiously captured. The Goths were on the rampage in Moesia and Thrace, having learned how to use boats for successful hit and run raids on rich cities, and the Franks and Alamanni and other assorted tribes were poised to attack the Rhine and the upper Danube. Gallienus was forced to use the limited resources that he had at his disposal. Lateral thinking, continual adaptation to circumstances, and changes in operational and organisational methods were the first priority, if Rome and the Empire were to survive.

13

Hard Times:
The Empire Fragments AD 260–284

GALLIENUS SOLE EMPEROR AD 260–268

After the capture of Valerian by the Persians, Gallienus ruled alone. From his reign onwards, the Roman world entered upon a period of change, and though the changes may not have been intended to be permanent, by degrees they became entrenched and in some cases irrevocable. Deprived of the troops and the revenues of the western and eastern areas of the Empire, and therefore forced to make the best use of what was immediately to hand, Gallienus adapted old established methods and produced something new, sometimes sacrificing hallowed traditions if they were not suited to his current circumstances. Gallienus reformed the army and the administration, but these reforms evolved from emergency measures rather than as a result of a co-ordinated policy. For most of his reign Gallienus was barely one step ahead of disasters, and was not granted the luxury of forward planning, but his achievements laid the foundations for the development of the later Roman Empire.

Remaining sole emperor, Gallienus did not appoint a colleague to replace his father. He could not spare troops for a military expedition to rescue Valerian without risking usurpation at home or invasion from the northern tribes, nor did he have access to sufficient wealth to offer a ransom payment. Gallienus's apparent lack of filial devotion derived from necessity, since the state had to take priority.

THE ARMY REFORMS

Gallienus had more need than most of an efficient and loyal army. In the west, all the legions of the Rhine and in Gaul, and most of the civilian population of these provinces supported the Gallic usurper Postumus. In the east, the Persians were stronger than they had been for many years, and if it had not been for the energetic defence of the east by the Palmyrenes under their leader Odenathus, the Persians would probably have taken over all of the eastern Roman provinces.

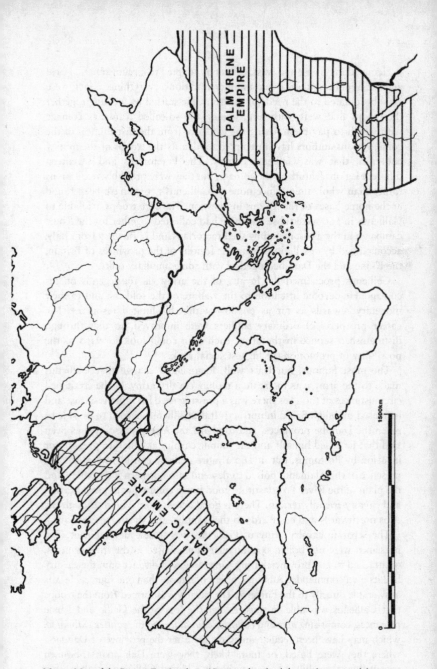

Map 2. Map of the Roman Empire about AD 260, after the defeat and capture of the Emperor Valerian by the Persians. His son and co-ruler Gallienus was confined to Italy and the Danube provinces, deprived of the armies and revenues of both eastern and western portions of the Empire.

Hemmed in on east and west, Gallienus adapted to circumstances. Fiscal and social policy, political and military traditions, everything in fact, were all subordinated to the needs of the army. He started by welding together the troops that were with him, issuing the so-called legionary coinage with which to pay them. Using the evidence from the distribution of the coins, various authors have attempted to identify the troops of the motley collection that was Gallienus's army. The Praetorians and seventeen different legions feature on the coinage, but they were probably vexillations rather than whole units, since none of Gallienus's coins have been found at the home bases of the legions in question. The core troops available to Gallienus in 260 were those which he had collected together for the Rhine campaign in the 250s, including the Praetorians and *II Parthica* from Italy, accompanied by vexillations from the legions of the provinces of Britain, the Rhine and the Danube, together with some auxiliary units.

Gallienus proclaimed the loyalty of the army via the legends on his coinage. He devoted attention to the welfare of the soldiers, and to their monetary rewards as far as possible within his limited resources. The career prospects of ordinary soldiers were improved, so that through distinguished service in the army, each man could look forward to the possibility of promotion the highest social rank.

The most famous, but least well documented change that Gallienus made to the army was to create a mobile cavalry army. In the straitened circumstances of the 260s there was a pressing need for rapid response and increased mobility. Based in northern Italy, Gallienus needed to be able to reach the Danube provinces, and to guard the Alpine passes. It has been said that he based himself and the mobile cavalry at Milan to prepare for invasion by Postumus, but in 260 a more realistic consideration was the presence of the Alamanni poised to descend into northern Italy. Milan and the plain of the River Po constitute good horse country, with good grazing and cavalry-friendly terrain. There is good access from Milan through the Alps northwards and eastwards to the Danube, and westwards to Gaul.

The separate cavalry army of Gallienus was a new development. The horsemen were not brigaded in auxiliary units based in the frontier posts, or attached to any provincial army. Operating as a distinct unit, the cavalry had its own commander, Aureolus, attested in more than one source. He was answerable directly to the Emperor. The cavalry was formed from the troops that Gallienus was able to muster after the loss of the Gallic and Rhine provinces, comprising *alae* and *cohortes equitatae*, and the *equites Dalmatae*, which may have been regular units, named after the province of Dalmatia where they were based, or more likely they were Dalmatian tribesmen recruited for their skill in horsemanship. In addition, Gallienus's mobile army contained the legionary cavalry, called the *promoti*, perhaps denoting an upgrade in status as they transferred from the legions to the cavalry army.

The Byzantine chronicler George Cedrenus says that Gallienus was the founder of the mobile cavalry army, familiar to ancient writers from the fourth century, but Cedrenus may have applied the term anachronistically. It cannot be stated categorically that Gallienus's cavalry army was the forerunner of the later mobile armies, because it is not certain how long it survived after his death. An inscription dating to the reign of Claudius Gothicus may refer to the mobile cavalry, since a distinction is made between the *vexillationes adque equites*, or the detachments and the horsemen, suggesting that the cavalry differed from the vexillations and did not fight under the same standard. The mobile cavalry was perhaps used to good effect by Claudius Gothicus against the Goths, and then by Aurelian, but it seems that after about 285 it was no longer at Milan, and subsequently it is not attested as a separate entity. It may have been disbanded, leaving Diocletian and Constantine to discover its usefulness all over again.

THE PROTECTORES

The title of *protector* first appeared in the joint reigns of Valerian and Gallienus. The *protectores* were drawn from diverse units and followed diverse careers, so they were not formed into a specific unit, making it unlikely that Gallienus intended to form a new bodyguard. *Protector* did not denote a rank, but it was a mark of distinction, proclaiming an acknowledged loyalty to the emperor. It was not awarded to senators, so it is possible that Gallienus wanted to establish a new kind of aristocracy of military men with proven ability. The suggestion that the *protectores* were members of a staff college is supported by the fact that at least one man was designated *princeps protectorum*, implying that there was a group who worked together and one of them was regarded as the leader. Some of the more distinguished *protectores* went on to higher offices, so that it is clear that the conferment of the title was a indication that such men were marked out for splendid careers.

THE GALLIC EMPIRE

Probably in 260 when the capture of Valerian by the Persians was known in the west, Marcus Cassianus Latinius Postumus, governor of Lower Germany, was proclaimed emperor by his troops. The Rhine army had no confidence in the ability of the legitimate emperor to protect the provinces from invasion, and chose the man whom the soldiers thought most capable of doing so. The Gallic Empire was firmly based on Roman institutions. Consuls were elected annually, the emperor assumed tribunician power each year, and he protected himself by means of a Praetorian Guard.

Postumus remained in power for a decade. The two Germanies, the whole of Gaul, with the possible exception of Narbonensis, then Britain and Spain joined him. He set up headquarters at Cologne, and attended to the repair and defence of the Rhine frontier and its hinterland. He promoted himself just as Gallienus did, advertising his successes, issuing good quality coinage that proclaimed him restorer of Gaul (*Restitutor Galliarum*) and the bringer of security to the provinces (*Salus Provinciarum*).

The restored provinces, somewhat battered, were restructured according to current needs. Archaeologists have shown that many if not all the frontier forts on the Rhine and through Germany were abandoned after 260, and there is evidence of widespread destruction. City authorities began to think very seriously of strong walls and fortified gates. The magnitude of Postumus's task occupied him fully for many years, perhaps preventing him from turning his attention to Rome and the struggle for supreme power over the whole Empire. It is debatable whether he ever intended to usurp Gallienus, who never officially recognized him, but no amount of discussion as to Postumus's ambitions can solve this problem.

Gallienus on the other hand tried to win back the Gallic Empire, perhaps on two occasions, in 261 and possibly in 265–266. He controlled the exits from the Alpine passes to protect the route into Italy, and he may have succeeded in regaining control of Raetia, but ultimately he failed and had to withdraw when he was wounded at Trier. Neither Postumus nor his successors marched on Rome to fight it out with the legitimate emperor, but further conflict was inevitable.

ODENATHUS & THE KINGDOM OF PALMYRA

When the senior Emperor Valerian was taken prisoner by Shapur I, the Roman army was extricated by Macrianus, an equestrian who had been put in charge of logistics and supplies for the campaign as *praepositus annonae expeditionalis*. He later broke with Gallienus, proclaiming his two sons Augusti, eventually marching on Rome with the younger Macrianus, leaving the other son, Quietus, with Callistus or Ballista in command of the eastern provinces, based at Emesa. Gallienus's general and cavalry commander Aureolus defeated the two Macriani in Pannonia, and possibly after this defeat the citizens of Emesa eliminated Quietus. Ballista disappeared. The Palmyrene Odenathus pursued Shapur as the Persian army headed back across the Euphrates laden with booty.

Palmyra owed its existence and its wealth to its fortunate geographical position, at a well-watered location in the desert, where crops could be grown, animals raised, and the inhabitants could conduct their long-distance trading ventures. It was not only a trading city in its own right, but a place of high culture with an established nobility, of which

Odenathus was one of the foremost members. His father Hairan had been granted Roman citizenship by Severus, and on inscriptions Odenathus calls himself Septimius. He was raised to senatorial rank, and by 258 he was of consular status (*vir consularis*).

Debate centres around the relationship between Gallienus and Odenathus. In 260 Gallienus was in no position to refuse the help of Odenathus against either the Persians or the usurpers. Odenathus had little choice except to take charge of the eastern provinces. Sandwiched between the Empire of Rome in the west and the rising power of Shapur and the Persian Empire in the east, it was possible that the Palmyrenes could turn either way, and it was thought by later chroniclers that Odenathus initially made overtures to Shapur before he began to act on behalf of Rome. Since Gallienus could not afford to mount a campaign of his own to win back the east, the better option was to allow Odenathus to continue as he had begun. Unlike Postumus in Gaul, Gallienus officially recognized Odenathus, possibly granting him a military command as *dux Romanorum*, leader of the Romans. This title is not definitely attested for Odenathus, but since Vaballathus, his son and successor held the title, it is assumed that it derived from Odenathus and that he was placed in command of troops in the east. It is not clear exactly how his command operated with regard to the existing military officers in the eastern provinces, and the provincial governors. With the sanction of Rome the Palmyrenes had for some time provided a military force under their own commanders, with which they patrolled the desert between Syria and the Euphrates, so Odenathus would have controlled these troops, but the major question is whether or not Odenathus was also placed in command of the Roman government personnel in the east, and all the available troops. It is likely that the arrangement with Gallienus may have allowed Odenathus a certain freedom of action within defined parameters.

In 262–3 and again in 267, Odenathus launched campaigns against Persia, reaching Ctesiphon and liberating Nisibis from Persian domination. In respect of these victories Gallienus took the title *Parthicus Maximus*, granting to Odenathus the title *corrector totius Orientis*. As with his title of *dux*, the inference is drawn from the titles displayed by his son Vaballathus, and not from direct evidence concerning Odenathus himself. Precisely what the title implied is not known for certain. It is reminiscent of Priscus, the brother of Philip the Arab, who was put in charge of the eastern provinces with the title *rector orientis*. Significantly, Odenathus was not granted official Roman posts such as proconsul, prefect or *praeses*. He awarded himself the title king of kings, but this did not signify that he intended to take over the Empire. The title was customary in the east, and since he had charge of the eastern provinces, Odenathus adopted a title that would be meaningful to the eastern population.

When the Goths invaded Roman territory in Asia Minor, Odenathus hurried to repel them, but before he had completed his task he was assassinated along with his eldest son, by one of his own men, in 267 or 268. The circumstances are obscure. The exact date of the assassination is unknown, and more than one murderer is named in the different ancient sources, including Gallienus himself as the instigator of a plot to remove the Palmyrene leader.

After the death of Odenathus and his son, it is possible that Gallienus could have reunited the eastern provinces with the rest of his Empire, but invasions by the northern tribes across the Danube preoccupied him. Zenobia, the young, energetic and ambitious wife of Odenathus, stepped into the power vacuum in the name of her young son Vaballathus. According to the ancient sources, she defeated the Praetorian Prefect, Heraclianus, allegedly sent by Gallienus to take charge of the east, but since Heraclianus is named as one of Gallienus's assassins in 268, this expedition, if it took place at all, may have been organized by one of Gallienus's successors. Since Gallienus failed to regain control of the east, he was regarded as a failure. It was Aurelian who brought the Empire back together.

THE EQUESTRIANS & THE SENATORS

Severus had promoted equestrians as military commanders and provincial governors, and Gallienus took the policy even further, appointing equestrians, including military men who had risen from the ranks, to high commands which had previously been the almost exclusive domain of the senatorial class. He employed men whom he knew and trusted, usually professional soldiers who had concentrated almost exclusively on the army and had not served their time simply in order to advance their political careers. In the early Empire ambitious senators usually combined their urban and civilian posts with a term of service with the army, as tribunes in a legion, then later as legionary legates, but these military appointments were merely stepping stones to a more glorious political career.

Gallienus preferred to put experienced equites rather than senators in charge of legions, not as *legati* but as *praefecti*, as in Egypt from the time of Augustus, where the equestrian commander was called *praefectus legionis*. Severus also appointed equestrian *praefecti* as legionary commanders of the three new Parthian legions. Gallienus built on these precedents, installing equestrian prefects at the head of all the legions in the provinces where his control was unchallenged. The post of legionary legate was not swept aside. The full title for the equestrian commanders, *praefectus agens vices legati*, reflects the fact that the prefect was acting as substitute for the legate.

Equestrians were also appointed as governors of some of the provinces. He had no influence in the Gallic provinces, but in the east, it seems that Gallienus still controlled the appointment of governors, while the Palmyrene Odenathus co-ordinated defence. There were precedents for equestrians as temporary governors, for instance when the original governor died or was killed and there was a need for someone to take over until a new governor could be appointed. The usual title, *agens vice praesidis*, made it clear that the equestrian substitute possessed full authority to act on behalf of the provincial governor. From about 260 onwards, Gallienus appointed equestrian *praesides* to certain provinces, not as temporary substitutes, but as authentic governors.

After 250, fully documented senatorial careers decline in number, and by about 262 the senatorial governors had disappeared from the Imperial praetorian provinces. Exactly how the change was put into effect is not elucidated. It cannot be said that Gallienus was motivated solely by his hatred of the Senate when he appointed equestrians as legionary legates or as *praesides*. The senatorial governors of large provinces with two legions were not affected, principally because equestrian prefects and not senators commanded the troops. The provinces to which equestrians were appointed were those which were threatened by the tribesmen from beyond the frontiers, or where there was internal unrest. Gallienus made no changes in the provinces where no troops were stationed, nor in the senatorial provinces, where he allowed senators to continue as proconsuls.

It has been suggested that Gallienus put an end to senatorial military careers, but in fact the military interests of the senators had been declining for some time. By the mid 250s, the military *tribuni laticlavii* had disappeared. A career pattern based on almost exclusively military or exclusively civil appointments had already begun to manifest itself as early as the reign of Hadrian, contributing to the development of specialization and professionalism, in administration and especially in the army. During the Marcommanic wars, Marcus Aurelius had found it difficult to find a sufficient quantity of suitable senators with military experience, but even after Gallienus's reforms, it is unlikely that all senators were divorced from the army. Nonetheless, senatorial participation in the government of the Empire diminished. The junior magistracies disappeared, except the quaestorship, and equestrians carried out many functions in administration and finance. The Emperor controlled the army, the finances, and significant appointments, so very little was left for the Senate to do. After Gallienus's reforms there were changes in the normal career pattern, the *cursus honorum*. The appointment as governor of a praetorian province usually paved the way to the consulship and then to further appointments. Divorced from posts in Imperial praetorian provinces and from commands in the army, senators had to find alternative routes to the consulship. From the mid-third century a spectacular senatorial career depended upon a good relationship with the emperor, a situation to which Gallienus was probably not entirely unsympathetic.

FINANCES

Gallienus had the army almost exclusively in mind in his monetary and financial policies. For a long time, income had failed to match expenditure, and there was no budgetary system in the modern sense. In the mid-third century there was an escalating degeneration in the Imperial finances. One response was to debase the currency and issue more of it, and both Valerian and Gallienus consistently adopted this procedure. The result was a rise in prices, the full effects of which were not apparent until after Gallienus's death, beginning around 270.

Cash payments to the army and some taxes were partly transmuted into payments in kind. The central treasury provided partial payment for the troops, but requisitions in kind fell most heavily on those areas where the troops were operating. Some areas could be denuded in a prolonged continuous war, or if successive short campaigns were fought over the same terrain before the next harvests could be brought home. Direct taxation, the source of much of the state revenue, fell most heavily on the wealthy landowners in Italy and the provinces. With regard to the payment of the army, Gallienus founded several mints near the various military headquarters, at Milan, Sirmium, Siscia and Smyrna, which reduced the risks involved in transporting coin across the Empire.

A major problem was that the values of the coinage were not standardized, so in general people judged the worth of the gold *aureus* upon what it actually weighed, not upon what Imperial power said it was worth. In the short term, the consequences of Gallienus's financial policies were satisfactory. The army was well rewarded and functioned as the Emperor wished, and the rest of the Empire managed as best it could. In the long term the policies were disastrous, and Gallienus did not survive long enough to reverse them.

GALLIENUS'S ACHIEVEMENTS

The chronology of events in the reign of Gallienus is far from clear. The Alamanni were soundly defeated near Milan in 260, and caused little trouble for several years after the battle. The revolt of Regalianus in Pannonia was ended when he was killed in an invasion by the Iazyges and Roxolani, while that of Macrianus was dealt with by Aureolus in the west and Odenathus in the east. Gallienus's general Theodotus put down another attempt at usurpation by Aemilianus in Egypt, in 261–2. Gallienus quelled an attempted mutiny in Byzantium at about the same time. Once these upheavals calmed down, by 262 Gallienus had re-established control over most of the Empire save for the extensive territories still loyal to Postumus. Though the east was still in the hands of Odenathus, the Palmyrene ruler was nominally Gallienus's chosen deputy.

During the few years of relative peace between 262 and 265, Gallienus found time to devote to philosophy, promoting his favourite Plotinus. He encouraged literature and the arts, and visited Athens where he was made exarch of the city and was initiated into the Eleusinian mysteries. His self indulgence in leisure pursuits was represented in the later sources as gross negligence.

Towards the end of 266 Gallienus marched to the Danube to fight the Goths. The first campaign produced no tangible result, and in 267 it seemed that the whole of the Roman world from Moesia to the Mediterranean was at the mercy of several tribes. The Goths poured across Moesia into Thrace, and the Heruli threatened Athens, Sparta and Corinth. Another group laid siege to Thessalonika. The Emperor and the army could not be everywhere at once, and the provincial troops were not sufficient in number to meet the invading bands and drive them out. Self-help was the only answer. Various communities built walls around their cities and sometimes it was necessary to arm the civilian inhabitants and lead them to war. An inscription from Augsburg refers to civilians fighting alongside the troops, and in Athens the defence was conducted by the civilian Dexippus, who resisted valiantly but still failed to save his city from capture, a fact which is subsumed in the rhetoric of his account of the episode.

Gallienus concentrated on Illyricum, where he defeated a group of Heruli, incorporating the survivors into the Roman army. He defeated another group at Philippopolis, but was unable to follow up the recent victory, because news arrived that the commander of the cavalry, Aureolus, had raised revolt in Milan. Leaving his general Marcianus in command of the campaign against the Heruli and the Goths, Gallienus marched to Italy, and besieged Milan. In July or August 268 a plot was hatched, led by Heraclianus, to assassinate Gallienus. The commander of the Dalmatian cavalry, lured the Emperor outside his tent by announcing that Aureolus was approaching with his army; not waiting for his bodyguard, Gallienus dashed out unprotected, and was killed.

The ancient sources are hostile to Gallienus, masking his real achievements in holding together the remnants of the fragmenting Empire and fighting off usurpers and invasions. It was only under Aurelian that the Empire was pulled back together, but without the efforts of Gallienus, there may have been no Empire to reassemble.

CLAUDIUS II GOTHICUS AD 268–270

The new emperor was Marcus Aurelius Claudius. The army officers supported him, but the troops were not happy, and he had to disburse lots of cash to persuade them to accept him. Claudius was an Illyrian army officer whose career had blossomed under Gallienus, becoming one of Gallienus's closest advisers and most experienced generals. There was apparently no stigma attached to his association with the previous emperor, so it does not seem that there was a conspiracy to remove the whole court circle and the top generals, and then start again with a new faction. Claudius's role in the assassination of Gallienus is not clear. The sources tend to whitewash him because Constantine claimed him as one of his ancestors, so all hints of a less than perfect life were expunged from the record.

Since Claudius was emperor for only a short time, he had no chance to undertake sweeping reforms or to establish coherent policies in the military, financial or social spheres, but the fact that he did not reverse any of Gallienus's policies suggests that the reign of his predecessor was not as dire as it was later portrayed. Claudius's relations with the Senate were at least cordial, but the retrospective favour shown him by Constantine may have improved and embellished the historical record. Careful to observe the formalities, Claudius went to Rome, where he persuaded the Senate to deify Gallienus. By this act, Claudius implied that the murder of Gallienus was illegal, but there was no witch hunt. Only Aureolus was put to death.

Claudius sent the prefect of the *vigiles*, Julius Placidianus, to bring the Gallic Empire back into the Imperial domain, and this officer won over part of Gallia Narbonensis and regained control of the Rhône valley, but failed to reintegrate all the provinces into the Empire. The bulk of Claudius's army was committed to the struggle against the Goths and the Alamanni. The Goths had discovered seaborne transport and were raiding the Mediterranean coastal cities. Claudius entrusted the prefect of Egypt, Tenagino Probus, with a fleet based in Greece to sweep the seas clear of the Goths and to protect the coasts.

Probably at this moment Zenobia, the widow of Odenathus, decided to take advantage of the preoccupations of the Romans to extend her control of the eastern provinces. Her armies swept into Egypt, defeating Tenagino Probus, who committed suicide. The Palmyrenes were now in command of most of the east, and of the bulk of Rome's corn supply, though there is no evidence that Zenobia deliberately disrupted the transport of grain from Egypt.

The Goths were still causing destruction on the Danube and in Greece, and had put Thessalonika and Marcianopolis under siege. Claudius claimed a victory over them at Naissus, but the Goths were not decisively defeated.

The Alamanni had been quiet since their defeat in 260, perhaps because they had made a treaty with Gallienus, which they regarded as a personal arrangement between two chiefs. When Gallienus was assassinated the agreement came to an end. Claudius defeated the tribesmen near Lake Garda, taking the title *Germanicus Maximus*. In summer 270 Claudius was at Sirmium, preparing a campaign against the Juthungi and Vandals in the Danube provinces, but he died of the plague that broke out in that year. For a short time his brother Quintillus stepped into the vacancy as emperor, but he did not have the support of the whole army. The rival contender, Aurelian, was proclaimed by his soldiers, and carried all before him.

AURELIAN AD 270–275

The origins of Lucius Domitius Aurelianus are unknown. His elevation from obscurity to supreme power was a result of social mobility based on military prowess. When Claudius died Aurelian was on campaign, probably against the Juthungi and Vandals. He was one of the most important officers in Claudius's entourage, and his proclamation as emperor was not a complete surprise. One of his first acts was purely practical; he seized the mint at Siscia, where he struck gold coins to enable him to pay the soldiers.

Aurelian had achieved a reputation for determination and energy, earning the nickname of *manu ad ferrum*, hand on hilt. Before the end of his reign he had earned a reputation for cruelty as well. Aurelian's priorities were to conclude the wars with the tribesmen. The Juthungi were on their way out of northern Italy, heading for home with their booty. Aurelian caught up with them in Raetia. He refused to grant them a peace treaty, but allowed them to continue homewards unmolested, if they would provide soldiers for the Roman army. In the campaign against the Vandals Aurelian devastated the territories all around them to starve them into submission, then he extracted 2,000 cavalry for the army, and made peace, giving food to the remaining Vandals so that they could return home.

When a temporary peace was restored Aurelian journeyed to Rome. The ancient sources indicate that one of the first problems that Aurelian dealt with was the revolt at the mint in Rome. There was a great deal of corruption among the mint workers, who were probably lining their own pockets. Aurelian made an initial attempt to reform the finances in the early part of his reign, and sometime later in 274 he began a more thorough reform of the currency and the financial system.

The attempted usurpations of Septiminus, Domitianus, and Urbanus, were quickly detected and eradicated. Suspicion was all that was necessary to condemn them, and whether they were guilty or not, the point was made that Aurelian would not tolerate opposition. It seems that all of these potential troublemakers appeared and disappeared early in Aurelian's reign, perhaps all of them in 271, possibly even before he arrived in Rome. As mentioned above, chronology is not one of the strong points in the documentation of the period from Gallienus to Diocletian, and for Aurelian's reign it is especially confused.

The Emperor needed to consolidate his supremacy over the Senate and people of Rome. Though the Roman mob no longer possessed the coercive power that it once had, it was always a wise move for new emperors to cultivate the goodwill of the populace, so Aurelian disbursed 500 denarii to each citizen in Rome, and cancelled debts to the Treasury, making a bonfire of all the records and gaining much popularity as a result. On the other hand he raised taxes, damaging the rich. The senators bestowed the usual powers on him, but the Senate as a body was weakened under Aurelian, losing the privilege of issuing bronze coinage, and its legislative powers disappeared as the Emperor evolved into totalitarian ruler and lawgiver.

News arrived that the Juthungi and the Alamanni were moving again, joined by the Marcomanni. The sources vary with regard to the tribes with which Aurelian fought, sometimes calling them all Scythians. Throughout the early part of Aurelian's reign there were rapidly changing military actions and wide ranging movements of troops. In 271 the Juthungi reached Milan. Aurelian chased the tribesmen from battle to battle in northern Italy, defeating bands of warriors in at least three different places, at Fanum Fortunae, Metaurus, and on the Ticinus near modern Pavia. The mobility of the tribesmen made it difficult to pin them down. After defeats they simply split up and then regrouped.

When some semblance of order was restored by running the tribesmen to ground, Aurelian returned to Rome and proclaimed a German victory. He knew well, as did everyone else, that his victories did not mark an end to war. He had gained a temporary respite, nothing more, and Rome was still vulnerable.

For centuries, the city of Rome had stood supreme, without protective walls, having long ago outgrown the old Servian walls enclosing the early city. Now in the late third century circumstances were much different. It had been demonstrated that the frontiers could not withstand determined onslaughts by large numbers of tribesmen. The prime purpose of the frontiers was to discourage attacks, controlling the tribes by a combination of alliances, gifts and subsidies, by patrolling, intelligence gathering, psychological intimidation and occasional aggressive wars. Once the tribesmen were across the Alps, however, the road to Rome was open. Aurelian called a meeting of the Senate to discuss the project of building a wall round the city.

Civilian workers were mobilized, because there were not enough soldiers to spare for building the wall. The circuit was too long to defend adequately, but the intention was not necessarily to enable the city to withstand a prolonged siege. The tribesmen did not generally attempt to besiege cities, because they did not have the ability to supply themselves for a long time in one place. They preferred to make hit and run raids, and move on. The walls of Rome were not finally completed until the reign of Probus, but even so they were built remarkably quickly, by incorporating several buildings within the circuit, and by the fact that the new walls did not take in the full extent of the city.

The Palmyrene Campaign

Aurelian turned to the reunification of the Empire. While he had been occupied on the Danube and also with the problems in Rome, he acquiesced in what amounted to a shared rule in the east with Zenobia's young son Vaballathus. Coins issued by the Alexandrian mint, on the orders of Zenobia, display the head of the Roman Emperor on one side, and on the other that of Vaballathus, but at this point Vaballathus had not assumed Imperial titles. Aurelian tolerated the situation but Zenobia knew that confrontation with the Emperor was inevitable. When he started to mobilize, Zenobia broke with him decisively, awarding to Vaballathus the titles Imperator Caesar Augustus, and calling herself Augusta, a direct challenge to Aurelian which he could not ignore.

Already on his way to the east in 271, Aurelian was waylaid by the Goths for a short time, but after his victory he marched towards the east, wintering at Byzantium in 271, and moving into Asia Minor in spring 272. Meanwhile one of his generals had reconquered Egypt, and by August 271 the Alexandrian mint was coining for Aurelian alone, indicating that Egypt was once more incorporated into the Empire. Aurelian swept through Asia Minor and into Syria. At Immae, about 40 km east of Antioch, he fought a battle with Zenobia and her army, commanded by her general Septimius Zabdas. Aurelian resorted to a ruse to draw the Palmyrene heavy armoured cavalry (nicknamed *clibanarii*, literally 'ovens') into an ambush. He ordered his Moorish and Dalmatian horsemen to turn tail and run when they saw the *clibanarii*. The stratagem worked. The heavy horsemen tried to pursue and were defeated. Zenobia evacuated Antioch, leaving Palmyrene garrison at Daphne nearby, but it did not hold up Aurelian for long.

The final battle was at Emesa. After his victory there Aurelian marched after Zenobia to Palmyra, and blockaded the city. During the action he was wounded by an arrow, but not seriously. Since supplies were not abundant in the middle of the desert, Aurelian came to a successful arrangement with the tribes who opposed Zenobia. The tribesman provided supplies for the Romans and helped to secure their communications.

Palmyra was not possessed of a complete circuit of walls and soon fell to the Romans. Zenobia fled once again, heading for the Euphrates and Persia, but she was captured. Her ultimate fate and that of her son is unknown. Some sources say that she soon died, or committed suicide, but others insist that she survived to be paraded through the streets of Rome in Aurelian's triumph, then was allowed to live in Italy, respectably married to a Roman senator. The house where she lived was pointed out to fourth-century Roman tourists.

Soon after the Romans left Palmyra, there were two revolts: one in Egypt led by Firmus, a wealthy merchant at Alexandria, and another in Palmyra, led by Septimius Apsaeus, who produced a relative of Odenathus and Zenobia called Antiochus, and proclaimed him king. The reappearance of Aurelian at Palmyra was so sudden that the Palmyrenes were taken by surprise. When he captured the city this time, he razed it. There would be no resurgence of Palmyrene power. Next it was the turn of Egypt. Alexandria was treated very severely and Aurelian took revenge on the Egyptians by raising the taxes. At the end of these campaigns Aurelian promoted his image as restorer of the east, *Restitutor Orientis*, as his coins proclaimed him.

THE END OF THE GALLIC EMPIRE

For nearly ten years, the Gallic Emperor Postumus had governed well. He had repaired and defended the Rhine frontier. His coinage was of a better and more reliable quality than the legitimate Emperor's and he had held out against the attempts at reconquest by Gallienus and his deputies.

Dissension began in 269 with the revolt of Laelianus. Postumus defeated him, only to face another usurper, Marius. While engaged in the struggle against the latter, Postumus was killed because he refused to allow his soldiers to sack the Roman city of Mainz. Victorinus, who had been Postumus's colleague in the consulship in 268, was proclaimed emperor in October or November 271, but was quickly assassinated. For a while his mother Victoria filled the power vacuum and brought to the attention of the troops, supported by substantial amounts of cash, the senatorial governor of Aquitania, Esuvius Tetricus, who was declared emperor and set up headquarters at Trier. He was recognized in Britain and the whole of Gaul, save for Narbonensis. Spain wavered and then joined him, as did the city of Strasbourg, but there the inhabitants soon changed their minds and declared for Aurelian. Invasions across the Rhine and along the coasts continued unabated. Some German tribesmen penetrated as far as the

Loire. The only response that Tetricus could make was to abandon forts and withdraw the troops. At least some of the coin hoards in northern Gaul must relate to this period of endemic insecurity.

Aurelian mobilized against Tetricus perhaps late in the year 273 or early in 274. The opposing armies met at Châlons-sur-Marne, but it is not even certain if there was a battle. Whatever happened, the Gallic Empire came to an end probably in March 274, when the mint at Lyons changed from coining for Tetricus and began to issue coins for Aurelian, declaring him the restorer of the east, and indeed the restorer of the world. The Empire was unified once more, not without certain false starts. A usurper called Faustinus was proclaimed emperor at Trier, but the rebellion was soon quelled. Britain returned to the fold voluntarily. In Gaul the army was split up and put into different garrisons, and Aurelian's reliable kinsman Probus was put in charge of the reconstruction and defence of the frontier zones. Tetricus survived, and was given an official post as *corrector Lucaniae*, preserving his fortune and his status intact.

THE EVACUATION OF DACIA

The date when Aurelian took the troops out of the Dacian provinces (modern Romania) is not known. The case for 272–3 is perhaps the most convincing, just before the campaign to quell the Palmyrene revolt. A buried hoard discovered in Romania, consisting of over 250 coins from the mints at Milan, Cyzicus and Siscia, contains nothing later than 272. In order to turn his attention to the Palmyrene revolt, Aurelian had to abandon the campaign against the northern tribes before he had achieved victory and a full settlement, so rather than leave behind him a threatened province, it is probable that Aurelian evacuated Dacia and brought the troops out at this juncture. He placed the population on the right bank of the Danube and created a new province called Dacia, carved out of territory that had belonged to the two Moesian provinces. Before 285, this new province was split into two smaller ones, called Dacia Ripensis and Dacia Mediterranea.

The territory of the old Dacia to the north of the Danube was now open to the Goths and Carpi. Though there is no firm evidence, Aurelian may have arranged a treaty with the tribes whereby they acted as defenders of the evacuated territory and kept it free from other incursions. How many of the civilian population came out of Dacia in the wake of the army is unknown. Many people would remain in their homes. Epigraphic evidence speaks for a continued Romanized population after the evacuation of the later third century.

AURELIAN'S REFORMS

Superlatives began to enter the titulature of the Emperor from 274 onwards, after he had reunified the Empire and he had become in truth the restorer of the world, albeit a world that was somewhat different from the Empire of Hadrian and Severus. The frontiers that were once so clearly marked were now a little ragged, and territory had been lost north of the Danube. Nonetheless the situation was such a vast improvement on the previous two decades. On inscriptions Aurelian, conqueror of the Carpi, the Germans, the Arabians, the Persians and the Palmyrenes, is described as eternal, invincible, the personification of Hercules, divine, and finally a god and lord in his own right, *Imperator deus et dominus*. This godly status may have been thrust upon him, in return for his services to the state, but he took to it well. He began to wear a diadem, and demanded obeisance from his subjects. Obviously he had learned a lot in the east, where such behaviour was normal. Aurelian took his role as saviour of the state very seriously. It was important that Romans should believe in him, and that enemies should fear him. The time of rough soldier-emperors sharing their soldiers' meals, marching with the lads, caring little for politics and statesmanship, was over. The emperor needed to be all things, military commander, politician, statesman, psychologist, performer, and god. For this it was necessary to be remote, lofty, ideal rather than real, creating echoing distance between ruler and ruled. Aurelian knew how to do it, and would have been more than a match for Constantine.

Although the Empire was reunified territorially, there were many things to put right within the state. Inflation had reached ridiculous proportions; the monetary system had foundered, and it required a strong hand to set it on course again. Aurelian had attempted a partial reform in 271, but he had not been totally effective. In 274 he began again. Unification brought in its wake increased revenues, and new taxes were raised. Aurelian taxed the wealthy men of the Empire, justifiably in his view since everyone ought to contribute to the well-being and defence of the Empire. The flow of precious metals from all parts of the Empire was resumed, sufficient to enable Aurelian to reform the coinage. He adhered to the traditional bronze, silver and gold currency, but the right to issue bronze coinage was wrested from the control of the Senate. Aurelian tried to withdraw all the old silver *antoniniani* of negligible weight. He eradicated the bad coinage in Rome and Italy, but not in the provinces.

The food supply of the Roman plebs also claimed Aurelian's attention. He reorganized the corn dole for the city, distributing loaves of bread instead of grain, and adding salt and pork to the rations, as well as oil, and wine at a reduced cost. These arrangements continued under successive emperors. The substitution of a bread ration for the corn dole was an innovative step. It involved a series of operations all under the supervision of the *Praefectus Annonae*, covering collection of the goods and transport by sea and by land, storage, processing and distribution. Grain was levied from Egypt as part of the taxation system, and delivered to the bakers free of charge; the weight of the loaves was increased but the price was held for the benefit of those who could afford to buy. The distribution of wine revitalized the struggling viticulture of Italy, and the transport of all the various goods was a boon for the shippers, the *navicularii*. The rudiments of the guilds and corporations of the later Empire derive from this reform of Aurelian's, but he probably did not intend to impose the inflexible rigidity that developed as part and parcel of the state control of the *annona*.

Religion was another sphere where Aurelian's reforming zeal introduced changes. The old gods had not been neglected by previous emperors, but there was a certain lack of coherence and cohesion in their policies. Aurelian introduced Sol, the sun god, as the supreme being. In the east he had seen the unifying force of the sun as a divinity, which all people, civilians and soldiers, Romans, Italians and provincials, could believe in without betraying their other gods. There were precedents in the reign of Claudius Gothicus, whose coinage had featured the sun god, and Aurelian's coinage accentuated the attributes of the sun god, with legends such as *Sol Invictus, Sol Conservator, Sol Dominus Imperii Romani*, celebrating the unconquered sun, the saviour of the state, and the lord and master of the Roman Empire. Since no cult could function without the focal point of a temple, Aurelian built one in the seventh region of Rome. It was consecrated in 274, an extremely ornate building that housed the trophies from Palmyra. The priests of the cult were drawn from the aristocracy, so that the bruised prestige of the upper classes was revived by the knowledge that the control of the state religion, if not of the state itself, was in their hands. Aurelian's religious policy was to restore old values in a new guise, to unify the Empire, to exclude no one except the most intransigent. He did not persecute the Christians or the Jews. He regarded himself as earthly but divine intermediary between the supreme god and the people of the Empire, but was granted little time in which to develop the theme of one state, one god. Constantine finalized that, on his deathbed.

The End of Aurelian's Reign

The defeat of Valerian by the Persians was still unavenged, and Aurelian was now in a position to prepare a campaign. It was an opportune moment to attack the Persians. Towards the end of 272 King Shapur I died. His successor Hormizd did not long survive him, dying at the end of 273 or at the beginning of 274. The new king, Vahram, had much to do to keep his Empire together and had no time for an aggressive campaign against Rome.

In the summer of 275 Aurelian set out for the east. He assembled his army in Illyricum, and declared war on Persia, but he never reached his objective. On the march through Thrace the Emperor Aurelian was assassinated. The sources are garbled, naming more than one man as the murderer. One story is that a list was discovered, or fabricated, of officers who had fallen out of favour, so they struck before they were eliminated. The fact that there was no candidate, ready and waiting in the wings to take over the moment that Aurelian was dead, supports the suggestion that the conspirators acted suddenly, in blind panic. There may also have been a few officers who were glad to rid themselves of both the Emperor and the need to go and fight the Persians.

Aurelian's promising career was terminated before he had been granted the opportunity to follow up his successes in pulling the Empire back together, or perhaps before he threw away all his credit by losing the war against Persia. He deserved his title *Restitutor Orbis*, Restorer of the World. He had built on the unacknowledged work of Gallienus and Claudius Gothicus, and had paved the way for Diocletian, who absorbed most of the credit that was really due to his predecessor.

TACITUS AD 275–276 & FLORIAN AD 276

The soldiers were very displeased at the murder of their emperor and made it clear that they did not intend to proclaim any of the generals in Aurelian's place. There was no heir, nor was there an obvious successor marked out by Imperial favour during Aurelian's reign. The important generals were dispersed in various parts of the Empire, so for a short time the Roman world was poised for complicated civil wars as the leaders of various armies fought each other until one of them emerged victorious. But this time there was no war. The sources all agree that the soldiers sent to Rome to ask the Senate to choose an emperor. The seventy-five-year-old senator Marcus Claudius Tacitus was persuaded to shoulder the task. He was in Campania when his name was put forward as emperor. His previous career is unknown. He was probably a middle class equestrian who had been adlected to the Senate.

The Emperor Tacitus was not a military man, but he spent most of his short reign fighting the Goths, earning the title *Gothicus Maximus*, for a victory or victories that have escaped documentation. He died after a mere six month reign, at either Tyana or Tarsus, perhaps because he had appointed one of his relatives called Maximinus to command in Syria, and Maximinus proved too severe, so the soldiers rebelled. The army declared for Tacitus's half brother Florian, who was Praetorian Prefect in the campaign against the Goths. At the same time Probus, commanding in Syria, Phoenicia and Egypt, was also declared emperor by his troops.

The east was almost wholly behind Probus. The conflict between the two Imperial candidates ended at Tarsus, where Florian decided to face Probus, but his soldiers were not accustomed to the eastern climate and their health declined. In direct proportion to their suffering, their commitment to the cause declined. Probus had only to wait, without giving battle. Florian's troops killed him, or perhaps suggested very strongly that he should commit suicide.

PROBUS AD 276–282

The reign of Probus was longer than that of Aurelian, and almost as important for the reconstitution of the Empire, but the source material is sparse. Probus's coins display his titles, making the usual claims that the emperor is invincible and unconquered, but the coinage does not help to establish dates for recorded events. The result is that the salient factors of Probus's reign can be described in broad outline based on the dubious foundation of a few overlapping statements in the works of the ancient authors, but the causes of events, and their consequences, can be reconstructed only with the help of speculation.

Probus benefited greatly from the achievements of Aurelian, but he inherited some unfinished business. The Rhine and Danube were still under threat despite Aurelian's victories, and the Persian campaign, aborted on the Emperor's death, was not regarded as redundant. Much of Probus's energies went into flushing the tribesmen out of Gaul and the Rhine frontier zones. It was said that he rebuilt sixty cities which had been damaged in Gaul, and re-established some of the Roman forts. There were wars on more than one front. Probus was victorious with the help of his generals against the Franks on the Rhine; he fought the Vandals and Burgundians, and carried the war into territory beyond the frontiers and was said to have established forts *in solo barbarico*, on barbarian territory. It was said that no less than nine barbarian kings submitted to him.

Beyond these brief notices very little detail is known. The identity of the nine kings, the tribes they represented, and the location of the forts that he established, cannot be listed. It can only be said that the Romans had returned, however briefly, to the ascendancy. Little of this energetic activity can be securely dated; it is probable that the campaigns in Gaul and Germany occupied Probus from his accession until the end of 278, and that in the new season beginning in the winter of 278–9 he turned to the Danube.

Probus had other ways of dealing with the tribes, apart from fighting them. He settled some of them in Roman territory, including 100,000 Bastarnae in Thrace. While these settlements potentially secured peace for at least one generation, providing a good source of recruits for the army and a partly Romanized zone between the Empire and the tribes outside it, the schemes did not always produce the desired results. The Franks were given lands, probably in the Danube area, but they were restless, and were soon on the move, sweeping through Greece, and then sailing to Sicily and Africa, pillaging their way round the coast, through the Straits of Gibraltar and back to the Rhine and their original homelands. This expedition typifies the sort of problems that Probus had to deal with, small-scale actions in localized zones, all of them nonetheless very disruptive, dispiriting and demoralizing. People were forced from their homes and resorted to brigandage. It was by no means a new problem; from the Republic and throughout the Empire infamous rebels and gangsters entered history, sometimes earning a grudging respect. There was considerable trouble in Egypt caused by the Blemmyes, tribesmen who had always been ready to harass the province from time to time. The rebellion was squashed by Probus's generals.

Several usurpers appeared in the east and in Gaul, but they were extinguished very quickly. A general called Saturninus was declared emperor, either in Egypt or more probably in Syria; the sources are confused as to exactly where his command lay and where he chose to stage his rebellion. It seems that the eastern troops killed him before Probus reached the scene. At Cologne there were two potential emperors, Bonosus and Proculus, who were both eliminated seemingly without much trouble. What does emerge from these scantily described events is that over most of the Empire Probus's government was working well enough. Governors of provinces and military officers did their loyal duty to the Emperor, communications were secure, the focal point was still Rome, and the army was ultimately successful when engaged in pitched battles, in suppressing other Roman generals, or in guerrilla warfare against plundering tribes.

Probably in 281, Probus celebrated a triumph. For the time being he had achieved peace over the Empire, dealt with usurpers and brigands, and could turn his attention to more peaceful pursuits. He encouraged vine growing in Gaul, Pannonia and Moesia. He employed his soldiers to plant the vines in some areas, and also set them to work on drainage projects in the Danube provinces. The fact that he had soldiers to spare for such tasks, testifies to the success of the long campaigns from the 270s to the early 280s. Probus is said to have remarked that very soon the Empire would have no need of its armies, a proud boast that satisfied the war weary inhabitants of Rome and the provinces, but not news that the army wished to hear. If Probus had promised to reward the soldiers for long service, pension them all off with lands, money, slaves, and everything they could wish for, perhaps he would have survived longer. Scepticism on the part of the Roman army was not without justification; in all periods before and since, and in all places, soldiers have often been treated in the same fashion, lauded when there is something to be saved from, reviled when they fail, and discarded without a thought when the danger is past.

Perhaps the army need not have been concerned for its future, since Probus had decided upon a Persian campaign. While he was otherwise engaged on the northern frontiers he had come to a peaceful if temporary arrangement with the Persians, compatible with both sides because King Vahram, beset by internal problems, was not in any position to fight the Romans. After the successful campaigns against the northern tribes, Probus was in a position to attack, but he was killed by his soldiers, at Sirmium.

CARUS AD 282–283, CARINUS AD 283–285 & NUMERIANUS AD 283–285

Dissatisfaction in the army probably had a long incubation period before it came to a head with the murder of Probus. The Praetorian Prefect Marcus Aurelius Carus, commanding troops in Raetia and Noricum, rebelled before Probus was killed. He was declared emperor by the soldiers, and it was said that Carus took power without reference to the Senate. His elder son Carinus, who came to northern Italy early in 283 for his marriage, may have contacted the Senate on his father's behalf. However, it is true that from the reign of Carus onwards, the role of the Senate in bestowing formal powers on the emperors was curtailed, and there was never any reversal of the trend thereafter.

Carus was an experienced military man. By the late third century it had become a prior necessity for the emperor to have a military background, and Carus was determined to take up the projected Persian campaign as soon as he could. He possessed what should have been a distinct advantage in that he had two sons and ought to have been able to secure the succession and found a dynasty that might have ensured peace and prosperity, building on and bringing to completion the work of Aurelian and Probus. Carus elevated Carinus and Numerianus to Augusti, Carinus early in 283 to take charge of the western provinces when the Persian campaign began, and Numerianus towards the end of the Persian campaign, perhaps in conjunction with the first victories. When Carus died the existence of two Augusti, one in the east and one in the west ought to have ensured a smooth transition of power, but it did not, nor did it cause a premature and irretrievable split into two separate Empires. Carinus in the west governed clearly demarcated territories with distinct boundaries, while Carus and Numerianus conducted the Persian campaign, but the arrangement was not a prefiguration of the division of the later Empire; it was more like a reiteration of the situation when Gallienus was left in charge of the west and Valerian embarked on his disastrous eastern war.

Carus fortunately met with considerably more success against the Persians, whose regime was not as strong as it had been under Shapur I. King Vahram II was still trying to establish his authority over his Empire, so he did not put up much of a fight, allowing the Romans to march into Seleucia and Ctesiphon almost unopposed. The title *Parthicus Maximus* was awarded to Carus.

At this juncture, Carus, who was in his sixties, died unexpectedly. He was probably killed by his Praetorian Prefect Lucius Aper. This ambitious individual was the father-in-law of Carus's son Numerianus, who also died during the withdrawal from Persia. Aper said that the young Emperor was suffering from an eye complaint and consequently had to travel in a closed litter as protection against light and dust. When the corpse began to emit an unsavoury aroma, Aper's subterfuge was discovered. This tale borders on the ridiculous, and all sorts of explanations are possible. Perhaps if Carus had indeed died accidentally or from disease without any assistance from Aper, then it would have been doubly difficult for the Praetorian Prefect to try to make the soldiers believe that the Emperor's son had suddenly died of disease as well. Perhaps Aper panicked and was unable to decide what to do, but he must have known that he could not travel very far in a hot climate with a dead emperor in a closed litter. A soldier called Diocles, the commander of Numerianus's guard, began to suspect that something was wrong.

14

Another World: The Empire Transformed AD 284–324

DIOCLETIAN AD 284–305

When it was discovered that the Emperor Numerianus was dead, the army declared for Diocles, proclaiming him Augustus on 20 November 284. Soon after becoming emperor, Diocles changed his name to Gaius Aurelius Valerius Diocletianus. For the remaining part of the year he made himself consul with a senator called Caesonius Bassus as his colleague. The Praetorian Prefect Aper was executed by Diocletian himself, fulfilling a prophecy made by a Gallic wise woman, that he would kill a boar (*aper*) and then become emperor.

Carus's elder son Carinus was still the legitimate emperor in the west, but he was opposed by a usurper called Julianus, who had been appointed *corrector Venetiae* in northern Italy. Diocletian simply had to wait until one or the other emerged victorious, and then fight the survivor, in this case Carinus. Their armies met in the valley of the Margus, near modern Belgrade. The Praetorian Prefect Aristobulus killed Carinus and the troops went over to Diocletian. It was probably by prior arrangement, since Diocletian confirmed Aristobulus in office as Praetorian Prefect, and made him consul for the rest of 285.

Diocletian was prevented from going immediately to Rome to have power conferred on him by the Senate, because he was involved in a struggle against the tribesmen of the Quadi and Marcomanni. He devoted his attention to the restoration of the frontiers and the re-establishment of law and order in the provinces, for which tasks he needed the co-operation of administrative and military specialists. He had served in the army, but he was by no means an experienced general, so he needed help. He had no sons, so it was advisable to designate his colleagues and successors. Joint rule had an established history, but it had usually been kept in the family. Marcus Aurelius had shared the burden with Lucius Verus and then with his son Commodus; the Severans had followed the same example, and the Emperor Carus had tried to establish a dynasty by giving his sons the title Augustus.

After the battle of the Margus, Diocletian appointed his fellow soldier Marcus Aurelius Maximianus as his Caesar. Maximian added Diocletian's

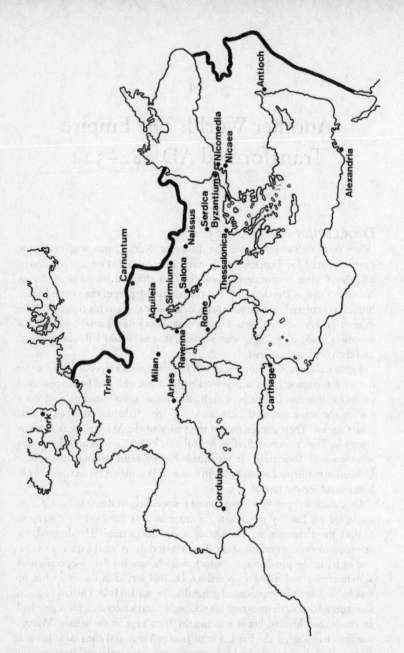

Map 3. Map showing the principal cities where the Imperial court set up headquarters at various times. During the third century the Roman emperors began to base themselves in large cities of the Empire rather than in Rome, so as to be close to the threatened areas. The presence of the emperors and the Imperial entourage brought prosperity to these cities, and the emperors were responsible for repairs, improvements, and new buildings.

family name Valerius to his nomenclature. The earthly association of the two men was equated with a partnership of the gods, Diocletian taking the name Jovius, the chief Roman god Jupiter, and Maximian that of Herculius, Jupiter's assistant. As a matter of urgency, the partners split up to attend to tasks at opposite ends of the Empire. From 285 until 288, Diocletian was occupied on the Danube, and then in the east, while Maximian took charge of the west.

Parts of Gaul had been overrun by a group of bandits called the Bagaudae, composed of displaced peasants, deserters from the army, and a collection of desperate people whose fortunes had been ruined by the invasions of the tribesmen from across the Rhine. The Gallic bandits of the third century were produced by a society in which an honest living was impossible to achieve, and everyone had to fend for himself. It is unlikely that the Bagaudae aspired to ruling the Empire, or even a part of Gaul. Maximian's successes against them are not fully documented, largely because the campaigns were better classified as police work rather than conquest.

By 286 Maximian was able to begin to concentrate on eliminating the Frankish and Saxon pirates who threatened the coasts of Britain and Gaul, and the Rhine mouth. The commander of the fleet in Gaul, Marcus Aurelius Carausius, achieved some success against them on both sides of the English Channel. It is not known whether he had been appointed by Carus and Carinus, or whether the appointment was made by Maximian soon after he took up his own command. Despite his victories, Carausius began to acquire a shady reputation. Rumours began to circulate that he knew when the Frankish raids would take place, and he waited until they had collected their booty, then captured them on their way home. It was said that the stolen goods went into his own coffers, and he was using the money to pay the Frankish soldiers that he had recruited. Maximian could not let this situation go unchallenged but the wily Carausius decamped to Britain, protected by his fleet and coastal defences, and in unchallenged possession of Britain. Maximian could do little to dislodge him.

Most of the evidence for Carausius's British Empire, or *Imperium Britanniarum*, derives from his coinage, which was of good quality. A sound coinage was a pre-requisite if the army and the influential people in Britain were to have any faith in him. He issued coins in 290, proclaiming that he ruled with 'his brothers' (*Carausius et Fratres Sui*), and depicting the heads of all three Emperors. The brotherly sentiment was not shared by Diocletian and Maximian, who never formally recognized Carausius or his claim to Britain and the coast of Gaul.

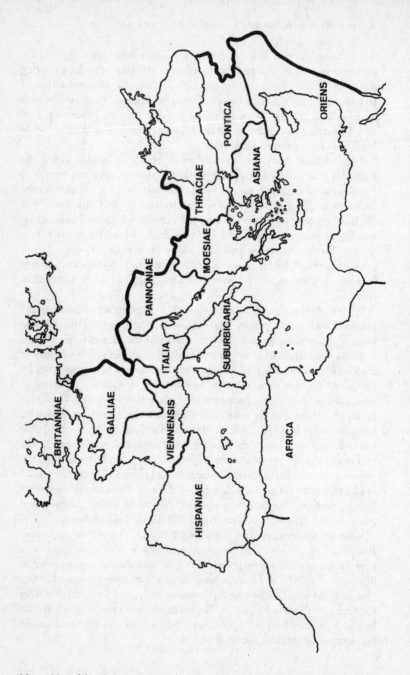

Map 4. Map of the administrative units called Dioceses, containing several provinces, created by Diocletian.

THE FORTS OF THE SAXON SHORE

Anyone who wished to make war on Carausius had to gather a fleet, cross the English Channel, and then do battle with his experienced sailors, and the soldiers of the coastal forts. The Saxon Shore forts are known to modern archaeologists by their collective name, which suggests that they were part of a homogeneous defensive system along the south and east coast of Britain, of long established antiquity. None of this is true. The Saxon Shore was probably not labelled as such when Carausius created his British Empire. The forts were not built all at once as part of a unified system for coastal defence. The fort plans differ from each other, and they were built at different times, originally for different purposes, between 250 and 300. The title Saxon Shore is attested in a late Roman document called the *Notitia Dignitatum*, which lists the garrisons and titles of the commanding officers all over the eastern and western Empires. By the time the British sections of this document were compiled there was a corporate system utilizing all nine of the forts on the British coast. The command extended to the coasts of Gaul as well, just as Carausius in his day controlled Boulogne.

It has been suggested, not without dispute, that it may have been Carausius who welded the so-called Saxon Shore forts of Britain into a functional whole. He had to defend Britain and himself against the pirates and the Imperial Roman fleet, so perhaps more than any of his predecessors who governed Britain, he required a strong defensive line of forts to guard and keep watch over the potential points of access to the island.

Before Maximian could attempt to recover control of Britain, he had to drive the Franks and the Alamanni out of Gaul and the Rhineland. Carausius was not necessarily considered a threat to the safety of Gaul. He had not shown any desire to make a bid for the whole Empire, but since Diocletian was not prepared to condone the independent rule of Britain, war was inevitable.

The potential threat posed by Carausius has been viewed as one of the most important factors in the elevation of Maximian to the rank of Augustus. One consideration may have been that Diocletian needed to find a way of binding Maximian more closely to himself, with the promise of adequate rewards, to pre-empt the possibility that he might join forces with Carausius. The loyalty of Maximian had to be secured, and he would have to be granted considerable power to enable him to operate independently and with credibility while Diocletian attended to his own problems in the eastern half of the Empire. Though it has been suggested that Maximian became Augustus at the very beginning of Diocletian's reign, it may have been in 286 that Maximian became Diocletian's full partner in Imperial rule.

In January 287 Maximian was at Trier, having fought the Franks and Heruli on the coast of Gaul and around the Rhine mouth in the previous year. During a series of campaigns that lasted until 288, he cleared the tribesmen from Gaul and the Rhine frontier. He received the submission of King Gennobaudes and all his people on the lower Rhine, and he settled Friesians, Franks and Chamavi between the River Waal and the Rhine, with obligations to protect their new lands from attack by other tribes, and to provide recruits for the Roman army.

While Maximian fought in Gaul and on the Rhine, Diocletian had defeated the Sarmatians on the Danube in 285 and then marched to the eastern frontier, where he had successfully completed a diplomatic mission and made peace. He was thus relieved of the necessity of gathering a campaign army for a war against Persia, and perhaps was able to spare manpower for a war in the west. Bringing troops with him he joined Maximian, probably at Mainz, and then embarked on a joint campaign against the Alamanni. Maximian operated from Mainz and Diocletian from Raetia, probably burning and destroying crops and food supplies as they went. By these brutal but effective methods Diocletian and Maximian regained control of the *Agri Decumates*, which had been overrun by tribesmen after the fall of the frontiers during the reign of Gallienus.

THE DANUBE & THE EAST

Immediately after his accession, and again four years later, Diocletian was embroiled in wars against the Sarmatians and other tribes in the Danube area. The tribesmen asked for lands inside the Empire, but Diocletian refused to allow them to settle. The problem was to recur in the later Empire as more and more tribesmen found the Roman world a better and richer place to live than their own lands.

Journeying to the east via Thrace and Syria, in 287 Diocletian came to an agreement with the Persians. The successful expedition of the Emperor Carus had paved the way for a peaceful settlement. The Persians were willing to negotiate, since their internal discord had not been solved. Diocletian strengthened Rome's position in the east, taking back the province of Mesopotamia and reorganizing the Syrian frontier, and installing the pro-Roman Tiridates on the throne of Armenia. This non-violent settlement of the east conserved manpower and resources, which Diocletian needed in the west in a combined offensive with Maximian against the Alamanni.

The campaign began in 288. Diocletian was probably based in Raetia, striking into the Alamannic territories while Maximian attacked from Mainz. By the following year, the Sarmatians had regrouped, and another war loomed. No details survive, but victory for the Romans was probably rapid. Inscriptions show that Diocletian took the title *Sarmaticus Maximus* four times during his reign, the second time after the campaign of 289.

Except for the embarrassment of Carausius, who still held Britain and controlled Boulogne, by 291 the Empire was more stable than it had been for many years. Diocletian and Maximian celebrated their successes, but in Milan, not in Rome, because in the north of Italy they were nearer to the Danube provinces and the routes through the Alps. Their choice of venue highlighted the fact that Rome was not conveniently situated to enable the emperors to deal with threats to the frontiers. Rome remained supreme as an ideological concept, but the government revolved around the emperor, and now more than ever before the presence of the emperor was necessary in the war zones. From Diocletian's reign, Imperial headquarters were set up in several cities all over the Empire, and Rome began to decline in importance.

THE TETRARCHY AD 294–324

The term tetrarchy was used in the Greek world to describe a territory divided into four areas, and is employed in modern times to describe the rule of four men that Diocletian imposed on the Roman world in 293. It was a response to circumstances, though no one knows when or how Diocletian conceived of the idea. For some years it had been clear that a single individual could not simultaneously direct the wars, fight all the battles, suppress usurpers, and also govern the Empire. Diocletian's answer was to create two senior emperors each with the title Augustus, and two junior emperors called Caesars, to attend to the different parts of the Empire, and also to provide undoubted successors. The two Caesars were Maximian's son-in-law Constantius, who adopted the name Flavius Valerius Constantius, and Galerius, who became Gaius Galerius Valerius Maximianus. The new names illustrated family connections with the two Augusti, further reinforced by marriage alliances. As a young soldier, Constantius married Helena, a tavern keeper's daughter from Naissus. They had a son, Constantine. When his career began to revolve around the Emperor, Constantius divorced Helena and married Theodora, the step-daughter of Maximian, probably in 289. It is not known when Galerius divorced his wife and married Valeria, Diocletian's daughter.

The four men who ruled the Empire were all Illyrians, and all military men. Diocletian chose men he knew from his own circle. The two Augusti both held the title Imperator, and the office of Pontifex Maximus. The Caesars were not given the title Imperator and did not share the high priesthood, but all four men shared the same victory titles, whether or not they had participated in the relevant wars. Constantius was equated with Maximian and adopted the name Herculius while Galerius was associated with Diocletian and became Jovius. Constantius took precedence over Galerius in official documents.

The creation of four emperors did not necessarily involve a fourfold division of the Roman world. It might seem from their attachment to certain groups of provinces as if each Caesar and each Augustus controlled an allocated portion of the Empire, marked out by official boundaries and a capital city as their headquarters, but at turn of the third and fourth centuries the four emperors were assigned to regions as and when they were needed, and not to specific areas as part of a fixed geographical plan.

The sources for the decade or so after the establishment of the Tetrarchy are not as abundant as they are for the earlier Empire, but what emerges from the available information is that the Empire was fully stretched at certain times, with wars of reconquest or aggressive punitive campaigns going on in the east and west while the northern frontiers were harassed. For the first few years Diocletian and Maximian recede into the background while the younger men went on campaign, but they reappear on the war front in 296–7.

Immediately after his elevation to the rank of Caesar in 293, Constantius launched an attack on Carausius, winning back control of Boulogne and the coast of Gaul. Despite the fact that the loss of his Gallic port reduced Carausius's credibility and led to his assassination by one of his officers called Allectus, Constantius did not follow up this success with an invasion of Britain until 296, being diverted to Germany to fight against the Alamanni.

Galerius in the meantime was in Egypt, where a revolt had broken out, probably as early as 293. There was also some action on the Danube against the Sarmatians in 294. Literary references indicate that Roman forts were built in barbarian territory opposite Aquincum and Bononia (*in Sarmatia contra Acinco et Bononia*). These forts have been interpreted as bridgeheads guarding the approaches to the main forts on the Roman side of the Danube, but others see them as forts built well inside Sarmatian territory, suggesting after a successful campaign, Diocletian occupied the territory of the Sarmatians, building forts to keep them under surveillance. Unfortunately there is as yet no archaeological proof of the whereabouts of these forts.

During the course of 294 there was disturbing news from Persia, where the warlike King Narses had seized power. He sent an embassy to the Romans, and for a while there was no action, but in 295 the Persians invaded Armenia and ousted Tiridates. This was a classic move, and it was not a situation that the Romans could tolerate for long, so after his operations in Upper Egypt, Galerius embarked on a war against Persia in 296, as Constantius was preparing to invade Britain. Diocletian was occupied in a struggle with the Carpi on the Danube and Maximian came to the Rhine to relieve Constantius of the task of guarding the area.

In the campaign against Narses, Galerius suffered a humiliating defeat. Constantius on the other hand, aided by his Praetorian Prefect Asclepiodotus, defeated Allectus and massacred the Frankish mercenaries who had fought for Carausius. According to Constantius they were about to sack London, and he saved the city from its fate. He issued the famous medallion from the Trier mint, proclaiming that he had 'restored the eternal light' to Britain (*Redditor lucis aeternae*). Given that Carausius had governed well for several years, looked after the interests of the merchant and land-owning classes, and issued a high quality coinage, there may have been some inhabitants of Britain who questioned whether they had really been in such terrible darkness.

During the next two or three years the theatre of action shifted from the west to the African and eastern provinces. Maximian campaigned in Mauretania, and Diocletian suppressed another revolt in Egypt, involving a prolonged siege of Alexandria that prevented Diocletian from joining Galerius in the renewed Persian campaign. It is testimony to the ability and goodwill of the army and the efficacy of Diocletian's system that the Empire was able to sustain warfare on several fronts at the same time. The long range movements of the army are illustrated by the Danubian troops that Galerius took to the east, and the German units that accompanied Maximian to Mauretania. The supply of food, armour and clothing, and above all of recruits to keep the army up to strength taxed the resources of the Empire, but the loyalty of the troops and their adherence to the ideology of Rome and the Emperor did not seriously break down.

The next four years saw an upsurge in Rome's fortunes and the achievement of peace on most frontiers. The siege of Alexandria was over by the summer of 298, and by the following year the Persians had been defeated. Negotiations followed. Diocletian travelled to Nisibis where he and Galerius formulated a treaty with the Persians, highly favourable to Rome. Tiridates was re-installed on the Armenian throne and Mesopotamia was recovered once again. Apart from the political significance of the treaty, it also carried great economic importance; all trade was to pass through Nisibis, which was under Roman control. The achievements of Galerius against the Persians were recorded on a triumphal arch at Thessalonika, Galerius's headquarters. Significantly the arch was not erected in Rome.

The pressure of the tribesmen on the frontiers was increasing. Galerius was soon occupied on the Danube fighting the Marcomanni and the Carpi, and Constantius was engaged on the Rhine against the Franks. Peace seems to have been established by 303. In that year Diocletian and Maximian went to Rome to celebrate their twenty-year rule, their

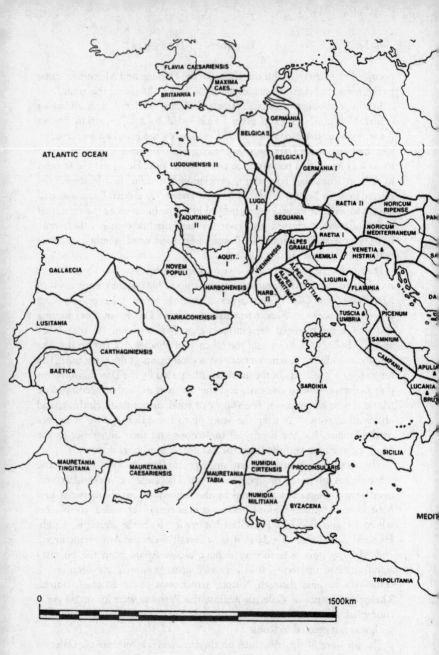

ATLANTIC OCEAN

FLAVIA CAESARIENSIS

MAXIMA CAES.

BRITANNIA I

GERMANIA II

BELGICA II

BELGICA I

LUGDUNENSIS II

GERMANIA I

RAETIA II

NORICUM RIPENSE

LUGD.

SEQUANIA

AQUITANICA II

NORICUM MEDITERRANEUM

RAETIA I

AQUIT. I

ALPES GRAIAL

VIENNENSIS

AEMILIA

VENETIA & HISTRIA

NOVEM POPULI

ALPES COTTIAE

LIGURIA

GALLAECIA

NARBONENSIS I

ALPES MARITIMAE

NARB II

FLAMINIA

TUSCIA & UMBRIA

PICENUM

TARRACONENSIS

LUSITANIA

CORSICA

SAMNIUM

CAMPANIA

CARTHAGINIENSIS

SARDINIA

APULIA &

LUCANIA & BRUT

BAETICA

SICILIA

MAURETANIA TINGITANA

MAURETANIA CAESARIENSIS

MAURETANIA TABIA

NUMIDIA CIRTENSIS

PROCONSULARIS

NUMIDIA MILITIANA

BYZACENA

TRIPOLITANIA

MEDIT

0   1500km

Map 5. Map of the provinces of the later Empire. As well as creating the Dioceses, as an extra tier of administrative units for the government of the Empire, Diocletian split up the provinces into smaller units, giving them new names or simply numbers.

vicennalia. The celebrations were recorded on the coinage; on one issue the Romans were exhorted to rejoice (*Gaudete Romani*), an instruction which practically begs for the addition 'or else'. There are some hints that while in Rome Diocletian persuaded Maximian that it would be politic for the two of them to renounce their powers together and let their junior partners progress from Caesars to Augusti, taking new Caesars of their own. It is said that Maximian swore to uphold Diocletian's plan, in a ceremony in the Temple of Jupiter.

Diocletian was already ill, and left Rome as soon as he could to return to his headquarters at Nicomedia. At the beginning of 304 he collapsed. At some unknown date, probably after this crisis, Maximian went to meet Galerius. Constantius remained on the Rhine watching the Franks. If Maximian hoped to forge some sort of alliance with Galerius to maintain his position as Augustus, he renounced it in 305 when Diocletian abdicated, and stepped down. Constantius and Galerius became Augusti. Diocletian retired to the famous palace at Split, while Maximian went to Lucania in southern Italy. They had both retired, but significantly they established themselves in the western and eastern halves of the Empire, but close enough together to be able to communicate.

The new Caesars were Severus in the west under Constantius, and Maximinus in the east under Galerius. Both men were colleagues of Galerius, which gave him the edge if it came to squabbling with Constantius. Severus was an experienced military officer from Pannonia; Maximinus had served in the Imperial guard. If Constantius and Galerius could achieve the same harmonious relationship as Diocletian and Maximian, with their Caesars able to take on the wars or administrative tasks that they could not attend to themselves, there was no reason why the system could not go on for several decades. But there were two other members of the Imperial households who had been overlooked. Maximian's son Maxentius, and Constantine, the son of Constantius, would soon tilt the balance.

DIOCLETIAN'S REFORMS

One of the advantages of Diocletian's long reign was that military, administrative and financial reforms could be set in motion, tested over time, and brought to conclusions. There is a lack of contemporary evidence for any of these reforms; most of the literary, epigraphic and papyrological information derives from the immediate post-Diocletianic period or more often from the reign of Constantine, with the result that it is difficult to disentangle the authorship of the original reforms. The only statement that can be made with certainty is that after the reign of Diocletian the Roman world was irrevocably changed.

Diocletian adopted some of the precedents that his predecessors had set. Aurelian had introduced the concept of the remote and sanctified emperor. Diocletian replaced Aurelian's sun god with Jupiter and Hercules. The cloth of gold, the diadems, the *adoratio* or obeisance, all remained and were refined into a deliberately elaborated system. The emperor-god found ready acceptance in the east, and in the west the sacrosanctity of the emperor had been established by Severus.

THE ARMY & THE FRONTIERS

Source material for Diocletian's reconstruction of the frontiers is so slender and so general that all that can be said is that he rebuilt forts on the Rhine and Danube and on the frontier from Egypt to Persia, but it not possible to name them, because in many cases it is difficult to distinguish the work of Diocletian from that of his predecessors or his successors. Diocletian may have consolidated the work begun by Probus on the new frontier connecting the Rhine and the Danube. In the east, the frontier road called the *Strata Diocletiana* is the classic Diocletianic or Tetrarchic frontier system, consisting of a road marking the boundary, protected by closely spaced forts, backed up by fortifications in the hinterland. Forts themselves began to change their appearance in the later third century, diverting from the classic playing-card shape of the earlier Empire. Gateways were blocked up, sometimes by projecting towers allowing for better surveillance of the walls. U-shaped towers were built at intervals along the walls, and on the Danube distinctive fan-shaped corner towers were built, allowing for greater protection of the defences. It is possible that this work is part of the Diocletianic refurbishment of the frontiers. The Emperor probably also attended to the various road posts, watchtowers, and fortified harbours, repairing existing structures and building new ones. Such features had always been part of the Imperial defence system where interior policing and exterior protection were necessary.

There was no corporate policy for the fortification of the cities of the Empire, where initiative was left to the inhabitants. From the reign of Gallienus there had been an increasing number of cities which had acquired walls to protect them against threats from invading tribesmen, or lawless bands such as the Bagaudae in Gaul, and on occasion from rebellious Roman troops. The wall-building is indicative of the lack of faith in the ability of the central government to protect the provincial population.

The Roman army at the beginning of Diocletian's reign was essentially the same army that had defended the Empire from the first century onwards, with the exception that the cavalry had increased in importance. Campaign armies were drawn from the frontier units, as they had always been in the early Empire, but campaigns had become more frequent and more prolonged. There had been an army in the field somewhere in the Empire almost without interruption from the reign of Marcus Aurelius, increasing the possibility that the commanders might use their troops to raise rebellion.

Diocletian attended to the command structure of the frontier armies. He sent back to the frontiers the vexillations and mixed troops that comprised the campaign armies. He may have split existing auxiliary units into smaller groups, dividing them up between different forts, and newly created auxiliary units may have been smaller than the older ones. The newly raised legions may also have been reduced in size, perhaps only 1,000 strong. This makes it easier to understand how Diocletian could afford to add over thirty new legions to the existing thirty-four that he inherited. Some of the existing legions may have been divided into smaller groups. In the fourth century on the Danube, the soldiers from *legio III Italica*, raised by Marcus Aurelius, were distributed over five different forts, and also contributed a unit to the campaign army. This may mean that the legion was divided into six groups of 1,000 men, so in effect there was no reduction in size of the old legion. The legionary fortress at El Lejjun, in modern Jordan, was not large enough to hold a legion of 6,000 men, but the smaller forts nearby could have held detachments. The evidence from these and other sites is not conclusive, but it is a strong possibility that the old legions remained at their original strengths, while the new ones that Diocletian raised were only 1,000 strong.

Before Diocletian's reign there was no permanent campaign army ready to march to threatened zones. By the fourth century, the Roman army had been split into two groups, the frontier units, and the mobile armies, the *comitatenses* of the later Empire. The antecedents of this mobile army are obscure. After 260 Gallienus created a cavalry army and placed it under a single commander, but it is not known for how long this separate army survived, so it cannot be demonstrated whether there was a direct connection between Gallienus's cavalry and the later mobile campaign armies.

The role of Diocletian in the formation of the *comitatenses* is debated. The argument revolves around the *comitatus*, or groups of friends and picked soldiers that accompanied any emperor on campaign. There is no doubt that such a body went on campaign with Diocletian, and probably also with each of the other Tetrarchs, but it is less certain how the *comitatus* functioned. Whether it was an embryonic mobile cavalry army or simply a bodyguard at this stage is not established.

In broad general terms it can be said that Diocletian reconstituted the frontiers. He probably did not establish the mobile army, which was more likely Constantine's contribution to the defence of the Empire; nor did Diocletian create the static troops called *limitanei* which formed a separate frontier force, tied to the land. This term should be treated with caution, since the ancient authors from the fourth century onwards used this term to describe frontier troops of the earlier periods, which is misleading.

In the sphere of administration, Diocletian did set the trend for later years in that he finally separated military and civil posts. Henceforth, except for a few small provinces where the governor was also the military commander, all armed forces were under the control of the *dux*, (plural *duces*) literally meaning leader. The *duces* were equestrian officers, whose authority often extended over more than one province, creating a unified command over frontier zones, regardless of who the civilian governors were. The military commander and the governor had to co-operate with each other with regard to supplies, but the duties of the *dux* were purely military and the duties of the *praeses* were purely civilian, judicial and fiscal. It meant that the wide ranging work load for governors and military officers was lessened, demanding less broad-based diversity and more specialist knowledge. Later emperors did not see fit to make radical alterations to the division of military and civilian commands.

One other military reform can be attributed to Diocletian. Though they are first attested only under Constantine, it was probably Diocletian who established the *scholae* or Imperial guards. The Praetorian Guard still existed, but its power was much reduced, and did not long survive the accession of Constantine.

FINANCE & TAXATION

The Roman Empire derived its income from taxes, spoils of war, the produce of mines and so on, but the economy was predominantly agriculture based, so if production declined, the income from taxation also declined. As for expenditure, by far the largest expense was the upkeep of the army and the buildings associated with it. Defence did not come cheaply, a point which Severus recognized when he increased army pay. The inability of the state to pay the troops increased during the third century, with the result that arrears of pay became the accepted norm, and in some cases payment in kind was substituted for cash payments. Weapons, clothing and food were originally paid for out of the soldiers' wages, but in the third century, these essential items became part of a soldier's pay. When the cash payment system broke down, hungry troops in need of food and clothing requisitioned whatever they lacked, which translates in many cases as stealing. This sort of abuse set the provincials against the army that was supposed to protect them, and landowners and city councillors protested that the state would bankrupt them.

It was necessary to find some method of tax assessment that spread the burden fairly and ensured that all provinces contributed to the defence of the Empire. Italy had for long enjoyed exemption from the tax burden, but this came to an end with Diocletian's reforms. The city of Rome itself was exempt, including territory around it up to a radius of 100 miles. In a predominantly agricultural economy, taxation was based on production, which varied from region to region, depending on the quality of the soil and the type of crops produced on it. Diocletian introduced a system of assessment based on an agricultural unit of production called the *iugum*, which varied in size according to the type of land and crop, and the amount of labour required to produce enough for one man to make a living. The labour (*caput*, literally meaning head) was also assessed; it was not strictly a poll tax, relative to the numbers of people on a farm or estate; for instance a woman's labour was sometimes assessed as half a *caput*. The *iugatio* and *capitatio* were inextricably related, and both were needed to make the fair assessment of taxes due from an area. Livestock was also included in the assessments, as the *capitatio animalium*.

For the purpose of assessment a census had to be conducted every five years. When the annual requirements for the state were set, the Praetorian Prefects were responsible for apportioning the amounts to be collected from each province. The municipal councils were then charged with the collection of the taxes. Any shortfall had to be made up by the members of the councils. City and town councillors could be rapidly impoverished if production declined. It became a matter of urgency to find people to cultivate vacant lands. Various emperors had tried to solve the problems of deserted land, sometimes offering incentives to farmers in the form of tax exemptions to help them to get started.

Diocletian attempted to reform the currency and to tackle the problem of inflation by curbing prices. The coinage had suffered during the third century, and Aurelian's measures had not solved the problem entirely. He had tried to fix the value of the coins and therefore their purchasing power, but traditionally coins were worth only as much as their metal content. While coins were issued with less and less precious metal, good coins were hoarded and disappeared, and prices inevitably rose. Diocletian issued better quality coins. In an effort to put a stop to escalating price rises, Diocletian issued the famous edict *de pretiis*, on prices. In the preamble, Diocletian reminds inhabitants of the Empire that wars have been fought on their behalf, the barbarian invasions and internal unrest have been successfully tackled, and tranquillity has at last been achieved. The edict goes on to list in minute detail products and their recommended retail prices that must not be exceeded. But it is easy to make laws and quite another matter to enforce them. The price edict did not work, and was allowed to sink into oblivion.

CONTROL OF PRODUCTS & SERVICES

Supplies for the army and the administrative staff were not fully provided for via the taxation system. Money payments did not die out altogether but a large proportion of goods were requisitioned. Mines and quarries had been under partial state control since the early Empire, but now, if privately owned manufacturing businesses possessed the slightest relevance to the army, they were taken over by the state. Factories producing arms and armour, textiles and clothing, were managed by military personnel. Skilled craftsmen were conscripted to work at their trades and in the fourth century it became compulsory for craftsmen to join a guild or corporation and to train their sons in their specific skills. No one was allowed to move to another profession or to another area to find work. The consequent loss of personal freedom gradually extended to all walks of life.

The rural population was no less constrained. Agricultural workers were compelled to stay on the land, and the produce was taxed. Bad harvests and insecurity drove many small farmers off the land, forcing them to ally with influential, wealthy people to enable them to survive bad harvests, or fight off the tax gatherers. Landowners needed workers to ensure that their farms were staffed and fully stocked, so a strong relationship was forged between the landowners and the farmers, the *coloni*, who were eventually tied to their patrons, almost like medieval serfs. Sometimes landowners and the military authorities competed for manpower.

Central administration of the Empire was also highly regimented, as demonstrated by the contemporary term for it, *militia*. Service in the army was distinguished from the civil service as *militia armata*, armed service. The administrators were organized in ranks, just like the soldiers. Separate departments to deal with specific sections of the administration had existed since the early Empire, and had grown and expanded as the Empire grew. Diocletian divided the administration into departments called *scrinia* after the boxes used to carry the relevant documents for each section. Officials called *magistri* were placed in charge of each section, not necessarily new personnel, but the existing ones were perhaps issued with new names. The *magistri* were members of the Imperial council, the *consilium*, which may have also been called the *consistorium*. It is not known when the *consistorium* was instituted, but whatever it was called, Diocletian's council was closer in spirit to the late Roman consistory than it was to the Imperial *consilium*, which was a circle of advisers, with no official appointments and constantly changing personnel. Diocletian's *consilium/consistorium* was the government, embracing administrators and department heads, all directed by the Emperor himself. Diocletian was the last Emperor of the Principate and the first Emperor of the Dominate.

PROVINCIAL REORGANIZATION

Diocletian made two major alterations to provincial administration. As a preliminary measure he grouped together several existing provinces into new administrative units which he called dioceses, governed by equestrian officials called *vicarii*, which means 'substitutes'. During the early Empire a *vicarius* was sometimes appointed as a temporary substitute for a provincial governor. Diocletian adopted the title for permanent appointments, representing an extra tier in the administrative hierarchy. The *vicarii* were senior officials, supervisors of the provincial governors and responsible to the Praetorian Prefects, though the emperors could and did communicate with them directly

The next step was to reduce the size of individual provinces. Severus had begun the process. Pannonia and Britain had each been split into two provinces, and Aurelian had created the two Dacian provinces out of parts of Moesia. Diocletian made further divisions, so that the number of provinces almost doubled. Consequently the number of officials also increased, giving rise to criticism that there were more officials than taxpayers. As mentioned above military and civilian commands were now separated, with the equestrian *duces* responsible for all the troops in the province, even if the governor was a senator. In some cases the *dux* commanded troops of more than one province. Only in a few cases in the smaller provinces was the governor also in command of troops.

The date of the changes in provincial administration cannot be ascertained. The document known as the *Laterculus Veronensis*, a list of dioceses and the *vicarii* in charge of them, and of the provinces and their governors, is the nearest evidence available for the Diocletianic system, but some of the entries have been shown to be Constantinian in date, obliterating the original arrangements under Diocletian. The provincial reorganization was probably carried out over a prolonged period, but it is not known how it was done. If it is correct that the dioceses were created before the provinces were divided, the *vicarii* may have undertaken the duties of the governors as they were replaced, until new officials were appointed.

The benefits of the subdivision of provinces were that each governor could devote more time to supervising the cities, transport and communications, the food supply, and to hearing judicial cases. They could exercise a tighter control over tax paying provincials. Control was the order of the day, as was the prevention of rebellion; some authors state that the creation of smaller provinces was designed to make it more difficult to usurp the emperor, but in the fourth and fifth centuries usurpation as a regular Roman recreational activity did not cease.

THE PERSECUTION OF THE CHRISTIANS

Diocletian revived and strengthened the old Roman religion but did not go so far as to enforce universal observance. The first onslaught against religious sects came with the attacks on the Manichaeans, who were firmly entrenched in the eastern provinces, and were numerous in Egypt and north Africa. They followed the teachings of Mani, who was considered a heretic by the Mazdean priests of Persia, but the Manichaeans flourished because King Shapur had forbidden the persecution of religious groups. The Romans suspected that the Manichaeans were sympathetic to the Persian kings, and that they were the agitators behind the Egyptian revolts against Rome. In 302 Diocletian visited Egypt, and issued an edict against the Manichaeans. The text is known; how it was put into effect is not elucidated.

Imperial attention then turned to the Christians. For some years there had been isolated examples of Christian intransigence, particularly with regard to the army. In 295 a certain Maximilian appeared before the proconsul of Africa because he refused to enlist in the army. A purge of the army was attempted to remove any Christians who might refuse duty. A refusal to serve in the army was subversive. If it spread, recruitment for the armies all over the Empire would be compromised, and if the Christians were to be officially excused from military service, there was nothing to stop men with an aversion to the army from undergoing a miraculous conversion to Christianity, and then refusing to serve.

In 298 a Christian serving in the army, a centurion called Marcellus, refused to take part in the celebrations in honour of Maximian, which presumably involved sacrifice to the emperors as gods, or at least to Jupiter and Hercules. Devotion to the chief gods of Rome was dangerously compromised, and the matter of sacrifice became the litmus test of a Christian's attitude to Imperial rule. Most religious groups who were accustomed to the worship of several gods or aspects of gods under different names, would not find any difficulty in sacrificing to the emperor or to the gods of Rome. The Christians, unfortunately, could not tolerate gods other than their own, and their missionary spirit meant that they were not content to live quietly in the background without drawing attention to themselves and their beliefs.

At the beginning of the fourth century the emperors applied themselves to eradicating Christianity. The blame for the anti-Christian policy is laid at Galerius's door. He was in a strong position after his victories in the east and on the Danube, and was said to have been violently anti-Christian throughout his career. Those who wish to exonerate Diocletian fall back on the assumption that he merely yielded to pressure from Galerius. The first edict was issued on 23 February 303, at the festival of the Terminalia at Nicomedia. The church was destroyed and fires broke out twice in the Imperial palace. Galerius ostentatiously left the city rather than be murdered by the Christians. Others said that he had started the fires himself to put the blame on the Christians and provide the excuse for persecuting them.

In the summer of 303 another edict was issued, aimed at the clergy, who were to be imprisoned. The prisons were soon overflowing. Another edict was issued ordering compulsory sacrifice to the gods, so that the die-hards would be weeded out. The edict was not strenuously applied over the whole Empire. The west escaped lightly because Constantius and Maximian did not share Galerius's zeal for burning people alive. Maximian limited his efforts to closing churches and confiscating books, and Constantius did even less to eradicate Christians. The uneven treatment of the Christians ensured that the edict could never achieve its goal; it was enforced rigorously in some parts of the Empire, but in other areas the officials did nothing and simply reported that everyone had sacrificed as instructed. At the time of Diocletian's retirement, the Christian problem had not been solved.

THE RISE OF CONSTANTINE AD 306–324

From the moment when Constantine came to power, recorded history depends almost totally upon the version that this ambitious ruler endorsed, little tempered by alternative sources. He rewrote the past to suit the present, and carefully orchestrated the history of his reign. Some cardinal facts are obscure, for instance it is known that Diocletian retired in 305, persuading Maximian to do the same, but no one knows exactly when Diocletian died. He ceased to play a major part in the political arena after his abdication, his presence influenced Galerius sufficiently to invite him to the conference at Carnuntum in 308, where he tried to persuade him to take power again, or at least to arbitrate among the rival factions that had grown up in the few years that had elapsed since the two Augusti had retired.

When the two new Caesars were proclaimed in 305, Constantine was at the court of Galerius at Nicomedia. His father Constantius was about to start his British campaign, and allegedly sent for his son because he was ill, which may be true, since Constantius died within the year. Galerius seemed reluctant at first to release Constantine, probably reasoning that he would lose his bargaining power with Constantius if he allowed his son to leave. Constantine thought that he was under threat, and proceeded as fast as he could to the west, melodramatically killing or maiming all the horses whenever he changed to fresh mounts at posting stations, so that he could not be pursued. It is indicative of the man.

Constantine arrived at his father's camp on the northern coast of Gaul, just as the British campaign was about to begin. Father and son proceeded to the far north of the island, but archaeology has little to show for this campaign. Only very slight traces of Constantius's progress are visible, and none of the many temporary camps in Scotland have been authoritatively assigned to this campaign. The similarities with Severus's British wars have been highlighted by several authors, especially since both emperors took their sons with them, and both died at York. The reasons for the war and what Constantius may have achieved in Britain is overshadowed by the fact that the army declared Constantine emperor in July 306, perhaps with a little encouragement from Constantius, and not a little from Constantine himself. The hereditary principle had not died out as far as the army was concerned and Constantine was not about to pass up the opportunity and nobly revert to the Tetrarchic principle of non-dynastic promotion. He tried to reconcile his new status with Galerius, and wrote to him to say that he had no choice but to concur with the wishes of the troops. Galerius compromised and made him Caesar.

In October 306 Maxentius, the son of Maximian, was declared emperor in Rome itself, with support from senators and the praetorians. There followed a scramble for survival in which alliances were made, broken, and made again. Galerius sent Severus to retrieve the situation, while he and Maximinus looked on from their respective parts of the Empire. Maximian reappeared, either on his own initiative, or perhaps he was invited to become emperor again by his son. Severus failed to dislodge Maxentius, and was besieged in Ravenna, where he committed suicide. Even Galerius, the conqueror of the Persians, was forced to leave Italy in the hands of Maxentius.

Maximian offered to ally with Constantine, who married Maximian's daughter Fausta in 307. There may have been a promise to make Constantine Augustus. At this stage, although Maximian was Constantine's senior partner, in fact he was nothing more than a usurper, so Constantine's dependence upon him cast a dubious light on his career, and he carefully disassociated himself from these less than perfect beginnings as soon as opportunity arose.

After Galerius left Italy, Maximian quarrelled with his son and tried to depose him, but Maxentius could call upon considerable support in Rome, and Maximian was forced to seek refuge with Constantine at Trier. For some time, Constantine remained in northern Gaul, attending to the Rhine frontier. A campaign or campaigns against the Bructeri are recorded, and there was activity at Cologne where Constantine built a bridge, and had perhaps begun to build the fort opposite the city at Deutz, though the archaeological evidence suggests that it belongs to a slightly later period.

While Constantine and Maximian were in Gaul, Galerius arranged a meeting with Diocletian on 11 November 308 at Carnuntum where an inscription from the Mithraeum records the reconciliation of emperors.

The Tetrarchic system was repaired, but not for long. Diocletian would not be persuaded to rule the Empire again, and Maximian was forced to retire once more. Constantine was relegated to the position of Caesar, along with Maximinus. The vacant slot for another Augustus was taken by Licinius, a colleague of Galerius. Maxentius was not even considered.

By 310, Constantine had rid himself of Maximian, who had allegedly begun to intrigue against him. Constantine marched to southern Gaul, besieged his erstwhile ally at Marseilles, where Maximian allegedly committed suicide. Constantine now purged himself of all connection with Maximian and sought for more respectable ancestry, insisting on the divinity of his father Constantius, and attaching himself to the house of Claudius Gothicus. Licinius countered by claiming descent from Philip the Arab. Hereditary power had a longer history than Tetrarchic principles. At about the same time as he created his new lineage, Constantine also departed from the Jovian-Herculian religious support structure, and turned instead to Apollo Sol Invictus, both sun gods. Constantine was emerging as an independent entity.

In the year 311 fate took a hand in the inexorable rise of Constantine. By the end of that year Severus and Maximian had already been eliminated, and it is possible that Diocletian had died, though some scholars have argued for 313 or even 316. It is well attested that Galerius fell ill and died in 311, probably in April or May. Before he expired he reversed the persecution of the Christians, issuing the edict of toleration that restored Christian places of worship and reinstated the clergy. By 311, only three emperors, Licinius, Maximinus and Maxentius, were powerful enough to oppose Constantine, but fortunately for him the three were far from united against him. None of the four rulers of the Roman world trusted each other, so there was a period of watchful suspicion while they decided who would ally with whom. Licinius was betrothed to Constantine's half sister Constantia, so in theory he was allied to Constantine, but if he suddenly threw in his lot with either of the other two the balance would tilt.

In 312 Constantine decided to move against Maxentius, who now ruled Italy and the African provinces, with all their agricultural resources at his disposal. After securing the Rhine, Constantine mobilized. The causes of the civil war are in reality the intolerance of one emperor for the other, and the grudges they held. Even though he had quarrelled with his father, Maxentius still wanted to avenge his death, since Maximian had more than likely been murdered by Constantine. On the other hand it was clear to contemporaries that Constantine wanted to rule the whole Empire, so he now represented himself as the saviour of Rome from the tyrant and usurper.

He marched from Gaul to the Alps with a conglomerate army that has never been fully documented, smashing through the troops sent to guard the Alpine passes by Pompeianus, Maxentius's Praetorian Prefect.

He stormed the town of Susa (ancient Segusio) where Maxentius had placed a garrison, but his own troops were held back and there was no bloody massacre or looting. It was an important point, and attests to Constantine's iron authority and command of his soldiers. This was going to be portrayed as a war to save Rome and the Empire from the unsuitable elements who had taken control, so it would have been extremely detrimental to the cause to behave in a worse fashion that the supposed tyrant Maxentius. At Turin where Constantine's troops defeated the guard that Maxentius had placed there, the town was once again spared. Assured of lenient treatment, other towns welcomed Constantine. Milan opened its gates to him. His eventual arrival at Rome was assured.

Maxentius decided to meet him outside the city, even though he had strengthened the Aurelian fortifications. It was a mistake to let Constantine get so far without stopping him, and when he had arrived it was a mistake to offer battle so soon, but Maxentius had already lost some of his popularity, despite his studied promotion of Roman values and traditions, partly because his building programme was proving expensive. If he had risked a siege of Rome he would merely have lost even more support in proportion to the length of time the siege went on, and when the food was running out and Constantine offered a better choice, his fate would have been sealed. So Maxentius met Constantine at the battle of the Milvian Bridge and lost. His troops were backed into the Tiber and he was drowned along with many of the soldiers. His death was convenient because now that he was removed Constantine could portray him as a tyrant, and more importantly everyone could choose to believe the propaganda without the embarrassing living reminder that he or she was betraying the erstwhile emperor. Besides there was an inevitability about it all; Constantine's victory was god-given, though which god had given it was not as apparent at first as it later became. The authenticity or otherwise of Constantine's Christian vision before the battle will never be proven. The tales are too deeply embedded in Christian iconography to be uprooted now by modern speculation, and such a pastime is doomed to failure because the various versions of what he saw and when he saw it are so inconsistent; they range from a simple cross in the sky some days before the battle, to a complicated Chi Rho symbol, combining the first two Greek letters X and P of Christ's name, seen or dreamed on the night before the battle. Allegedly he was informed that in this sign he would conquer, and allegedly he ordered the soldiers to put this Christian device on their shields, which conjures up the scenario of lots of soldiers milling about looking for some paint when they could have been getting a good night's sleep. Veracity is not the important point; it is the legend and the use that Constantine made of it that count, because he re-shaped the Roman Empire and by extension, the western world.

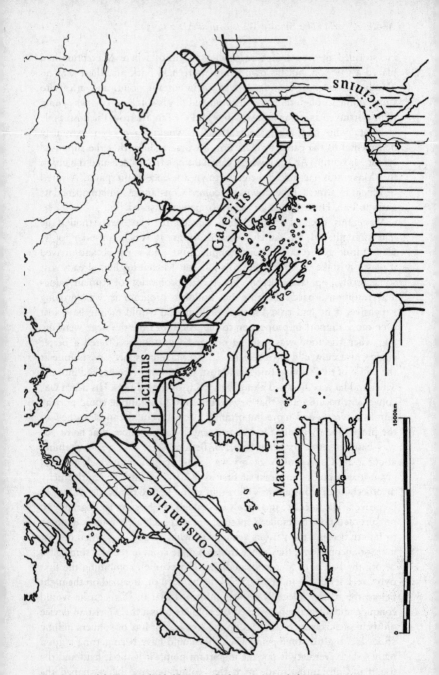

Map 6. Map of the Empire divided between the four emperors, before Constantine defeated the other three and became sole ruler.

The Elimination of Maximinus & Licinius

Shortly after the battle, when he was established in Rome, having conciliated as many groups as possible with promises that he was just as Roman as other emperors, Constantine wrote to Maximinus to try to persuade him to end the persecution of the Christians in his territories. His letters were probably ineffective. Maximinus was steadily marginalized as Constantine and Licinius drew closer together. Early in 313 the two met at Milan, where Constantine's half sister was married to Licinius, and an edict was issued declaring toleration of all religions. Licinius's part in this undertaking is overshadowed by the glory of Constantine's later reign, and because towards the end of his life Licinius resorted to persecution of the Christians again, but in 313 he deserved as much credit as his brother-in-law.

Equality was never in Constantine's personal vocabulary for long; in his own territories, inscriptions made it clear that he was the senior emperor, and he began to describe himself as Maximus Augustus, or at least he made no move to prevent others from addressing him as such. Licinius acquiesced, perhaps because he thought that he could eliminate Maximinus and build up a power base in the east that would secure him against anything that Constantine could put into effect against him. He picked a fight with Maximinus because the latter had invaded Thrace; Licinius won the victory and took over Maximinus's provinces. He also made sure that few of Maximinus's family or adherents survived; no risk of any resurgence in his name was to be countenanced, and while he was about this grisly business Licinius seems to have decided to remove any possibility that Diocletian's or Galerius's families might make a bid for power. Whatever his reasons, in 313 or perhaps in 314, Diocletian's daughter Valeria, the widow of Galerius, and Prisca, Diocletian's widow, were killed. Maximinus fled to Tarsus and committed suicide. Constantine now had only one main rival.

Relations remained stable enough through the following years. In 315 Constantine celebrated his ten-year rule. The festivities of the *decennalia* were crowned by the dedication of the arch of Constantine, still visible in Rome near to the Colosseum. It was magnificent but somewhat second hand, in that some of the sculptures were borrowed from other monuments. The text outlines Constantine's achievements, in phrases not unlike the beginning of the *Res Gestae* of the first Augustus, who advertised the fact that at the age of nineteen he had raised his own army to save the republic from faction; Constantine attributes his success to inspiration of the divinity and his own noble mindedness, by which he was enabled to save the republic from the tyrant and his faction. This refers to Maxentius, but could just as well be taken as indicative of any other dissenting elements. Consolidation of his power was achieved in the west.

There remained the east, and Licinius. Constantine waited upon events until 316, when he appointed his brother-in-law Bassianus as his Caesar. This man's brother Senecio was a friend of Licinius, and Constantine probably used this relationship to weave a little intrigue. It was said that there was a plot against him, engineered perhaps by Senecio, perhaps by Bassianus, possibly with the support or encouragement of Licinius. It was all rather mysterious, no doubt by design, to increase the aura of subterfuge. Bassianus was executed, and Constantine asked Licinius to surrender Senecio. This was the test of his loyalty, perhaps; he refused to hand him over. Manoeuvring began. Licinius moved up with his army to the borders with Constantine's territories. He appointed an Augustus of his own called Valens. The inevitable war resulted in defeat for Licinius, and a compromise. He ceded territories to Constantine, the frontier province of Pannonia, part of Moesia, and part of the Balkans. The unfortunate Valens was eliminated, and in his place three young Caesars were appointed. These were the fourteen-year-old Crispus, Constantine's son by his first wife, and two very young children, the infant Constantine, and the son of Licinius, not yet two years old. Hereditary succession was back in fashion. From 317 to 323 there was an unofficial truce while each emperor attended to his own territories Consulships were shared, in 318 by Licinius and Crispus, and in 319 by the young Constantine and the young Licinius. During the same year, Constantine campaigned in the Danube provinces while his son Crispus fought against the Franks on the Rhine. Harmonious relations were brief. Licinius departed from Constantine's plan when he began to persecute the Christians. Constantine's response was to take up the Christian cause. Relations deteriorated, and when Constantine crossed the boundaries of his own territories into Thrace while he was campaigning against the Goths in 323, Licinius suspected that Constantine was about to launch an invasion of his territories. Constantine was reasonable; he said that he had defeated the Goths and thrown them back across the Danube, so the methods by which he had accomplished this were less important than the result.

Despite Constantine's studied innocence, preparations for war escalated. Licinius appointed yet another Augustus, Martianus. His reasons may have been to provide himself with administrative assistance, freeing him to concentrate on the war, but it is notable that Constantine kept any promotions within the family, giving the command of his fleet to his son Crispus. Licinius and Constantine faced each other at last in July 324 at Adrianople. Licinius was defeated and fled to Byzantium, but Constantine's fleet under Crispus forced its way through the Hellespont, threatening him with blockade or capture, so he moved on. Constantine won the final battle at Chrysopolis, opposite Byzantium. Licinius surrendered, persuaded by his wife Constantia that her half brother Constantine would be merciful. He made terms, ceding all his territories to Constantine in return for a life of leisure under house arrest. After only a few months he and his son were killed along with Martianus, the new Augustus. It had taken nearly two decades for Constantine to extend his rule over the whole Empire. His path had not been easy or direct, and there had been many casualties, but he had achieved sole rule, and could now devote his attention to reshaping the Empire.

15

New Rome: Constantine to Theodosius the Great AD 324–395

CONSTANTINE SOLE AUGUSTUS AD 324–337

As sole ruler Constantine created a new world. He brought to fruition all the mid-third-century developments, of the adaptations of Gallienus and of the Diocletianic and Tetrarchic innovations. Once he had all the Empire under his control, Constantine could rewrite his origins, and put his policies into effect. He emphasized his descent from Claudius II Gothicus, with the result that this emperor's achievements were praised by the historians. His press agents were Christian writers, notably Lactantius and Eusebius. Constantine's promotion of the Christian Church is his most enduring achievement, and the one that has received the most attention from the ancient authors and many modern scholars. His first allegiance to a single god, Sol Invictus, never faded entirely, and pagan symbols rather than Christian ones appeared on his coinage, until later in his reign. It is a matter of opinion whether he believed in the Christian message or whether he simply used it for political ends. To some authors he was a true convert to the Christian faith, largely because he had no pressing need to promote it and there was no advantage in doing so. All he needed to do was issue and uphold an edict of toleration and allow all kinds of religion to flourish. He was baptized only on his deathbed, but this was not abnormal at the time, and cannot be used as proof that he was only playing along with the Christians. Some scholars insist that Constantine wished only to establish some kind of unifying force throughout the Empire, and used Christianity to achieve it. Since the early Church was rent by schisms from its infancy, it was not the most effective unifying force that he could have chosen.

Constantine was drawn into the dispute of the Donatists in Africa, when the Bishop of Carthage died. The Carthaginian Christians elected Caecilian as the new bishop, but a rival group opted for another candidate, who also died and was replaced by Donatus, who gave his name to the sect. In 312 or 313 the Donatists appealed to Constantine for arbitration as to who was the true Bishop of Carthage. At a hearing in 313 and again at the council of Arles in 314, the claims of Donatus were rejected. In 316 Constantine declared firmly for Caecilian, but by this time the Donatist church had gained many supporters in Africa. The significance of the episode is that the appeal was not directed to the Bishop of Rome as head of the Church, but went straight to Constantine, who was not yet sole emperor.

Constantine took an active part in the councils and synods of the Church, the most famous being the Council of Nicaea in 325, which at first seemed to produce all the answers to thorny questions of doctrine and to quell the factions within the Church, bringing about the hoped for unity. It did not prove wholly successful on this score, though the Nicene Creed still forms the basis of Christian belief. The Church was favoured by Constantine, but it never emerged from a position of subordination to him, losing its erstwhile independence. The clergy were allowed considerable freedom, enjoying the benefits of tax exemptions and being excused municipal obligations, but Constantine remained the master while calling himself the servant. If he had changed his mind about the Church, he still had the power to outlaw Christianity, and would probably have succeeded. The fact that he did not do so indicates that the Church gave him what he wanted. In return he encouraged the foundation of Christian churches, which were not mere copies of pagan temples, but a new form was chosen for them derived from the basilicas, civil buildings with administrative and legal functions. The basilica of St Peter had been founded before 319, and was completed during Constantine's sole reign, in 329. Prudently, most new church foundations were on Imperial lands, or in the case of Rome, they were built either on lands that Constantine owned, or placed outside the city.

Constantine's social policies were bound up with his attitude towards the Christians. He insisted that the men who were eligible to serve as decurions on their town councils should do so, despite the fact that growing impoverishment made it more and more difficult for such individuals to meet the expenses involved. The large number of laws that were passed to try to force eligible councillors to undertake municipal obligations merely highlights the fact that the legislation was not working. Since the clergy were exempted from their municipal obligations, it was hardly surprising that resentment built up against the privileges of the Christians, but at the same time more and more men sought a way out of their municipal burdens by entering the Church, reducing still further the number of people who could serve their communities in the practical sense rather than in the spiritual realm. Eventually the wealthiest men were forbidden to enter the clergy, to try to retain men of means within the sphere of local government of the towns and cities.

There was a distinct advantage in belonging to the Christian fraternity. The officially sanctioned state religion was Christianity, which meant that personal alliances and networks could be built up within Christian circles in the Imperial administration. While promoting Christianity,

Constantine tried to retain religious freedom. Although he was less tolerant of paganism after he became sole emperor, it was not stamped out, and those who refused to join the Church still had a part to play. As a means of conciliating the pagan aristocracy of the Empire, Constantine created new senators, bestowing senatorial rank without the obligation to live in Rome or to attend meetings of the Senate. These senators were appointed prefects of Rome, or as governors of the consular provinces, and as *correctores* in Italy.

Constantine did not much alter the arrangements that Diocletian had made with regard to the government of the provinces. He did not attempt a full scale removal of the equestrians as governors and did not radically alter provincial boundaries. The large numbers of experienced personnel necessary for the government of the provinces and command of the armies made it unlikely that he could turn his back on equestrians as a source of supply, so he promoted them and adlected some of them to the Senate.

In view of the potential shortage of manpower, he did nothing to halt or reform the crystallization of professions that Diocletian had instituted. Constantine's policies did not include liberating the inhabitants of the Empire from their hereditary obligations. The *coloni* continued their descent from free men to virtual slaves, while the power of the great landowners, whose nominal tenants they were, increased to the point where they were eventually able to challenge the state itself and defy the attempts of the emperors to control them.

The army was a different matter. There Constantine did make some changes, though controversy still reigns over who created the mobile field armies. The balance of probability is that Constantine remoulded Diocletian's armies and developed something new. The pagan author Zosimus accused Constantine of destroying Diocletian's system, because the latter had secured the frontiers by putting the troops back into their forts, while Constantine took the troops away again and put them into the cities, where they were not needed in the first place. That was perhaps how it seemed to contemporary observers as the mobile cavalry armies (*comitatenses*) and the more static frontier armies (*limitanei*) were developed. The old system whereby the legions and auxiliary troops were stationed on the frontiers made it more difficult to assemble a campaign army and march it to the threatened areas, and in any case, denuding one area of its troops, in order to come to the assistance of another region, invited further trouble at the lightly-garrisoned points. On the Rhine and particularly on the Danube, the tribesmen were fully aware of what was happening on the frontiers, and ready to seize their chance for raiding, or sometimes to force their way into the Empire and settle down because life seemed better on the Roman side.

From the middle of the third century the importance of cavalry units had increased, and Constantine responded to the need for greater mobility by developing the mounted units. The new deployment of the armed forces was reflected in the new military commands, the *magister equitum* in command of the cavalry and the *magister peditum* in command of the infantry. Constantine's contribution to the protection of the Empire was not radically altered by his successors.

The Praetorian Prefects had already been given tremendous responsibilities in the administration of the Empire, and under Constantine they lost all their military functions. One of their tasks was to administer the *annona*, the all important supply system. The Praetorian Guard was abolished after the battle of the Milvian Bridge, and replaced with a new bodyguard called the *scholae*, first established by Diocletian. This bodyguard was commanded by the chief of the civil administration, the *magister officiorum*, who was in charge of all the departments of the administration.

Apart from introducing Christianity as the official religion Constantine's next most famous or notorious innovation was to reinvent Rome in the east, at Byzantium. It was not a complete surprise since the emperors had not lived in Rome for many decades, and some of the short-lived emperors never even saw the capital city. New capitals had been established at different cities nearer to the frontiers at Trier, Milan, Sirmium and Nicomedia; Constantine had chosen Serdica (Sofia) as his residence, and now his choice was Byzantium. Strategically this city offered tremendous advantages. It was eminently defensible; Septimius Severus had reduced it only after very a long siege. Supplies could be brought in directly by sea, unlike Rome which had to be supplied from the port of Ostia. And it was close to the eastern provinces, where the greatest threat to security derived from the Persians, and to the Danube, continually harassed by the tribes from the north. Prime requirements for defence of the Empire were that the emperor and the armies should be close to the potential trouble spots, and Byzantium fulfilled those requirements.

Byzantium officially became the city of Constantine, Constantinople, in 330, but there is evidence that it was already labelled *altera Roma*, another Rome, at least four years before the official foundation date. Probably as soon as he became sole emperor, Constantine decided to create another capital city. In itself the establishment of yet another Imperial headquarters was not a revolutionary move; it only imitated what had happened in other provinces. What was revolutionary was that Constantine transported to his new city the whole of the government administrative machinery. The city had seven hills and fourteen administrative districts, just like Rome, and Constantine gave his new capital a Senate, a Forum, and a circus, and instituted a free corn dole, everything that mirrored Rome itself.

In Rome there remained a shadow of what had gone before. Constantine repaired some of the major buildings and completed the huge basilica that Maxentius had begun, but otherwise he paid the city little attention, except for celebrating his twentieth anniversary as emperor in 326. Without the Imperial presence, commercial and social life went on much as before. Senators still lived out their lives in the city, debates were still held in the Senate House, and some senators took up provincial posts. But the government of the Empire was no longer centred on Rome. For many years the administrative machinery had not been located in the city, but lumbered after the emperor wherever he was; as Herodian recognized at the beginning of the third century, Rome was where the emperor was. But in the end, Rome did not lie down quietly and die. It remained a symbolic centre, part of the ideology of the western Empire, and a focus for the kingdoms that emerged when the Empire lost its cohesion.

After the experiment of the Tetrarchy, the hereditary principle in the Imperial house reasserted itself. Constantine prepared for the succession by proclaiming as Caesars his sons by his wife Fausta. The first born son Constantine was made Caesar as an infant in 317, and his siblings Constantius and Constans were given the same rank in 324 and 333. Crispus, Constantine's son by his first wife, had been given army commands, but was not otherwise promoted, and for reasons unknown he was executed in 326. There may have been palace conspiracies which have not come to light, or Constantine simply grew suspicious. He accused Crispus of having an affair with his wife Fausta, and had her killed as well.

In 328, Constantine the younger was sent to Trier, while Constantine senior campaigned on the Rhine. There were further campaigns against the Goths in 332, when Constantine made a treaty with them, and then against the Sarmatians in 334. The frontiers were secured for the rest of Constantine's reign. The three sons of Constantine had to be content with the rank of Caesars, since the Emperor did not share power with any of them, and did not elevate any of them to the status of Augustus. He raised another of his relatives, Dalmatius, to the rank of Caesar in 335. Echoes of the Tetrarchy were revealed when Constantine divided the Empire into four regions, with one of his Caesars in control of each. His intentions are puzzling to modern scholars. The Diocletianic system had patently not worked, and no one knew its weaknesses better than Constantine. Equality among four rulers would be short-lived, even among the most well balanced individuals, but on the other hand, if Constantine had designated a sole successor, it would have simply promoted rivalry among the other Caesars and led by a different route to civil war. This is exactly what happened after Constantine died in May 337, but it took three years for the fighting to start.

CONSTANTINE II AD 337–340,
CONSTANS AD 337–350 & CONSTANTIUS II AD 337–361

For about six months after Constantine's death, the Roman world held its breath. The four Caesars made no move until the army made it clear that no one except the sons of Constantine should rule. Dalmatius was quickly assassinated by the soldiers, along with other peripheral members of Constantine's family. Only two boys were spared, Gallus aged twelve and Julian aged six, who were to play a part in the Empire nearly two decades later. The Empire was divided into three parts under each of Constantine's sons, who awarded themselves the title of Augustus. The partition was not an amicable agreement. Constantine II ruled the west, Constantius the east, and Constans controlled Italy with Illyricum and Africa. As the youngest of the brothers he was supervised by Constantine II, the senior Augustus, but the arrangement did not last long. Constans challenged his brother, who responded in 340 by bringing his army to Italy. At Aquileia, Constantine II was defeated and killed, and Constans quickly took over his territories. In the east Constantius was preoccupied with the resurgence to power of the Persian King Shapur II and approved the extension of Constans's Empire.

Constans devoted attention to the defence of the Rhine frontier and the provinces of Britain. He was far from popular with either the troops, because he had restored discipline with a rather heavy hand, or the people who faced increasing impoverishment, so it was easy for conspirators from the army and civil government to form a conspiracy against him. Less than a year after taking over the west, Constans was dead, having been defeated by a Germanic army officer favoured by the troops, called Magnentius. He was acclaimed by the army and accepted by the people, except for the inhabitants of Illyricum, where Constantius's sister had encouraged another so-called usurper, Vetranio, to seize power, because he was preferable to Magnentius. Constantius temporarily patched up the problems in the east and set off to eradicate Magnentius. Vetranio was content to step down, having preserved Illyricum, and his soldiers joined Constantius, who defeated Magnentius at Mursa, leaving Constantius sole ruler in 351. Magnentius was still a free agent, having escaped from Mursa, but he did not represent a serious threat. Two years later at another battle in the French Alps, Magnentius was killed.

The relative peace of Constantine's reign was ended in the 350s, only a few years after his death. Constantius was faced with invasions across the northern frontiers and mounting trouble in the east, and the multiple problems of internal security and frontier defence proved too much for one man alone, so in 351 he turned to his surviving relatives for assistance. He summoned the twenty-eight-year-old Gallus, made him Caesar, married him to his sister Constantia, and sent him to guard the eastern frontier.

By 353 it was apparent that he had made the wrong choice, so in 354 he brought Gallus back to Rome and executed him.

For the next few months there was almost continuous fighting. There was a revolt in Gaul, when a Frankish officer called Silvanus was accused of treason, and raised rebellion, then the tribes of the Franks and Alamanni crossed the Rhine. More than ever, Constantius needed an assistant whom he could trust, and his next choice was Gallus's half brother Julian, who was studying at Athens. In 355 he was made Caesar, married to Constantius's daughter Helena, and sent to Gaul where he was appointed military commander in 357, despite having no experience or training in military matters.

Julian's lack of experience was no problem. In a famous battle near Strasbourg he brought the Alamanni to battle and trounced them. The survivors fled back to the Rhine with Julian in pursuit. For the next two campaigning seasons in 358 and 359 he led further expeditions across the Rhine, and repaired the frontier installations. Constantius then asked him to send troops to the east, where he was preparing a campaign against Shapur II, because the Persians had invaded Roman Mesopotamia and destroyed the city of Amida. This period of Roman history is fully documented by the historian Ammianus, who was a contemporary commentator and had personal experience of what he described.

Julian did not trust Constantius because he suspected that it was he who ordered the army to massacre all his relatives in 337, to remove any opposition after the death of Constantine. Likewise Constantius did not trust Julian because he was not in the habit of trusting anyone, and Julian had been successful and made himself popular with the army, so it was probably no surprise to Constantius to hear, while he was preparing the eastern campaign, that in 360 the troops in Gaul had proclaimed Julian emperor, and that Julian had not refused the offer. The trouble was supposed to have started when Julian was about to obey orders and send his troops to the east. Some of his German soldiers had been enrolled on the basis that they would not be asked to serve anywhere beyond the Alps, and Julian's instructions contravened that agreement. They protested, and the eventual result was the proclamation of Julian.

Constantius refused to recognize Julian as emperor, so war was now inevitable. Rather than wait in Gaul for the onslaught, Julian set off for Constantinople. Constantius also set off from the east, but before the two rivals could meet, he died in Cilicia in 361. It was said that he had named Julian as his successor, which avoided further wars. As sole emperor, Julian inherited the Persian war that Constantius had prepared for. For the few months before he mounted his own Persian campaign, Julian tackled the financial problems of the Empire. He tried to reduce state expenditure, revoked tax exemptions to increase revenue, and stopped civilians from using the Imperial postal service, the *cursus publicus*. The Christians suddenly found themselves out of favour after their prosperous development under Constantine, because as a young man Julian had devoted himself to classical studies while he was divorced from public life, and had been converted from Christianity to the old religion. He did not persecute the Christians at first, but he harassed them, removing support for the clergy, demanding that temples converted to Christian use should be restored, and encouraging various writers to produce pamphlets attacking Christian beliefs and doctrine. Since his rule was very short and his successor was a Christian, this glitch in the progress of Christianity was soon repaired.

Preparations for the Persian campaign began in May 362, when Julian marched to Antioch. In spring 363 Julian took a large army down the banks of the River Euphrates, marched to the Tigris, and finally reached the Persian capital at Ctesiphon, where he won a battle. Several times in the past a Roman army had reached this Persian capital and won a battle, but none of these battles had ever resulted in permanent occupation of Persia, nor had they helped to solve the problem of enmity between the two Empires. Julian's expedition was no exception to the rule. Shapur II arrived with the main Persian force, and Julian marched homewards up the Tigris, dogged all the way by the Persians, who made small attacks but did not join in a main battle. During one of these skirmishes Julian was wounded, possibly by a Persian spear, but some said that one of the Christians in his army had attacked him. He died that same evening. The army immediately chose a successor, the commander of Julian's bodyguard, called Jovian.

JOVIAN AD 363–364

The new Emperor was in a highly unenviable position, similar to that of Philip the Arab a century earlier, who also took over after the death of the emperor, and had a choice of fighting and losing, or negotiating his way out of Persia. Jovian chose to make peace. It was costly, but the army was extricated, to fight another day. Jovian gave up territory, never a popular move for the Romans. The eastern parts of Mesopotamia were relinquished, along with the important site of Nisibis, where Diocletian had signed a treaty in 299, favourable to the Romans. Jovian also agreed to renounce control of Armenia, and to pay subsidies to the Persians.

Jovian had no opportunity to reveal any plans or policies, save for allowing freedom of religious worship all over the Empire, and repealing Julian's enactments against the Christians. His reign lasted only eight months. He died of natural causes rather than assassination. He was one of the very few emperors to die a natural death. The military high command,

assisted by civil administrators, chose Flavius Valentinianus, an army
officer from Pannonia, to succeed Jovian, but the army was not content,
because the soldiers had concluded that there was a need for two emperors
to take charge of the east and the west. They approved Valentinian's choice
of his own brother Valens, and both took the title Augustus.

VALENTINIAN AD 365–375 & VALENS AD 365–378.

Valens went to the east, while Valentinian took control of the western half
of the Empire, and devoted himself to clearing the Rhine provinces of the
tribesmen who endangered them. By a combination of warfare, diplomatic
efforts and strengthening the frontiers, he brought peace to Gaul and the
Rhineland. He fought the Alamanni, the Franks and the Germanic tribes,
made lasting treaties with some tribal chiefs, recruited large numbers of
tribesmen for the Roman army to keep it up to strength, and rebuilt the
chain of forts and bridgeheads from the Upper Danube area, along the
Rhine all the way to the western coast. He sealed the gap between the
Upper Danube and the Rhine with a chain of forts running along the
southern edge of Lake Constance to Basel, and joining the frontier along
the west bank of the Rhine to Strasbourg. He was a prolific builder,
with the result that it is difficult to discern the work of other emperors
who came after him, and he was so thorough that it is tempting to label
everything from the fourth century as Valentinianic. His work secured
Gaul for some considerable time.

While Valentinian attended to the Rhine and Danube, his trusted
general, Count Flavius Theodosius was in Britain. His proper Latin title
was *comes*, plural *comites*, originally meaning companions, but the term
was given official status by Constantine and granted to high officers of
the civil and military administration. Theodosius repelled the tribes of
Picts and Scotti and Saxons, who had invaded all at the same time in 367,
giving rise to the theory current in ancient times that there had been a
barbarian conspiracy. Theodosius strengthened the British frontier, and
also the forts and towns of the interior. He may have been responsible
for the addition of towers to some town walls, which would support
artillery to keep attackers from coming too close. Theodosius went on to
put down a rebellion in the provinces of North Africa, which had begun
probably in 373. A chieftain of the Mauri called Firmus was supported by
the populace, but he was defeated by Theodosius in 374. Intrigues at the
Imperial court led to the execution of Theodosius in the following year,
possibly because he had gained knowledge of some serious corruption
among senior officers and court officials, who struck him down before he
could reveal names.

The first challenge in 365 for Valens was the attempted usurpation of

Procopius, one of Julian's extended family and a close associate who had perhaps expected to be named as his successor. He established his base at Constantinople, and controlled Thrace and Bithynia. He stressed his relationship to Julian and Constantius, which engendered considerable support for him. The dynastic principle, and loyalty to the house of Constantine was not dead. However, he had insufficient military strength to sustain a rebellion, let alone make a bid for the whole Empire. More detrimental still, he had not been able to sway the officers of the army to support him. They deserted him after about a year, and went over to Valens in May 366.

War broke out in Thrace, where the Goths continually invaded and devastated the country. Valens defeated a group of them in 369 and made a treaty with the leaders of the tribe. This entailed a levy of tribesmen (*foederati*) for service in the army, and a solemn promise to cease hostilities, but the oath was sworn by a tribal individual to a Roman individual, not to the tribe or state, so the tribesmen in particular considered the treaty invalid once either of the individuals died.

In 367 Valentinian fell dangerously ill, and designated his nine-year-old son Gratian as Augustus, to try to ensure the succession. He recovered, and in the early 370s he went to Pannonia. Tribesmen were again proving troublesome and threatening the security of the Danube provinces, so Valentinian mounted several expeditions against them. After returning from one of these expeditions in 375, he allowed an embassy from the Quadi to see him. They complained that they were not responsible for the raids on Roman territory, which had been carried out by other tribes turned brigands, who had settled near the Danube. Then they complained about the frontier installations that had been built opposite their lands, at which point Valentinian, angered beyond endurance, fell dead of an apoplectic seizure.

Valentinian's son Gratian, now aged about sixteen, succeeded his father, but to make sure of the dynasty, the military leaders persuaded Valentinian's widow to make their four-year-old son Augustus, as Valentinian II. Gratian remained in Gaul and Valentinian II was to govern Illyricum with the help of the military commander Merobaudes, probably of Frankish origin, but a competent general. In 371 Valens went to the eastern frontier to wrest control of Armenia from Shapur II, and bring the country back into the Roman sphere of influence. Between then and 377 he guarded against further encroachments of the Persians, and drove them out of Mesopotamia, but then news came of a serious incursion of the Goths into the Danube provinces.

This time the tribesmen were not simply making raids. The fierce Huns had come sweeping out of Mongolia and entered Gothic territory, massacring the population as they advanced. The Goths were obviously terrified of them, and wanted to settle in Moesia and Thrace, where life seemed much sweeter. A group of Goths known as the Tervingi, under their leader Fritigern, was allowed to settle, but then another group, the Greuthungi, crossed the Danube without official permission and joined them. The Romans treated them badly, denying them food supplies unless high prices could be extracted. Unable to go back home, and prevented from moving further into the Empire, the Goths took to raiding. The military force sent to assassinate the Gothic leaders failed, and war broke out in 377.

Valens hurried to Constantinople, and then to Adrianople where the Goths who had been drafted into the Roman army had rebelled in support of their fellow tribesmen. The major battle was fought there, where so many other battles had already been fought. Gratian had sent troops from the west, but before they arrived, Valens committed his forces in an attempt to stem the tide. His defeat was total, and he lost his life. His body was never found. The Goths spread out over Thrace and Illyricum, and the problem of how to deal with them was bequeathed to Gratian. He decided to ask for help. He chose Theodosius, son of Count Theodosius who had restored order in Britain after the disasters of 367. When his father was denounced and executed, Theodosius had shared the disgrace and had been dismissed from his post as *Dux* of Moesia Superior and/or Illyricum in 374. Traditionally, Gratian called him from his retirement Spain, but some scholars now think that Theodosius was already reinstated and held a command on the Danube. Wherever he came from, Theodosius was made *magister militum* under Gratian in 378. In January 379 he was elevated to Augustus, and given command of the eastern Empire.

THEODOSIUS THE GREAT AD 379–395

The Empire was ruled by three emperors: Gratian in the west, Valentinian II, who had been made Augustus at the age of four, in Italy and Illyricum, and Theodosius in the east, specifically Moesia, eastern Illyricum, and the new Dacia, carved out of Moesian territory. The Goths had taken over Thrace and Moesia Inferior, and eventually spilled out into Macedonia and Thessaly. Theodosius took advantage of the endemic disunity among the Goths, and for a while he was able to play rival factions off against each other, to occupy them in internecine struggles instead of attacking Roman territory. He then concentrated on building the garrisons up to strength in Macedonia, and in 380 he arrived in Constantinople.

The policy of letting the Goths fight each other paid off when one of the Gothic leaders, Athanaric, was expelled by his own people, and asked for asylum in Constantinople, where he died soon afterwards. In 381 Theodosius was reinforced by troops from the west under Arbogast and

Bauto, Frankish generals. Theodosius had held military commands, but he was not an outstanding military leader, and was content to let these generals drive the Goths out of Macedonia, Thessaly and Illyricum. The tribesmen marched back to Thrace.

Theodosius made a treaty with them in 382, an arrangement for which he was censured by contemporaries and later historians. The terms were that the Goths could settle on the lands they had overrun in Thrace, and were to be ruled by their own leaders. This treaty did not reflect the same conquering spirit as previous ones. Normally the Romans remained in the ascendancy, monitoring the tribes settled on Roman territory, and the treaty stipulated that they should provide soldiers for the Roman army. Theodosius had concluded the sort of treaty that might have been made with tribes outside the Empire. He promised subsidies of food, one of the most important factors in the Gothic eruption that led to the battle of Adrianople, because the Romans short-sightedly withheld food from them.

The contribution of troops was probably one of the most important parts of the treaty of 382, but it is not known on what basis this was carried out, and it is possible that the Goths levied in this way were commanded by their own officers and not by Romans. This would distinguish them from the Goths who were already serving in units of the Roman army, and make them more like the auxiliaries of the Republic, who were not a permanent part of the Roman army, being raised from tribesmen who were commanded by their nobles, and went home after the campaigns ended. Unfortunately, with regard to Theodosius's treaty, none of this is known for certain.

The arrangement with the Goths polarized the Roman world. Romans who hated the so-called barbarians thought that the tribes would simply imagine that the Empire and Theodosius, were weak, and would not keep their word. Others advocated Romanizing the Goths, and making them into good Christians. The orator Themistius said that it was better to fill Thrace with farmers and potential soldiers than with corpses.

In truth the Empire *was* weak, if only for lack of recruits for the army. The battle of Adrianople had decimated the eastern army, and there was now a growing reluctance to serve in the ranks. Theodosius recruited wherever and whenever he could, in an attempt to keep up the numbers, and he employed thousands of Goths, who fought well for Rome. Most of them would probably not consider that their military service for Rome was at odds with their Gothic nationality. Tribal organization and cohesion was flexible. Tribesmen were able to join other tribal groups without incurring the charge of betrayal, and provided that the men were accepted by the others and obeyed the leaders, groups were formed and dissolved quite quickly. Nationality was an embryonic concept in tribal organization. A gravestone of a tribesman, admittedly a Frank and not a Goth, epitomizes the easy acceptance of dual identity. His epitaph reads *Francus ego cives, Romanus miles in armis*, meaning I am a Frankish citizen and a Roman soldier.

In 383, a rebellion broke out in the west. A commander in Britain, Magnus Maximus, was hailed as emperor by his troops. He was accepted in Gaul and Spain, where discontent with the rule of Gratian was increasing. Maximus gathered troops, perhaps reducing the garrison of Hadrian's Wall to the danger point, and crossed into Gaul. Gratian took flight, but was captured and handed over by his own soldiers, and executed. Theodosius was not strong enough to challenge Maximus, so he recognized him as emperor, and Maximus remained in command of most of the west for a few years. In 387 he appointed his son Victor as Caesar, and invaded Italy, part of the realm of Valentinian II, who fled to Thessalonika with his mother and his half-sister, Galla. Theodosius could not allow this action to go unpunished. He had stopped a group of Goths, labelled the Ostrogoths, from crossing the Danube, and he had arranged a peace treaty with Shapur II, whereby he agreed to partition Armenia and share it with the Persians. There was a lull in hostilities in the east, leaving Theodosius free to attend to affairs in the west. He had elevated his elder son Arcadius as Augustus in 383, so he left him in Constantinople, and marched against Maximus. His fleet ensured that Maximus could not leave Italy except over the Alps, and he brought the usurper to battle at Siscia and then at Pola, defeating him in both encounters. At Aquileia, Maximus's troops surrendered him. He had become very unpopular, financing his expedition by seizing the property of the rich and not so rich. He was executed in 388, but he is immortalized in the Welsh heroic tale of the Mabinogion, as Macsen Wledig.

Valentinian II was restored to power, and Theodosius married Galla, Valentinian's half-sister. Valentinian was sent to Gaul, where Victor, Maximus's son, was killed. The Frankish *magister militum* Arbogast accompanied Valentinian, to watch over the young man. Theodosius went to Milan, remaining in the west for some time. At this point, St Ambrose, or Ambrosius, began to exert an influence over the Emperor. He interfered when a Christian mob, incited by local monks, burnt down a Jewish synagogue in Mesopotamia. Theodosius wanted the Christians to rebuild the synagogue, but Ambrose persuaded him against the idea. Two years later, in Thessalonika, a popular charioteer was imprisoned and the general who refused to release him was killed in a riot. Theodosius gave orders for the soldiers to round up and kill the rioters, and in the end it was said that the casualties amounted to 3,000 civilian dead. St Ambrose demanded that the Emperor should perform a public penance, or face exclusion from the Church. After a delay of eight months Theodosius complied. His dilemma was that as an ardent Christian who persecuted heretics, he ought to display unity with the Church. But the episode illustrated how easily the Church and state could be involved in a power struggle.

Theodosius returned to Constantinople in 391, to deal with various troubles. His son Arcadius had quarrelled with Galla, and the Goths had taken to raiding again, but the tribesmen were pacified without a war. The Praetorian Prefect Rufinus, and the general Stilicho, stopped the raiding and exploited the mutual antipathy of some of the Gothic groups. These men were Theodosius's trusted assistants. Stilicho was the son of a Vandal tribesman, a good general and loyal to the house of Theodosius. He married the Emperor's niece and was made *magister militum* in 392. Two years later, Stilicho accompanied Theodosius to the west, to eliminate the usurper Eugenius.

Arbogast had exceeded his brief as protector of Valentinian II, and had gained so much power that he was able to ignore an attempt by the Emperor to dismiss him. In May 392 Valentinian was found dead, the verdict being suicide, but suspicion attached to Arbogast. Since he was a Frankish soldier, Arbogast did not try to make himself emperor, but instead he raised Eugenius, an official at Valentinian's court, as Augustus. Theodosius refused to recognize him. For the best part of two years, Eugenius tried to mollify Theodosius. He asked St Ambrose to mediate, and issued coins depicting Theodosius and Arcadius, much as Zenobia in the 260s had issued coins depicting the Emperor Aurelian. Theodosius responded by appointing his younger son Honorius as Augustus in the west in 393, and gathering an army to face Eugenius in 394.

At the battle of the Frigidus, Arbogast and Eugenius with an army composed mostly of Franks were defeated by Theodosius and Stilicho with their army of Goths. Eugenius was captured and killed, and Arbogast committed suicide. Once again three emperors ruled the Roman world: Arcadius in Constantinople, Honorius based initially at Milan and their father Theodosius on his way to Rome to celebrate the victory. But soon the emperors were reduced to only two, because Theodosius died in January 395 in Milan. Stilicho assumed responsibility for Arcadius and Honorius, and for a while he was the most important man in the Roman world.

From the end of Constantine's reign the problems that he had faced began to increase. The perennial dilemma of the later Roman Empire was that it was threatened or attacked on more than one front, and was too large to be ruled by one man. Various methods of sharing power had been tried since the second century, not always successfully. Even when Imperial rule was kept within the family, with a senior partner as Augustus and a junior Caesar, or with two or more Augusti, the emperors had not always been able to keep the frontiers safe or prevent usurpers from claiming power. The Tetrarchy, theoretically a better system, had shown that non-dynastic power sharing did not always work either. Quartering the Roman world between four rulers ought to have provided better government and protection, but only if all the personnel co-operated with each other and kept to the tasks that were given them. The Empire needed a strong hand to co-ordinate it, and trusted subordinates in different regions to govern and protect it. After the reign of Valens, the emperors no longer led their troops on campaigns as they had done throughout the third century and most of the fourth. By Theodosius's reign, the military leaders, the *magistri militum*, or masters of the soldiers in different parts of the Empire had risen to prominence, sometimes acting on their own initiative, and even influencing policy. These men were often of barbarian origin, good generals, resourceful and capable. They knew their own power and did not hesitate to use it, but without them the Empire would probably have collapsed or been overwhelmed in the fourth century.

Similarly large numbers of barbarians served in the Roman army, particularly the Goths. Among the Romans, service in the army had become very unattractive, to the point where recruitment was well nigh impossible. A series of laws issued by Valentinian I and Valens demonstrates the difficulties of finding enough men to fill the ranks. In 365 the Emperors adopted stern measures to round up deserters, and to punish anyone who sheltered them. Then they tried to identify the men who were eligible to serve but had somehow escaped the recruitment process. Some men preferred to become camp followers or even servants rather than join the ranks, so they were rooted out and turned into soldiers. Casting the net wider, Valentinian reduced the height qualification for soldiers. In 367 he passed laws to force men who had chopped off their fingers, or otherwise mutilated themselves, to join up and serve in some capacity or other. This presumably did not produce the desired result, since he lost patience altogether and passed another law in the following year, where the penalty for self-mutilation to avoid army service was to be burnt to death, and the masters of these evaders were also to be punished for not preventing them from chopping their thumbs off. The lack of willing recruits was countered by drafting large numbers of barbarian soldiers, who either volunteered, or were provided by the terms of a treaty. Viewed in this light, Theodosius's use of Gothic soldiers is the only reasonable alternative that he could have adopted at the time.

The civilian sphere was not much better off. Large scale impoverishment affected many parts of the Empire, cities declined, local councillors were as reluctant to serve their communities as eligible soldiers were to serve in the army, because they too were impoverished and taking a place on the town council was a very expensive business. There were some rich and influential men in civil administration, but they were in the top echelons, close to the emperors. In the first century administrative posts had been filled by freedmen, then as time went on by equestrians, and now by higher class men, who used their proximity to the emperors to advance their own careers. If the civil administrators combined with the military chiefs, they could control the emperors, or even rid themselves of unfavourable ones and set up new emperors in their place. Corruption and self-seeking was rife, and it was a brave man who would try to put an end to it.

Everyone in the Roman world had always been subordinate to the wealthiest men, and in the fourth century the great landowners became more and more powerful. Farmers were forced off their lands through war or impoverishment, and looked to the landowners for protection, becoming tied to them more closely for their livelihoods, while the landowners headed growing communities of men and became powerful enough to protect their estates and their people. Eventually they were strong enough to defy tax collectors and emperors alike. Even Constantine had not been able to prevail against them.

The late fourth century was a time of great upheaval among the tribesmen across the frontiers. It was not a new phenomenon in itself, but the scale of the movements was too vast for the Romans to stem the tide in all parts of the Empire. When Theodosius died in 395, the seeds of fragmentation, both internally and externally, had already taken root.

16

Lost World: The Transformation of the Western Empire & the Survival in the East AD 395–476

ARCADIUS AD 395–408 & HONORIUS AD 395–423

After the death of Theodosius the Empire was shared between his two sons, Arcadius, aged about eighteen or nineteen, based in Constantinople, and Honorius aged ten, based at Milan. AD 395 is traditionally the date when the eastern and western Roman Empires parted company, but the people who lived through the end of the fourth century and the beginning of the fifth would not interpret the recent events as the start of a new era. Emperors had shared power and territory on several occasions in the past. Gallienus and Valerian took charge respectively of the west and the east in the third century, Constantine created a new capital while business carried on at Rome, and more recently Valentinian and Valens had shared Imperial power in the two halves of the same Empire, without giving rise to any suggestion that the Empire had split into two separate entities. The date AD 395 only becomes significant when viewed retrospectively, because from then onwards there were two emperors, several of whom were too young to rule alone, and despite efforts to reunite the Empire, which continued sporadically until the middle of the sixth century when Justinian launched expeditions to win back territory, the Empire that had once stretched from Britain to Syria and from Africa to the Danube, was never reconstituted.

The fourth century had seen the rise of a class of military men who directed events and assisted, or in some cases dominated, the emperors. The extreme youth of succeeding emperors in both west and east ensured that this state of affairs was not reversed. The last emperor to lead his armies into battles was Valens, and the last to accompany his armies for some time thereafter was Theodosius I, who relied on his generals to win his battles. After his death, the two young Emperors Arcadius and Honorius remained in their capitals while their armies and commanders fought battle on their behalf. Increasingly, the safety of the Empire depended on the skill of the generals who led the troops. The various *magistri militum* became military dictators, and began sometimes to squabble with each other in their ambitious scramble for power. They could be assisted or opposed by the chief officials in the civil administration, who sometimes ousted the generals from their positions, or even had them executed, and then assumed control of the Empire. Neither the military commanders nor the civilian administrators held onto their power for any significant length of time. At certain periods history descends into a list of who killed whom, like who begat whom in the Bible. Alarmingly, the internal struggles often occupied the attention of commanders and administrators to the detriment of the protection of the Empire and its inhabitants.

The military commanders were mostly of barbarian origin, as were the armies that they led. The *magistri militum* were usually highly Romanized, literate and capable. Stilicho was the son of a Vandal cavalry officer in the Roman army, and a Roman mother. He had served under Theodosius, leading troops at the battle of the Frigidus. At Theodosius's death, Stilicho was the most powerful commander in the western half of the Empire. There was no proof that Theodosius, on his deathbed, had entrusted to Stilicho the care of both his sons, and therefore responsibility for the whole Empire, but Stilicho insisted that this was the case and pursued his aim diligently, opposed by officials at Constantinople, in particular Rufinus, Praetorian Prefect at the court of Arcadius. A war of words was carried on for some time as Stilicho utilized the poet Claudian to extol the exploits of the deceased Theodosius, and to revile the men of the eastern court. It was always useful to have the ear of the local press, and if newspapers and television had existed in his day, Stilicho would have appeared in the columns and on the news programmes.

When the east was threatened by the Goths, Stilicho set off with his army to check them, but Rufinus persuaded Arcadius to refuse the help but demand the return of the troops from the east which had taken part in the battle of the Frigidus. Stilicho complied, but Rufinus did not profit from his machinations, since the leader of these troops, a Goth called Gainas, murdered him. He was replaced by the eunuch Eutropius, an official in the civil administration, who made himself *magister officiorum*, the chief of the administration, and more or less ruled the eastern half of the Empire for four years. Eutropius was definitely not in favour of the Goths, or any of the other barbarians who proliferated in the army.

The so-called barbarization of the Roman army, once considered detrimental, is actually the trend that enabled the battered Roman Empire to survive as long as it did. The Roman field armies still had a part to play, and are sometimes glimpsed in action in the sources, but the rank and file were increasingly drawn from the tribesmen who clustered around the periphery of the Empire or were settled inside it. The various tribes represented a source of manpower that the Romans had always exploited, and during the later Empire the tribesmen were virtually the only source of recruits. They fought well, but as time went on and the tribes realized their power, their usefulness was partially offset by their growing demands. The Goths, for instance, had helped Theodosius to win the battle of the Frigidus against the rebels Arbogast and Eugenius, but they considered that their rewards were not commensurate with their services. At Theodosius's death, a leader had emerged among a group of Goths, called Alaric. He approached Constantinople with demands for food, money and lands, hoping for an official appointment for himself as commander of troops. It was rumoured that he had come to some arrangement with Rufinus, Praetorian Prefect under Arcadius. Whether or not there had been an agreement, it could not be honoured before Eutropius took power after the murder of Rufinus.

Achieving nothing in Constantinople, Alaric moved into Greece at the end of 395 or the beginning of 396, and sacked Athens. Stilicho arrived, brought the Goths to a standstill, and allowed them to settle in Epirus, approximating to modern Albania. Alaric was to feature largely in the history of both halves of the Empire for the next few years. He commanded a large force, and lengthy debate centres on the nature of Alaric's Gothic army. It has been argued that he led a collection of family groups, encumbered with wagons full of women and children, so only part of his group would be fighting men. Other scholars prefer to interpret Alaric's group as a military force, continually seeking employment by the Romans, sometimes successfully when it suited either the east or western governments to use him, and sometimes unsuccessfully, in which case Alaric resorted to pillage, to try to force the Romans to give him a military command. The group was occasionally settled on the land, but the men were unable to sustain themselves on a permanent basis, and if employed by the Romans the men and their commander would be supplied from official sources.

Alaric was not in command of the entire Gothic nation. There were Goths employed or settled over a large part of the Empire, with a foot in both east and west. In Thrace, and around the Black Sea and the Crimea, Gothic tribes were settled on the land. When the Goths arrived at the Danube in 376, seeking asylum, there were two groups called the Tervingi and Greuthungi. At a later time, another two groups began to be distinguished, possibly derived from the Tervingi and Greuthungi, the western groups called the Visigoths, and the eastern groups labelled the Ostrogoths. Then there were the Amal Goths, whose leader Theoderic has received the best press notices of his day. None of these labels denote homogeneous ethnic tribes or nations, or even names that the tribesmen themselves would have recognized.

The Romans did not always bother to distinguish different tribes, lumping them all together under the general heading of Scythians, whatever their original tribes had been. Eutropius disliked all of them, but he was perfectly willing to despatch the Goths on military expeditions, which backfired on him in 399. There was a rebellion in Asia Minor, and the Gothic leader Tribigild was sent to restore order, but joined the rebels instead. Eutropius then sent Gainas to deal with the rebels. Instead, Gainas and Tribigild joined forces, and then persuaded Arcadius to demote and execute Eutropius. The Goths gained nothing from the elimination of Eutropius. Encouraged by the Empress Eudoxia, the civilians of Constantinople rose up against the Goths, and killed thousands of them in the city and surrounding area. It was not wholly a racial hatred that spurred on the populace of the city, but also the fact that the Goths were Arian Christians, and the orthodox church of Constantinople did not approve. Arcadius appointed a new military leader, Fravitta, another Goth who was on friendly terms with him. Fravitta forced Gainas to flee to the Danube, where he was killed by the Huns, but Fravitta himself lasted only until 401, when he too was killed. From then on, the Goths in the east never recovered their superior position. The western tribesmen were denied access to military commands, and recruitment of Armenians and local eastern tribesmen filled the ranks of the eastern Roman army instead of Goths. This was partly necessity at first, in order to replace the Gothic troops who had been killed in the rising at Constantinople, but it became eastern policy to keep recruitment local, employing eastern tribes who would have a vested interest in protecting their territory.

In 401–402 Alaric descended on Italy. It is possible that he had been given a command by the eastern government, and then his supplies or payment had been cut off. If the eastern high command never actually deflected tribal movements towards the west, then the various emperors certainly derived some benefit from such events, and did little or nothing to stop the movements. There was no interference from the east when the Goths marched into Italy. Fortunately, Stilicho was able to stop Alaric after two battles at Pollentia and Verona in northern Italy, but he did not eradicate them. He had other uses for the Goths. The province of Illyricum was partitioned between the east and the west, and Stilicho was determined to win back the eastern section to join it to Honorius's half of the Empire. Alaric and his Goths would be able to help him to do so, so he gave a military command to Alaric in anticipation of battling with the eastern Empire.

Before he embarked on the project, another group of Goths under Radagaisus invaded in 406, so Stilicho turned aside to deal with the threat. In Liguria he defeated the Goths, recruited about 12,000 men for the army and enslaved the rest, flooding the slave market in Italy. There was great rejoicing in Rome, statues were commissioned for the hero Stilicho, and then the news arrived that a commander in Britain had been acclaimed as emperor by the troops. He was called Constantine, labelled the third of that name. He soon crossed the Channel into Gaul, which was attacked from across the Rhine by hordes of Vandals and the Germanic Suebi in 406–407. The usurper Constantine was able to hold everything together in Gaul for the next few years.

Having waited in vain for the launch of Stilicho's project to reclaim Illyricum, Alaric re-entered the scene, demanding the payment that Stilicho had promised him. Honorius and the Roman Senate were inclined to refuse, but Stilicho insisted. His credibility would have been destroyed if it was clear that he could be overruled, so Alaric received 4,000 pounds of gold, raised by the senators and people, somehow.

In 408 Stilicho's ascendancy started to wane. Arcadius died, and Honorius and Stilicho fell out over who should travel to the east to preside over the installation of the next emperor. It was decided that Honorius should attend to the west to try to root out the usurper Constantine, and Stilicho would approach the eastern court, but in the meantime, the *magister officiorum* Olympius, whose influence over Honorius prevailed, spread rumours that Stilicho intended to raise his own son to Augustus in the east. The rumours caught the imagination, and in the end Stilicho virtually gave himself up rather than start a civil war to retain power. He went back to the court of Ravenna, and was executed. Honorius had just rid himself of the one man who could perhaps have protected his Empire.

Olympius decided to take a hard line with the Goths, refusing to meet any of Alaric's demands for cash, food and confirmation of his military command. Legions were summoned from Dalmatia to fight against Alaric, but were defeated. The Praetorian Prefect Jovius was sent to negotiate with Alaric. The Goths were probably hungry by now and their demands were scaled down, this time for food supplies and permission to settle in Noricum, near the Danube frontier. Jovius refused even these terms, so Alaric seized Ostia and cut Rome's food supply, which meant he could scale up his requests to a higher level than before, and Jovius and the Senate capitulated. This time, Alaric appointed his own emperor, Priscus Attalus, who gave him the military command that he wanted. The Goths then went off to besiege Honorius in Ravenna. Attalus was supposed to have gone to Africa to win back control of the provinces, and the food supply, but he did not fulfil his part of the bargain so Alaric removed him, and marched on Rome in 410. The Goths held the city for three days, looting private houses and public buildings, but this famous sack of Rome is now played down. Its moral effects were tremendous, but there was no great destruction of buildings and no wholesale massacre of the population. The Goths were Christians, and spared all the people who took refuge in the churches of St Peter and St Paul. Alaric captured Galla Placidia, the daughter of Theodosius, and sister of Honorius. The

Goths took her with them when they moved off. The seizure of Rome provided lots of portable wealth, but did not solve the problem of feeding the Gothic army, so Alaric moved south towards the coast, intending to cross over to Sicily, but a storm wrecked his ships, and on returning to the mainland, Alaric died, in 411.

Tradition holds that in the same year that Alaric captured Rome, the province of Britain was abandoned. There is little mention of it in the ancient sources after the usurper Constantine crossed into Gaul, but Britain was probably not relinquished entirely. If Honorius did withdraw the troops as tradition states, there may not have been very many of them in the province after Constantine took units of the army to Gaul, and of those that were left, it is to be supposed that many of the soldiers remained where they were, with their families. The end of Roman Britain was not a single, sudden event. A lingering *Romanitas* survived as communities carried on as best they could, but the corporate security and supply systems disappeared, so communities shrank to self-sufficient groups. Some people sought sanctuary in Gaul, perhaps once they had realized that the Romans were not coming back to reclaim the island. How long that hope survived is not known, but the Celtic resurgence began quite rapidly, once Britain was divorced from the crumbling western Empire.

Alaric was succeeded by Athaulf, his brother-in-law, who led the Goths into Gaul in 412. For a while he joined the usurper Jovinus, who made a bid for Imperial rule on the Rhine, supported by tribesmen of the Burgundians and Visigoths. But Athaulf abandoned him in favour of the Romans. By this time, the western Empire had begun to pick up the pieces, as Flavius Constantius took command of the army and enabled the Empire to strike back. The assistance of Athaulf's Goths turned the tables and led to the surrender of Jovinus. This success ought to have raised Athaulf's chances of an alliance with the Romans, and a military command such as Alaric had held, but he overdid things. In 414 he married Gallia Placidia, kidnapped from Rome by Alaric. In due course they had a son whom they called Theodosius. As the nephew of Honorius, who had no heirs and had not named a successor, the child was a highly important figure who could be used to persuade the Romans to agree to whatever Athaulf asked for. But the Goths were to be thwarted by Constantius.

Flavius Constantius was a native of the Balkans, whose early career was with the army of the eastern Empire. He may have arrived in the west as part of the force that was sent from the east to help Theodosius in the war that ended at the battle of the Frigidus. It is presumed that he was a supporter of Stilicho, who survived the fall of the general, and became *magister militum* in 410. By the simple policy of keeping the Goths away from supplies, he eventually forced Athaulf out of Gaul and into Spain in 415. Lack of food, combined with the dismal prospect of a continuous trek to find it, led the Goths to assassinate Athaulf, but his murderers survived for only a short time, then a leader called Wallia took over.

In return for supplies from the Romans, Placidia was now released and sent to Ravenna. Her son Theodosius had died as an infant, so there was no bargaining tool for the Goths. Constantius authorized Wallia to attack the tribes who had taken over much of Spain, the Vandals and Suebi, and this Wallia did with considerable success, but he had not completed the task when Constantius recalled him and his tribesmen to Gaul, and settled them in Aquitania. It was said that Wallia had been a little too efficient for Constantius's taste. The new Gothic settlements may have been on Imperial lands, or abandoned farms, since there seems to have been no outcry from displaced Gallic landowners and farmers. The Gothic kingdom in Aquitania survived until the early sixth century.

The power of Constantius at Honorius's court steadily increased. He made sure that he was surrounded by loyal supporters and found posts for them. In 417 he married Galla Placidia, who bore him a daughter, Honoria, and a son, Valentinian. In 421, Constantius was made Augustus, to share power with Honorius. It seemed as though the western Empire might be reconstituted. Then in the same year, Constantius died. Two years later, Honorius also expired, after a thirty-year reign.

There was now the threat of civil war. Honorius had never produced children and had not appointed another successor after the demise of Constantius. To make matters even worse, he had fallen out with Placidia in the year before his death, and sent her packing to Constantinople with her son. The vacuum was soon filled, as one of the palace officials called John took over the western Empire, supported by a general called Castinus, but opposed by Bonifacius in Africa, who refused to declare for John. For about eighteen months John was able to cling onto power, but in the end he was overthrown by forces sent from the eastern Empire. Placidia and her son, the young Valentinian, were brought to Thessalonika, where Valentinian was declared Caesar, and then in the autumn of 425, mother and son arrived in Italy and Valentinian III was declared emperor in Rome. Placidia was the pre-eminent personality at the western court, but she had to work hard to remain in that position. Her main adversary was to be the general Aetius, called 'the last of the Romans'. He was the general who almost welded the western Empire back together, but was catastrophically interrupted by a seemingly unstoppable force that first threatened the Empire of the east: the Huns under their leader Attila, who first appeared in the east during the reign of Theodosius II.

If the Romans themselves thought of the Empire as a unified whole, modern historians usually treat the east and the west as separate entities from the early fifth century. The chronological approach to the history of both halves of the Empire becomes more difficult as the reigns of the emperors do not coincide, and there are only rare instances of mutual co-operation between the two Empires. It is significant that during the period from 408 to 491, there were only five emperors in the east, two of them sharing power for a year, while in the west there were sixteen, some of them reigning for only a few weeks. The east was not immune from attempted usurpations, but the emperors managed to overcome the usurpers and cling onto power. Their armies were recruited from the tribes within the eastern Empire or on its immediate periphery, and attacks from the northern barbarians were fewer than those in the western Empire. The cohesion of the eastern Empire, where no territory was ceded or taken over permanently except by agreement, meant that the eastern emperors did not lose the revenues and taxes that paid their armies. From the early fifth century, history takes a different course in the east and west.

THE EASTERN EMPIRE FROM THEODOSIUS TO ZENO AD 408–491
THEODOSIUS II, EMPEROR OF THE EAST, AD 408–450

When Arcadius died in 408, he was succeeded without opposition by his eight-year-old son Theodosius. Fortunately there were good advisers for the new child emperor, one of the most important being the Praetorian Prefect Anthemius, who started by building new walls around the city of Constantinople, making it virtually impregnable. It is significant that during Theodosius's long reign, while the western Empire was more often than not fighting for its life, the officials of the eastern Empire could devote their energies to wall building and to the compilation of the laws known as the Theodosian Code, which was published in the 430s, the exact date being uncertain. The Code contains over 2,000 laws from the western and eastern halves of the Empire, dating from the reign of Constantine. The laws were collated under subject headings, and divested of unnecessary verbiage with the object of making the main points clear and unequivocal. The Theodosian Code is an invaluable source for modern historians, and formed the basis of the laws of the later barbarian kingdoms that arose in the western Empire after Roman rule declined and disappeared.

The expulsion of the Goths from Constantinople in the reign of Arcadius, and the subsequent recruitment of home-grown soldiers gave the eastern Empire an advantage that was not available to the west, since there was no internal source of troops for the western leaders to exploit, and the west was more highly pressured by the barbarians than the east. It is suggested that one of the reasons why Stilicho was determined to win back the eastern portion of Illyricum was to exploit its manpower for the army.

Compared to the troubles of the west, there was little warfare on the eastern frontiers. The eastern rulers profited from a determined policy of diplomacy with the potential enemies on their frontiers, especially with their most powerful opponents, the Persians. The eastern armies fought wars only occasionally, since the regime preferred to buy off attacks and only went to war if the schemes failed. This was made possible by another advantage that the east enjoyed, which was the preservation of its revenues. Taxes were collected, wealth accrued at Constantinople, territories were not ceded to the barbarians. In the west it was a different story, lands were lost and with them the revenues that ought to have been collected by the government, and taxes were further reduced because the farmers on devastated lands were unable to pay, and had to be given a few years' grace to recover. Although the Empire was still considered a single entity, the cracks were already visible, leading remorselessly to the transformation of the west and the survival of the east.

Two short wars with the Persians were fought, the first in 421–422, and the second after an invasion of the Roman Empire in 441–442. In each case the Romans were victorious. They were less successful against the Huns, a nomadic tribe from Mongolia. The effects of the first movements of the Huns had resulted in the displacement of the Goths *c.*370, which resulted in the great influx into the Roman Empire, and the disaster of Adrianople in 378. The Huns were brilliant horsemen, and many of them had been employed as cavalry in the Roman armies of the west. But the power of the Huns was turned against the Roman Empire when their dynamic new leader Attila emerged and succeeding in welding the tribesmen into a cohesive and destructive force, which was used to threaten the eastern Empire.

By means of annual subsidies, the court at Constantinople managed to buy off attacks, but Attila and his brother Bleda continually demanded increases. In 434 the amount was doubled to 700 pounds of gold. An agreement had been reached that, among other things, restricted the places where the Huns and the Romans could trade. This was standard procedure that had been adopted from at least the second century, but on one market day at Margus, in Moesia, the Huns disguised themselves as traders, then suddenly threw off the pretence and killed the guards and many of the Romans. They took over the city of Margus because the terrified Bishop handed it over to them, but they also managed to take the old legionary fortress of Viminacium on the Danube, and the city of Naissus (modern Nis), which they besieged and sacked. It was the city where Constantine the Great had been born, and held some symbolic significance for the Romans. This was a frightening development. Barbarians were not usually capable of besieging and taking cities. For one thing they could not remain in one place long enough before they ran out of food or started to succumb to disease, or both. For another they did not usually possess the technological skills to build and utilize siege equipment. Modern scholars have expressed extreme doubt that Attila and Bleda had been able to organize a siege train, but perhaps the technicalities do not matter. Naissus fell to them, and the fortress of Viminacium. This was a more formidable force than the Goths or the Vandals, and they had been dangerous enough. The Huns had demonstrated their potential strength and were now able to blackmail the government at Constantinople for higher payments. The agreed amount of 700 pounds of gold was tripled, reaching an annual payment of 2,100 pounds.

Probably in 445, Attila and Bleda quarrelled, for reasons unknown, and Bleda was killed. It was said that Attila had ordered his brother's murder. Still receiving subsidies from Constantinople, Attila moved into Thrace and Greece. Then in 450, two things happened: Theodosius II died, succeeded by Marcian, and Attila began to think of heading west.

Marcian AD 450–457

Theodosius's formidable sister Pulcheria chose, and married, the new Emperor Marcian. He was an experienced military officer. She claimed that he had been Theodosius's choice. Marcian took a firm stance against the Huns, taking steps to recover the Balkans, and he also stopped the annual subsidy payments. There was no retribution, since Attila veered off to find what the west had to offer. Marcian's reign brought peace and prosperity to the eastern Empire, largely due to the absence of the threat from the Huns. Finances improved, enabling Marcian to lighten the tax burden for many of his subjects.

There was some localized trouble with the Blemmyes in Egypt, and the Arabs raided Syria, but these problems were more or less endemic and were dealt with by the Imperial troops. Marcian formed a peaceful relationship with the Vandals in Africa, and he settled various tribes within the eastern Empire. A group of Ostrogoths were settled in Pannonia under the terms of an agreement whereby they contributed troops for the army.

As his successor, Marcian favoured his son-in-law Procopius Anthemius, but at his death in 457 he was succeeded by Leo I, and Anthemius had to wait for another decade before being chosen by Leo as Emperor of the west.

Leo I AD 457–474 & Leo II AD 473–474

Leo was made emperor though the machinations of the *magister militum* Aspar, an Alan, who had fought against the Vandals, the Persians and the Huns under Attila. Aspar may have hoped to achieve the predominance of the western generals who were able to control their emperors, who represented Imperial power, while in reality it was the generals who ran the show. Leo was a Dacian, and too shrewd to become the mere tool of an ambitious general. About 460, Leo recruited a bodyguard from the Isaurian tribesmen, as a counterweight to Aspar, and he married his eldest daughter to one of the foremost Isaurians, Zeno. In 467 Leo nominated Anthemius, Marcian's son-in-law, as emperor in the west, when there was an interregnum after the death of the Emperor Libius Severus in 465.

Although Marcian had come to some arrangement with the Vandals, their sea-borne raids on Italy and Greece did not cease, proving detrimental to both halves of the Empire. Leo decided to mount a naval expedition against them in 468, but it ended in complete disaster, with the Vandals as dangerous as ever. The eastern Empire unable to put together another expedition. The west was equally powerless to deal with the Vandal menace, but by a diplomatic arrangement, the western general Ricimer appointed as emperor a candidate who was related by marriage to the Vandal King Gaiseric, and therefore acceptable to them.

In the penultimate year of his reign, Leo raised his grandson, Leo II, to Augustus, and shared power with him. Leo II was the son of the Isaurian Zeno, but there was an upsurge of antipathy towards the Isaurians at Constantinople, so Leo deemed it prudent to avoid further trouble by raising his son-in-law to Augustus. In the same year, Leo tried to dominate the western Empire by sending Julius Nepos as his chosen candidate as emperor in place of the short-lived Glycerius, who was deposed. Unfortunately for Nepos, Leo died in February 474, and his chosen co-emperor, Leo II, also died in November. Nepos left Italy and returned to Constantinople.

Zeno AD 474–491

When Leo I died, Leo II made his father Zeno his partner as emperor, sharing power with him for only a few months before his own death in November 474. Zeno's reign was challenged by Gothic tribesmen and by more than one usurper. As soon as he succeeded Leo II, the Goths in Thrace, under Theoderic Strabo rebelled, and as soon as the revolt was put down, the brother-in-law of Leo I, Basiliscus, was proclaimed at Constantinople in 475. The ex-Empress Verina, the widow of Leo I and sister of Basiliscus was one of the driving forces behind the usurpation, which was at first successful. Zeno was exiled. Basiliscus and his son Marcus enjoyed a brief joint reign, but soon lost support because of their heretical religious beliefs, which enabled Zeno to re-enter Constantinople and resume power.

His next problem concerned two rival Gothic factions under Theoderic Strabo and Theoderic the Amal. Zeno was not partial to Theoderic Strabo, who had already tried to rebel, so he employed Theoderic the Amal to crush him. Tribal loyalties proved stronger, however, and the two Gothic leaders joined forces to strike against Zeno, who managed to come to an agreement with Strabo in 479. He failed to bring the Amal to heel, probably because he was distracted by the plotting of the *magister militum* Illus and Verina to raise Leontius, an Isaurian general, as Augustus. The struggle went on for the best art of four years, until Zeno's forces captured the usurpers, and executed them in 488.

Zeno's last years were more peaceful. The western Empire had already been carved up into tribal kingdoms, and Rome and Italy had been ruled since 476 by the barbarian Odoacer. Theoderic the Amal had ambitions to replace him, and it was in Zeno's interests to encourage him to descend on Italy rather than linger in the east as a potential threat to stability. Theoderic was still engaged in warfare with Odoacer when Zeno died in 491. He was succeeded by Anastasius, who rid himself of all Isaurian officials and military men, and ruled until 518. By then the eastern Roman Empire had become the Empire of the Byzantines, taking it into a different era and bridging the gap between Rome and the middle ages.

THE FRAGMENTATION OF THE WESTERN EMPIRE AD 423–476
VALENTINIAN III, EMPEROR OF THE WEST, AD 423–455

When the child-Emperor Valentinian, was proclaimed in Rome, the general Flavius Aetius was on his way to Italy at the head of 60,000 Huns in support of John, the chief of the palace staff, who was for a short time the ruler of the west. Aetius arrived too late for the final showdown, and was therefore on the wrong side with thousands of menacing troops at his back. He escaped punishment, however and gained much credit for sending the Hun army back home, and Placidia, acting as Regent for her son, helped by paying them off. From then onwards she and Aetius were rivals at the western court.

Flavius Aetius was the son of Gaudentius, who had been *magister militum per Gallias*, in command of the armies in Gaul. As a young man Aetius had been sent as a hostage to the Goths and then to the Huns, so he had gained considerable knowledge of tribal customs. His standing among the Huns is demonstrated by the fact that he could raise a large army to fight for John in the west, and then dismiss them when their services were not needed. It took Aetius ten years to ascend to the supreme position of virtual ruler of the west, but even when he had achieved this, he never tried to proclaim himself emperor. During the decade from the accession of Valentinian III until 433, he tried to restore order in the west. The provinces were much reduced and fragmented when he embarked on this task. The short-lived Emperor Constantius had begun to make some progress, but by the time

Aetius picked up where he had left off, the Visigoths who had been settled in Aquitania were beginning to agitate for home rule, and to be recognized as an independent unit. The Franks, the Almanni and Burgundians were on the Rhine and in the Alps, or beyond the frontiers with a foothold in Roman territory. In Spain, Wallia the Gothic leader had suppressed but not eradicated the tribes who had settled there, and the Suebi were still in possession of part of the country. The Vandals held the two Mauretanian provinces and part of Numidia, but in Africa, the commander Bonifacius was holding the province. Unfortunately Bonifacius was no friend of Aetius, being a firm adherent of Placidia.

Aetius was a capable and energetic commander, fighting many battles and travelling long distances all over the west, but the sources are not complete and the chronology of his exploits is confused. Some of his battles may be duplicated in the accounts of his first years as commander, for instance he is said to have driven the Goths, by now better described as the Visigoths, from Arles on two occasions, which may be a repetition of the same story. He fought the Franks on the Rhine, probably in 427–428, and the Juthungi north of the Alps, then dealt with the rebels in Noricum, preserving the western Empire from further encroachments by the tribes.

In 432 Placidia and Bonifacius decided that it was time to dispense with Aetius's services. Bonifacius sailed to Italy, and defeated Aetius in battle, but died later of his wounds. For some months Aetius had to lie low and retired to his estates, but he re-emerged stronger than ever in 433 or 434, backed by an army of Huns. He restored the situation in Africa, but had to confirm the Vandal possession of Mauretania and part of Numidia. On the Rhine, Aetius attacked the Burgundians and may have restored the frontier, and he cleared Gaul of the troublesome Bagaudae. The problem is that no one knows precisely who the Bagaudae were. The common rendition of the term is bandits, but this perhaps only applies to hard-pressed Gallic peasants of the late third century, when the Bagaudae are first noted. By Aetius's day the Bagaudae may have gathered together and formed a tribe of sorts, or the term may have been applied to any disruptive group, perhaps disguising a mixed group of tribesmen. Whatever they were, Aetius seems to have stopped them in their tracks in 439, earning the gratitude of the Gauls, especially the landowners.

The year of triumph was marred by bad news from the African provinces. The Visigoths under their vigorous leader Gaiseric seized Carthage, and acquired a fleet. The history of the Republic was about to be repeated, since any people who controlled Carthage and the sea could cripple Rome. This time, though, the Romans were not in the same state of military and political health as they were when they went to war with the Carthaginians. Nonetheless, Africa had to be recovered and the Vandals had to be stopped, so Aetius made a treaty with the Visigoths in order to turn aside to deal with the Vandals. The treaty may have re-affirmed the terms arranged with Constantius in 418, but it gave the Visigoths what they wanted, independence and recognition as a separate state in part of Gaul, which was now lost to the Romans. It was a necessary expedient to enable Valentinian III and Aetius to begin a recruitment campaign to assemble an army to take to Africa. Troops were also sent from the eastern Empire, and the combined army began to move into Sicily, ready for jumping off into Africa.

The campaign to restore Africa never took place, most likely because the Huns under Attila had started to put pressure on the eastern Empire. The Persians had invaded and been repulsed, but now the eastern troops destined for Africa were needed at home. With only the army of the west, Aetius could not conduct a campaign in Africa and defend the northern frontiers at the same time. The African project fell through and a treaty was made with the Vandals, recognizing them in possession of Africa, including Carthage. Like the Carthaginians centuries before, the Vandals also controlled Lilybaeum in Sicily. The Romans took back the two Mauretanias and part, but not all, of Numidia. Gaiseric was recognized as a friendly king and ally of Rome (*Rex socius et amicus*), and his son Huneric was betrothed to Eudocia, one of the daughters of Valentinian III. Now both the Visigoths in Gaul and the Vandals in Africa were independent of Rome, free to conduct their own affairs, form their own policies and alliances, and collect their own revenues, which were henceforth denied to the western Roman Empire.

For the next few years it is not known where Aetius operated. Opinion differs as to the date of the treaty with Gaiseric and the Vandals, some authors placing it in 442 and others two years later. Aetius reappears in 450–451, when Attila and the Huns moved into Gaul, probably reinforced by contingents from the peoples they had conquered and absorbed on their expeditions. The Visigoths of Gaul, under their King Theoderic, fought for the Romans, with a vested interest in protecting their own territory from the Huns. Aetius had assembled several other allies in his large army, and in June 451 he drove Attila away from Orleans. He then caught them near Troyes, in a battle variously labelled the Catalaunian Plains or the Mauriac fields. The site is not precisely known. It was a resounding victory for Aetius, but the Visigothic leader Theoderic was killed.

Attila was not accustomed to defeats, and it is said that he even contemplated suicide, but he pulled himself together and went on to attack Italy. Aetius was unable to stop him. One by one the cities of northern Italy fell and suffered accordingly, but for some reason Attila did not march on Rome. The legend grew up that the Pope Leo had an interview with him and dissuaded him from doing so, which tale should be taken with more than a pinch of salt. Fortunately for Rome and the western Empire, in

453 Attila married a new wife, had an energetic nuptial celebration and died in the night from a massive nose bleed. The story goes that he was buried in the bed of a river which was diverted while he was interred and then allowed to flow back over him. Thus Attila, the Scourge of God, came to an end, and his vast Hunnic Empire quickly began to fall apart. Modern scholars have pointed out the incredible qualities of the man, his skill in battle, his genius in leadership, his cunning, his knowledge of the psychology of his own men and his enemies. All this may be true, but these sterling qualities may not have been the first things that struck the minds of the inhabitants of the cities that he took and destroyed. With sublime indifference Attila and his Huns destroyed lives and livelihoods, carried off portable wealth from all sources that he could terrify into submission, and produced nothing permanent from it, except a trail of destruction and a lasting fame or infamy.

Aetius did not long survive Attila. Valentinian III executed him in 454. Aetius had been trying to arrange a marriage for his son, to connect his family with that of Valentinian, and so secure his own position in the western Empire. If the Huns had still been at large, threatening Italy or the northern frontiers, Aetius might have survived a little longer, but there was no pressing need for his services now. He had done his job too well, and he had enemies at court, who persuaded Valentinian that he could now take full control of the western Empire without the general. In September 454 the Emperor himself, assisted by the head of his household staff, attended a meeting with Aetius to discuss the finances, and killed him. Then many of Aetius's supporters were killed, but Valentinian had reckoned without the soldiers of the Guard, who resented the death of the general. Two of them set upon the Emperor in March 455 when he went off on horseback to practise archery on the Campus Martius in Rome.

PETRONIUS MAXIMUS AD 455

The man behind the assassination was probably Petronius Maximus, who wanted to be emperor. He got his wish the next day, was proclaimed emperor, and set about shoring up his regime. He made a good start by marrying Valentinian's widow Eudoxia, and sent an ambassador, a Gallic nobleman called Eparchius Avitus, to the Visigoths in Gaul to solicit their support, or at least their non-aggression. Maximus made the mistake of arranging the marriage of his own son Palladius to Eudocia, the daughter of Valentinian and Eudoxia. This would break the arrangement made with the Vandals, since she had been betrothed to Huneric, the son of Gaiseric. Using this as a reasonable excuse, Gaiseric invaded Italy and headed for Rome. Maximus did not stand and fight, but found a horse and tried to leave the city, but was killed before he could do so. Rome was given up to Gaiseric and the Vandals, and unlike Alaric, they made a proper job of sacking the city. When they left, they took Eudoxia and her two daughters back to Carthage, with several other prisoners.

Avitus AD 455–456

The western Empire was now leaderless for a short time, until Avitus, who had been sent to the Visigoths on behalf of Maximus, made a bid for the throne, and immediately negotiated with the eastern Empire. The army accepted Avitus, conscious of the fact that he could call upon Theoderic II, King of the Visigoths, for assistance if he was challenged. Avitus was declared emperor at Arles. Waiting in the wings was an army officer called Ricimer, and his comrade in arms Majorian, who both kept a low profile as long as Avitus could count on the support of the Visigoths. In 456, operating under Avitus, Ricimer won a victory over the Vandals at Agrigentum and destroyed their fleet. He was now on his way to power. He and Majorian plotted to overthrow Avitus, and finally confronted him and his troops at Placentia, where they won a decisive victory. They spared Avitus's life and made him a bishop, but he died soon afterwards. While Ricimer held power in the west, several men died at tremendously opportune moments, giving rise to the suspicion that the deaths were not always from natural causes.

Majorian AD 457–461

The Emperor of the east, Leo I, seems to have recognized and condoned Ricimer's command, or at least no protests have been recorded from the eastern court. Nor did Leo insist on raising an Augustus of his choice, so Ricimer was free to appoint his comrade Majorian, perhaps because he thought that he would be able to control him. As a barbarian, Ricimer preferred not to claim the throne for himself. He was the grandson of Wallia, leader of the Goths after Athaulf and Alaric.

It was said that Eudoxia would have chosen Majorian, but before she could do so Petronius Maximus pre-empted her. If she endorsed the choice, it may have encouraged acceptance of Majorian, who was the first emperor who bore no relation to the Theodosian family. He was also the first emperor since Theodosius I to take the field with an army. He operated against the Visigoths in Gaul and the Vandals in Africa, reversing for a short time the usual pattern where the emperor remained in the palace and the barbarian general directed the expeditions. This time, Ricimer remained in Italy while Majorian fought the battles. It showed that the new Emperor was not willing to be the malleable tool of Ricimer, and so when he returned from his campaigns in August 461, Ricimer met him and suggested very strongly that he should abdicate. Majorian complied, dying soon afterwards, of dysentery, or so Ricimer claimed.

LIBIUS SEVERUS AD 461–465

Some three months passed without an Augustus in the west, with Ricimer in undoubted command. Then in an attempt to reconcile the Senate and the Italian aristocracy, Libius Severus was made emperor, elected by the senators in 461. For four years the partnership worked, though it was clear that it was Ricimer who was directing affairs. During this period, Ricimer tried to negotiate with Gaiseric and the Vandals in Africa, hoping to put an end to the raids on Sicily, but the negotiations came to nothing. The eastern emperor, Leo I, was more successful in 462. Gaiseric had arranged the marriage between his son Huneric and Eudocia, but had kept Valentinian's widow Eudoxia and their younger daughter Placidia in Carthage. Now he agreed to release them both and return them to Constantinople. Placidia was married to Anicius Olybrius, who was to play a small part in the crumbling government of the western Empire a few years later.

ANTHEMIUS AD 467–472

When Libius Severus died in 465, no emperor was appointed for two years until Leo I chose Anthemius, the son of the Praetorian Prefect under Theodosius II who had refortified Constantinople. Anthemius was also the son-in-law of the eastern Emperor Marcian. His credentials were good, his reputation was sound, and he was a capable general, which made him acceptable to most of the inhabitants in the west except Ricimer, who had no desire to operate as a subordinate of a capable Roman general turned emperor. But he had little choice, since he could not control the Vandals without help, so acceptance of Leo's candidate was inevitable. To seal the bargain, Ricimer married Anthemius's daughter Alypia.

Ricimer was hemmed in and his independence curbed, exactly as Leo had planned. To make matters worse, Anthemius brought with him his own general, Marcellinus, who had been a supporter of Aetius, and Ricimer's enemy. Fortunately for Ricimer, Marcellinus was murdered in 468, by officers of the army scheduled to fight the Vandals. It was very timely for Ricimer, but Anthemius was steadily divesting him of his barbarian supporters and replacing them with Roman appointees to various posts. Ricimer was facing annihilation. Then the Vandals started to raid Sicily and the coasts of Italy, and Ricimer developed a plan that would perhaps enable him to kill two birds with one stone. He needed to come to an understanding with the Vandals, and he needed to be rid of Anthemius. He raised a new emperor in opposition to Anthemius, who would bridge the gap between the house of Theodosius and the Vandals. This was Anicius Olybrius, married to Placidia, and therefore the son-in-law of the deceased Valentinian III, but also the brother-in-law of the Vandal Prince Huneric, who was married to Placidia's sister Eudocia. Although Olybrius was by no means clamouring for the role, Gaiseric had been agitating for the appointment for some time, and now it suited Ricimer's purpose as well.

Anthemius started to lose support in Italy, save for the few who remained in Rome with him when Ricimer besieged the city in 472. The turning point came when the relief army sent to rescue Anthemius was defeated and the survivors joined Ricimer. Anthemius tried to escape disguised as a beggar, but was discovered and killed, in July 472. Ricimer and Olybrius were now unchallenged – that is, for another month. In August, Ricimer died of a haemorrhage, and two or three months later, Olybrius expired.

GLYCERIUS AD 473–474, NEPOS AD 474–475 & ROMULUS AUGUSTULUS AD 475–476

There was another interregnum after the death of Olybrius until March 473. In his few weeks as ruler, Olybrius had replaced Ricimer with Gundobad, the son of the chief of the Burgundians in Gaul, with whom Ricimer had always been on very good terms. Gundobad was also the nephew of Ricimer, so the appointment would appease Ricimer's supporters. Gundobad's only contribution was to raise as Augustus his candidate Glycerius, and then he returned to the Burgundians as their king, shedding all his Roman titles. The eastern court was not prepared to recognize Glycerius. Leo I despatched Julius Nepos to take over in the west. Glycerius was deposed and sent to Salona as bishop. Presumably he was allowed to survive because he represented no threat and had no supporters who would raise rebellion on his behalf.

Julius Nepos may have survived if he had been able to reconcile the barbarian troops to his rule, but he more or less ignored them. In 475 he chose as his military commander Orestes, who was a Roman, but who had experience of the barbarians, having worked for some time with Attila as his secretary. It was not a good choice, since Orestes quickly raised revolt and expelled Nepos, who fled, but lingered in the vain hope that the new eastern Emperor Zeno would reinstate him. Orestes elevated his young son Romulus to the rank of Augustus, soon rendered as Augustulus, little Augustus, by the people.

Orestes arranged a treaty with Gaiseric and the Vandals to ensure peace and quiet from that quarter, but at home he faced the age old problem of troops demanding settlement on the land. In this case it was the Germanic soldiers who wanted to settle in Italy, to which Orestes and the Senate were opposed. Their policy was short-sighted. Barbarians had been settled on Roman territory almost everywhere else, and the western government was not in any position to argue, especially when the troops suddenly found a leader who had been in Anthemius's bodyguard and then gone over to Ricimer. This was Odoacer, a Roman citizen of barbarian origin, who was declared king of the tribal troops that he led, not a homogeneous group, but a collection of different tribesmen united by a common cause. Odoacer defeated Orestes and killed him, and then deposed the young Romulus, who was packed off to a villa and allowed to live out his life in Italy.

ODOACER AD 476–493

The year 476 as an end date for the western Roman Empire is as artificial as the dates of many other turning points in the history of Rome, but it does mark the transition from Roman Imperial rule to rule by the kings of various tribes. Long before Odoacer took control of Italy, other parts of the Empire had been ceded to tribal rulers. Much of Gaul was already divorced from Roman control by the early fifth century. Constantius settled Wallia and the Visigoths in Aquitania, which was not an unusual procedure in the Roman Empire, but soon after Theoderic II was recognized as an independent ruler, with jurisdiction over the Romans as well as his own people. After he was murdered by his brother Euric in 466 or 467, the Visigoths began to extend their control. By 475 Euric controlled the Auvergne and was eventually recognized as ruler of Gaul between the Atlantic seaboard, the Rhône, the Loire and the Pyrenees. Shortly afterwards the Visigoths took over part of Spain. Under Ricimer, the Burgundians were settled in Gaul.

In 476, the same year that Odoacer took over control of Rome and Italy, the eastern Emperor Zeno was forced to acknowledge the Vandal kingdom of Africa, and their possession of Corsica, Sardinia and the Balearic Islands. Africa had been lost to the Romans since the treaty that Aetius made with the Vandals in the 440s, but there had always been the slight possibility that the provinces could be regained. After 476 the western Empire was too fragmented to mount a corporate campaign against the Vandals, and even the well-organized cohesive eastern Empire could not hope to extend control over Africa. In the sixth century the Byzantine Emperor Justinian made the attempt to recover the lost territories of the west, but failed. Spain was lost to the Romans when the Vandals and the Suebi established themselves there, but the Vandals were defeated by the Visigoths under Wallia, and turned to Africa. By the sixth century the Visigoths had established complete control over the former Hispanic provinces.

Odoacer maintained control of Italy for nearly twenty years. He respected the senators of Rome, appointing a consul each year from among the

Romans, and reserving civilian offices for them. He was sensitive enough to refuse to call himself king on his coinage. Military appointments were given to the barbarian soldiers, but this was by now quite customary. The eastern Emperor Zeno did not formally recognize him, and was deliberately vague in dealing with him, waiting for an opportunity to attempt to oust him. It came in 487–488 when he encouraged the Germanic Rugii to invade Italy. Odoacer campaigned against them, but realized that he did not have the military capacity to hold the Danube frontier, and abandoned Noricum, bringing the population to Italy to resettle them. The following year, Zeno tried again, using the Amal Goths, or Ostrogoths, under their King Theoderic to mount another invasion. The war dragged on, until Odoacer died in 493. Zeno had promised Theoderic that he could take Odoacer's place, but refused to recognize him as independent ruler of Italy. Theoderic called himself king without waiting for approval from Constantinople, but he received recognition of a sort from Anastasius, who succeeded Zeno in 491. There was no clear definition of Theoderic's status, and no acknowledgement that he was subordinate to the eastern emperor. It was really just an acceptance of the status quo, while in denial about the split between the two Empires.

The Roman Empire of the east survived and evolved for many more centuries. Its geographical cohesion was not fragmented as was that of the west, enabling the eastern emperors to maintain control of their revenues and taxes, so in the fifth century the east was much wealthier than the west. The barbarian assaults that brought the west to its knees were not experienced to the same degree in the east, and whenever there were threats, more often than not the assailants veered, or were turned, towards the west, where the eastern emperors did not always send military aid. The policy of recruiting soldiers from local tribes enabled the government of Constantinople to create an army that had a vested interest in defending its own territory, whereas the western rulers and military commanders were forced to take whatever they could get, from warriors who were affiliated to the tribes who threatened the Empire. The wonder is that these tribesmen fought so well for the Romans.

In reality, although they caused massive devastation, the various tribes such as the Franks, the Alamanni, the Goths and the Burgundians, who established their kingdoms in the provinces of the western Empire, were not sworn enemies of Rome, but wanted to be part of the Empire and be like the Romans. Their influx did not always entail displacement of the existing population, and thousands of them were officially settled on Roman territory. When they took over lands by force, it may have been a different matter. When Gaiseric and his Vandals took over Africa, he redistributed the land to his own followers, and Roman refugees found their way to Italy, but in Gaul there seems to have been plenty of land to go around. At least one barbarian who had taken over an estate in Gaul went to find the owner so that he could pay for it. Many of the Gallic landowners came to terms with the barbarians in their midst. There was little else they could do, since the army could not always help them, so fighting the tribesmen was no longer an option. When Sidonius Apollinaris, Bishop of Clermont-Ferrand, encouraged the populace to defend their city and homes, the result was a disaster, but Sidonius's letters show how Roman life continued in fifth-century Gaul, with races in the circus, games and shows. When their kingdom was established, the Visigoths used the laws of Rome to formulate their own codes, and in Italy under the Ostrogoths, Latin and Greek literature was preserved, administration continued as it had under the Romans, coins were issued, trading continued, and peace and prosperity reigned until the sixth century.

Looking back over the centuries, it can be seen that Rome and the western Empire never really fell, but were transformed slowly into the kingdoms of medieval Europe, underpinned by Roman law, administrative systems and language. It is, however, undeniable that there were many casualties during the upheavals of the fourth and fifth centuries, and it is questionable whether the survivors of the various cataclysms were able to take the long-term view, comforted by the fact that what was happening to them was simply a transformation.

Glossary

Aedile: city magistrate originally responsible for supervision of the *aedes*, or the temples of the plebs. During the Republic there were two aediles subordinate to the tribunes of the plebs, and later two more were elected from the patricians (*aediles curules*). In the Empire the main duties of the aediles were care of the city, including keeping the streets clean, keeping public order, attending to the water supply and markets. They were also in charge of the public games (*ludi*) until Augustus transferred this duty to the praetors. All the municipalities of the Empire employed elected aediles fulfilling the same purposes as they did in Rome.

Aerarium militar: military treasury set up by Augustus in AD 6 to provide pensions for veterans.

Ala milliaria: auxiliary cavalry unit of *c.* 1,000 men.

Ala quingenaria: auxiliary cavalry unit of *c.* 500 men.

Annona militaris: provisions for the army; in the later Empire the Praetorian Prefects were placed in charge of the supplies for the troops.

As: lowest denomination Roman coin, made of bronze.

Atrium: the central reception area of a Roman house, with a square or oblong opening in the roof to let in light. Rain water was caught in a sunken area in the floor, called the *impluvium*, corresponding to the roof opening.

Auctoritas: a measure of the reputation and social and political standing of Roman senators and politicians. The literal translation 'authority' does not convey its true meaning. *Auctoritas* could be earned and increased by political or military achievements and lost after disgraceful conduct.

Aureus: Roman gold coin, worth twenty-five *denarii*.

Auxilia: literally 'help troops', the term used by the Romans to describe the units recruited from non-Romans, organized as *alae* and *cohortes* during the Empire.

Caldarium: the hot room of a bath house.

Canabae: the civilian settlement outside a legionary fortress; see also *vicus*.

Capitatio: a poll-tax, paid in cash.

Capitum: fodder; in the later Empire payments to the soldiers were made partly in kind. *Capitum* and *annona* were the terms used for food for the horses and the men.

Cataphractarii: heavy-armoured cavalry, perhaps armed with lance and shield.

Centuria: a century, or a division of a cohort, nominally of 100 men, but in practice of 80 men, from the late Republic and throughout the Empire; also a voting unit of the people of Rome.

Centurion: commander of a century, or *centuria*.

Clibanarii: slang term for heavy-armoured cavalry, derived from *clibanus*, meaning oven. It is not certain whether these troops were the same as *cataphractarii* or whether they were armed and fought in a different way.

Cohors: a cohort, denoting two types of unit, the first a division of a legion containing six centuries, and the second denoting an auxiliary infantry unit, either 500 or 1,000 strong.

Cohors equitatae: part-mounted auxiliary unit.

Colonus: tenant of a landowner.

Comitatenses: collective name for the units of the late Roman mobile field army, comprising cavalry and infantry.

Comes: the entourage of an emperor consisted of his friends (*comites*) on an unofficial basis at first, but Constantine gave the title *Comes*, usually translated as Count, to his military commanders and provincial governors. There was originally no connotation of rank in the title, but with the passage of time three grades were established, called *ordinis primi*, *secundi*, and *terti*.

Comitatus: derived from *comes*, initially describing the entourage of the emperor; by the fourth century *comitatus* denoted the field army.

Consul: senior magistrates of the Republic, elected annually in pairs, responsible for civil duties and command of the armies. During the Empire the consuls were still elected annually, but with reduced military responsibilities and subordinate to the emperor.

Consul ordinarius: during the Empire there were often more than two consuls in the year. The *ordinarii* were the officially elected consuls, who might hold office for a month or two, giving way to the *consules suffecti*. The *ordinarii* were the eponymous consuls, giving their name to the year.

Consul suffectus: the suffect consuls were those who held office after the *ordinarii*, gaining experience and rank before going on to other appointments.

Constitutio Antoniniana: act passed by Caracalla in AD 212, making all freeborn inhabitants of the Empire Roman citizens.

Contubernium: tent party or the soldiers sharing one barrack block, normally eight men.

Corrector: (plural *correctores*) Roman officials with the title *corrector* were appointed from the reign of Trajan, originally for the purpose of attending to the financial affairs of free cities which did not come under the jurisdiction of the provincial governors. *Correctores* held military and civil powers and their responsibilities, which eventually extended to any of the cities in a province if the emperor wished to investigate their affairs.

Curiales:members of the city councils.

Denarius: Roman silver coin worth four *sestertii*.

Diocese: administrative grouping of several provinces, instituted by Diocletian.

Dromedarius: camel rider.

Dux: (plural *duces*) literally, leader; the term used for equestrian military officers in command of troops in the frontier regions, usually with the title *dux limitis,* accompanied by an explanation of where they operated, such as *dux limitis per Africam*. Their commands sometimes covered more than one province. *Duces* were raised to senatorial status by Valentinian I.

Equites legionis: cavalry of a legion, initially thought to number 120 men, but increased by the Emperor Gallienus to over 700 men.

Foederati: literally those who are allied in war, derived from *foedus*, a treaty, and denoting troops raised according to the terms of a treaty. To be distinguished from the sixth century *foederati*, which were regular troops.

Imperium: the early kings of Rome were holders of *imperium*, comprising command of the armies and exercise of legal power. During the Republic, this power passed to the higher magistrates, the annually elected consuls and the praetors, and the dictators for their six month term of office. It was extended to the proconsuls and propraetors as commanders and later governors of the provinces. In Imperial times, only the emperors held *imperium*, which was delegated to his appointed commanders and governors.

Iugum: a unit of land for tax purposes, not always a standard measure since the type of land and the crops grown were taken into consideration by the assessors.

legion: the term *legio* originally meant the choosing, or the levy, and was eventually applied to the main unit of the Roman army. Around 5,000 strong, the legion was an infantry unit, but also contained some cavalry. Legions of the late Empire were smaller, newly raised units being only about 1,000 strong.

Limes: (plural *limites*) frontier(s).

Magister equitum: master of horse; in the Republic this title was given to the second in command of a dictator; in the late Roman army it was an important military post in command of the cavalry units.

Magister militum: master of the soldiers; like the *Dux/Duces* the various *magistri militum* could be in command of the troops of a province or a region, but the title sometimes denotes a supreme commander, otherwise expressed as *magister utruisque militiae*.

Magister officiorum: late Roman head of the secretarial offices.

Magister peditum: master of the infantry of the late Roman army.

Maniple: literally 'a handful', a term denoting a unit of the Republican army consisting of two centuries.

Peristyle: the courtyard of Roman house, usually planted as a garden, surrounded by a colonnade.

Pilum: missile weapon used by legionaries, consisting of a long thin metal shank with a pyramidal tip, attached to a wooden shaft. There were various different sizes and types of *pila*.

Praefectus: prefect, a title given to several different civilian officials and military officers. The summit of an equestrian career was to be appointed to one of the four great prefectures, *Praefectus Annonae* (the Prefect of the *annona*, in charge of military supplies), *Praefectus Vigilum* (the Prefect of the *Vigiles*, the fire brigade in Rome), the Praetorian Prefect, or the Prefect of Egypt.

Praeses: (plural *praesides*) provincial governor of equestrian rank, common from Severan times onwards.

Praetor: the praetorship had a long history. Originally the praetors were the chief magistrates in early Republican Rome, but were superceded by the consuls. When the consuls were absent the praetor was in charge of the courts, acted as president of the Senate, and had the right to command armies.

Proconsul: as the Romans extended their power over wider territories, more magistrates were required to govern the provinces or command armies in wars, so the powers of the consuls could be bestowed upon men who had held a magistracy, or in emergencies upon private individuals for an appointed time.

Protectores: a title used by Gallienus for his military entourage, not simply a bodyguard, but perhaps the foundation of a staff college formed from officers loyal to the emperor.

Quaestor: originally the lowest ranking magistrates of the Republic appointed to assist the consuls in financial matters. The office was held by young men at the start of their career, before they had entered the Senate. As the Empire expanded more quaestors were created to deal with provincial administration. Quaestors acted as deputies to consular governors, and could hold commands in the army. Sometimes in modern versions of ancient works, quaestor is translated in the military context as quartermaster, which is not strictly accurate.

Schola: late Roman cavalry guard unit; *scholae palatinae* were the emperor's guard.

Sestertius: Roman silver coin; four *sestertii* equalled one *denarius*.

Stipendium: military pay, also applied to a period of service.

Triclinium: dining room in a Roman house, with three couches arranged around the central space where the food would be served.

Triumph: during the Republic, a triumph was granted by the Senate to victorious generals, who valued this opportunity to show off their captives and the spoils of war by processing along the Via Sacra in Rome, to the Temple of Jupiter. The *triumphator* rode in a chariot with his face painted red, and was supposed to approach the temple on his knees to dedicate the spoils, with a slave at his side constantly reminding him that he was mortal. Augustus recognized the inflammatory nature of the triumph and took steps to limit it to members of the Imperial family. Other generals were denied the procession, and were granted *ornamenta triumphalia*, triumphal insignia, instead of the procession through the streets of Rome.

Vicarius: governor of a diocese, answerable to the Praetorian Prefects.

Vicus: a term that could mean an area within a town, or a rural village, but in the military context it refers to the civilian settlement outside a Roman auxiliary fort; see also *canabae*.

Vigiles: the fire brigade of the city of Rome, organized in military fashion by Augustus to cover the fourteen regions, or districts, of the city of Rome.

Select Bibliography for Further Reading

Books about the Romans are, as it were, legion, with new books appearing all the time. With the new publications and all the past to catch up on, reading about the Romans could become a full-time occupation. The following list represents only a small percentage of what is available, but the reading lists in each book will cover much of the rest.

ANCIENT SOURCES

The surviving sources for the history of the Roman Empire are vast, but fragmentary and uneven. For certain periods such as the foundation of Rome, the rule of the kings and the development of the Republic, and the later Roman Empire of the third century, the sources are frustratingly inadequate. The full panoply of sources from ancient times includes not only literature, but art and architecture, Greek and Latin inscriptions and archaeological evidence. Books on these topics are listed below, while this section includes some of the more accessible translations of ancient works.

A good place to start is with the *Loeb Classical Library*, published by Harvard University Press, with the Latin or Greek text on one page and the English translation on the opposite page, complete with explanatory notes and indexes. This is a brief selection of the more important works for Roman history:

Ammianus Marcellinus: (no title given except the author's name) 3 volumes. Ammianus was a military commander during the second half of the fourth century AD, and wrote a history of his own turbulent times, using other historical sources and his accounts of events, including the expeditions under the Emperor Julian, which he had witnessed for himself.

Appian: *Roman History*. 4 volumes, covering the Civil Wars between Marius and Sulla, Caesar and Pompey, Octavian and Antony.

Caesar: *The Gallic War, the Civil Wars,* and *The Alexandrian, African and Spanish Wars.* 3 volumes, covering most of Caesar's career, as presented by Caesar himself.

Cicero: *Letters to Atticus* and *Letters to his Friends*. 8 volumes, written during the lives of Pompey the Great, Julius Caesar, Octavian and Mark Antony, and providing a detailed and very human account of the political machinations of all the leading men of the times.

Dio Cassius: *Roman History*. 9 volumes. Written at the beginning of the third century, Dio's work covers the period from the earliest years until AD 229, but some of the original books are lost and only some of the gaps can be filled from references in later works.

Livy: (Titus Livius) *History of Rome*. 14 volumes. Livy worked in the reign of Augustus and wrote a history of Rome from its foundation to 9 BC, in142 books, of which only 35 are extant.

Polybius: *Histories*. 6 volumes. Covers the rise of Rome to the later second century BC and is of particular importance for the organization of the Republican army.

Scriptores Historiae Augustae: supposedly written by different authors, but now referred to more commonly as the *Historia Augusta* since it has been shown that there was only one author, picking up where Suetonius (see next entry) left off with biographies of the emperors of the second and third centuries. A good sensationalist read, but use with caution.

Suetonius: *The Lives of the Caesars*. 2 volumes. Suetonius worked in the reign of Hadrian, and wrote biographies of the emperors from Augustus to Domitian.

Tacitus: *Agricola*. 1 volume. Writing in the later first century AD, Tacitus wrote about the exploits in Roman Britain of his father-in-law, the governor Gnaeus Julius Agricola, during the reigns of Vespasian, Titus and Domitian.

Tacitus: *Histories* and *Annals*. 4 volumes. Covers the period from the death of Augustus in AD 14 to the assassination of Domitian in AD 96.

The works of some of these authors are available in English, with introductions, notes, maps and indexes, published in paperback by Penguin Books, of which this is a small selection:

Ammianus Marcellinus: *The Later Roman Empire*, trans W. Hamilton, 1986.

Cicero: *Selected Letters*, trans. D.R. Shackleton Bailey, 1986

Livy: *The Early History of Rome*, trans. Aubrey de Selincourt, 1960.
  Rome and Italy, trans. Betty Radice, 1982.
  The War with Hannibal, trans. Aubrey de Selincourt, 1965.
  Rome and the Mediterranean, trans. Henry Bettenson, 1976.

Pliny: *Letters of the Younger Pliny*, trans. Betty Radice, 1974.

Tacitus: *The Annals of Imperial Rome*, trans. Michael Grant, 1956, revised 1996.

Histories, forthcoming, June 2009.

REFERENCE BOOKS

Oxford Classical Dictionary eds. S. Hornblower and A. Spawforth, Oxford: 3rd ed. 1993. An invaluable reference tool, with alphabetical entries on people, places and topics in Greek and Roman history, each entry accompanied by lists for further reading.

Cambridge Ancient History: several volumes covering Roman history from the earliest times to the later Empire, with chapters written by specialist scholars, and brimming with notes explaining where the information comes from. The price tags for each volume indicate the vast amount of work involved.

Routledge History of the Ancient World: an up to date (1990s to *c*.2004) series devoted to the history of Greece and Rome, available in affordable paperback volumes, bristling with notes to explain details and to give the sources for the information. Specifically, in chronological order for Roman history:

T. Cornell, *The Beginnings of Rome; Italy and the Rome from the Bronze Age to the Punic Wars*, 1995.

M. Goodman, *The Roman World 44 BC–AD 180*, 1997.

D.S. Potter, *The Roman Empire at Bay AD 180–395*, 2004.

A. Cameron, *The Mediterranean World in Late Antiquity AD 395–600*, 1993.

Examples of text-book style works for students, with analyses of events and trends, references to ancient literature, and bibliographies, are the following:

M. Boatwright (et al.), *The Romans from Village to Empire*, Oxford, 2004.

M. Leglay (et al.), *A History of Rome*, Blackwell: 3rd ed. 2005.

ATLASES

T. Cornell and J. Matthews, *Atlas of the Roman World*, Phaidon, 1982. Coloured maps of the provinces with the main cities, towns and fortresses, but this book is much more than just a series of maps, containing a historical survey from the earliest times to the sixth century AD, and it is fully illustrated throughout.

C. Scarre, *The Penguin Historical Atlas of Ancient Rome*, Viking Press and Penguin, 1995. This book follows the development of Rome from the beginning to the sixth century, well illustrated, with sections highlighting certain topics, all supported by the coloured maps.

STUDIES OF SPECIFIC PERIODS & RULERS

This list is potentially endless, so here are just a few titles, in chronological order from Republic to Late Empire.

P. Matyszak, *Chronicle of the Roman Republic: the rulers of ancient Rome from Romulus to Augustus*, Thames and Hudson, 1993. A good read as well as a popular reference tool. It concentrates on the various personalities as the title suggests, with timelines, background history and potted biographies of each personality, well illustrated.

R. Syme, *The Roman Revolution*, Oxford University Press, 1936. Very scholarly, still the revered text book for the transformation of the Republic into the Empire under Augustus, written in an unforgettable idiosyncratic style at a time when tyrants were gaining individual power in Europe. Essential for serious students.

E.S. Gruen, *The Last Generation of the Roman Republic*, University of California Press, 1974. Covers the same period as Syme, awesomely detailed and scholarly but readable, not revised since 1974, but for the paperback edition a new introduction contains an annotated bibliography to document the major new work since it was first published.

A series of books on the lives and reigns of various emperors has been published by Batsford, and continued by Routledge:

P. Southern, *Augustus*, 1998.

B. Levick, *Tiberius the Politician*, 1999.

A.A. Barrett, *Caligula: corruption of power*, 1990.

B. Levick, *Claudius*, 1990.

M. Griffin, *Nero: End of a Dynasty*, 1987.

K. Wellesley, *The Year of Four Emperors*, 3rd ed. 2000.

B. Levick, *Vespasian*, 2005.

P. Southern, *Domitian: Tragic Tyrant*, 1997.

J. Bennett, *Trajan: Optimus Princeps*, 1997.

A.R. Birley, *Hadrian: the Restless Emperor*, 1997.

A.R. Birley, *Marcus Aurelius a Biography*, rev. ed. 1996.

A.R. Birley, *Septimius Severus: the African Emperor*, rev. ed. 1988.

A. Watson, *Aurelian and the Third Century*, 1999.

S. Williams, *Diocletian and the Roman Recovery*, 1997.

C.M. Odahl, *Constantine and the Christian Empire*, 2004.

P. Southern, *The Roman Empire from Severus to Constantine*, Routledge, 2001. Chronological history from the accession of Severus to the sole rule of Constantine, with chapters on the contemporary histories of the northern barbarians and the Persians, and how the various threats on the Roman frontiers engendered usurpations and rebellions within the Empire. Lucidly written, it says on the cover.

A.H.M. Jones, *The Later Roman Empire 284–602*, Blackwell, 1964. 2 vols. Once the bible for the study of the later Roman Empire, some points have been revised by succeeding scholars, but it is still invaluable for the amount of references and notes.

S. Mitchell, *A History of the Later Roman Empire AD 284–641*, Blackwell, 2007. Scholarly book, covering chronological history from the reign of Diocletian to the sixth century, then covers topics such as the Roman state, the barbarians, religion, economy, society, with a chronological list of emperors, usurpers and the kings of Persia.

P. Heather, *The Fall of the Roman Empire: a New History*, Macmillan, 2005. Extremely readable on a very complicated period, the first two chapters covering the Romans and the barbarians, followed by the various wars against the tribes. Attila gets a chapter to himself. There is an appendix containing short biographies of the major Romans and leading tribesmen.

SOCIAL HISTORY

D. Cherry (ed.), *The Roman World: a Sourcebook*, Blackwell, 2001. Latin and Greek source material in translation, derived from literary works, inscriptions, papyri, grouped under chapter headings, such as women, marriage and family, politics and government, economy etc. Accessible and readable history, with an introduction to each section and notes

J.A. Shelton, *As the Romans Did: a Sourcebook in Roman Social history*, Oxford University Press, 2nd ed. 1998. More source material in translation, scholarly but easy to read, and well organized, easy to find relevant sections from the contents list and index, all entries well annotated.

P. Grimal, *The Civilization of Rome*, Allen and Unwin, 1963. Getting on a bit now, but still a good read, packed with black and white photos, and a historical and biographical dictionary.

U.E. Paoli, *Rome, Its People Life and Customs*, Bristol Classical Press 1990. Classic work available in several editions, first published in the 1940s, containing lots of photos and notes on sources.

GOVERNMENT & ADMINISTRATION

Apart from the source books listed above:

A. Lintott, *The Constitution of the Roman Republic*, Oxford University Press, 1999. The Roman Republic did not have a formal written constitution, but this book brings together all the customs and procedures of the popular assemblies and the Senate, and describes how the magistrates functioned.

F. Millar, *The Emperor in the Roman World*, Duckworth, 1977. Although over thirty years old, this is still a valuable work explaining how the emperors governed, their relationship with the senators and equites, the provinces and cities, and latterly the Church. Readable and full of sources and references.

THE ROMAN ARMY

B. Campbell, *The Roman Army 31 BC to AD 337: a sourcebook*, Routledge, 1994. Various sources from literature, inscriptions and papyri, all translated into English dealing with aspects of the Roman army, readable and well organized.

L. Keppie, *The Making of the Roman Army*, Routledge, 1998. Covers the army of the kings of Rome and its transition into the early Republican army.

A. Goldsworthy, *The Complete Roman Army*, Thames and Hudson, 2003. Covers the whole period from early Republic to later Empire, concentrating on the Imperial army of the second and third centuries, very well illustrated and a good read.

P. Southern and K.R. Dixon, *The Late Roman Army*, Batsford, 1996. Brings together the sporadic evidence for the organization of the late Roman army, arranged in sections including the history of the army from Constantine to Justinian, recruitment, conditions of service, fortifications, and what happened in the end. Criticised for not pushing back the frontiers of knowledge, but then, it was never meant to; it collects what there is.

THE BARBARIANS

P.S. Wells, *The Barbarians Speak: How the Conquered Peoples Shaped Roman Europe*, Princeton University Press, 1999. Covers Rome's relationship with various tribes from the earliest times, including the way in which the barbarians and the Romans interacted beyond the frontiers, and how the blend of cultures affected both.

M. Todd, *Migrants and Invaders: the Movements of Peoples in the Ancient World*, Tempus, 2001. Looks at the relationship between Romans and barbarians from the earliest times to the sixth century AD, in a series of chapters originally designed as lectures. It examines the attractions that the Roman world offered, and concentrates on the transformation of the western Empire.

T.S. Burns, *Barbarians Within the Gates of Rome: a Study of Roman Military Policy and the Barbarians ca. 375–425 AD*, Indiana University Press, 1994. A study of the relationship between the Romans and the tribesmen in the later Empire, how and why the Romans employed some tribesmen in their armies, the different ways in which they employed them, and the policy of settling whole tribes or groups of barbarians on Roman land.

Illustration Credits

All illustrations are from the author's collection unless otherwise stated.
All maps are drawn by Graeme Stobbs.

Index

Except for Roman Emperors, who are indexed under the names by which we know them, other personalities are found under their family names, eg: Gaius Julius Caesar belonged to the family of the Julii and is listed under that name.

Also available from Amberley Publishing

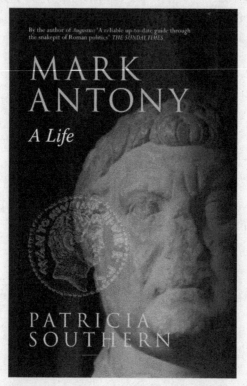

THE up-to-date and authoritative biography of Mark Antony

The life of one of the towering figures of Roman history, Mark Antony, politician, soldier, ally to Julius
Caesar, lover of Cleopatra. History has not been kind to Mark Antony, but then he was probably his own
worst enemy, fatally flawed, too fond of wine and women, extravagant, impetuous, reckless, always in debt,
and attached to all the wrong people. In modern eyes, influenced by Shakespeare, Antony is perhaps the
ultimate tragic hero, who gave up everything for the love of a woman, Cleopatra VII, ruler of Egypt.

£12.99 Paperback
52 illustrations
288 pages
978-1-84868-0863-1

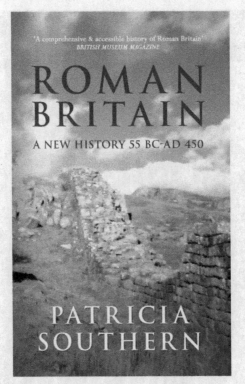

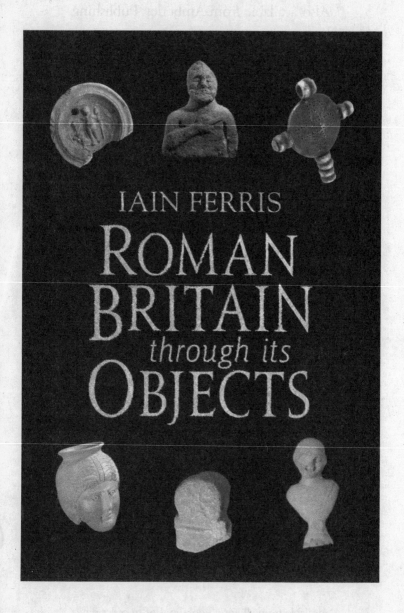